SO-BIQ-281

PRAISE FOR
Shooting from the Lip

"Al Simpson is an American original. Among the many important events recounted in Donald Loren Hardy's lively biography are gems from Simpson's close friendship with Ronald Reagan and George H. W. Bush, which reveal as much about Al as they do about the presidents—that he is altogether without pretension, honest, never boring, and always good-hearted."

David McCullough, Pulitzer Prize–winning author of *John Adams*

"Al Simpson was a Senator with the right touch. Because of his integrity and his humor, he had many friends in the United States Senate—deservedly so."

George H. W. Bush, 41st President of the United States

"Don Hardy has captured every mood, idiosyncrasy, beauty spot, and wart of this great American. The wonderful friendship between Al Simpson and me and our strong respect and love for each other are not based on our thinking alike on every political issue, but on our respect for the public policy–setting process, our advocacy for preserving the liberties and freedoms for which others have given their lives, and our belief in the opportunities this great country offers. This book is about a warm, wonderful person who has devoted his life to straight talk, unabashed patriotism, and a willingness to work 'across the aisle' to make this a more perfect Union."

Norman Y. Mineta, U.S. Representative (D-Calif.; 1975–1995) and
U.S. Secretary of Transportation (2001–2006)

"This lively biography of Al Simpson brilliantly captures a man as wide open and free-spirited as the West itself. *Shooting from the Lip* is refreshingly funny and irreverent—and never more timely than now, when the nation is once again turning to Simpson for straight talk about government spending."

Andrea Mitchell, Chief Foreign Affairs Correspondent, NBC News

"Reading *Shooting from the Lip*, you quickly discover that Al has built a remarkable career, and our nation is sure as hell the better for it!"

Neil Cavuto, Anchor and Managing Editor, Fox News Channel and Fox Business Network

"Those who know of Simpson or who might have met him at some event or another surely have wished to spend time with him to get to know him better. Hardy provides that opportunity—in spades."

Wyoming Tribune Eagle

SHOOTING
FROM THE
LIP

~

The Life of
Senator Al Simpson

BY DONALD LOREN HARDY

University of Oklahoma Press : Norman

For Rebecca, my everything

~

Library of Congress Cataloging-in-Publication Data
Hardy, Donald Loren, 1945–
    Shooting from the lip : the life of senator Al Simpson / by Donald Loren
Hardy.
        p. cm.
    Includes index.
    ISBN 978-0-8061-4211-1 (hardcover : alk. paper)
    ISBN 978-0-8061-4320-0 (paper) 1. Simpson, Alan K. 2. United States.
Congress. Senate—Biography. 3. Legislators—United States—Biography
4. Legislators—Wyoming—Biography. 5. United States—Politics and
government—1977–1981. 6. United States—Politics and government—
1981–1989. 7. UnitedStates—Politics and government—1989– 8. Wyoming—
Politics and government. I. Title.
    E840.8.S5448H37 2011
    328.73'092—dc22
    [B]
2011007485

The paper in this book meets the guidelines for permanence and durability
of the Committee on Production Guidelines for Book Longevity of the
Council on Library Resources, Inc. ∞

Copyright © 2011 by the University of Oklahoma Press, Norman,
Publishing Division of the University. Paperback published 2012.
Manufactured in the U.S.A.

All rights reserved. No part of this publication may be reproduced, stored in
a retrieval system, or transmitted, in any form or by any means, electronic,
mechanical, photocopying, recording, or otherwise—except as permitted
under Section 107 or 108 of the United States Copyright Act—without the
prior written permission of the University of Oklahoma Press.

4 5 6 7 8 9 10

CONTENTS

~

ILLUSTRATIONS

~

PREFACE

~

IN EARLY 2005 my wife Rebecca and I were navigating our sailboat-home, *Pioneer,* near a Caribbean island when my former boss, retired U.S. senator Al Simpson, phoned from Cody, Wyoming. After pleasantries, he came to the point. "Don, several people have contacted me about writing the story of my life. I'm sure they are fine authors, but you know everything there is to know about me. Are you interested in coming out of retirement?"

In a beautiful anchorage that evening, Becky asked how long it would take to draft such a book. A year or so, I underestimated by a factor of five. Would it include other members of Al's family, or his ancestors? No idea. Would it focus on his personal life, his humor, his politics? All of those, I supposed. How would I organize it? Organize?

But, wait! The diaries! Over the years, and especially while a Senate leader, Simpson logged nearly everything of importance that he witnessed, heard, and said in the U.S. Capitol, the Oval Office, and similar venues. With access to his diaries, my story of his life could become a portal, a fly-on-the-wall view of historic moments. His nineteen-volume diary would surely contain jokes shared by President Reagan, even as the Iran-Contra scandal threatened his presidency. There would be conversations in Moscow with Soviet leader Mikhail Gorbachev before the fall of communism—and in Baghdad with Iraqi president Saddam Hussein before Operation Desert Storm.

Simpson's logs would describe dinners in the private quarters of the White House, laughter-filled rides in the president's limousine, and whether he actually rejected a shot at the vice presidency.

They would explain why he mocked the White House press corps and his irritation during the Clarence Thomas and Robert Bork Supreme Court confirmation hearings. They would illuminate his close friendships with political opposites, such as George H. W. Bush and Ted Kennedy. Looking farther back, I could explain how a teenager on probation for breaking federal laws had managed to become a U.S. Senate leader writing them.

When Simpson offered unlimited and exclusive access to his diaries—and to his expansive collection of photos, documents, intimate correspondence, and handwritten notes—I cautioned that I would reveal not only achievements but also his most painful public and private moments. His response was immediate: "Don, just tell the truth, the whole truth, as you always have. Go to it. Dig through the darkest recesses of my life. Leave teeth, hair, and eyeballs on the floor, if that results from telling the truth." Becky and I changed course, sailed back to the United States, sold *Pioneer*, moved west, and began rooting relentlessly into Simpson's life and ancestry.

There was much to discover. Finn Burnett, Al's great-grandfather, was a noted frontiersman, a sutler (civilian provisioner) who built stores in army forts and was the sole survivor of a savage Indian attack. Later he befriended Chief Washakie and taught Indians to sow and reap crops. "Broken Ass Billy" Simpson, Al's grandfather, was a friend of Butch Cassidy but later prosecuted the famous outlaw for horse theft. In separate incidents, Billy shot two men—one a banker who had bounced his check.

Lorna Simpson, Al's mother, faced a formidable challenge: taming Al's fierce temper and instilling in him a sense of social responsibility, before he too began shooting antagonists. Milward, his father, clashed bitterly with Harvard Law School professors before becoming Wyoming's governor, U.S. senator, and Al's political and personal inspiration.

Readers of this book will come to know scores of people who influenced Simpson's life, and vice versa. The narrative follows the sometimes destructive antics of his childhood, his deep depression as a young adult, and his growing maturity and rise to national prominence in the U.S. Senate. It tracks his friendships and conflicts with presidents and world leaders and with people who never held a title. We come to know his wife Ann, the most durable thread in the tapestry of his life.

In 2006, the U.S. Congress appointed Simpson as one of the ten members of the bipartisan Iraq Study Group, charged with assessing the U.S.-led Iraq War and making policy recommendations. Then in early 2010 President Barack Obama asked seventy-eight-year-old Al Simpson to co-chair the National Commission on Fiscal Responsibility and Reform—commonly known as the Deficit Commission, or Debt Panel. He saw the task politically as a "suicide mission" but approached it with trademark verbiage. *Newsweek* reported Al saying: "The people who distort the commission and try to scare people into doing nothing, let's say they win the day, and we don't do anything to try to bring down this debt. Well, great. They've got grandchildren, too, and in 40 years they'll be sucking canal water and picking grit with the chickens."[1]

For years, Al said, people had sent their representatives to Washington to do one thing: bring home the bacon: "Go get the money. Get money for the YMCA, the airport terminal, the dam, the road, the VA hospital. They worshiped the great God of reelection. They brought home the bacon—and now the pig is dead."

True in every aspect, this is the story of Al Simpson's odyssey through the peaks, valleys, and evolution of politics—and life.

SHOOTING
FROM THE
LIP

Chapter One

PIONEER SPIRITS

~

AT MY REQUEST, eighteen members of the Cody High School class of 1949 gathered one frozen Wyoming morning in early 2006 to tell me about their famous classmate, Al Simpson. The retired U.S. senator spoke first.

> Don, you are about to hear some things about me that I am not proud of in any respect. I am not trying to hide them because, sadly, they did happen. No book of my life would be complete without them. However, I would pray it might be clearly understood that I was not in any way in these latter years "bragging" or "cocky" about being reckless, dumb, rebellious and irresponsible as a kid. Many of the things I did were just plain damn stupid.
>
> Looking back, I am very sorry my friends and I did them. But we did. We were teenagers, goofy kids seeking thrills in a destructive way that can't be explained by any of us—even to the present day. We were very fortunate to have lived in a loving and forgiving community and been able to go on with our lives—after serving our probation and making restitution—without being marked for life, as many might be in today's world.

The room grew quiet. Al's stories were always the best—especially those involving gunfire and explosions. "My dad won a car, a Nash, at an Episcopal Church raffle. We got to driving around in that thing. We were all excellent shots, crack shots, so we often drove around shooting at things. It always seemed like a good idea at the time." After school one day in 1948, Al and a few friends

motored the Nash along a small road near Cody. Armed with
.22-caliber rifles, they shot enthusiastically at every inviting target,
meaning everything within range. They found one roadside mailbox of particular interest. Seventy-two bullets left it in shards.

"The bullets were going through the mailbox and landing near
old man Basinger's porch, which was a half mile or a mile away.
Oh yeah, we got out of the car and shot the hell out of it—left
pieces of lead all over the place." Reports of shots being fired, and
the death of a cow, soon led to the boys' capture. Seventeen-year-
old Alan Simpson and several cohorts were charged with the federal offense of destroying mailboxes, and more. "We shot the tires
on a road grader, because they were filled with water and when we
shot them, the water just squirted out. That was really exciting!"[1]

A classmate went on to describe the day they blew up a house.
Simpson listened quietly, then offered a correction: "It was not
a house. It was just an old shack, a health hazard, to our way of
thinking. People had been in there drinking and *all manner* of
things." His tone suggested that dealing unmercifully with the
building would be an appreciated service to the public. Another
friend picked up the story, which involved a World War II internment camp hastily constructed near Heart Mountain, northeast of
Cody: "The house came from the old Japanese camp. It was one of
those old tarpaper shacks that someone had moved after the war.
We filled a coke bottle with gas and stuffed a rag in it. We lit it and
threw it through a window."

Again, Al objected. Nobody had thrown anything through a
window, since the glass was already missing—although he did concede that a homemade fuse may have ignited gasoline that somehow came to be inside the house, and that soon the entire structure
was missing.

This reminded him of the day he and his pals passed sentence on
an old car owned by a family friend. The auto's "crime," punish-
able by immolation, was having allowed itself to be long abandoned
on Simpson family property by an owner unaware of the lads'

eagerness to address such effrontery: "That car sat there behind our house for three or four years. It belonged to a friend of my parents, and it just sat there. But I was not the one who suggested that we take it across the bridge and set it on fire—and then push it down that steep hill toward the river below." The hill in question was just north of town, above the Shoshone River canyon. Any car doused with gasoline, ignited, and pushed over the edge would be certain to tumble wildly hundreds of feet into the ravine, a vision the boys gleefully anticipated.

"The engine didn't run, so we hooked the car up to this other vehicle, intending to pull it to its 'accident' site. While we were pulling it down the main street, a cop came along and asked if he could help. We said, 'No, we think we've got it.' He wished us good luck and we went across the river and perched the car atop a rugged, rocky, sagebrush-strewn hill," Al recounted. In preparation for the event, the boys siphoned five gallons of gasoline from a tank in the back of a stranger's pickup. Even though several of the lads, including Simpson, later became Cody volunteer firefighters, on that day they enthusiastically sloshed the purloined gasoline into the doomed vehicle and struck a match. In an instant, the car was violently ablaze.

Simpson interrupted the story to emphasize his devotion to project safety. "While some of the others went below to watch from there, I stayed on top to flag passing cars and warn of any danger," he explained.

Pushing the blazing vehicle over the edge of the cliff proved more difficult than anticipated, since the doomed machine was now blistering hot. Fearing that its gas tank might explode, one of the boys scrambled wildly over the cliff's edge and began pulling on the front bumper. As others shoved on the rear, the doomed vehicle grudgingly lurched forward. It pitched and then tumbled down the steep hill at alarming speed, spewing flaming gasoline in all directions. Having cheered its thrilling descent, Simpson demonstrated the seriousness with which he took his safety responsibilities by dashing back to the highway.

I knew the first guy who came along [in his car]. He was very excitable. I ran up and said, "Fred! A car just went off the cliff. I'm afraid to look."

He said, "You crazy bastards! I knew you kids would kill yourselves! I'll go to the hospital and let them know, and I'll be back in a minute."

He was just absolutely beside himself, shrieking, cursing and carrying on. Off he went, but by the time he got back, nobody was there. The car was still there, of course, at the bottom of the cliff, in flames.

As months of their childhood passed, the rowdy boys began to mature and even to make amends. They had fired thousands of rounds of .22-caliber bullets in their early days, ammo they could afford because they had stolen it from a store in Cody. "I think we got up about thirty dollars, a bunch of us. We clipped letters of the alphabet out of the newspaper and made a note saying, 'We stole shells from your place over the years. We feel badly about it.' We took the letter to Powell [twenty-four miles away] and mailed it from there, so it wouldn't have a Cody postmark. We signed it, 'Guilty Boys.'" Store owner Stan Lundgren operated his business for several more decades, never learning the thieves' identities.

Al's menace with a rifle and keen marksmanship were established facts. He remains proud of his ability to throw objects into the air and shoot them from the sky. "As a kid, I read about Annie Oakley. I thought that if she could shoot like that, surely I could do it. Actually, all you do is wait until it stops. You just throw something up into the air. When it stops going up, you shoot." Marksmanship was one thing, but brinksmanship elevated the boys' interest in guns to an art form. "We shot at *each other*. We got behind rocks down on Sulfur Creek and we'd see how close we could get to each other with .22-caliber 'shorts.' We never actually shot each other, but when the ricochet came close we would say, 'Boy, that was a good shot. That was pretty close—and it didn't even hurt.'" Al once shot so close to a friend's foot that the bullet pierced the side of his shoe. Since no blood was drawn, the boys interpreted the achievement as irrefutable evidence of amazing and daring marksmanship.

HUMOR

As a youngster, Al observed how well humor worked for his father. As the guest of honor at a Cody High School prom, Milward addressed the students solely in "Chinese." Al's classmate Jim Nielson laughed while telling the story: "I remember the class of '49 junior-senior prom, and Al's father getting up and speaking Chinese to us. We were impressed, since the theme of the prom was 'In a Chinese Garden.' We couldn't wait to report to everyone how great his father was." Milward's "Chinese" had been complete gibberish. He knew the sound of Chinese but had no idea how to speak actual words. Six decades later, Al commented on that evening.

> I was kind of embarrassed—you know, to have Dad and Mom there. But Pop got up and said, "All this takes me back to when Lorna and I lived so many years in China. We love China." He named some cities, having read the book *The Good Earth*, by Pearl Buck. He had also been a friend of Nelson T. Johnson, who was ambassador to China prior to WWII.
>
> Dad said, "I think on a night like this we should think how the Chinese would say aah . . . [extensive expressions in tonal faux Chinese]." I just stared. My date, Jim Nielson's sister Joanne, said, "Wow! I didn't know your father spoke Chinese!" I said, "Neither did I!"

Al continued to observe his father's use of humor and was soon emulating it as a way of making an impression or dealing with conflict.

Although Milward and Lorna cherished their sons' many accomplishments later in life, their early years were challenging. In 2006 Al reflected on the anguish he caused:

When a cop car would drive up in front of the house, my mother would just go into shock. I know it's terrible, but in those days I considered it a success if I could make my mother cry.

I had a vicious temper. I would just sit in my room, after getting into trouble. She would shut the door and lock it. I would be pounding on it and shouting, "I'm going to kill you!" It is not a very nice thing to tell your mother. She would say, "I'm lying here on the bed. I'm sick, I'm heart-sick." I thought, Well, okay!

Mrs. Simpson once told *Time* magazine about her son's legendary temper and her deep frustrations with him as a child. A woman of soft voice and firm resolve, she was determined to keep him from perfecting his budding delinquency. Al came to know her as "the velvet hammer—soft as velvet, strong as steel."[2]

During the classmates' storytelling session, Al's earliest friend, Bob Borron, piped up about a time when the Simpson brothers, then young boys of six or seven, "entrapped" him.

Dad was hired to tear down an old building on the Simpson property. When Pete and Al came over, Dad said to me, "Why don't you play with those little Simpson boys?" So I went over to the garage and pretty soon they were handing me rocks. They encouraged me, so I started throwing rocks at the garage windows.

I was having a nice time knocking holes in the garage when a lady came along and said, "Little boy, why are you tearing up our garage?" Al said to her, "Mother, I was trying to get him to quit!"

I was still sore at him about the garage deal when [in school, several years later] I saw Al creasing the pages in his textbook. I said to the teacher, "Look at that, look what our class president is doing. What if every little kid destroyed our books like that?"

She asked, "What do you think we should do about that?" I said, "Well, we've been studying impeachment. Let's impeach him!" So that's what we did.

Once again, Simpson leaped to his own defense. "All I was doing was folding the pages like butterflies. I was not crimping them! They looked kind of like a fan. I wasn't breaking the backing or tearing the pages." The group laughed heartily. They loved their "Alibi Al."

On July 3, 2006, four and a half months after Bob Hoagland Borron joyfully shared his story, Al Simpson fought back tears while delivering Borron's eulogy: "I cherish the near lifetime of years that I was a beneficiary of this wonderfully kind man's love and good fellowship. He drew people like a magnet—because he was pure fun. And who in the daily course of life doesn't love to be around someone who is just plain fun? We had many leaders in our class. Bob was the leader of mirth and laughter."

While Al and his brother were growing up, it was generally conceded that Pete's antics were less bizarre than those conjured up by his irrepressible younger brother. "I joined Al on several occasions, but I was always the 'getaway car,' not the perpetrator," Pete explained. "I used to try to discourage him from those things, and I used to make excuses for him with our parents." A family friend had a simple and astute way of defining the difference between the Simpson boys: "Pete would always let a sleeping dog lie. Al would go over and jerk its tail."

Pete was considered the more responsible son in part because many people never learned of his having served federal "probation" long before Al was arrested. Sitting comfortably in the house where the two grew up, Pete described the events of decades earlier. "I had thrown a cherry bomb into a mailbox in front of the post office in Jackson [Wyoming]. It blew up all these letters. I escaped the scene, but it was too small a town and they knew who did it. I was put on probation, but never had to contact a probation officer. At the time, I thought I was going to the penitentiary." To make a lasting impression, Milward had rigged a courtroom charade, using real judges, officers, and lawyer friends.

"They had this formal hearing. I thought, 'Christ, I'm going to Worland!'" Worland was the site of the state reformatory for boys. "Dad was in the back of the courtroom, not saying a word. I kept looking around, hoping he would come to my aid." After "testimony" was presented, the judge "sentenced" Pete and an accomplice to federal probation. Years passed before he realized that the hearing had been a mock sentencing. One might assume Pete's traumatic ordeal had an impact on his brother. It did not. Like some of his highly spirited ancestors, Al remained steadfast in his determination to learn life's lessons his own way—the hard way.[3]

SIMPSON PIONEERS

In 1835 John Porter Simpson, Al and Pete's paternal great-grandfather, was born to Robert and Nancy Simpson of Huntingdon, Pennsylvania. The family ventured west, and in Bear Creek, Colorado, on Christmas Day of 1865, John married Margaret "Maggie" Susan Sullivan, eleven years his junior. On January 26, 1868, in a house near Fort Reynolds, east of Pueblo, Maggie gave birth to a son they named William. A free spirit from an early age, Billy was fifteen years old when he ventured into the Wyoming Territory to find work as a cowhand and later to pursue his interest in becoming a lawyer.

In 1889 his parents, after numerous relocations and family tragedies, also moved north and took up residence on a ranch in the Wind River drainage north of Lander. In 1892 they relocated to Lander, near their son Billy. In September of the following year they moved for the last time, to Jackson Hole. That fall, in one of the nation's most beautiful settings, they built the first house with a shingled roof, and Maggie became the settlement's first postmaster. She and John were formative in laying out the original Jackson town site.[4]

Billy's future wife Margaret "Maggie" Burnett was born January 24, 1874, not in Wyoming but in Utah. Her mother, Eliza Ann

McCarthy Burnett, had been taken there for the birth because of dangerous conflicts with the Bannock Indians near their Fort Washakie home in the Wyoming Territory. Maggie, whose father was well-known frontiersman Finn Burnett, departed for Texas at age fifteen to attend Green's College in Dallas and St. Ursula's Catholic convent in San Antonio. She returned to Wyoming and became a volunteer teacher of English and Latin to Indian students at St. Stephen's Catholic mission. There she met Billy Simpson, who, despite little formal education, was seeking Latin instruction in his quest to take the state bar exam and become a lawyer. He successfully completed an oral examination on the law, and on July 11, 1892, he was admitted to the Wyoming Bar as a practicing attorney. He was twenty-four years old. In October of the following year Billy Simpson married nineteen-year-old Maggie Burnett.

Billy

Commonly known as "Broken Ass Bill" since he had been afflicted with polio at age eleven and walked with a limp, Billy loved to brag about having been expelled from the fourth grade back in Colorado for witnessing a public hanging—something he laughingly considered "a twofer."

He became known as an accomplished lawyer with a penchant for drinking and gambling and, during the following decades, lived with Maggie in Lander, Jackson, Meeteetse, Thermopolis, and Cody, Wyoming. His grandson Al says they moved often. Billy— also known by the pet name "Popoo"—was prone to getting drunk, gambling, and losing their home. "Three times, he came home to say, 'Pack up, Maggie. We don't own this place anymore.' That really irritated my grandmother."

The couple had three children: Virginia, Milward, and Glen (also spelled Glenn, and further known as Burnett). Milward was born in a log cabin in Jackson on November 12, 1897, and was destined to play a significant role in public life. He was only seven years old the day his father shot a Meeteetse banker.

The incident occurred in 1905, while Billy, a candidate for Park County attorney, was serving as chairman of the county's Democratic Party. He was also its treasurer and secretary, since there were few Democrats in the area. The local banker in question was W. Dean Hays (also spelled Hayes in some Meeteetse Museum District documents), who bounced Simpson's Democratic Party check—even though sufficient funds were on deposit. A popular family man, Hays had been elected Meeteetse mayor the previous year and was a principal at the Wilson, Hays and Company Bank. The Simpsons lived on a street bearing the banker's name. In 2008 Al Simpson explained what happened:

> Popoo entered the bank and said, "Hays, you bounced my check, and our Party has money on deposit in your bank."
>
> Hays reportedly said, "Well, Mr. Simpson, maybe you ought to realize that we really don't care for Democrats here in Park County. We could get along without them, so maybe you would like to choose another bank." Popoo warned him not to bounce another check, and left.
>
> Sometime later, the bank did bounce another one of Popoo's checks. He went into the bank, laid his pistol on the teller counter, and said, "You did it again, didn't you Hays?" Hays responded, "Yeah, I did."
>
> Popoo reacted by picking up the gun and shooting. The bullet grazed the side of Hays's head and nearly blew his ear off—probably "deafed" him too.

Simpson was not charged with a crime, although he did pay a price of sorts. Because a number of voters felt that shooting bankers in the head was bad form, he lost the election, by three votes.

Billy had a much more serious encounter eighteen years later, and thirty-two miles away, in Cody. Based on court testimony and research reports, this is what happened. In 1922 a Cody barber named Edward Uriah Raines and his attorney Ernest J. Goppert were involved in a lawsuit over property ownership. Simpson, representing the opposing party, lost the case. Nonetheless, the conflict left Raines so angry that he was occasionally heard to mutter threats against Simpson.

On Sunday, August 19, 1923, at eight o'clock in the evening, Raines sneaked up behind Simpson as he strolled along Cody's main street, Sheridan Avenue. When he got close enough, he bashed Simpson in the head with a large rock, collapsing him instantly and partially dislodging one eye from its socket.

Witnesses assisted Simpson, barely conscious, into the Mint Café and pool hall. He remained there half an hour before two friends helped him to his own office. Meanwhile, Raines entered the Cody Drug Store, where he encountered town marshal Clarence Sirrine. Although aware of the assault, the officer did not arrest Raines but instead collected a fifteen-dollar bond. Raines would have been better off in jail than strolling, as he then did, into the Mint.

About this time, Billy, still seriously dazed and in considerable pain, picked up his .38-caliber pistol—(a conflicting story says he grabbed the pistol of an attending doctor, Frances Lane)—and staggered onto the street and from there into the Mint. Spotting Raines, he wasted no time clubbing him in the head with the pistol. This ignited a vicious fight. During the melee, Simpson fired several shots. Two bullets struck Raines, the first impacting a silver dollar in his pocket. That might have been his lucky dollar, had he not been hit a second time.

As the two were scuffling on the floor, with Raines on top, the café's butcher, John Mathisson, rushed up. Raines screamed, "For Christ's sake, Butch, get this gun." Mathisson grabbed Simpson's wrist and gun and said, "Let go of this pistol."

Simpson yelled back, "No, I won't do it. I am afraid of this man."

Mathisson tried again. "Turn loose of the gun and I will take the man off from you."[5]

Simpson finally released his grip, and as Mathisson dragged Raines away, it became apparent to participants and witnesses alike that one bullet had passed completely through his abdomen. He was taken to the doctor's office across the street, examined, given a shot of morphine, and transported to the hospital at Powell. He died the next day.

Simpson was taken into custody by Park County sheriff W. H. Loomis and charged with first-degree murder. His attorney friends from as far away as Cheyenne quickly put up his $10,000 bail and began working on a defense strategy.

The trial was scheduled sixty miles away, in Basin, Wyoming, and began on April 9, 1924, Judge James H. "Harry" Burgess of Sheridan presiding. The prosecuting attorney was Ernest Goppert, the same lawyer who had defeated Simpson in the case that sent Raines into a rage in the first place. Goppert's seriousness became clear when he subpoenaed thirty-four witnesses.

Near the conclusion of the two-day trial, Judge Burgess ruled that since no evidence had been presented that Simpson knew Raines was in the Mint Café when he entered, and since he had earlier asked for coffee to deal with his throbbing head and announced that he was going to the café for coffee—and since he had every reasonable right to be carrying a gun, having been recently attacked—he could not be convicted of premeditated murder. The jury pondered the matter to a stalemate on April 11. When they announced they were unable to come to a unanimous decision, Judge Burgess discharged them from duty.

William L. "Billy" Simpson continued to be a flamboyant and controversial figure and died of a heart attack in Jackson on Sunday morning, December 15, 1940. Gravediggers at the frozen hillside cemetery in Jackson had a formidable challenge burrowing into the rocky hillside graveyard in the freezing cold of winter. Al remembers the extraordinary measures required. "They had to blast his grave. In the bitter cold, they had to use pieces of dynamite to blast into the rock and frozen ground. Nanny [Maggie] said she could hear the blasting during the day, and knew what it was."

Maggie put her hand on the casket, Al recalls, and said, "Didn't think I would stick with you, did you, Billy?"

In 1991, more than fifty years after his grandfather's burial, Al met a man who had been the mortician's assistant in Jackson that day. "I worked for the guy who buried your grandfather—I was just a kid," the man said. "I don't think you ever knew that when most people had left the burial site, a huge rock fell from the uphill side of the open grave and crushed the casket. One of the other guys who knew him was there that day. He said, 'That'll keep old Billy from getting down to the bar tonight!'"

Milward

After graduating from Cody High School June 16, 1916, Billy and Maggie's son Milward departed for Tome Prep School in Port Deposit, Maryland. With WWI inevitable, he left Tome to join the army. Following service at Camp Pike, Arkansas, he was transferred to the Presidio in San Francisco. Although he was an infantry officer, his only combat involved being seriously injured by an attacking bulldog.

Milward was honorably discharged and entered the University of Wyoming. He graduated in 1921 and joined the United Mine Workers Union, working briefly in a coal mine in Red Lodge, Montana, earning $7.92 per day. Family members say he returned to Red Lodge years later as an attorney defending an alleged horse thief. It is not clear whether the jury was intentionally stacked with Milward's former coal-mining buddies or if it just happened that way. His grandson Bill laughed while explaining the trial's outcome: "It was kind of a special verdict for them. The jury found the defendant not guilty, but then sought an admonition from the court that said, 'But we'd like the horses returned.'"

THE KOOI BRANCH

In Chicago a Dutch man named Peter Kooi (pronounced "Coy") married Mary Helen Brown, a woman of Scottish and English descent. They had two daughters, Doris and Vera. More than ten years later, on August 19, 1900, a third daughter was born.

So it was that not quite three years after Milward L. Simpson was born in that little cabin in Jackson, Wyoming, his future bride, Lorna Helen Kooi, began life in Chicago. She was still a child when her father became interested in the coal-mining business and moved his family to northern Wyoming. Before long he founded a coal-mining town bearing his name.

As a child, Lorna rode horseback from Kooi to Monarch and then boarded an inter-urban trolley for the ten-mile ride to the public school in Sheridan. As a teen, she returned to the Chicago area to enroll at Lewis Academy. Next she entered a private school, Miss Mason's Castle School in Tarrytown, New York, where she studied art, music, history, and sculpture. Later, while briefly a student at the University of Illinois, she was advised that although she was an excellent musician, there would be no professional opportunities for her in music.

In 1929 Peter Kooi, after enjoying unprecedented business success and serving in the Wyoming State Senate as a Republican, sold his properties to the Sheridan-Wyoming Coal Company. The wealth he had accumulated allowed his family the almost unheard of luxury of international travel. This influenced Lorna's life as much as formal education, as her son Peter explained: "She was highly educated just by the fact of travel, because not many women went to college. Mom only went one year to the University of Illinois. Miss Mason's was a finishing school, where she went to the opera and took other cultural trips to New York City. She was a gifted pianist and became an educated woman, but not in the formal sense you would know today."

Lorna traveled with her family to Egypt, France, the British Isles, Turkey, Greece, Algeria, Brazil, Chile, Argentina, and Peru—and once flew in a single-engine plane over Sugar Loaf Mountain in Rio de Janeiro. She shot movies everywhere she went, including one of Rudyard Kipling emerging from a Rio hotel.

Back in Sheridan, Lorna met Milward Simpson at her friend's wedding. "I was maid of honor and a man by the name of 'Simp' was to be the best man. It was sort of a strange name," Lorna told the *Casper Star Tribune* in 1980. She was on time for the rehearsal dinner, but Simp failed to show up. Her frustration grew to irritation the following day, when a man scheduled to help decorate the church suddenly departed to rescue Milward, whose car had broken down on the top of a mountain. From her perspective, Simp clearly lacked the judgment and mechanical aptitude required to keep his car running properly when he was expected at an important engagement.

Milward did arrive in time for the wedding at St. Peter's Episcopal Church in Sheridan. Afterward, he told a friend that he was "agog" while watching her from the corner of his eye as they walked down the aisle and he thought to himself, "*This* is the girl I am going to marry." In the months that followed, he stayed in touch with the pretty Kooi woman, courting her aggressively and sending roses to her every port of call. Her opinion shifted so completely that on June 29, 1929, in Sheridan, Lorna Helen Kooi became Mrs. Milward Simpson.

The couple moved to Cody but returned to Sheridan for the birth of their first son, Peter, on July 31, 1930. Because he had been nearly nine pounds at birth, Lorna was taken to Mercy Hospital in Denver as a precautionary measure for the delivery of the couple's second son, Alan, on September 2, 1931.

ALAN KOOI SIMPSON

Back in Cody, Alan developed normally in every way but one; he did not speak. He made sounds like other infants, but nobody could understand what he was trying to say—other than his brother.

> Al would be sitting in the corner and my parents would ask me, "What is he saying?" He wasn't saying anything they could understand, but I understood everything. He didn't say an actual word until he was nearly three—and then it was a whole sentence. I had been translating for him all the time.

Mom left him in the kitchen one time, in a high chair, and
he was going through this razzmatazz. Finally, she heard him
say, *"I want to get down."* He said that full sentence the first
time he spoke actual words.

For decades Milward and Lorna repeated the story about Alan's
reluctance to begin talking, always laughing and punctuating it
with, "and then we couldn't get him to *stop!*"

Al's earliest clear recollection is of an airplane and its pilot. He
believes his initial fear of flying may have been sparked when aviator
Bill Monday told him and a group of other children to stand in the
middle of Cody's main street, look to the sky, and watch for his plane.

We were all out there when he just cut his plane's engine and
did this "falling leaf" thing. He gunned it again, did a roll,
and came down. It looked like he was within about twenty
feet of the stores on Main Street. It was an absolutely vivid
and beautiful day. He waved. I could see him up there.

I also have early memories of sheep. The sheep would be
driven from their fields to the top of the hill and down to the
highway. Thousands of sheep would move down that street,
right in the midst of the Yellowstone Park buses. They finally
stopped the sheep drive because the sheep dung on the street
was about a foot thick. Wow! As a kid, you don't forget things
like that!

During his childhood Al found his father's profession something
of a challenge: "Dad would be representing someone that people
really didn't like. Tough kids would say, 'Are you Milward Simpson's
son?' I would say that I was, and they'd say, 'Well, he's representing
a crooked son of a bitch!' Then they would slug me. We remember
who they were. Pete and I really learned to stick together."

In 1940, at age forty-two, Milward also provided Al with some
early exposure to politics by running for the U.S. Senate against
incumbent New Deal Democrat Joseph O'Mahoney. During the
campaign Simpson repeatedly denounced communist subversion,

asserting, "The little red school house is redder than you think." The snappy phrase failed to stir Wyomingites. He lost resoundingly.

How did eight-year-old Alan feel about his father running for public office? "I couldn't figure it out. We had spent time with our grandparents in Sheridan, and it seems like during the campaign in the fall of '40 we spent a lot of our time in Jackson. I remember getting punched in the face for wearing a Wendell Willkie for President button in the midst of Roosevelt country, so I came to think of politics as a contact sport."

HEART MOUNTAIN

Alan Simpson was twelve years old when he and fellow members of a church group stepped guardedly through the barbed-wire gate at the Heart Mountain Relocation Center near Ralston, twelve miles northeast of Cody. Inside were nearly eleven thousand Americans of Japanese heritage forcefully transplanted from their homes in the western United States by the government, in the wake of the Japanese bombing of Pearl Harbor. Most were U.S. citizens.

Al somberly recalls the anti-Japanese hysteria of the day and that towns throughout America, including Cody, routinely conducted air attack drills. When the sirens went off at night, Al and Pete helped their parents cover or extinguish any lights that might be seen from the sky. "We were always watching for enemy planes, Japanese planes," Al remembers.

That day at the "Jap camp," as it was known locally, Al visited hesitantly with a few internees his age—holding back fear that their relatives in Japan might be planning an attack on Cody. But what, he wondered, had *these* children done wrong? Why were they caged behind barbed wire fences? Not long afterward, Cody's junior high school principal joined the Simpson boys' scoutmaster in arranging a second trip to the camp. In 2009 Al's brother Pete described it:

Principal Glenn Livingston and our coach Bill Waller were two of the most profoundly influential men on young boys growing up in Cody. Glenn's talk to us was, and I paraphrase: Boys, we're going to have a day with the Boy Scouts at the Relocation Center. They're Japanese-Americans. They pledge allegiance to the flag just like we do. They swear the same Boy Scout oath. They use the same salute, and they wear the same uniform. We're going there to learn more about them and to teach them some things about ourselves, and we'll have a great day!

At the camp they encountered a boy wearing a similar uniform. His name was Norman Y. Mineta. Al remembers him as "a bright, curious, fun-loving, knot-tying, pesky, rambunctious young scout." The two became friends and stayed in touch by mail long after the war ended and the camp was abandoned. Neither dreamed that one would become a U.S. senator, the other a member of the U.S. House of Representatives—and U.S. secretary of both Transportation and Commerce. Both also became members of the Smithsonian Institution Board of Regents.

Al characterizes their chance meeting as one of the "profound lessons shaping my life." In 1999, during a banquet meeting of the Heart Mountain Wyoming Foundation, he described himself as having been "a child torn between two cultures." One he had always known. But Japan presented a threat to his country. He told the crowd, "My trip here [from Cody] was twelve and a half miles." Then he turned to his old friend Norm Mineta and added, "It was so much longer, and more painful, for you."

In a 2006 interview for the Academy of Achievement, a Museum of Living History in Washington, D.C., Mineta explained how he and Al reconnected after they had fallen out of touch.

I was elected Mayor of San José, California, and the Associated Press had a short story about me being elected. . . . It read, "Mineta was one of 120,000 Japanese Americans evacuated and interned in camps during WWII. He and his family were at Heart Mountain, Wyoming."

Well, the *Cody Enterprise* picked up on the story. . . . Alan was practicing law in Cody. The next thing, I get a note, "Dear Norm, congratulations on being elected Mayor of San José. I have been wondering what the heck you'd been up to all these years."

In 1974, I got elected to the Congress, and in 1978, he got elected to the United States Senate. Our friendship went back together as if we were sitting in that pup tent in 1943.

The Heart Mountain campsite is recognized by the Department of the Interior as a National Historic Landmark, a status held by only 4 percent of the properties listed on the National Register of Historic Places. Legislation is pending to include the site in the national park system. In June 2007 Mineta and Simpson stood side by side at the campsite, proudly announcing plans by the Heart Mountain Wyoming Foundation to build an 11,000-square-foot Interpretive Learning Center.

In August 2009 the two met again at Heart Mountain, in public celebration of the center's progress. Mineta told those present, some of whom had also been rounded up by their own government, that he would never forget May 29, 1942, when his family was forced from their California home and onto a train. When they reached their tar paper barracks home at the foot of Heart Mountain, they found it surrounded by barbed wire and guarded by soldiers. Their guns were facing in.

When he concluded, his old friend Al Simpson rose and walked toward the podium. He paused to peer through a doorway and noticed that a soaking rain was falling on the mountain. Reflecting on Mineta's story, he turned to the crowd and said somberly, "I think Heart Mountain is crying."[6]

Chapter Two

CREEPING MATURITY

~

IN 1948 MILWARD and Lorna sent their son Peter to Cranbrook Schools in Bloomfield Hills, Michigan, for a postgraduate year of education and refinement before college. Al followed a year later, and before long made a discovery: "I became aware of Stroh's Bohemian light beer. I didn't drink much beer in high school, didn't want to. It didn't taste good. But boy, beer started to taste good at Cranbrook."

This was not the kind of refinement the senior Simpsons were hoping for, but at least Al was cutting the apron strings without severing all of them. When he found himself too busy to do his own laundry, he mailed it from Michigan to his parents' home in Cody to be washed and returned.

As a postgrad, Al was assigned his own room in Marquis Hall and in short order discovered the campus tower. "It had a secret entrance, and I had a key. We went up these stairs and there were things like *Playboy*—no, wait, there wasn't a *Playboy* in those days. Well, there were books and magazines that would certainly stir the imagination—and we could smuggle a little beer in there." He also found it possible to travel the area, since day students from Detroit had cars. "We could just leave, leave at night and go into Detroit. There was a burlesque theatre there. It was quite important to go to that."

Wisely, he was not too busy to write progress letters to his parents.

September 23, 1949

I got to get ready for "Physical Science." I might not have told you about that change. But when I saw you had French down for me, I said that stuff "was for the birds" (a new saying here). Anyway, the Phys Sci is really a good course. Most is lab work and glass blowing and making nitro-glycerin. (Isn't that terrible, Mom?)

In December he received his first grades. About his C in English, his instructor wrote, "A fine worker whose English efforts are beset by difficulties in spelling, punctuation and organization." He scored an A− in American government ("excellent!") and a B+ in modern European history, dropping from an A due to a disappointing final exam. His last grade was in physical science, where he was given a B− and the note "Good Work." Apparently, the nitro had not exploded.

May 9, 1950

On Saturday night, May 20, I am the Master of Ceremonies at the Ameture Amature Amerature Amateur (what a word to spell) Night Program. I thought you could give me some tips, Dad. Just give me an introductory phrase and some of your good jokes and I'll put it across. . . . I got a date for the Commencement Formal and also a gal asked me to the big dance at the K'Wood . . . but of course I haven't quit studyin' yet. I'll get some black shoes. I hope they won't cost too much. . . . Say, Mom, I'm in dire need of pants. That's right, just plain slacks. I have only two pair other than suit pants. Maybe you could purchase 2 pair to send to me. I wouldn't ask if I really didn't need them. Size 36–38 waist and 36 pant leg would do the trick. I sure need them. It's really urgent. I'm practically naked. . . . PS: Don't forget my M.C. job on Saturday, Pop.

THE GIRL FROM GREYBULL

Eighteen-year-old Al Simpson's next challenge was the University of Wyoming, where he soon had one eye on a bachelor of science in law degree and the other on a former cheerleader from Greybull. Looking back, Ann Schroll Simpson describes their unpromising start. She and her twin sister Nan were tall, "but all the boys that I was interested in were about my height or smaller. Back in high school, we had been on the lookout for the Simpson boys at the next basketball tournament, where I was a cheerleader. We spotted them, and they spotted us. Unfortunately, they didn't know how to dance. Right away, we ruled them completely off our list."

Al confirms the rejection. "That's right. We didn't dance. We were the 'zit kings' of the world. I was knock-kneed and heavy. I had good hair, though—like Tony Curtis! Ann didn't mind that, but was unimpressed once she found that I couldn't dance."

Ann didn't realize it, but she had met her future husband—a tall boy who could shoot a basketball like a laser, but had a difficult time running fast, and certainly could not dance. "He was a great shot on the court. But he was heavy. I remember that we called him 'fatso' in high school. He made so many baskets that we had to think of something disparaging." The object of her ridicule was not oblivious to the name-calling. "People used to boo me," he said. "I could hit the bucket, but I would waddle up and down the court. I had spent years outside the house shooting buckets, and was good. But I couldn't run. They called from the stand—'Hey, fatso!' All that did was goad me on to score more points."

At the time, Ann had her own challenges. Her father, fifty-six-year-old Ivan Schroll, had fallen seriously ill during a hunting trip.

He died of a brain tumor when we were just beginning our junior year in high school. It came on quickly. He had been having headaches and didn't say anything because he thought it was just his glasses. After he passed out and was revived, he made the others promise not to tell my mother. By the time he went to the hospital and was diagnosed, it was too late. He died within about ten days of that. It was just before my sixteenth birthday.

At the University of Wyoming, Ann had new opportunities to check out "fatso." Not only was he still unable to dance; he was now drinking beer, "in astounding quantities." Again Al confirms her observation. "I preferred drink over women. Beer was my date, and I drank a lot of it. I loved it, glass after glass. I was a social fellow and went to the dances, but for me it was more fun to go to the Buffalo Bar and get ten draft beers for a dollar. We would see how long it would take to work through that Hamm's draft beer." Nonetheless, the two began dating, which eventually led to the phone call Ann received late one night. It was her boyfriend—calling from jail, as Al later explained.

> I went down to Poor Bill's bar that warm night. A guy I knew had just staggered out of the place. He had a couple of cuts on his chest, and his shirt was torn open. I said, "Gee, what happened to you?" He said, "I've been in a fight with a nigger."
>
> I said, "*What?* You must be the dumbest . . . " He came at me, so I just took him like that [he made a sweeping motion with his arm] and he fell into the hedges. Just as he was climbing out, the cop car came up. They heard there had been a knifing or a fight, so they grabbed me.
>
> They said, "Well, well—look what you've done to this guy." I said, "I didn't do a thing to this stupid son of a bitch." The cop said, "You may think you didn't, but we just saw you throw him into the hedge—so you did *something* to him, didn't you there, big guy?" I said, "No!" Then the drunken guy pointed at me and said, "That guy is an *asshole.*"

Given Al's strong aversion to being called an asshole, the situation deteriorated. "When the cops said, 'We saw this happen,' I got furious . . . I was half-tight, and I just wheeled on the guy, swung on him, the cop. Then he tapped me [with a nightstick], and that little white mark is still right there today. . . . He said, 'You are going to jail!' " Al pointed to the scar just above his left eyebrow.

Both young men were charged with disturbing the peace, and bond was set. Because Al did not have enough money, he spent the night in jail. "There were guys who had shit their pants in there, and there was urine all over the floor. It was a *great* experience."

In the morning, Pete sprang his brother from the slammer. The future U.S. senator was fined two hundred dollars, given a six-month suspended jail sentence, and stripped of his "Who's Who on American Campuses" honor. "I was heartbroken, absolutely heartbroken. I tried to hide it. I said it didn't mean anything to me. But I tell you, it meant a lot."

Through it all, Ann stuck by her man. She recalls an important conversation they had late one night.

> We were in the car, probably smooching. I was about to graduate and was talking about my two job offers, one in California and the other in Cheyenne. The California one panicked him. "*California?*" he said. "Well, if you went to Cheyenne we could get *married* in a year."
>
> *That* was my proposal! He didn't even *give* me a ring until the following *Christmas!* He said he needed another year before we got married. That was okay. I needed that year to make sure he wasn't drinking so much beer.

Her concern was not groundless. Al had earned a widespread reputation as a phenomenally prodigious consumer of the product. His capacities left even his brother Pete in awe:

> There was an ATO fraternity party at a crossroads called Reeds Ranch outside Laramie. Al had a *five gallon can* full of beer and bet that he could drink that whole can. He did. The party was most of a whole day, and he put away five gallons. I can remember somebody throwing a little sheep shit—a little manure—into the container, and Al just brushing it aside. We have a picture of him with the can. It was an *astonishing* feat.

TAKING ON THE PRESS

A fellow university student named Paul Holtz was editor of the school's weekly newspaper, the *Branding Iron*. Al Simpson was one of three student senate members of the election committee, which was in charge of student body leadership elections. The fiasco that followed that year's balloting represents the first of his many intense confrontations with the media. In 2007 Holtz gave his version of the conflict:

> After the students had voted, I learned Simpson had told one of the *Branding Iron* reporters he did not intend to give us the actual number of votes cast for two candidates. He said he thought it would be embarrassing to the guy who had ended up in second place.
>
> I sat down and put together an editorial—for the front page, no less—that reminded Al of the need to reveal the number of ballots cast for each candidate. I likened it to having the head of the University's Athletic Department return from an away football game and decreeing he would provide no information about the contest because the Cowboys hadn't done very well.

Simpson and his fellow senators fired back with a lengthy explanation, but the paper stung them with another editorial. Simpson was learning how difficult it is to challenge the power of the press.

ON BENDED KNEE

Al graduated in spring 1954 with a bachelor of science in law degree and with two years of law school remaining. Not long afterward, he and Ann participated in the most meaningful event of their lives, though they could not know at the time what a long and rewarding marriage theirs would be. Early in the morning on June 21, 1954, Al paced nervously inside tiny St. Andrews Episcopal Church in little Basin, Wyoming. "I got over there at seven in the morning for the ten o'clock ceremony and just *sat around*. Nobody was paying any attention to me, so the anxiety just built."

When the time came to repeat the wedding vows, he nearly collapsed. Pete, who served as best man, remembers the moment his brother began to lose it. "I was standing right beside him. The sweat broke out on his head, and he started to go down. I grabbed his belt and held him up. He said, 'Oh Jesus, I'm glad you did that.' We joked about it afterward. I said, 'If you had fallen, it would have been like felling a six-foot-seven timber right in the church.' "

That summer Al had his first job that came with benefits. "I was working in Laramie for the University of Wyoming Buildings and Grounds Department, working on the garbage truck. It was a physical job. You picked up the barrel, dumped it into the truck, and put it back on the curb. It paid two hundred fifty bucks a month—*and all you could eat* [hearty laughter]."

Soon there was more to celebrate than marriage and paid work. Al's father had remained politically active after failing in his 1940 bid for the U.S. Senate. In mid-1954 he campaigned successfully for the Wyoming governorship. His slim 56,275 to 55,163 victory over William S. "Scotty" Jack produced relief and family jubilation. Milward Simpson was the first person born in Wyoming after it achieved statehood in 1890 to become its governor.

The newlyweds' celebration of Milward's victory was brief, however, as Al honored his Reserve Officers' Training Corps (ROTC) commitment and was soon on his way to the army—and the greatest emotional crisis of his life.

LIEUTENANT SIMPSON

At Fort Benning, Georgia, Second Lieutenant Al Simpson was taught how to protect the nation before being assigned duty in Germany. During their transatlantic flight, Ann made an intriguing discovery about her new husband: "We flew to Frankfurt first, on Flying Tiger Airlines. During the flight, we ran out of water, and the plane was filled with crying babies. Al kept saying to me, "Don't be afraid." I said that I wasn't, but he kept comforting me. I suddenly realized that *he* was the one afraid." He remembers it the same way.

I was terrified on the flight over. Once there—well, I
had been trained as an infantry officer. I was a crack shot,

obviously, but instead of sending me to the field, they found out I had one year of law school. They said, "Aha. You're going to be the assistant adjutant of the Tenth Infantry Regiment of the Fifth Infantry Division, the Big Red Diamond."

I said, "What the hell is *that*?" They told me it was an administrative position.

That was the first instance of the total failure of Alan K. Simpson as an administrator. I didn't have any idea what I was doing. None. I'd read manuals and memos from the Colonel. My God, it was like they were written in Egyptian.

Ann soon noticed that her husband was sleeping a great deal. He became sluggish and distinctly uninspired by his service. "He hated the army. I think it was the discipline, not being able to do whatever he wanted. He does not like someone telling him what to do—his wife or anybody else." After complaining of severe stomach pains and high blood pressure, Al was hospitalized in the 11th Field Hospital.

I said, "Look, I have ulcers, I know I have ulcers. You should treat me." I took the barium test and all this stuff. The doctor said, "You don't have ulcers. You are just so filled with anxiety that you don't even know what is going on. But if you think you are sick and that you have ulcers, I can keep you in the hospital until you figure out what's eating on you." That is what that doc said. I thought, "Man, what a barbaric bastard *this* guy is."

Ann would come and see me every day. I would say, "How is it out there Ann, dear?" She would say, "I went to a museum today. Why don't you get up and come with me?" I would respond, "I can't. I am sick, you see. I'm *sick!*"

The army doctor finally diagnosed Ann's role in her husband's situation. It was a conversation she never forgot. "When Al's doctor said to me, 'My dear, you must remember that you are not his mother,' that was the best lesson I ever had." Ann went to Al and said, "I love you, Al, but I am not your *mother*. Your mother is eight thousand miles away, and she is not here to hold your head up out of the toilet bowl. So you can be there with your little fevered brow, like you were a little boy, but I am *not* your mother. She is *not here!*" Al began putting things into perspective.

> I was in a room with some guy who'd had his legs shot off
> and yet had a cheerful attitude about life, and I began to real-
> ize that self-pity is the blackest hole you can get into. It is all
> self-induced. There is nobody cranking it from the outside,
> not your mother, not your wife. It is *you* hand cranking that
> big old crank with a barrel of shit under it called self-pity. I
> tell you, you don't want *any* part of that.

Al was changing, but not fast enough, as he demonstrated one evening shortly after being released from the hospital. He and Ann were having dinner when she looked at him and delivered distressing news: she would not be able to conceive and would never be a mother. Decades later, she recounted their exchange. "He looked at me and said, 'I've had such gas on my stomach all day.' I said, '*Did you hear what I just said, Alan*? You are so filled with self-pity that you are only concerned with *yourself*.'"

Ann's anger in a little German restaurant that night was a major turning point in the life of twenty-four-year-old Alan Simpson. "He finally heard it," she said emotionally in 2006. "In all our arguments and discussions after that, Al always hears what I say—even if he doesn't like it." Looking back on that moment decades later, Al said, "That's where I decided I was going to be either a boy-man, or a man-boy. That's when I began to grow up." The couple's relationship survived that dangerous moment, and a few weeks later Ann discovered that the doctor was wrong about one thing: she was pregnant.

Al completed his army service and was honorably discharged after the two flew home. Before Al returned to law school at the University of Wyoming in the fall of 1956, he decided to reveal to his mother the details of his emotional breakdown in Germany.

I came back from Germany weighing 188 pounds. Guys who knew me were just stunned. My mother thought I had pernicious anemia. After Pop went to bed one night—he was governor then—and Ann had gone to bed, I told my mother, in confidence, about my situation, what had happened to me. She never said a word. She just listened with her eyes wide.

When I finished the whole revelation, in thirty minutes, she smiled, placed her hand on mine and said, "I know that did not happen." She was dead serious. Her cherished son had a flaw, a great big flaw, and she refused to accept that.

I went upstairs and told Ann, "I just poured out my soul to my mother. She told me she knew it *didn't happen*."

That was the power of my mother. She had the great ability to will the world away.

LAW SCHOOL AND POLITICS

In 1956 Al Simpson, largely recovered physically and emotionally from his army experience, was a newly invigorated student of life—and a somewhat invigorated student of law at the University of Wyoming. He and Ann moved into married student housing, which Ann recalls as clean but chilly and breezy. "When the cold wind blew, it came right through the cinderblocks." William Lloyd Simpson was born half a year later, on February 24, 1957. The new parents were thrilled with their fine, healthy baby, and found it deeply comforting to know their child would carry on the family heritage.

To get by financially, Al initiated a unique austerity measure— brewing his own beer. The enterprise went well until the day an increase in apartment temperature caused a problem. Forty-eight years later, in a 2006 letter to his friend Ed Hunter, he was still chuckling.

Who can forget the batch that somehow escaped our brewers' skills and blew up! . . . It was when a shard of glass went through the partitioned door between the storage closet and the kitchen that Ann said, "No more of that, because that's your son who crawls on the kitchen floor right there!"

So much for the beer making, but it really wasn't too savory anyway. . . . Certainly, you and I can never forget the day I bought that fresh, clear bottle of Budweiser and scrubbed the label off, removed the cap, put our own cap on it and invited you over to test [it]. You said, "My heavens, that's *glorious!*" And so it was!

Al graduated on schedule in spring 1958, although not at the top of his class. "No, I wasn't at the top, but there were five guys who graduated cum laude. Later, when people asked, I proudly told them I graduated in the top eighteen." It was a class of eighteen. Simpson took the bar exam and was gratified to learn that his score was near the top. In mid-July, his entire class was sworn into the State Bar and invited to lunch by his father, Wyoming's governor.

Al, Ann, and little Bill returned to Cody and moved into a modest house. Al was eager to begin the practice of law. It was a good time to settle down, since Ann was now pregnant with their second child, Colin.

That summer and fall, Milward ran for a second term as governor but lost, largely because of his opposition to capital punishment and a controversy over the routing of future Interstate 90 in northeast Wyoming. His loss to Democrat Joe Hickey would have ended his political career but for a remarkable turn of events. In November 1960, popular Wyoming Republican Keith Thomson was elected to the U.S. Senate. Before being sworn in, he suffered a heart attack and died. Governor Hickey, now halfway through his first term as governor, found Thomson's death an extraordinary opportunity. Wyoming law allowed him to resign the governorship and have himself sworn into Thomson's Senate seat. He could serve on an appointed basis for two years, until a special election for the remaining four years of the term could be conducted in November 1962.

Milward, still stinging from his loss of the governorship to

Hickey two years earlier, was particularly displeased by this "political opportunism." Announcing his own candidacy for the remaining four years of the six-year Senate term, Simpson—with his son Al serving as campaign manager—labeled Hickey the "instant senator."

Late in the contest Hickey suffered a heart attack. Milward ceased his own campaign activities out of respect for his stricken opponent and on November 6, 1962, won the contest with 57.8 percent of the vote. He served in the Senate until announcing in 1966 that he would be unable to run for a full Senate term, due to the onset of Parkinson's disease.

With his father in the Senate, Al began thinking about his own career. When he found an opportunity, he gathered his family to reveal his intention to run for a seat in the Wyoming House of Representatives. He was elected on November 3, 1964.

Of the numerous initiatives Representative Simpson spearheaded during his years in the state legislature, none more exhilarated him than House Bill 208, which pitted him and a handful of colleagues against the Union Pacific Railroad. The issue involved what Simpson saw as unfair competition.

As a provision of the original development of the railroads, the federal government gave Union Pacific alternate sections of land across the state within twenty miles of the rail line. Some of those mile-square sections lay adjacent to deposits of trona, which is mined underground and used to make glass, paper, and detergents. Union Pacific was attempting to keep trona-mining companies from combining federal leases into a profitable unit by denying them the right to make tunnel crossings under the checkerboard U.P. sections. The railroad owned competing trona operations and thus sought to put competitors at a disadvantage by this action.

> We had a friend in the attorney general's office who found the confidential documents saying that if a trona company would give Union Pacific *forty-eight percent* of the action [value of the trona transported], then they could transit U.P. property. That was damn sure overreaching. I put in a bill. It said that if the

trona company needed to cross the corner of a U.P. section underground, they could do so by condemnation. The Union Pacific went insane.

Simpson and two colleagues—Republican Harold Hellbaum and Democrat Ed Herschler, who later became governor—took the battle to the House floor. On February 7, 1967, the *Casper Star Tribune* reported: "Rep. Alan K. Simpson (R-Park) slashed out at the Union Pacific Railroad in one of the most bitter attacks ever heard on the floor of the House as House Bill 208 came before the Committee of the Whole Monday." Decades later, in an interview for this book, Simpson cheerfully told of the day he backed down Union Pacific and its ivy-league lawyers: "The last night there was a big party. The New York lawyers were there, and the Los Angeles lawyers and all the other U.P. people. This one New York lawyer got up and said, 'I want to tell you something. I am so God damned sick and tired of listening to stories about you poor old country lawyers. You sons-a-bitches cleaned our clock!'"

During Al's more than thirteen years in the state legislature, the Simpsons had a third child, Susan, and Al rose through the leadership ranks, achieving the positions of majority whip, majority floor leader, and speaker pro-tem. Then in 1977, while he, Ann, and their daughter were visiting Ann's sister and her daughter in Paris, a wire arrived from Milward. It reported that two-term senator Cliff Hansen of Wyoming—elected when Milward retired—had announced his retirement from the Senate. "I didn't even play it coy," said Al. "I went right down and got a bottle of wine, some goat cheese and a big baguette. I said to Ann and Sue, 'Here we go—we're going to run for the Senate.'"

Late that year, forty-six-year-old Al Simpson resigned his Wyoming House seat and announced his U.S. Senate campaign. Initial reaction was generally positive, with one vocal exception. Their youngest child, Sue, was a sophomore in high school. "No!" she pleaded. "What will I do without my friends? Are you are trying to *ruin my life?*"

Simpson was not without competition in the Republican primary. A professional engineer named Hugh Binford, one of several other candidates leaping into the race, referred to himself as "Bigfoot," which was not the reason Simpson didn't like him.

> Bigfoot was bombastic. He had money. He made it in the oil and gas business. Like a lot of guys with money, he thought it gave him power. He was saying things about me, like I was a "100 percent environmentalist," which wasn't that bad, but he was also saying that I hadn't been pure enough on gun control. Man, I finally just had enough of him; I had a bellyful.
>
> He kept smarting off, so one day at a picnic rally in Casper, I walked over and said, "I wanna tell you, I'm tired of your shit. I am tired of you. I'll bet you a thousand bucks I'm going to whip your ass. Not only that, if you keep mouthing off about me, I'm going to *punch your lights out.*"
>
> "I don't think I have to take this," Bigfoot sputtered.
>
> "Well then, maybe you should put your money up—or *shut* up!"

Simpson defeated Binford 37,332 to 26,768, with the remaining votes split among the others. "Bigfoot," whose feet were actually smaller than Al's size fifteens, never officially accepted or paid the bet.

In the general election, Simpson faced feisty Democrat Ray Whitaker, a trial lawyer. It was a spirited and occasionally contentious campaign, but on November 7, 1978, Simpson took 62 percent of the vote to become Wyoming's next U.S. senator. He was gratified and proud, but had one more campaign to wage before moving to Washington.

He realized that if he could be sworn into office before the other newly elected senators around the country, he would gain a dozen positions in Senate seniority. To accomplish this, he asked outgoing Republican Senator Cliff Hansen to resign a few days before the official end of his term. Hansen did not agree immediately, but when he did, Simpson asked Democratic governor Ed Herschler to appoint him to the remainder of Hansen's term.

In Cody's Christ Episcopal Church the night of December 31, 1978, personal friend Justice of the Peace Richard W. Day administered a brief oath. With the words, "I will well and faithfully discharge the duties of the office on which I am about to enter: So help me God," forty-seven-year-old Alan K. Simpson became the nation's 1,782nd United States senator.

Chapter Three

Big Steps

"It's like working in the sewers of Paris!" the new senator muttered while peering up through the glass pane separating his small basement office in the Senate's Russell building from the window well outside. He watched as the soles of shoes appeared and disappeared on the grate above, people walking importantly up and down Constitution Avenue.

"I'm not sure *this* is the kind of office I had in mind," he chuckled to his small band of wide-eyed staffers. "But it certainly serves to keep one humble." The employees, several in their first day on the job, stared at the little window, then at their boss, then at one another. "So this is the United States Senate," one of them observed with a tone of disappointment.

The cramped office was basic in every respect but served satisfactorily as a temporary home while more appropriate facilities were being prepared across the street, on the sixth floor of the Dirksen building. Until then, Simpson and his fledgling crew would labor in subterranean chaos—which they did by unpacking boxes, setting up shop as best they could, and spending considerable time wondering what to do next.

Senator David Pryor of Arkansas, a Democrat also just elected, appeared at Simpson's door bearing a gift. It was a large plant that he felt would perfectly match the Simpson office décor. Al stared at the gift for a moment, then burst into laughter. The plant was dead.

Although several staff positions were yet to be filled, the dozen people already on the job crowded close for their first staff meeting. Most were happy just to have found their way from Wyoming to Washington, then via subway and bus routes to the Capitol building, and through the intimidating bowels of the Senate. Excited, intimidated, and more than a little confused, they awaited their assignments. Al didn't have any. "Well, I don't like job descriptions. They can be limiting. I can only say that each of you has a general idea of your job, and you have a title. I told the people of Wyoming that if they elected me, I would work hard and try to make them proud. That is *my* job description. As of right now, it is also *yours*."

Legislative aides set off to obtain copies of Senate bills and to consider how issues discussed and debated during the campaign might be addressed legislatively. Several others gathered at the nearby coffee shop to ponder the situation. As the senator's press secretary, I set off to investigate the Senate's recording and printing facilities.

The scheduling secretary phoned her counterparts in the office of Wyoming's senior delegation member, Senator Malcolm Wallop. He had been elected two years earlier and had previously served with Simpson in the Wyoming Legislature. Other staffers chatted with their counterparts in the office of Dick Cheney, who was beginning his first term in Wyoming's sole seat in the House of Representatives.

One challenge was clear to everyone. Something had to be done with the mountains of congratulatory letters and cards that Senate Post Office employees seemed eager to deliver in large wheeled bins. From the beginning, responding to the flood of incoming mail was a tall challenge. For eighteen years, it grew.

Several initial staff members were experienced in office procedures, having previously worked for Senator Cliff Hansen. Among them was Paul Holtz, who, as editor of the University of Wyoming's student newspaper, had sparred mightily with Simpson back in 1957 over the paper's reporting of student leadership elections.

> I stayed on, with several other Hansen staff members, to help his newly formed staff get used to their new jobs. At the end of about two months, when I got ready to move on, Al called us all into his office to wish me goodbye. He used the occasion to recount the story about the student body president election at the University of Wyoming. He ended the story

by saying the encounter made it clear to him that "you should never argue with people who buy printing ink by the barrel." It made for a good story, but it was advice Big Al found very hard to follow during his three terms in the Senate.

A first order of Senate business was doling out committee assignments to the new senators. Simpson sought one in particular. "When I came to the Senate, Strom Thurmond of South Carolina asked me what committees I wanted to be on. I said I wanted to be on Judiciary. Strom said, 'I'll talk to Ted [Kennedy], and we'll get that done.'"

THREE MILE ISLAND

They did get that done, and because of Simpson's seniority jump courtesy of Senator Hanson's resignation three days early, Simpson was named the highest-ranking Republican on the Environment and Public Works subcommittee on Nuclear Regulation. Democratic Senator Gary Hart of Colorado was its chair.

On March 28, 1979, less than three months after Simpson began service, a member of Hart's staff rushed up. "Senator Simpson, there is a problem. You need to contact my boss right away. This is serious! There could be a meltdown at the Metropolitan Edison nuclear power plant near Harrisburg, in southern Pennsylvania." The problem was at Three Mile Island (TMI).

Arrangements were quickly made to transport Simpson and Hart to TMI by helicopter. Prior to liftoff several Republican colleagues advised Simpson to be careful of Hart, who had expressed presidential aspirations. They feared he might use the TMI incident to partisan advantage. During the noisy northbound flight, Simpson was distracted by the helicopter's condition.

There we were, in this shitty helicopter. Hell, you could see through the floorboards! I had been in them in the army and I had never seen a crappier one. I put that out of mind a moment, and turned to Hart.

"Gary," I said, "I don't know you that well, but I just wonder if you are going to use this [power plant incident] as a tool to destroy nuclear power in America."

"Who said *that*?" Hart demanded.

"That doesn't matter. I just want to know," I answered.

Hart said he had no such agenda. He added, "Alan, just watch what I do and say."

A few minutes later, Simpson wasn't watching Hart at all; he was watching in disbelief as the helicopter began to hover over the stricken power plant, a facility reported to be venting radioactive gas. His blood pressure lowered when the craft landed but rose again when the crippled plant's operators described what had happened: "We listened to the most inept people running the most inept organization. When we came out of the briefing—well, I never saw more media in my life. They were talking about the ghastly 'plume' of radiation. Of course, the plume was about the size of a sparrow fart."

Following a yearlong investigation, the senators issued their report on the accident. Before a roomful of reporters, Simpson joked that "before TMI," he had hair. Some correspondents laughed. Others grimaced. "We prepared the only report about the incident that had everything in it attributed. There was no rumor. It was all attributed, with footnotes, and was signed off by Gary and me. I still think it is the finest such report I ever saw, in all my time."

DRIER BEHIND THE EARS

Another challenge awaited Simpson in the Environment and Public Works Committee, where Chairman Ed Muskie of Maine was not amused by the Wyoming senator's suggestion that funding for the Corps of Engineers be reduced 10 percent. Simpson felt the agency was wasting money, an impression fueled by its invitation to fly him around America on a tour of Corps facilities. Why, he asked, was it necessary for the Corps to be flying around the country in all these government airplanes?

Muskie glowered while Simpson pressed his case, hour after hour. Finally the chairman could take no more. Addressing the committee but focusing on his junior colleague, Muskie said somewhat bluntly that perhaps the senator from Wyoming was too inexperienced to understand Corps needs, as would a more seasoned member. Simpson refused to back down. He wanted a vote and got it: a 10–2 shellacking.

When the session ended, he stepped into an elevator with Muskie, who said, "You hung in there, young man. I admire that. In order to succeed around this place, Simpson, you have to be about half son of a bitch—and I see you are that!" As the elevator arrived at its destination, Muskie gave Simpson a reassuring pat on the shoulder. In a way perhaps only fully understood in the Senate's rarified air, the Wyoming senator considered himself highly praised. So did a reporter who by happenstance was in the same elevator. Bruce Kennedy, who owned a chain of weekly community newspapers in Wyoming, wrote that Muskie had shown the Wyoming freshman that if you come to Washington to rock the boat, you might get wet. Simpson countered that his experience had left him "drier behind the ears."

In the months that followed, he continued vigorously opposing Corps initiatives such as the Tennessee Tombigbee project, an expensive canal designed to run barge traffic from Alabama into Mississippi. In an editorial on July 21, 1981, the *Washington Post* saw it Simpson's way:

> It took 25 years from the time the Tenn-Tom was first autho-
> rized for Congress to become sufficiently persuaded of its
> merit to appropriate money for it. Congress was right the first
> 25 times. . . .
>
> Nearly everything about the project is uncertain, including
> where the canal could sensibly end, which direction barge traf-
> fic on it will travel, who would use it and for what, and whether
> the benefits would ever exceed the costs of construction.

The waterway project was funded at a construction cost of $2 billion and was completed on December 12, 1984, over Simpson's ongoing objections.

The Wyoming senator was also heavily involved in "Superfund," the goal of which was to identify and clean up the nation's worst toxic waste dump sites—and in separate efforts to assure clean air, clean water, acid rain reduction, and the protection of endangered species. As difficult as these initiatives became, they were no greater than yet another significant challenge. In May 1979 President Jimmy Carter appointed Simpson to the Select Commission on Immigration and Refugee Policy. The Wyomingite knew little about immigration law but quickly came to appreciate the depth of the problem—and to admire the commission's chairman, Father Theodore Hesburgh, president of the University of Notre Dame. It was the beginning of a long friendship.

Family Ties

Meanwhile, Ann Simpson was wasting no time adapting to her new Washington environment. "The big issue for me was allowing enough time to get everywhere. I certainly was excited about it, and I didn't feel overwhelmed at all. The congressional group [elected] that year remained very strong friends and we saw each other all the time."

Ann joined the Senate Wives Club and began networking in Washington's social circles. Before long, she decided to go back to work. "I was in real estate sales in Wyoming. When I came to D.C., Antoinette Hatfield [wife of Senator Mark Hatfield of Oregon] had just opened her new brokerage. She asked me to come in with her, so I took the test. I passed quickly and became more and more involved. After daughter Susan left home, we had college tuitions for two sons and a daughter. It was wonderful to be able to pay them."

Although Susan had reacted negatively to the possibility of moving while still in high school, her anguish faded. Having learned from her father and grandfather that opportunity can be found in challenge, she went to work on her future. The National Cathedral School soon had a new junior class president named Sue Simpson, who the following year became president of the student body. Looking back, she said her father's decision to run for the Senate was "the best thing that could have happened to me."

War on Gibberish

By Simpson's second year in office he had grown weary of the way official Washington communicated with the public. Speaking both humorously and seriously in his statement titled "War on Gibberish," he said, "I have launched a drive to return *English* as the official language spoken in Washington."

He charged that people around the nation had become frustrated and confused by Washington "bureaucratese." Numerous newspapers and magazines picked up his statement, which said in part:

> I have long ago come to believe that the relationship between the government and our nation's citizens has been unduly strained because nobody could understand what the government was trying to say—including the people who said it. . . .
>
> No wonder people become annoyed . . . when they receive explanations such as the following gem gleaned from agency correspondence.
>
> > Innovative mechanisms of input by the techno structure can finalize solutions to societal dysfunctions. . . . Submitted attached is our response to your position relative to our answer concerning your question about the statement regarding our facts relating to your allegation superseding the remark on the correction to the addition of the omission in your programming specification. Should your evaluation of our review of your changes lead to revision of the amendment to your omission, our response may require discussion.
>
> I request that those who work for me—and with me—try to follow these basic rules: if an ordinary word fits, why not use it? Write short sentences. Don't look for original and creative ways

to repeat yourself. Don't use words that continually send people running off to the dictionary or out on a coffee break. Do not assume everyone knows exactly what you are talking about. Omit needless words. Vigorous and lively writing is concise. A sentence should contain no unnecessary words for the same reason that a machine has no unnecessary parts. Let's promise that:

> "At this point in time" will be "now."
> "Heretofore" will be "before."
> "Effectuate reductions" will be "reduce."
> "To impact on" will be "influence."
> "A query relative to the status of" will be "a question about."
> "Aforesaid" or "aforementioned" will be "previous."

I direct that the following words and phrases, among others, will no longer be [used] in my office: infrastructure, interface, parcelization, conurbation, disaggregation, full time temporary employees, and part time permanent employees.

Simpson's decree was well received in Washington but had little practical impact outside his own office.

On May 12, 1980, *Washington Post* staff writer Timothy Robinson wrote about it, focusing on the Wyomingite's irritation with the writing style of committee staff lawyers.

> The senator says he plans on invoking what he calls the Simpson terrorization process the next time a committee staffer brings him an unintelligible document.
>
> If the staffer admits to writing the document, Simpson said, he is going to ask, "Why didn't you use English, and what were you trying to say?"
>
> He said he has concluded that "the only thing they (Hill lawyers) fear is embarrassment. I don't want to humiliate the fellow, but accountability has to be part of it."
>
> Simpson said he has been presented "the goofiest-looking legislation known" by committee [staff] members who "just sit around all day ginning up stuff."

His point is to have laws written more clearly and to "make laws more understandable to the governed." If that can't be done, he asks, "why bother?"

Star *Power*

Not all newspaper commentary about Simpson was approving. His first major skirmish with Wyoming's largest newspaper, the *Casper Star Tribune*, occurred during his second year in the Senate. The paper was upset by his comments and legislative efforts on the issue of newsroom searches by the police. On July 29, 1980, Simpson released an eight-page statement, a portion of which read:

> My recent comments about newsroom searches seem to have struck a raw nerve at the *Star Tribune*. Their article and subsequent editorials on the topic would seem to leave one with the impression that I believe the police should have the right to march unimpeded in lock step into newsrooms throughout the country and rummage desks and files whenever the urge strikes. Nothing could be further from the truth. . . .
>
> I fully agree with the *Star*'s argument that law enforcement agencies should not routinely use newsroom documents as an extension of their investigative activities. However, there are times when an individual or business—newspapers and television stations included—may have possession of documentary evidence that may be critically needed in the investigation or prosecution of a crime. In those cases there should be, and there already is, a legal and proper course of action.

Because the *Star* was also concerned about amendments their senator had put before the Senate Judiciary Committee, he explained those too:

> I felt that warrant searches of the press should have been permitted if the offense being investigated or prosecuted was related to espionage, treason, or sabotage, and if there was probable cause to believe that the delay required to obtain

the materials through a subpoena would have substantially reduced the usefulness of the materials, or that the giving of notice pursuant to subpoena would have resulted in the destruction, alteration, or concealment of the materials. . . .

The press does have very special importance in our system, and is being given very special protection. If, however, an irresponsible member of the press ceases to serve, but rather seeks to frustrate justice, then this special protection should not apply.

Simpson and the *Star* batted the issue back and forth for months, both sides remaining adamant. Irritations arising from their first major confrontation evolved into significant disagreements on scores of other issues. Their relationship never fully healed.

Sweet Suite

After operating from offices in the Dirksen building for nearly two years, Simpson was given the option to relocate his staff to the comparatively opulent new Hart building. Because of the structure's cost and spaciousness, he feared his Wyoming constituents might disapprove. He finally opted to make the move but issued a public statement emphasizing his reluctance. Congressman Dick Cheney, who had been assigned a cramped office on the House side, was quick to respond by letter.

Dear Al:

C'mon! You're breaking our "Harts" with all that hand-wringing over your move to the Hart! Fess up, now—you-all just can't wait to get over there where you'll have three acres per staffer.

Have you given any thought to renting out a few square feet to a deserving member of the Lower Body—someone clean-cut, with no bad habits?

My staff is planning a nice "house-swarming" gift for yours when you get settled in. We've rounded up a couple of our choicest cockroaches—a strapping stud named "Crusher," and his very prolific mate, "Daisy." We guarantee an abundance of hearty offspring in no time, who will be constant companions to your staff. A nice batch of robust cockroaches can eat more paper in a day than you can file in a week, and we've developed a special breed that thrives on Congressional Records—"Cannon Courageous," we call them.

Enviously yours,
Dick Cheney and staff

PS: Don't worry—if anyone from Wyoming mentions anything about your moving into the Hart, we'll be sure to say that you hate the place and had to be dragged kicking and screaming into its disgusting opulence and depressing spaciousness.

THY ROD AND THY STAFF

The two-hour time zone difference between Washington and Wyoming meant that when Simpson arose each morning, most Wyomingites were still asleep. Because he considered it a functional and political necessity to be handed a current Wyoming news summary as early as possible each day—no matter where he was—employees in Wyoming arose early, snatched up the morning papers, watched the television news, and madly typed summaries. In the early days before Senate offices were computerized, it required six minutes to fax each page to Washington.

When he reached his office, additional memos awaited—lists of births, deaths, awards, marriage notices, and similar matters around the state and nation. If it was important to his constituents or anyone he knew, anywhere, he wanted to know about it, pronto. Ann too received news summaries and wrote scores of congratulatory and condolence letters. At times, staff members became intimidated and even infuriated by the barrage of correspondence.

Dear Senator

The flood of incoming mail only accelerated. Many inquiries were routine. Some were sad and even bizarre. One woman in Dallas wrote repeatedly about her discovery that mutants in the sludge ponds of a Texas oil refinery had grown to become "giant killer worms." She feared they would soon be slithering about the country, killing everyone they encountered. She felt that Simpson was the only person of national prominence who would dare confront the situation.

One day she appeared in the office. Simpson was in the Capitol at the time, so I met with her. After our long conversation, she seemed satisfied that "appropriate action" would be taken, and returned to Texas. She phoned a few days later to say that oil company officials discovered she was trying to blow the whistle on their killer worm problem. "Poison gas is being pumped into my kitchen," she said in her last communication with the office.

More Mail

While some senators were sending canned responses to constituent inquiries—or no responses—Simpson relished answering every question in detail: "Some guy would write concerning five or six topics, and we would respond to each of them, in detail. Then the person would write again and say, 'Hey, I didn't ask for a letter *that* long.' I would write back again and say, 'Well, you *asked* for those issues to be addressed.' I *loved* that."

On rare occasions, the exchanges grew harsh. Excerpts from this response to a constituent (and friend) demonstrate how irritated Simpson could become:

> God, it must be tough for you to write a letter like that one of December 9, 1985, and then sit around the fireplace in Jackson and say you just wrote me kind of a "heavy piece." It was not heavy—it was hostile and nasty. I didn't like it a damn bit. . . .
>
> It was just like some of that pathetic drivel and crap you leveled at me during the wilderness bill—and then when it

was all done you were right there kissing my old arse. You can't have it both ways, pal. . . .

The interesting thing about the brazen arrogance of your drivel is that you always seem to indicate that if people don't come out on your side, then they don't understand one whit about what the hell is going on . . . and you really missed the full reality of all human life there in that first paragraph. If you "got a burr" under a saddle, I sure as hell didn't put it there. . . . Take that ten-foot umbilical cord you're hauling around and ram it into some other navel. . . .

The classic lesson in all this exercise is to remember that whenever you "got a burr under your saddle," you put 'er there, friend. Nobody else. The horse didn't—and neither did the horse's ass out here.

Al often dictated lengthy letters to people who never expected one, since they had only signed a petition. One of the most tedious office jobs involved pawing through stacks of Wyoming phone books, tracking down the mailing addresses of people who had signed petitions, leaving no contact information. Over time, numerous individuals, having forgotten they had signed a petition in the first place, received letters from Simpson—and then wrote back to ask why he was writing.

Eagle Eye

On countless occasions a staffer was dismayed to find that during Simpson's nighttime work sessions at home, he had discovered a single typographical error in a lengthy letter. This meant, in the days before computerized correspondence, that authors would "learn accuracy" by retyping entire documents.

After the office received its first computers, I explained that small errors could easily be corrected and documents could be reprinted in seconds. This irritated him. "Well, if it is *that* easy to fix mistakes, how are they going to learn to be more careful in the first place?"

Sometimes Al's requirement that staff pay keen attention to detail avoided significant embarrassment. Multiple copies of his July 12, 1981, letter to constituents were stacked on his desk for signature when I spotted an unfortunate error in the lead paragraph: "Thank you for your postcard regarding the explicit scene of sexual intercourse on the Pubic Broadcasting System April 16. I do very much appreciate your concerns." Before the letters were mailed, the word *pubic* was corrected to read *public*.

No matter what kind of draft document Simpson was handed, he could be counted on to edit it, usually several times. Ann is among those keenly aware of this.

> I hate to give him something that I'm writing. I know he's going to edit it. Then, when I give him the edited version—he edits *that*. But, if you actually *want* an editor, he's the best.
>
> I have sometimes said to him, "Alan! This is *my* letter. I'm not using that word, that isn't the way I do it. I'm briefer than you are and that's my style. Don't make your style my style."
>
> If I edit *his* stuff, I just take out all kinds of descriptive over-the-top things. He is an amazing writer. He is so thorough. I admire that, although it is sometimes maddening.

The Simpsonizers

Each day the staff logged incoming telephone calls. Some names remained on the list for months, since Al didn't have time to return them but refused to delete them. On at least two occasions, callers died before he found time to phone them back.

The office "black book" was a significant project. The huge database contained details about tens of thousands of people the Simpsons knew, or who had contacted him or any of his offices for any reason. When he and Ann traveled, they carried segments of the black book. By the time they arrived, they had reviewed the names of people they might encounter and the issues that might be mentioned.

Simpson was and is a creature of the night, often working into the wee hours. Each workday evening, senior employees crammed memos, schedule requests, draft letters, news clips, and a variety of related items into his large briefcase—from which he worked at every opportunity. It was his practice to "mark up" memos by jotting comments or questions on them. This was known in the office as "Simpsonizing," or "Simpsonization."

Over the years he underlined significant points, circled key words, and scratched notes in the columns of hundreds of thousands of staff-authored memos and was able to quote from some of them months or years later.

Researching and drafting tens of thousands of personalized, detailed letters soaked up a lot of staff time. Simpson was unsympathetic. At one point he became so irritated with staff "sluggishness" that he instituted a financial penalty system. Anyone assigned a constituent question who failed to produce a draft response within a specified period was subject to a fifty-dollar salary penalty—per letter.

Simpson himself was one of the most significant factors in correspondence delays, since he demanded to see, amend and approve everything leaving the office over his signature. He altered drafts extensively and asked to see them repeatedly. Outgoing letters bore the date of the first draft, no matter when they finally left the office. Many recipients presumed that their letter from Simpson had been lost in the mail for weeks.

Black Monday

One Monday Simpson summoned his entire staff into his office and said, "I don't like rooting out mistakes in staff paperwork while you are off somewhere having a good time." He asked whether they were working for him, or vice versa. Eyeing each person in the room, he announced that henceforth, they would redouble their efforts. If burning the midnight oil was required of him, "sure as hell" everyone could do that.

An individual with a doctoral degree and issue mastery, but weak interpersonal skills, said he felt that digging up information for people in Wyoming was a poor use of his valuable time. His talents should be put to better use.

"*I'm* the senator here!" Al almost hissed. "Answering the mail is important to *me*. It is not beneath *me*. So if you would like to continue your labors here among us, helping with the mail will not be beneath *you!*" When reminded of Black Monday two decades later, he still felt the same way: "I just *motivated* them. They didn't like doing the mail. They thought it was demeaning. I was up dictating in the night. I figured everybody should do that too. I said that we don't represent Pennsylvania, where there are a lot of people, we represent Wyoming where there are few people—and dammit, those people *know* me and expect an *answer.*"

His staff ran up against other kinds of surprises too. He often ate lunch in his office, usually a plate of fruit and a slice of pecan pie. He liked the pie filling but not the pecans. One day a staffer noticed him sucking the filling off each pecan and returning the nuts to his plate. "Al! Do you always suck off the juice and spit out the pecans?" He confirmed that he never ate the pecans. "But Al!" she gasped. "Every day when we take your tray out of your office, we see that pile of pecans—and we *eat them!* Sometimes we fight over them. We had no idea they had been in your *mouth!*"

Because of Simpson's unique approach to politics and constituent service, *Washington Post* reporter Ward Sinclair singled him out in an article headlined "Freshman Simpson: Western Breeze through Stuffy Senate" on January 11, 1980:

> A senator who finds renewal in Thurber and Mencken, keeps Western originals by Russell and Remington on his walls and sees the Senate as something of a funny farm deserves a closer look.
>
> Actually, the word about Alan K. Simpson, a Republican from Wyoming, got around rather quickly after he showed up in the Senate last year.
>
> The guy is different, they were saying. He talked back to senior senators, always with courtly deference, but he talked back. Don't tell me how to vote, he cautioned committee staffers accustomed to telling senators how to vote.

Simpson, 48, came here last year labeled as one of those new hard-core conservatives hell-bent on standing big government on its head.

The game of politics, alas, is played with labels and codes and Simpson is stuck with his label. What a yuck.

He is conservative and big government doesn't enamor him, but his link with the label pretty much ends there. He idolizes some of the liberals he's supposed to abhor, cosponsors their bills and trades ribald stories with them.

Simpson turns out to be one of the most refreshing breezes that occasionally gentle their way through Congressional pomp and fustian to remind that all is not lost; it hasn't even been found.

CHRONICLING LEADERSHIP

In early November 1984, Al Simpson was elected by a wide margin to a second six-year Senate term. He was grateful for voters' confidence in him and relieved that Republicans had retained control of the Senate. For him personally, the best was yet to come. When the Senate Republicans met in secrecy later that month, they selected Bob Dole as party leader and—in a decision that changed his life— Al Simpson as assistant leader, or "whip."

Voting on chairmanship of the Republican Senatorial Committee was up next, and competing for the job were Al's old Wyoming friend and Senate colleague Malcolm Wallop and Pennsylvania's John Heinz. Unfortunately for Wallop, many Republican senators were disinclined to fill two leadership positions with senators from the same state—and Simpson had just been elected to the number two spot.

Simpson intended to vote for Wallop. To be straightforward about his choice, he showed his marked ballot to Heinz. A senator sitting behind the two witnessed their brief exchange and thought Simpson was demonstrating his intent to vote *for* Heinz. He did not, but Heinz still won, by a single vote. Later, the observing senator incorrectly told Wallop that he thought Simpson had voted for Heinz. Wallop stormed straight to Simpson, who explained that the other senator simply had it wrong. Wallop remained unsure for a period but eventually accepted the explanation. His wife did not.

After stewing about it for days, French Wallop decided to vent her irritation—not at Al but at Ann. Decades later, Ann described their confrontation: "French Wallop invited me for lunch. Then she assailed me about what Al had done to Malcolm on the vote, saying that he had voted for somebody else. I finally said, 'I don't want to hear any more.' I was rattled, but I held firm and told her, 'I'm going to call Al right now.'" Al assured her that he had shown his ballot to John Heinz in order to be upfront about his voting for Wallop—and that the observing senator had relayed an incorrect assumption to Malcolm.

Ann returned to the table and repeated the explanation. Mrs. Wallop was not at all persuaded, and their discussion devolved into an angry confrontation. Ann, emphasizing her husband's ongoing support of Malcolm over many years, finally cut loose. "Let me tell you something, lady, this is how it is. Malcolm has always enjoyed Al's full support. I don't care what you have been told or what you think. Any suggestion otherwise is just plain wrong."

"That terminated for all time," she said without a hint of regret, an "already unfavorable relationship."

Looking back on his sixteen years of Senate service with Malcolm Wallop, and their years of state legislative service and friendship before that, Al said in 2006, "Malcolm and I have a very warm and wonderful relationship. I wouldn't want to taint that in any way." He did not distance himself from Ann's assessment of French, now Wallop's former wife.

Whipping Post

Everything was coming up roses as Simpson's second six-year Senate term began. At home late one night, he picked up the microphone of his tape recorder and made this commitment:

I am going to start something as a New Year's resolution. I am going to make notes when I get home in the evening, as to what happened during each day. It will be a diary entitled "The Odyssey of Big Al and His Travels through the Peaks and Valleys of Politics."

I will relate some of the things that happen from the beginning of my second term, after being elected the assistant majority leader of the United States Senate on November 28, 1984, as I begin my job as majority whip on January 3, 1985.

He honored that commitment, eventually amassing a private diary amounting to more than five thousand pages.[1] His first entry:

A fine young man assigned to me as driver picked me up at the house. Too ostentatious for me. I will ride in the front seat. There is a little reading lamp there. Since time will be a precious commodity for me, I will fall for the bait.

A meeting with all Republican senators in room 207 [of the Capitol building], the Mansfield room. A rambunctious crowd. [Senator] Dan Quayle presented his reforms of the committee system and got rocks rained down on his head. . . .

Into the Senate chamber. I now sit down in the center of the well, next to Bob Dole. I will miss my seat in the back. In all of my years as a legislator, I have always had the very furthest seat in the back on the center aisle, in order to watch those rascals. I will probably lose some of my prowess.

Vice President George Bush swore me in for another term, and did so again later in informal ceremonies in the Old Senate Chamber. With the media present, George became quite solemn and said, "Will you raise your right hand and place it on the Bible, and do you solemnly swear—and I understand you do often . . ." That broke the whole thing up. It was a delightful event and George is a most delightful friend in every respect.

On January 7, 1985, Simpson attended the opening of the Senate and House sessions. The ceremony began with the reading of the reports of the Electoral College vote, followed by certification of the national elections, state by state.

> A very interesting ceremony. Each state submitted a sealed envelope with a ballot. There was a special "letter opener" for each of the envelopes and the Sergeant at Arms of the House presented one to me. It is a small letter opener about five or six inches long of pressed metal with the seal of the United States Congress on it, in a circle.
>
> I will keep that very instrument in a separate small box. I marked the handle with my penknife. I scratched in '1/7/85—AKS.' You know me—a pack rat.

Over the years he collected an impressive array of memorabilia, ranging from a Capitol building brick to doodles by renowned Americans. Sometimes, when he spotted someone sketching on a pad during a meeting, he asked if he could add it to his collection.

The Western Front

Through it all, Al was actively monitoring his aging parents' deteriorating health. In mid-January 1985 he and Ann flew to Phoenix, where Milward and Lorna were spending the winter. The trip had a secondary element, the "Senator's Cup" tournament at John Gardiner's Tennis Ranch in Scottsdale. "I played thirty-six games of tennis in one day and won more than I lost. That is real progress for this kid. I came in about the middle of the Republican senators. We won the tournament 80–75 over the Democrats. Great fun."

The event featured more footwork than was required solely for tennis. Ann had taught Al to dance, and until that night the Simpsons' dancing abilities had remained relatively unknown to his colleagues. "The evening's entertainment included a dancing contest. Annie and I did a very swift and spirited jitterbug, alone, and we won the cup. We couldn't believe how we jigged around."

Returning to Washington, Al took his son Colin, who had arrived for President Reagan's second inauguration, to his Off the Record Club dinner at the Monocle Restaurant. "I am the president and the host of that outfit. We had about twenty journalists asking questions. . . . It was a good session and a rather long day with the brethren of the Fourth Estate. Then Colin and I drove home and I worked until past midnight, preparing for a speech at eight in the morning."

During the evening, Al spoke on the phone with Bill Walsh, head coach of the San Francisco 49ers football team. The two, who had met during the tennis tournament in Scottsdale, spoke of the coming Super Bowl game. "I told him that I was the only guy in America *not* asking for a Super Bowl ticket. I wished him well and we had a nice visit. He said he thought he had a chance in the game."

Of more immediate importance was the 1985 inauguration. It proved most notable for its brutal weather.

Sunday, January 20, 1985: It is beginning to get cold as hell. An icy northern wind really rips through your underwear. However, it was not too tough for the *Wyoming* people. They had all gathered at the Wyoming State Society congressional delegation champagne reception at the Capitol Hill Hotel. It was great fun—a nice little buffet, with drinks. Neither Malcolm Wallop nor Dick Cheney could be there, so Ann and I held court with all of the Wyoming people.

Al, Ann, brother Pete, and his wife Lynne jumped into the "company car." Al drove, since it was Sunday and he had given his driver the day off. A short while later they arrived at the home of Sandra Day O'Connor, an associate justice of the United States Supreme Court, and her husband, John. "Sandra and John have become lovely friends of ours," Al told his diary. "Brother Pete and I were called upon to share our musical talents. We sang a verse or two of 'Detour' and one of 'We Three'—without accompaniment.

We told a few jokes and did our 'Brother Routine.' It was fun and everyone seemed to like it."

The event's warm camaraderie seemed at odds with the cold winter scene outside. "During the gathering, the beautiful hard, crisp south sun was shining across the Potomac and through the window on this very stark but bright and sunlit winter day. The windows were covered with frost, but there was warm company and delightful food. A very lovely, warm, snug luncheon ran into the afternoon and past three thirty." Later that day, as San Francisco was "trampling" Miami 38–16 in Super Bowl XIX in Stanford Stadium in Palo Alto, California, it was decided that the bitterly cold D.C. weather would trample the next day's outdoor activities. The inaugural committee moved the ceremony inside the Capitol, resulting in significant crowding.

> There were a few seats in the rotunda for Chief Justice Burger and his wife Vera, and for Tip O'Neill and his wife Millie. There also was room for [Senator] Mac Mathias and Mac's wife Ann. Mac was chairman of the inaugural committee. There were seats for the president and vice president and Nancy Reagan and Barbara Bush, and that was about it. Everyone else stood. I mean everybody. There was no room for House spouses, and limited room for Senate spouses.
>
> I kept Ann right on my arm as we walked from the Senate chamber to the Rotunda. Strom Thurmond and his wife Nancy were leading, and Ann and I were second. Oh, leadership! We pressed close to the podium and the platform within the Rotunda and were about fifteen feet from the presidential party and from President Reagan as he gave his inaugural address. It was a warm and conciliatory message laced with pleas for bipartisanship. . . .
>
> The impressive moment for me was when we said the Lord's Prayer. The sound of those voices going up a hundred and eighty-three feet into the air to the top of the Capitol Dome—and looking up and seeing the windows, frosted

from the cold, and the crisp sunlight and blue sky—and the sound coming back down and reverberating the religious commitment to the presidency and to the United States was a goose-pimpler indeed. It was "powerful medicine," as the Native Americans call it.

After the ceremony, Simpson told NBC reporter Roger Mudd, both humorously and seriously, "We'll have to slay a few sacred cows." Indeed, he was ready to attack costly federal programs considered by many citizens to be untouchable. He would continue the quest far beyond his Senate days.

Next came a Statuary Hall luncheon with President Reagan, Vice President Bush, members of the congressional leadership, and ranking government and military officials. Not all the leaders present were Americans. "Ann was seated with [Soviet] Ambassador Dobrynin. She and Anatoly have a nice friendship cooking there, since our dinner with them at the Argentine Embassy several weeks ago."

Later that day, GOP whip Simpson officially closed down the Senate session. He had not previously performed that leadership responsibility. "It was impressive, being down in that seat next to the leader and participating in the closing of that remarkable institution. A great thrill it is. I seem to be confident at that desk. It's a good feeling."

The Simpsons drove home, changed clothes, and soon arrived at a *USA Today* buffet and reception for Jim and Sarah Brady. They admired Brady, who had been shot and permanently disabled during the assassination attempt on President Reagan on March 30, 1981. "Jim is a lovely friend. I came to know him in 1979, when he was press secretary for [Senator] Bill Roth. Jim and I used to visit. Sarah is a dear woman of inspiration deluxe. She said that I ought to run for president. I demurred."

Al and Ann chatted at length with Cathie Black, president of *USA Today*. They had become such close friends that the Simpsons sometimes spent weekends in her New York City apartment.

At the Inaugural Ball in the Shoreham Hotel they joined visiting Wyomingites and hundreds of other people decked out in tuxedos and formal gowns. "We did a hell of a lot of dancing—worked up a real sweat. Annie looked beautiful in a black dress with velvet bodice and scalloped black sleeves. Later we had a glass of wine in the Shoreham garden court with Pete and Lynne, and were home by two in the morning—pooped."

The Pace Quickens

Day after day he debated issues on the Senate floor and in committee. Night after night he returned home late and worked in his den well past midnight. On a majority of weekends he flew to and from Wyoming. He became so busy that on occasion he was obligated to change clothes in his car. "January 30, 1985: I spoke at Georgetown University, in Gaston Hall. . . . I spoke to the Center for Immigration Policy and dropped by the reception afterward. I rushed like hell to my next event at the Sheraton Washington Hotel. I changed into my tuxedo shirt in the car. One of these days, I will be arrested for indecent exposure."

His staff marveled that he seemed invigorated rather than decimated by his pace. No matter the aggravations, delays, frustrations, and confrontations, his daily journal often concluded with the words "fascinating day." He seemed to rejuvenate himself with additional activity.

At the end of one busy week he and Ann flew to New York City. After he delivered a speech, the two visited the Brooklyn Art Museum and toured the city for hours before heading to the Jockey Club for dinner. Afterward, they attended a "sub-par" Broadway play. In the morning they had a quick breakfast, flew back to D.C. for a television interview, and then began a packed meeting schedule. "I think I met with half the people in Wyoming today," he said. Indeed, he had dealt with representatives of the postal service, a telephone company, food dealers, and a dozen other organizations and individuals.

He was often so busy that members of his own staff, hoping for a few seconds to confer with him, queued outside his door, waiting for visitors to leave. Then they would dash in and fire questions until he picked up the phone or the next appointment arrived. Al once irritated his entire staff by publicly comparing them to coyotes scratching on his office door.

Duty Dawns

Even though Al was up working as late as four in the morning, he had even less a chance to sleep past daybreak after Senator Dole announced that Senate sessions would commence each morning at eight. At first, Simpson was all for it. "We need to kick these guys off their butts so we can get moving on these appropriations bills." Then he realized the problem. "Guess who gets to open the sessions and be there before anyone else?—yours truly."

Never a "morning person," Al felt that if he could stay up half the night working and still arrive in time to open the next morning's Senate session at eight, showing up at a reasonable hour should be a snap for everyone else. On the morning following Dole's announcement, he was front and center—of almost nobody. "I looked like a one-acrobat troop at the Big Top. I related to my colleagues that we were 'getting addicted to sloth,' in the words of Aldous Huxley" [author of *Brave New World*].

One day Al took time to visit with Eppie Lederer—also known as advice columnist "Ann Landers." He had met her several years earlier and enjoyed their friendship. Among her numerous notes to him was this one.

> I had a great time a couple of weeks ago with our mutual friend Ted Hesburgh. We both received honorary degrees at St. Leo's College in Tampa, and it was great fun being with that delightful Padre for nearly two days. The place was loaded with Catholic clergy, and I kept asking myself, "How did a nice Jewish girl like you get invited to this shindig?"
>
> Do you ever get to Chicago? If so, please rattle my cage in advance. The home phone (very unlisted) is . . .

Now she was suggesting dinner with the Simpsons the following Tuesday. He could not accept because of an event at the embassy of Sweden. He ransacked his calendar. "Damned if I ever thought I would turn down a dinner with Ann Landers—at her invitation." He finally discovered a possible opportunity—the following February, nearly four months hence.

Strom

Simpson was inspired to maintain his swift pace by elderly Senator Strom Thurmond. One day in 1985 the two rode together from the White House back to the Capitol.

> He looked sharp and alert, and yet he told me he had given a speech the night before—in Los Angeles. He left there at 9:45, caught a 10:30 plane, flew all night to Philadelphia, and continued on to Washington for his meeting with the president this morning. He slept just a bit on the plane and he looked great. He is the damnedest guy I ever saw. No one will ever be like him, or ever was.

If Thurmond could do that, surely Al could fly to Wyoming and back the next day. He already had plenty of motivation, having learned a bitter political lesson the previous year when Senate votes precluded his scheduled appearance before the Wyoming Stock Growers Association. They had been griping about it ever since.

Once again this year, Senate activities threatened his appearance. Rather than endure another year of recriminations, he took an early morning flight from Washington to Salt Lake City, and then flew up to Billings and back down to Sheridan, where the convention was underway. He delivered his remarks, took questions, and in the process made certain the stock growers understood how difficult it was to get there and back to Washington in the middle of hectic Senate activity. He did not appreciate their unwillingness to understand that he couldn't attend the previous year, since he had been stuck in Washington, "working day and night on *your behalf*."

He chartered a plane back to Billings and flew commercially from there to Denver and Chicago. It was not possible to make it all the way home, so he slept briefly at an airport hotel and continued to Washington at the crack of dawn. On arrival he said, "There, *that* ought to keep some of the ranchers from running around the state saying I don't care about them. It took a year to unwrap my entrails from their axle."

On another occasion Al and Ann missed their scheduled westbound flight out of Dulles Airport, but caught later flights to Chicago and on to Denver, arriving at an airport motel well after midnight. As the sun rose they were boarding a tiny craft bound for a GOP breakfast in Laramie. He later told his diary, "It was nice to see about thirty or forty people out that early. I don't know why the hell they came out at that hour—must have been gluttons for punishment."

They chartered a plane to Cody and joined his parents, who had recently returned from Arizona. Early the following morning they flew to Denver and back to Washington. Their baggage was late, and one piece was lost. Still, he still did not feel like a glutton for punishment. "We rushed to the Safeway store and then home. After bolting down some soup and salad, we got into formal wear and were off to the Ford's Theater Gala." They missed the White House reception preceding the event but were in their seats prior to the president's arrival.

Snafus

Long-term staffers began wondering how long their boss could maintain his pace and were awed by his ability to multitask. He often brushed his teeth while changing clothes for an evening event, even while talking with people in person or via speakerphone. This occasionally led to problems. One evening he was walking out of his office when he looked down to discover a large blob of white toothpaste hanging from the zipper of his pants. "My God," he gasped. "What if I hadn't seen that? Can you imagine what people would *think*?"

On rare occasions he simply could not keep up. One day in spring 1988 he was late for a luncheon honoring Brian Mulroney, who was prime minister of Canada and leader of the Progressive Conservative Party. As he stepped gingerly through the back door, Mulroney said, "Ah, that Simpson. He has good timing, doesn't he?"

A more serious disconnect occurred later that spring, on May 11. Early that morning Simpson was taken by Senate driver Eugene Barton to the Washington Hilton to deliver a speech. Then he was whisked to the Madison Hotel, intending to address the American Industrial Health Conference. He dashed inside, only to discover he was in the wrong hotel. He should have been taken to the Washington Sheraton. He phoned his driver and told him to return immediately. Eugene, frantic to get back to his waiting boss, found himself blocked at every turn by heavy traffic and one-way streets. He lurched the Senate car toward the Madison, dodging and weaving as if his very life depended on it. In a state of trauma, he finally picked up his irritated passenger.

Even though Al abbreviated his next speech, he was late for a meeting at the White House. President Reagan accepted his tardiness with good grace, but Simpson was still upset as he dictated into his diary that evening. "It was the damnedest most frustrating son of a bitching situation in a long time."

He was exaggerating, of course. Such frustrations had become commonplace.

Chapter Four

MILESTONES

~

THE OPTIMISTIC SPIRIT of Ronald Reagan's second inauguration remained in the air the following morning. Simpson sensed it during a session at the White House.

> It was truly one of the most fascinating meetings I have ever had in the Cabinet Room of the White House, or anywhere in the White House. There was a great deal of jocularity and good fun. We talked for thirty minutes about not much of substance. A few great stories were told and it was a lovely time. The jellybeans were passed around and House Speaker Tip O'Neill even patted Ronald Reagan's hand a couple of times. If we can get those two old warhorses together, we might make progress in this country. There is hope.

Simpson told his diary that Reagan was in a "conciliatory mood," as was Vice President George Bush. The friendliness waned briefly when O'Neill charged the president with "taking us down the heaviest deficit road we have ever been on." That provoked Senator Strom Thurmond. "Who, exactly, has been controlling the Congress during the last fifty years of spending increases?" he demanded. With the descent into partisanship thus stalemated, the group returned to lighthearted banter. Simpson later wrote, "The president told us about the three attractive female military persons in front of the White House during the Inaugural parade. He said that when eighty-two-year-old Strom saw them, he wondered if he could get their phone numbers."

Simpson reported that after he recently made "a few smart cracks" about the defense budget, "Cap Weinberger called up to say, 'Alan,

I just want you to know that I have activated your reserve unit.'"
Everyone knew the camaraderie would not last. But as the group
left the White House that day, they thought it an excellent beginning to the new session of Congress and President Reagan's second
term.

VENI, VIDI, DEFICI

Al was always ready to deploy humor, and the exclusive Washington organization called the Alfalfa Club proved the perfect venue.
Each year the club conducts a banquet and selects a "presidential
candidate," whose campaign motto is always the same: "Veni, vidi,
defici"—which they translate as "I came, I saw, I lost."

Al had served as their candidate the previous year, 1984, and his
acceptance speech was well received. He told the gathering:

> I do graciously, and humbly and with great alacrity, accept the
> nomination. I do so with great humility, knowing full well
> that those who travel the high road of humility in this town
> are not really troubled by heavy traffic. . . .
>
> I shall soon have some serious nominations for my Cabi-
> net appointments—although I remain alarmed, as I presently
> perceive quite a significantly shallow level in the quality of
> applicants. One recently filled out an application form. On
> the blank where it asks, "Church preference," he wrote, "red
> brick." . . .
>
> I have come to know the difference between a horse race
> and a political race. In a horse race, the entire horse runs. . . .
>
> These are times of cynicism toward politicians, perhaps
> best evidenced by the two guys sitting in a penitentiary. One
> turned to the other and said, "The food was better here when
> *you* were governor." . . .
>
> They were doing a movie on Congress. When they got to
> the part where the Congressman refused a bribe, they had to
> use a *stuntman*. . . .

In our nation, there are serious problems with alcohol. This winter I saw an old cowboy coming out of a bar in Wyoming with a pint in his back pocket. He slipped on the ice and fell flat on his can. He lurched up, reached back, and felt something warm running down the back of his leg. He said, "Oh God, I hope that's *blood*!" . . .

I have been working graveyards, getting together some voter registration lists. You might imagine that my rather grim and risky task was lightened somewhat by viewing a beautifully scrolled obelisk in Baltimore, home of the champion Orioles. The inscription read:

> Here lie the bones of Tilly Jones,
> For her life held no terrors,
> A virgin born, a virgin died,
> No hits, no runs, no errors

I have just the person in mind for the Federal Reserve, a little old lady I met at a savings and loan branch in Eureka, California. I saw her go to the savings window and this young, officious and obsequious clerk smiled thinly at her and said—as she laid out on the counter several hundred dollars in one-dollar bills, and fives, and tens—"My, it must have taken you quite a while to hoard that up." The old lady never stopped counting as she said, "No, not really. My sister whored up half of it."

Near the end of his remarks Simpson shifted gears and expressed a few serious thoughts about service, dedication, and patriotism.

The essence of America is striving, hoping, experimenting, innovating, and searching. Sometimes we get pretty deadly serious about ourselves and the great issues that confront us. Politicians do fail to keep many of their promises, which may be one of the main reasons why this country has survived for more than two hundred years.

But amid the ruffles, flourishes, spotlights, laughter, flags, and music, recall a phrase of that great American patriot Will Rogers, who brought a sense of self and kindly good humor to our lives in times of turmoil when he said, "It's great to be great—but it's greater to be human."

A year later, Al was looking forward to another night with the real president, members of the Supreme Court, the Joint Chiefs of Staff, and hundreds of other luminaries. As the outgoing Alfalfa presidential candidate, he was again seated at the head table, and again noted the comments of other speakers.

> Senator Nunn said, "Being the presidential candidate on the Alfalfa Club ticket is the equivalent of receiving a kidney transplant from a bed wetter."
>
> Of Vice President Bush, someone referenced the tedium of his job. "George spends his time searching for Halley's Comet—on the days when there are no funerals."
>
> Bush said, "There is a time for healing the nation's wounds—and a time to kick a little ass!"
>
> President Reagan said, "I am assured of a place in history. In the Cabinet Room there will be a brass plate that will say, 'Ronald Reagan Slept Here.'" He added, "The recent switch in Cabinet members worked beautifully. There was not one leak about it—even to *me*."

Later that January Al attended the Washington Press Club Dinner. When it was Vice President Bush's turn to speak, he said, "Simpson has served with distinction in Congress. He has taken on the tough issues of immigration reform, nuclear matters—and then there was the Wilderness Act." He paused a moment. "That's what they caught him doing up there in Yellowstone Park last year."

STATE OF THE UNION

Al enjoyed President Reagan's 1985 State of the Union speech, in part because his new leadership role entitled him to a special privilege.

I went up to the Senate chamber at eight thirty, as I was part
of the escort committee to take the president to the podium
for his State of the Union address in the House of Representatives chamber. The order of march was Bob Dole, Robert
Byrd, Al Cranston and myself. Quite a treat. We had an informal five minutes with the president, and then took him to
the House floor. He gave an absolutely tremendous address. I
never saw him more relaxed, confident, at ease and authentic.

Thus ended January 1985, a month of significance to Ann and
Al Simpson, the junior senator from Wyoming and now second-
ranking Senate Republican. It had been a month of fascination and
exhilaration, even before the commencement of any real legislating. He was ready to take on major new challenges he knew were
lurking just around the corner.

DOWN TO BUSINESS

Simpson's log of February 20, 1985, describes an effort by several
senators to delay a vote confirming the appointment of Ed Meese
as attorney general. "Three Democrats are filibustering against the
Ed Meese nomination confirmation until we deal with the farm
problem in America. I never heard so much demagoguery. You
would think that every damn farmer was lying dead between his
cornrows." Even though farm subsidies had nothing to do with the
Meese confirmation, the debate did make him think further about
the situation.

Forty-two percent of government wheat money goes to less
than 8 percent of the wheat growers in America. It is not
going to the guy with the Oshkosh B'Gosh overalls who is
out slogging around with the pigs. The farm programs are a
mess. This Administration put fifty billion dollars into the
farmers in the last four years, and more of them went out of
business than in any four-year period in our history. That says
something. Damned if I know what.

The Iron Lady

Later that day he helped escort the United Kingdom's prime minister, Margaret Thatcher, to the House Chamber for her speech before a joint session of Congress. She hit a chord with Simpson when she said, "Wars are not caused by the buildup of weapons. They are caused when an aggressor believes he can achieve his objectives at an acceptable price."

Simpson found her "powerful and superb. It was absolutely poignant and extraordinary. She is indeed the 'Iron Lady,' and a class act." The two visited a few minutes before she presented Congress with a small bronze statuette. It bore the image of Sir Winston Churchill, his hands on his hips, peering forward with his best bulldog look. "It is a hell of a piece of bronze," Simpson remarked later. "She was very charming as she presented it."

During her speech, she blasted the Irish Republican Army (IRA) as "the terrorists" in Ireland. House Speaker Tip O'Neill came up afterward and gave her a big hug and kiss, but cautioned, "Don't tell the IRA I did that!"

Still later that day, in an office just off the Senate chamber, Al lost his cool over farm subsidies.

> I blew my cork. I told [Senator] Jim Exon that he could make
> anything partisan—even a water cooler. He blustered a bit
> at that, but I told him I damn well meant it. I also told him
> I had watched the whole uranium industry go down the
> tubes in Wyoming and *they* never came to hang around like
> poor relatives looking for federal support. I said I saw the oil
> and gas business go to hell, and I never came in asking for a
> handout for them. So what the hell are we supposed to do for
> farmers when 42 percent of the wheat support goes to about 8
> percent of the wheat farmers? It is a nutty way to do business.

Simpson said that if he were running the Senate, the filibustering senators would do well to cancel their Friday and Saturday engagements, because the session would carry right through the weekend.

"I really came into that one like a heavy chump, but a guy can get fed up in this league."

He also found himself in rare discord with the president. At a White House meeting, he mentioned the pending farm bill and said he hoped Administration officials would "get off their butts and help advance their cause" by publicly stating the total amount of federal subsidies paid to farmers during the past four years. "That story doesn't seem to get told. What a bunch of horse crap that it doesn't."

He met later with the deans of agriculture and graduate studies from the University of Wyoming. "I asked them all what they would do on the agriculture issue if they were in Congress. They had rather academic and goofy responses. It surprised me, and that shows why we keep giving money to agriculture. Their answers sure as hell didn't seem to come to the root of it." His diary entry for February 27, 1985, expressed hope that his criticisms had caught the president's ear: "To the White House for breakfast with the senators just elected. Someone asked the president if he would veto the Farm Bill. He gave that smile and said, 'I'm just dying to veto *something*.'"

Tipping Cows, Butting Heads

During early 1985 Simpson participated in intense budget discussions among Republicans. It was one of Washington's most exasperating, vexatious, and never-ending topics. He joined a group of Republican committee chairmen who had gathered to hash things out. "Pete Domenici of New Mexico really laid it on the line. He said, 'Either you are Republicans and you support the leadership procedure, or you don't. We need to get one vote on the budget and stick with mathematical consistency. If a guy wants to put Amtrak funding into the bill, then he has to figure how to transfer funds from another program.'"

Morning brought a procedural war of wills. Simpson noted that the Senate's "Lone Wolf," Robert Byrd, was now at the center of the pack. "I spent all the remaining hours of the day on the [Senate] floor with regard to the budget and the use of the 'five amendment tree.' Bob Dole keeps his equanimity, and Bob Byrd loves his role as the 'whale in the pond.' Of course, Byrd knows enough parliamentary tricks to tie you into a pretzel and you wouldn't even know it."

Numerous issues now under consideration had become so contentious and evenly divided that voting outcomes sometimes depended not only on South Dakota Senator Larry Pressler's predictably unpredictable last minute decisions, but also on various senators' health problems. On May 9, 1985, Simpson reviewed the most recent round of budget votes. "We brought Pete Wilson out of the hospital to vote. He had an appendectomy the day before. We could not get John East to the Chamber because of his serious medical difficulties. In addition, Jim Exon went into the hospital the day before to have his gall bladder removed. It was not so much a 'whip check' as it was checking pulses in a M.A.S.H. unit."

Senate floor activity continued hot and heavy through the month, as members worked to complete the Defense Authorization Bill before the Memorial Day break. Very late one night, Simpson dictated this: "Barry Goldwater is managing the bill, and is impatient as hell. Malcolm Wallop really bridled about the cuts in the defense budget and the MX missile program. He may filibuster. I spent the day working out ways to avoid that. We went out of session about eleven in the evening and I will open the Senate back up in the morning."

By July Simpson found himself gripped by a different emotion—disappointment. "The president blew a hole in the Domenici-Dole budget deficit reduction proposal. Pete and Bob are deeply disillusioned and irritated, and I can't blame them a damned bit." Indeed, a significant rift was brewing. Many Senate Republicans felt the president was not supporting their agenda and that his officials were not counseling him to be supportive.

The Boycott

A few days later Simpson had no choice but to miss a meeting at the White House. Media pundits jumped on it as a sign of intra-Republican discord. They overlooked the reality that Senator Thurmond had already scheduled Simpson's longstanding immigration reform bill for final markup in the Judiciary Committee at the same hour. With expressions of concern, gravelly voiced pundits told the nation that Simpson and Thurmond had "boycotted" a White House meeting. Something must be terribly wrong with Republican unity, they speculated, since the two had "refused" to go to the White House. In his office, Simpson sighed. "So goes the media in this joint. Fascinating, isn't it? It's an absurd situation, how things are played up."

When the revised version of the budget finally passed the Senate, 67–32, Simpson was philosophical: "Well, it certainly isn't what we all wanted. But as they say out in Wyoming, it's better than a kick in the butt with a sharp boot." During the debate Simpson had become testy. "I came down hard on Republicans Mark Andrews and Ted Stevens. A few harsh words were bandied about," he wrote after one session. The crusty Alaskan Stevens had ten years' seniority on Simpson, and a reputation as the wrong man to cross. Given that, Al went on a fence-mending mission.

The Pledge

After he made peace with Stevens, Simpson thought about his recent blustery exchanges with other colleagues and decided it was time to mellow out. At a meeting of Senate Republicans, he made a commitment: "I kind of bared my soul and pledged that I have given up my intensity. I said that I would just kind of 'roll with the river' from here on in. It was a good visit with a nice, warm group." Twenty years later he was asked about his pledge. "I don't remember that. I had probably read that in some philosophical magazine or something, about rolling with the river, or letting life flow—the kind of babble you post on the locker room wall." Whatever the case, Simpson's pledge to "go with the flow" vaporized in a flash.

> Some heavy remarks from [Senator] Lowell Weicker about aid
> to people in need were directed at [Budget Director] David
> Stockman. Lowell said that Stockman was "a liar" and that
> he was involved in giving fraudulent budget figures. It was an
> extraordinary display of belligerence.
>
> I intervened and indicated to Lowell that I have known
> him for a long time, and that he was a softie down under that
> harsh exterior, but that he was being in every sense just a
> plain damned bully. I spelled it: "b-u-l-l-y."

Weicker began to stalk out of the room, but returned. Later the two made their peace. "We two big lugs went forward and gave each other a big hug, and moved on to other action. Lowell has little objectivity in this area of aid to the handicapped and the disenfranchised and to the blind and infirm, since he has a dear son with Down syndrome. It is natural enough to see why he comes on strong. In this case, he really was blatantly abusive." Weicker stood six and a half feet tall and weighed about 250 pounds. Simpson was an inch taller and weighed 200 pounds. He noted that if they had put on the gloves, the others could have sold tickets.

Protection of sacred cows had pitted friends and colleagues against each other—with major debates over immigration reform yet to come. Bracing himself for legislative turbulence, Simpson said, "It's time to hang on tight."

BORDERING ON WAR

After the "Reagan Revolution" swept a Republican majority into the Senate back in 1981, Strom Thurmond, chair of the Judiciary Committee, and Ted Kennedy, ranking minority member, decided it was time to establish an immigration subcommittee. They picked Al Simpson to chair it, thereby thrusting him into a paramount challenge of his Senate career.

From the beginning he felt the success of any effort to stem illegal entry into the United States through comprehensive immigration law reform would hinge on being able to determine every worker's identity and employment eligibility. He offered several options, including enhanced border security and a counterfeit-resistant national identification system. The latter was not universally well received.

New York Times columnist William Safire was among those most alarmed by the idea. In an opinion column on September 9, 1982, he called Simpson's proposal the "computer tattoo." Safire wrote: "In a well-meaning effort to curb the employment of illegal aliens, and with the hearty good wishes of editorialists who ordinarily pride themselves on guarding against the intrusion of government into the private lives of individual Americans, Congress is about to take this generation's longest step toward totalitarianism." Simpson did not believe his ideas would lead to "totalitarianism," but a growing public fear of government invasion of liberty and privacy became one of the legislation's key stumbling blocks. Others included a provision making it illegal to hire illegal immigrants knowingly and the possibility of "amnesty" for long-term illegal immigrants.

For three years Simpson's efforts were debated heavily on Capitol Hill and around the nation. After scores of hearings and hundreds of revisions, the legislation he had promoted day and night died in the final hours of the 98th Congress.

Round Two

Now in his second term, Simpson decided to resume the effort. To announce it, he conducted one of the few press conferences of his career. "The damnedest thing I ever saw. I pulled up a chair in front of about twenty-one microphones. Every network was there, about ten cameras, reporters from all around the country. There must have been about a hundred reporters in the room. The media's 'immigration groupies' were all there. I answered all their questions and it seemed to go very well."

In short order, opponents brought out the big guns to kill his bill. The more shots they fired, the more determined he became to keep his "no win turkey" alive. One day he appeared before the Federation on American Immigration Reform (FAIR). "It was a spirited group of groupies. I advised them that I was going to go ahead with the bill and we would work on it some more—and, because it was so contentious, I must be a 'perverse bastard.' My language was a little rich. I won't say that the next time, but they seemed to like it anyway."

In the following weeks he visited with numerous members of the House and Senate and with scores of reporters and leaders of government and industry. Among them were Labor Secretary Bill Brock and AFL-CIO president Lane Kirkland. Both were interested in exempting the agricultural industry from sanctions against employers who knowingly hire illegal aliens. "It might work," he conceded, "since only about 8 to 15 percent of the illegal, undocumented workers are in agriculture. We will hold some hearings on it."

June 17, 1985, brought the first judiciary subcommittee hearing on Simpson's latest effort, known as Senate Bill 1200. Near the end of the session, he took flak from several Hispanic witnesses. "Some of it was just radicalized beyond belief," he griped afterward. After another year of effort, the road to immigration reform seemed more rutted than ever.

Full Court Press

Finally, it was time to deal with members of the American Bar Association. "They knew what I have been up to. I laid it on them, as to their holding back for so long on immigration reform, especially in the area of employer sanctions"—penalties against those who knowingly hire illegal immigrants.

His effort to shore up the lawyers' support was followed by a trip to the White House to shore up President Reagan's. Before their discussion turned serious, Al commented on the president's upcoming medical appointment to check for colon polyps. The exchange that followed was not typical of chats between citizens and their president.

> I told him the one about the old cowboy who said he had been eating a lot of cheese, jerky and hardtack, and was constipated. The doctor asked, "Why don't you take these suppositories and let me know how that works?"
>
> A week later, the cowboy came back. The doc asked, "How did they work?"
>
> "Oh hell, Doc," he exclaimed. "For all the good they done me, I shoulda stuck 'em up my ass!"

Since they had consumed two minutes of their scheduled five-minute session, Al came to the point. "I told him we have been slogging along on immigration reform for about four years. I said that he has been very helpful, but many around him [members of his Administration] are not. I said that the first duty of a sovereign nation is to control its borders, and we do not. We have no sovereignty over our borders. The more than one million [illegal entrants] apprehended last year came from *ninety-two* different nations." Simpson told Reagan that if the United States were only then applying for admission to the United Nations, it would not qualify, and he warned that it would be easy for terrorists to enter the United States with a flow of illegal economic migrants. He stressed that he was taking a humane approach, but the country should be ready to resort to "tougher methods," if necessary.

In preparation for the session, he had reviewed Reagan's debate statements, in which the president had committed his support of immigration reform. "This is that chance," Al said emphatically. "We have to think about getting away from the *Wall Street Journal* theory of immigration, which is a lot like child labor. It might be good for the economy, but it really is not good for our judicial or social systems. . . . We're not dealing with any changes in legal immigration—no asylum changes, no criminal penalties on employers, no alien age discrimination."

He estimated an annual cost of implementing the proposed leg-islation at $600 million to $1 billion per year and advised the presi-dent of growing support for immigration law reform. "Finally, the Chamber of Commerce is aboard—and the National Association of Manufacturers, the Business Roundtable, the National Federation of Independent Businesses and every major employer organization."

He asked Reagan to encourage House Judiciary Committee Chair Peter Rodino to pursue the effort there, and he concluded the session with a strong personal appeal: "I told the president that I had toiled for him, and would do a hell of a lot more of that because I think he has done a tremendous job. I said, 'I know how greedy those bastards get around here. They [some members of Congress] just hang around you like poor relatives, asking for favors, but never me—until now. I am pushing all of my chips into the pot.'"

Torres and Wilson

Because immigration reform was of primary concern to the League of United Latin American Citizens (LULAC), its national execu-tive director, Arnold Torres, was of primary concern to Al Simp-son. The two had clashed repeatedly, so Simpson was heartened to learn that the local LULAC chapter had been clashing with Torres as well.

> I was quite pleased to be invited to their meeting. They asked me about the immigration bill and said they were taking an objective look at things and wanted to work with me. I said I would be deeply pleased and honored, and that the person I had the most difficulty with in all of America was Arnold Torres. They said, "You think *you* had trouble? *We* had worse trouble with him than you did—and if he were here right now, he would tell you the same thing."

Simpson pledged to work thoughtfully with LULAC and said he appreciated their conciliatory tone. At least they were no longer threatening him.

He was less optimistic the next day, after meeting with California Senator Pete Wilson about "special problems" being expressed by representatives of the perishable fruit growers industry. Frustrated, Al said, "I think we can get some things moving, once we remove the growers' *greed*. It may be a terminal ailment for them."

On July 24, 1985, Congressman Rodino phoned to say he would be introducing an immigration reform bill in the House, one similar to the Senate effort. Congressman Ron Mazzoli of Kentucky, a Democrat and fourteen-year veteran of the House, would be a key cosponsor. Simpson and Mazzoli, already friends, were destined to labor together for many months.

Later that month, the Senate Judiciary Committee passed Senate Bill 1200, but only after Simpson accommodated Senator Metzenbaum on two modifying amendments and Senator Simon on two others. The vote was 12–4.

Now it was a matter of getting the bill before the full Senate. On September 11, Al persuaded Senators Carl Levin and Al Cranston not to filibuster the motion to proceed with its consideration. "This has been cooking a long time. The interest groups get heavier and tougher. The lobbying gets more intense, the money laid out to lobby the issue gets more lavish—and things get gummier and gummier."

Finally the bill was scheduled for debate, and Simpson turned to a friend and particularly formidable opponent, Ted Kennedy. As the senior Democrat, and Simpson's counterweight on the immigration subcommittee, Kennedy could cause big trouble. On this day, he did not. "Ted Kennedy was co-manager of the bill. He kept a steady pace and did not go into any histrionics as in past floor debates. It was a steady day. We will try to get the bill completed by Friday. Hope we can get it done."

When debate continued into the following week, Simpson cleared everything from his calendar and focused exclusively on immigration. "I cancelled out of *Crossfire* and *Good Morning America* [television interviews]. No time to do those. I have to stay in the fray. Handled five amendments on the floor—patiently I might add, since some of them were real doozies."

He soon resumed his battle with Senator Wilson of California, a state heavily impacted by immigration—legal and illegal. "Pete and the 'perishable fruit growers' were back for another try, and this time drank deeply at the well and won the amendment to establish a temporary farm worker program. That will make final passage of the bill more difficult, since the House of Representatives is certain to object." Al warned his Republican colleague that establishment of a 350,000-person guest worker program would come back to haunt him.

Heinz

On September 19, 1985, after five days of fulltime consideration that included thirty-one hours of Senate debate and the processing of twenty-seven amendments, Simpson still felt the revised bill worth passing. Then another problem presented himself: "John Heinz of Pennsylvania has a non-germane amendment in there about *Social Security*, and insists upon debating it. It could screw things up, because then other people are going to get very creative. I think we can hold it together with a vote of at least 55–45, but if we don't get it wound up soon, that could deteriorate." Al took Heinz aside and lowered the boom.

> I said, "John, I've known you for a long time. You are a great guy, and I love to fish with you and I love you as a friend— but I tell you, if you had managed this bill on the floor of the Senate for seven days and were ready for a final vote, and you had *my* extraneous non-germane amendment pending, you would be *offended.*
>
> Well, *I am* offended, John, and I tell you this—either you get the damn thing off the bill, or I am going to *stick it up your ass!* I am tired of it. It is tedious, it is ponderous, and it doesn't have a damn thing to do with immigration! If you want to keep screwing around, I am just as good at that as anybody else!"

Within fifteen minutes the Heinz amendment was gone and Simpson's bill passed, 69–30. "It tickled my old butt. . . . It was a long haul this time, the longest debate we have had on immigration. Hopefully, this time will be the charm." With Senate passage in hand, attention turned to the House of Representatives, where the effort was destined to stagnate well into the following year.

Protests

Al Simpson arrived in Colorado Springs to deliver the Colorado College commencement address and be presented with an honorary law degree. He soon encountered a professor and a dozen students in full protest mode.

> I had a fascinating session with them. Obviously, [the professor] had been feeding them a great pile of distortion about my legislation. He kept babbling, but I said, "Why not let the students talk?" Finally, he did. They had good questions but very little background. Then I said, "I feel that a teacher lacks academic integrity if he doesn't teach both sides of an issue, or at least give his students some food for thought."

Al was prepared to be loudly heckled during the graduation ceremony but was not challenged. "I gave a hell of a good commencement address. I had prepared that baby thoroughly, and they seemed to love it. They even gave me a very fine standing ovation. I was deeply moved." As the graduates were receiving their degrees, one young man stepped forward wearing a white armband representing opposition to Simpson's legislation. He paused a moment, said "I won't be needing this," ripped the band off his arm, and handed it over. Simpson was moved, and that night told his diary, "That made the whole thing worth it."

Intensive Care

In the fall of 1986 immigration reform was still struggling in the House of Representatives. To help keep it alive Simpson conferred with Congressman Chuck Schumer. He came away dejected. "Because of him, we may have to drop employer sanctions—penalties against employers who knowingly hire illegal aliens—at least for agricultural workers." Then he visited House Judiciary Chair Peter Rodino, who said he hated to see the bill die, but there would be no way of working out conflicts over illegal employment in the agriculture industry.

Unwilling to accept defeat, Simpson responded by launching a verbal blitz on everyone even peripherally involved in immigration reform. At one point, he told his staff, "The damned bill is still alive over there and I'm trying to pump a little plasma into the corpse." A few days later he reviewed the adjustments made by the House and decided that since the core of his effort remained intact, resuscitation efforts should continue. Finally, he received good news: "They intend to get a rule today to put the immigration bill on the House floor. They will try to pass it on Thursday and send it to conference with the Senate on Friday. Who would have believed it? You don't want to watch laws, or sausage, being made. That is for damn sure."

His relentless work and personal relationships with key members of the House inspired a wonder of legislative rebirth. The House passed the bill and sent it to conference to hash out differences with the Senate version. Simpson chaired the conference committee. "There were lots of arguments and much fluff and bluster. It seems easy for them [House members] to raise hell with the bill, then stop and chew the fat, and then return to shoot the crap out of the bill some more. We adjourned at seven in the evening, in some turmoil. I said we would resume at nine the next morning."

When the conferees gathered that Saturday morning, Simpson surprised them by announcing there would be no votes. "We are here because we are going to do all the 'root canal' work and get every issue laid out on the table—and get the maximum amount of shrieking and gnashing of teeth out of the way right now. Next Tuesday, since Monday is Columbus Day, the bill will be ready for final consideration." After a great deal of wrangling, the committee finally agreed to a compromise version of the complex legislation. The committee had yet to vote on it, but the agreement gave Simpson yet another opportunity to employ his "back from the dead" analogy: "I feel like Dr. Frankenstein creeping over to that slab, with the lightning flashing, and attaching an electrode to a grayish looking toe and shooting a charge in there—and then watching that big lug get up off the table and stagger out into the marshes."

Arriving early for the final session, he visited first with Congressman Rodino, then privately with the conferees. During the following five-hour open session, the Senate conceded on forty-three issues, the House on forty-six. "It was an extraordinary accommodation and true compromise. It was done with good humor, ill humor, obscenity, profanity and tenderness. It was a wild-ass time. Democrat Howard Berman . . . could drive you crazy. [He] wanted the last full pound of flesh, and he damn near got it with the agriculture workers programs. . . . I decided to concede rather than let those greedy sons of bitches bring down the whole pile."

Veto Threat

Precious little time remained in the legislative year, but before Simpson could get his House–Senate conference report before the full Senate for final consideration, he was stunned by a significant setback. In part because the bill had been heavily amended, the Justice Department was now recommending a presidential veto. Incensed, Simpson stormed over to meet with the attorney general and his top lieutenants. "I told them to go to hell, and that I would be *terribly* disappointed in the president if he did that. I said I would do some real ripping and snorting, and made certain they understood that I did not intend to be the gentle and cooperative soul of my past relationships with our fine president." The lawyers responded by scheduling additional meetings.

The last days and hours of the 99th Congress in 1986 were among the most pressured of Al Simpson's legislative life—perhaps his entire life. He finally wedged his multiyear immigration reform effort onto the Senate floor for a final vote, only to encounter Senator Phil Gramm of Texas lying in wait. "He really was juiced up about the bill. He ripped into the agriculture provisions with great gusto and glee, and some ridicule. He was right on some points because that is the weakest part of the bill."

Al fended him off, and slipped down to the White House to put the "final grip" on an important friend.

> I told the president that I remembered my very first visit with him on immigration, many years ago. I said that when I first sat in that chair by the fireplace in the Oval Office, I was filled with some trepidation and awe. Not this time. . . .
>
> I told him that I had gone into conference and had gotten just what he wanted, that I had done exactly what he told me to do. He listened intently and asked questions, demonstrating that he really did follow the issue. He said he remembered the exact funding mechanism and the promises made.
>
> We visited about some specific provisions of the bill for half an hour. Then he looked over at [Chief of Staff] Don Regan and said, "Let's go with it. I'm ready to sign it."
>
> I think I floated out the door of the White House. I told the waiting press that the president would sign the bill, if we could get it passed. They seemed a bit incredulous.

The next morning, Al again seized the first opportunity to put the conference report up for a final vote—and once again encountered senators ready to filibuster its consideration. "Phil Gramm again asked some very bright questions on the farm workers program. Then Jim McClure really teed off on me, and the bill. He let 'er rip. Jesse Helms came in with his objections." As the pitched battle finally neared conclusion, Simpson urged passage by reminding his colleagues that although America is a country of immigrants, illegal entrants have often been victimized. He closed with the following:

No fair quoting from the Statue of Liberty, because it does not say on it, "Send us everybody you have got, legally or illegally." That is not what it says. . . . Prattle on all you want about rights and humanity and everything else. But let me tell you, when you have a United States of America that is going to be populated from stem to stern with illegal, undocumented people who have lesser rights than the rest of the citizens . . . if you think you have problems now, you try [maintaining] the status quo.

It Lives!

When the opposing senators ran out of steam, several commended Simpson for years of work on immigration reform. "Terribly moving to me were the tributes of my colleagues, Democrats and Republicans alike. When I say I sniff that stuff but don't inhale it, well I guess I really did inhale it that day. I was very moved by it all." After years of toil, an exhausted but exuberant Al Simpson stood on the Senate floor bursting with joy as the clerk announced the bill's passage: 63–24. "It was like giving dry birth to a porcupine," he joked afterward.

He was on top of the world. His previous immigration reform efforts had been killed, and this one had been pronounced dead so many times that almost nobody expected its resurrection. He had persevered, using all his energy and every ounce of his intellect and credibility to get the job done. He was proud. "Damn proud." He took his top immigration staffer—the same Dick Day who, as justice of the peace back in Cody, had sworn him into office—out to celebrate, but briefly. "This is a very, very special time, but there is little of it. That is the fascinating part about this adventure. You don't really have time to savor a victory any more than you have to anguish in defeat, and that is good. I just feel a sense of real purpose and mission accomplished."

After sleeping a mere three hours each night during the previous two weeks, he went to bed at 2:30, arose at 5:00, and went to the airport. Two hours into his westbound flight, he picked up his recorder. "I really do not need sleep or sustenance. I think I could fly to Denver today under my own power. Last night we passed the Immigration Reform and Control Act of 1986. . . . It was absolutely one of the most extraordinary days of my life. I cannot really even sleep. I'm high as a kite."

On November 6, 1986, "Simpson-Mazzoli" was signed into law by President Reagan in the Roosevelt Room at the White House. One senator notably missing was Ted Kennedy. Simpson regretted his absence, even though Kennedy had voted against the bill. That night Al told his diary, "Ted was of immeasurable help through the six and a half years, guiding me through issues with the ACLU, Hispanic groups, and other concerned parties." During the signing ceremony, Al's hand was the only one shaken by the president, who said, "Al, you really did work like hell on this one."

Thus Simpson-Mazzoli became the law of the land amid a great outpouring of hope that it would resolve the problem of illegal immigration. Had it been aggressively funded and fully enforced in the years that followed, and if Simpson had not been compelled to save the legislation by dropping provisions such as secure universal identification for every person legally in the county, it would have been more effective.

According to the Center for Immigration Studies, about 2.7 million people received lawful permanent residence ("green cards") in the late 1980s and early 1990s as a result of the amnesties contained in the Immigration Reform and Control Act (IRCA) of 1986. At an event in San Diego, Simpson was moved nearly to tears. "That was one of the greatest thrills in all my days in the immigration field. What a tingling sensation, to go into the room and have people of all colors, sizes and shapes applaud and say, 'Viva Simpson.' Boy, I loved it." Not present was the *Casper Star Tribune's* editorial cartoonist who had sketched a tall, skinny Simpson wearing a button that read, "Never give an Hispanic an even break."

LIFE IN THE SENATE

Although the tremendous effort devoted to immigration legislation was a priority, a range of many other things commanded Al's attention as well. Some entailed further sparring among senators; others brought interesting encounters with various luminaries. Destined to overshadow those things was the controversy over U.S. policy in Nicaragua that would become known as the Iran-Contra affair, the first trickle of which appeared in 1985.

The Contras

In a nutshell, the Iran-Contra political scandal involved senior Reagan Administration figures using arms sales to Iran, a country under an arms embargo, to fund the efforts of anti-Sandinista and anti-communist rebels known as the Contras, in Nicaragua. Israel was to ship weapons to a group of Iranians. The United States was to resupply Israel and receive the payment made to the Israelis. The Iranians involved would try for release of six U.S. hostages being held by the Islamist organization Hezbollah in Lebanon. The scheme to sell weapons to Iran in exchange for the release of American hostages was modified at the hands of Lieutenant Colonel Oliver North of the National Security Council in late 1985 so that some of the weapons sales proceeds would go to Nicaragua.[1]

In mid-April of 1986 Simpson met with Secretary of State George Shultz about this. He came away vexed.

> It seems to me that the Administration is a bit muddled on that one. We do not want to overthrow Nicaragua, but we sure want to tell them what to do. Somewhere, this is going to break down. I don't know the best course, unless we find that the nation is exporting arms to the insurgents in El Salvador or spreading their activities through Central America. Then our options will be clearer.
>
> [President Reagan] wants fourteen million dollars in [U.S. government] aid for the Contras, who are opposing the

Nicaraguan government. Tip O'Neill feels just as strongly
that the Contras are "butchers."

If the Sandinistas were that terrible, thought Simpson, why was the
United States conducting $60 million worth of trade with them
and maintaining an embassy there?

At a White House meeting months earlier, the president had said
of the situation, "Our job is to simplify, simplify, simplify." Still,
matters were not at all clear. Simpson added his own perspective,
warning the president that chaos in Nicaragua could prove both
politically and physically threatening to America: "When that
happy band begins to trickle out of Nicaragua, if it goes down the
tube, just wait until a terrorist enters illegally with them into the
United States and slaps a piece of plastic explosive on the light plant
in El Paso." Later in the session the president said something that
Simpson found curious. "He looked at me and said, 'Well, I'll tell
that to Teddy Roosevelt when we meet again. We often visit by my
bed, at night, on how to do Central America.'"

Dam It

Closer to home, Senators Simpson and Wallop had been working on
funding for a water projects bill that contained money to heighten
and renovate the Buffalo Bill Dam and hydroelectric power plant
just west of Cody.

> I've been haggling like hell on the water projects appropria-
> tions bill. Appropriations like the Buffalo Bill Dam are in
> there, and even though the state is paying $47 million of the
> $116 million tab, we still can't get that passed.
>
> Failure would be embarrassing to both of us, especially
> since the state of Wyoming already committed a large share
> of the total. Several other senators resist funding because the
> federal portion is too *small*. They fear such a precedent might
> result in their own states having to fund a greater percentage
> of similar projects.

After a protracted struggle, the project was finally funded, and construction was completed in 1993.

Imputed Irritation

In Washington, Senator Howard Metzenbaum of Ohio was focused on the real estate profession. This irritated Simpson.

> He is raising hell with the real estate profession, telling them what a windfall "imputed interest" is. That is a great hypocrisy, in view of the fact that he took a "finder's fee" on the sale of the Hay Adams Hotel, after [doing] nothing more than making about three phone calls. The fee was $250,000. When that became public, he returned the money. It is not a very good time for him to lecture, pontificate, rip, and snort.

A few minutes later Metzenbaum asked Senator Dole for additional time on the Senate floor to discuss the real estate issue. Simpson relished their exchange: "Howard said, 'Well, Bob, surely you can bend a little on my request.' Bob replied, 'You can bend on mine when you are majority leader, Howard. Right now I am majority leader and we will find out who is running the Senate—you or me.'"

The U.S. Senate is sometimes called "the world's greatest deliberative body." One might question that, based on a following day's dramatic explosion at the Judiciary Committee. It was sparked when Senator Metzenbaum and several colleagues provoked eighty-two-year-old Strom Thurmond. The exchanges among several senior senators soon devolved into what seemed more like a schoolyard dustup, complete with repeated forced apologies. Simpson described the session as "one of the toughest and harshest Judiciary Committee meetings ever."

The president had nominated William Bradford Reynolds to become associate attorney general for civil rights. The Judiciary Committee was considering whether to confirm or reject him. Simpson recorded what happened.

When Senator Thurmond, who was chairing the hearing, called for a vote, Senator Biden said, "I want not only to suggest the absence of a quorum, but I want to assure it."

Biden got up and walked out during the roll call vote, and was followed by fellow Democrats Kennedy, Metzenbaum, and DeConcini. This infuriated Strom, who commanded the clerk to continue calling the role even as they were departing.

Metzenbaum then came back and really laid into Strom, saying that he had seen Strom involved in lots of situations, but had never seen him be as discourteous or harsh or as partisan as he was being right then. That made Strom even madder, so he continued to require that the roll be called.

Biden came back in and unloaded on Strom, as did Democrat Howell Heflin, "mister steady" himself, that old former chief justice of the Alabama Supreme Court. He sought the floor, but Strom said that Democrat Paul Simon of Illinois had the floor. Howell really got mad. I have never seen him like that.

The Republicans decided to have Senator Orrin Hatch of Utah ask the committee clerk to read back what Senator Biden had originally said, in order to determine the nature of the offense that had triggered Thurmond's irritation.

The suggestion slowly evolved—and I was a part of that discussion—that Joe Biden would indicate his apology and say that he really had not intended to walk out and break up the quorum, but rather his intent was to call a recess so they could get their ducks in a row.

However, Strom wanted another apology, and Joe agreed to give it. Then Joe asked Strom to go ahead and complete the roll call vote. Strom graciously agreed to do that. When the meeting opened up again, Biden apologized profusely to Strom, and Strom insisted on it, several times. Then Metzenbaum apologized to Strom for his harsh comments, and Strom apologized to Howell for not recognizing him, and Howell accepted that graciously.

Other senators were engaged that day in an unrelated conflict on the Senate floor. Republican Jesse Helms was "raising hell," as Simpson described it, about several of the president's nominees for key Administration positions. "There was no way to break him loose on that. So what we thought would be getting done on the floor of the Senate today didn't happen. Bob Dole is very frustrated, and I can't say I blame him."

INTERLUDES

Simpson escaped combat by walking across the street to the Supreme Court for a chat with Chief Justice Warren Burger. "This is about the third time the two of us have visited over a cup of tea. He poured! He was in his old clothes, since he and Vera have just moved to their new house. He had on a pair of Hush Puppy shoes and was in a delightfully reflective mood. He is a prince of a guy," Simpson observed. The two talked about their love of practicing law and some of the cases they had tried. Then they reviewed Simpson's new leadership challenges and several matters of particular interest to Burger. "He mentioned some of the things he is going to address with the Bar in future speeches—such as greed and attorney fees and the need for a new type of appellate clearance system. He didn't lobby me on that, and we tried to stay out of things that we know would come back to trouble both of us under the 'separation of powers.' It was a very pleasant hour that flashed by."

Another pleasant half hour came a few days later, when Sharon Fritzler Pederson dropped by for a visit: "Sharon was my first grade girlfriend in Cody. In fact, she was my girlfriend until she got into the seventh grade and left Cody. It was a great visit and we covered all the old ground. We shared with her husband [Charles] what an 'advanced' group we were, since we always used to play 'post office' together—focusing especially on 'special delivery letters.' Charles seemed a bit nonplussed about it all."

Fredericks of Nevada

That evening Al attended a black tie "stag event" where President Reagan was the only other invitee apparently not advised that the event was formal. Since Reagan was late, Simpson was asked to speak first. Embarrassed to appear before the formally attired crowd in a blue suit, he had just begun when the president entered, in a brown suit. The room fell silent as the two stared at each other. Simpson finally said, "Well! When I came in here I felt as out of place as a rat turd in a canary cage. Now another chap has come to take the heat off me."

Because the dinner was one of Nevada Senator Paul Laxalt's annual "lamb fries," it was only natural that both men ended up telling a number of jokes centering, as Al put it, on the "vagaries of the behavior of sheep." He revealed that the preferred shopping venue for sheepherders buying their wooly friends Christmas presents was "Fredericks of Nevada."

Rogers of Hollywood

The tone was quite different one subsequent evening when Al enjoyed a conversation with the famous actor and dancer Ginger Rogers.

> I went over to the Library of Congress where Ruth and Dan Boorstin, the Librarian of Congress, were having an event for Ginger Rogers. What a thrill that was. She is still a striking lady in every respect.
>
> They showed black and white movies of Fred Astaire and Ginger Rogers dancing—indeed, dancing in that inimitable way as only they could. It was a treat. In addition, she was dancing backwards, and in high heels—and you think *he's* good? Wow.

Gandhi of India

At another event, Al came to the aid of his friend Bob Dole. Prime Minister Rajiv Gandhi of India and his wife Sonia had just arrived in Washington for a special dinner. Senator Dole and his wife Elizabeth were the ranking Americans present—or would have been, had they arrived. Al later explained:

> They asked me if I knew where Bob was. When I called Elizabeth at their apartment at the Watergate, there she was, having pizza and working on a transportation liability issue.
>
> It is one of those things that can happen to all of us in this rat race. They forgot, or they cancelled and the staff failed to tell the event organizers. Bob was out attending six other receptions and Elizabeth was really quite embarrassed. The dinner went ahead without them.

As the highest-ranking American official in the room, Simpson returned the Indian prime minister's toast and was pleased that his impromptu remarks "didn't seem to set off any kind of international diplomatic ruckus."

For Al, the evening's highlight was the chance to chat with Nancy and Henry Kissinger. "Nancy's father, Al Maginnes, and my father were roommates at Harvard Law School," Al recalled. As children, Al and Pete had traveled with their parents to White Plains, New York. Nancy Maginnes, who was then in her late teens, had taken care of them for an afternoon.

A Well-Traveled Joke

During a White House conversation with President Reagan, Simpson told a joke that traveled halfway around the world and back in less than a day.

> I shared a story about the old cowboy buying some generic toilet paper—and coming back later and saying, "I gave the stuff a new name."
>
> The clerk asked, "What did you call it?"
>
> "John Wayne Toilet Paper."
>
> "Why is that?"
>
> The cowboy said, "Because it's rough, tough, and it don't take no shit off anybody!"

Just before a meeting the following day, Reagan was laughing as he approached Simpson. Two weeks earlier an anti-terrorist military group known as the Delta Force had left North Carolina for an undisclosed location in the Middle East to deal with a hostage situation involving passengers on a TWA plane taken over by terrorists. Now Reagan told Simpson:

> Alan, I have to tell you what happened after you told me that great story yesterday. I ended the National Security Council meeting by telling that story. It just busted them up.
>
> I gathered that they spread it around, because this morning at another meeting of the Security Council, General John Vessey [chair of the Joint Chiefs of Staff] said, "Let me tell you one, Mr. President. I called our commander in charge of the Delta Force. I told them I hoped everything was going well for them. I said I knew it was a tough time for them and asked if there was anything they need or anything we can do for them."
>
> The commander said, "Yes. Could you send us some good toilet paper? All we have over here is that damned John Wayne stuff!"

The commander had no idea the story had originated with Simpson in the White House the previous day. Al told his diary that the president "really busted a gut," while explaining the tale's journey halfway around the world and back. The White House photographer snapped a shot of the two of them, doubling over in laughter.

But Al grew somber when recalling a letter of concern he wrote to Wayne after it was revealed that the famous actor had been diagnosed with stomach cancer. Wayne penned this response: "Dear Al: I want to thank you and your lovely wife for the thoughtful note and sentiments that are inspiring and needed sometimes when the going is rough. God knows the people in this county have bestowed on me more than my share."

President for a Day

On Saturday, July 13, 1985, Vice President Bush served as president, briefly. His role as commander in chief began at eleven that morning, while President Reagan was undergoing surgery for removal of an intestinal polyp. From the moment of his incapacitation until he signed a letter eight hours later stating that he was ready to resume the duties of the presidency, Acting President of the United States George Bush was in charge.

His brief elevation to the presidency was the topic of discussion that evening, as he and Barbara dined with the Simpsons and several friends in common at the vice president's residence. Bush was eager to report that the country had been in good hands.

In the Grove

Al was elated to have been asked to give the "Lakeside Lecture" at the midpoint of the prestigious two-week "Bohemian Grove encampment" in California. By intent, the Grove was not well known to the public, although on August 2, 1982, a *Newsweek* article provided a glimpse: "The world's most prestigious summer camp—the Bohemian Grove—seventy-five miles north of San Francisco is a fiercely guarded, 2,700-acre retreat. It is the country extension of San Francisco's all male ultra-exclusive Bohemian Club to which every Republican president since Herbert Hoover has belonged." Al told his diary about his special time at the Grove.

> Friday, July 19, 1985: I drove by myself into the Grove, where I was stationed at the Pelican Camp. It and all the camps have an enclosure, a boundary. There are places for lodging that hold about twenty-four bodies. I had a room of my own, like one of the old cabin camps in Yellowstone Park in the 1930s. The whole place was built out of redwood. There were about 140 of those camps in various stages of opulence or simplicity.

Among two thousand people in the Grove that weekend, Al met musicians, artists, entertainers, and statesmen—an array of much of America's top talent. The weekend was filled with music, from impromptu jam sessions to full-on concerts, and from old-time tunes to opera. The essence of the whole experience was "music, music, music, and good fun and fellowship." There was "marvelous food and wine—and more music."

> The only minor aberration of sorts—one that quickly inspired me to the conduct of my earlier life—was that one of the rituals of over a hundred years was to piddle upon the base of redwoods, when one had to humor one's functions. There was a lot of that going on because there was a great deal of liquid refreshment. It is a rather different kind of situation to be standing next to a Nobel Prize winner, both of us pissing at the base of a two-hundred-foot tree.

The first night, he attended a variety show featuring Metropolitan Opera singers and talented duos from New York, Los Angeles and San Francisco. "I topped off the evening by having a remarkable drink they called Nembutal, "Nembie" for short. It must have consisted of about five ounces of hot rum and about a half-cup of cocoa with butter and cinnamon. It was a real knockout, in every sense of the word."

The next day, he was the featured attraction.

> I readied myself for my talk, which was to begin at 4:30 at the lakeside. Mine was the principal one of the weekend. Charles Black, husband of Shirley Temple, introduced me. There was quite a crew there—Henry Kissinger, former attorney general William French Smith, Walter Cronkite, Joe Foss, Jimmy Doolittle, Caspar Weinberger, and many others. I mentioned several topics, and this is what I told them.
>
> Defense: They are wallowing in charges of mismanagement and chaos. I have never had more letters from my own constituents about expensive toilet seats, coffee pots, ashtrays, and contractors.
>
> Agriculture: We have programs that emphasize production,

while other programs are paying to take crops *out* of production.

Social Security: A typical couple gets all their contribution back in six and one half years. On average, a single person gets back his contribution in three years, and ends up getting back three bucks for every buck put in. Yet the perception is that somehow everybody over the age of sixty-five is foraging in alleys.

Veterans' Benefits: I don't think all veterans should receive the same benefits. A person who never left the United States and has never been involved in combat and doesn't know a mortar tube from either end should not receive the same benefits as a combat veteran. In the Senate, the most hysterical debate comes from those who never served in the military.

Medicare: Lord's sake! Try to add $7.50 more a month [to an individual's cost] and the howl is deafening. It was originally supposed to be paid 50 percent by the beneficiary and 50 percent by the government. Now it is 76 percent paid by the government. When we tried to change that by one percentage point, to 74/25, the mailroom broke down again.

Tax Reform: Thirty-nine thousand lawyers in Washington, D.C., and many of them make a tidy salary simply by protecting one word or one sentence in the tax code.

Immigration Reform: Illegal aliens are responsible for 67 percent of the births in the Los Angeles County Hospital. Unpaid medical bills for illegal aliens totaled $145 million in Los Angeles County alone in 1983—and recall that each illegal alien mother is giving birth to a United States citizen. Refugee welfare dependency in California for those who have been here less than three years is approximately 85 percent, while in the rest of the country it is about 35 percent.

He amplified each point and touched on a score of others. Then he revealed his definition of politics.

I said that in politics, there are no right answers, only a continuing flow of compromises among groups, resulting in a changing, cloudy, and ambiguous series of public decisions—where appetite and ambition compete openly with knowledge and wisdom.

I was really quite overwhelmed by the response. As I gathered up my papers from the podium, people rose from the grass where they were sitting and came forward to thank me for my remarks. I knew that I had prepared well and was going to *make* them like me!

After wrapping up the weekend with more feasting, music, and socializing, Al joined Ann in Monterey, where their hotel room overlooked the eighteenth green at Pebble Beach Country Club. After dinner and dancing, they retired to their room, where "Ann lit a fire—and we kissed and giggled!"

Hatching Checks

Back in Washington, Senator Orin Hatch of Utah was proposing federal compensation to sheepherders in his state who had been exposed to atomic testing that began in the 1940s and continued until 1958. Hatch argued that since the citizens of the Marshall Islands—located in Micronesia, in the Pacific Ocean—were to be compensated for atomic testing at Bikini Atoll, Utah sheepherders should be compensated as well.

Simpson feared that once the door was opened to cash compensation for people living downwind of atomic test sites, whether or not they suffered any health problems as a result, the precedent could lead to even more creative means of tapping the federal treasury. "I am going to have to resist that tooth and fang on the Senate floor, or else it will open the door to 'atomic veterans,' and then compensation for exposure to Agent Orange and all kinds of other things—and we will end up breaking the bank."

Wolf Scat and Stinking Water

On September 2, 1985, Al celebrated his fifty-fourth birthday by driving Ann to their Bobcat Ranch. Originally a homestead, later a part of Buffalo Bill's TE Ranch, the Bobcat is southwest of Cody at the confluence of a creek named Ishawooa (a Shoshone word meaning "wolf scat") and the south fork of the Shoshone River, which was originally named Stinking Water.

As explained by Colin Simpson in 2007, the Bobcat, which is in a physical setting more attractive than the nearby creek names infer, was named by a rider in Buffalo Bill's Wild West Show. It came into Simpson family possession in 1933.

> Carly Downing was one of the Rough Riders in Buffalo Bill's Wild West Show. I have a copy of the agreement that granddad wrote. I think it was for $1,250. Unless Carly could pay it back within a certain time, then granddad and Nana [Milward and Lorna] would own it. However, if he did pay it back, they would still own what was called the "Sayles Cabin."
>
> Carly never could pay it back, so it was a kind of a foreclosure. It was an agreed-upon thing, where Carly just said that if he could not pay it back, it's yours.

Not long after the Bobcat became theirs, Lorna and Milward were cleaning one of the cabins and found a handwritten note penned years earlier by "Buffalo Bill" Cody. It was an apology for having to break in and borrow something he needed.

Al sat on the porch of the main building that day in 1985, reveling in his heritage and reviewing the scores of precious family memories spawned there. He shifted to his father's medical problems, and drove to Cody to visit him. "Pop is not doing as well as he did. It is just awfully tough for him as it becomes harder and harder for him to walk. He is a person of extraordinary courage and spirit, as is Mom. It was tough to leave them."

Back in Washington, he recorded thoughts about his children. Bill, Colin and Sue were then twenty-eight, twenty-six, and twenty-two. "Our three are well and seem to be busy and active in their life's pursuits. Colin stumbled a bit, but he will pick up the slack quickly. He knows just how to do it. A fascinating crew they are. They were the best investment we ever made in our lives. We spent a lot of time with them assuring that. It was better than investing in anything else I could imagine on the earth's surface."

That night, Al seemed especially eager to resume Senate combat, saying to his diary, "Bring on the United States Senate and its accompanying phantoms, specters, dragons, brigands and thieves."

Chapter Five

HEADLINERS
AND HEADACHES

~

IN LATE 1985 two radically different high-profile international events played out wholly within the United States. One involved a fairy-tale visit by a prince and princess. The other saw a Russian so desperate to land on American soil that he repeatedly swam the final yards.

MEDVID

On October 24 Soviet seaman Miroslav Medvid jumped forty feet into the Mississippi River from the deck of the Soviet ship *Marshal Koniev*, which was docked near New Orleans. The U.S. Border Patrol interviewed him, but because his intentions seemed unclear to agents, he was returned to his ship. He jumped again and swam to shore. This time he was caught by a pursuing Soviet officer and dragged back aboard his vessel.

When the incident became publicly known, the Reagan Administration ordered the ship held. The State Department persuaded the Soviets to let American representatives—including a navy doctor and an air force psychiatrist—talk with seaman Medvid. Under the watchful eyes of Soviet diplomats, and presumably fearing retaliation against his family back home, Medvid told the Americans that he had simply fallen overboard, twice, and had no desire to defect.

As chair of the Senate committee bearing oversight of the Immigration and Naturalization Service (INS), Al Simpson made careful notes of the situation. He soon came to believe the INS "botched the initial interview very badly—as did the interpreter." As the incident took on international significance, he became concerned that it could result in an ugly confrontation with the Soviet Union. "There are many United States ships in Soviet waters. Something not appropriate will occur in retaliation," he warned. "Medvid's choices may have been stupid or suicidal, or under coercion, but a twenty-four-year-old electrician who speaks three languages has those choices. If that is suicide to him, that is his business. If he ends up defecting, what does he gain? Probably the death of his parents in the Soviet Union."

Complicating the situation was the president's upcoming "Superpowers Summit" in Geneva with Soviet leader Mikhail Gorbachev. With that less than three weeks away, Simpson attended a meeting at the White House and listened carefully to the president. He noted later that Reagan said, "We are going to be tough but reasonable. Realism is the key." Reagan also said, "If the Russians say to me that they do not want to let us verify [weapons reductions], then I'm going to tell them it must mean they want to cheat." The president laughed and told the senators he would bring back some vodka, since he was sure he would run into a sale. Whether or not he intended to buy vodka, he seemed in no mood to buy any excuses from the Soviets; he was using spirited language, such as, "I'll do whatever the hell has to be done."

Simpson brought up the Medvid situation and expressed annoyance that some members of Congress seemed to be using the issue simply to aggrandize themselves. "The problem with Medvid hearings is that everybody in Congress thinks they might get a seven-camera hearing out of it, or a twelve-camera hearing. That is what makes the job so tedious. How did foreign policy of the United States come to be conducted by the *Agriculture* Committee of the United States Senate?" Simpson stressed to the president that four U.S. federal courts had ruled Medvid was not seeking asylum and should be returned to his country, and six times he confirmed that judgment.

After the meeting, Congressman Jack Kemp approached Simpson and asked if he was the one being accused of seeking a "seven-camera hearing."

"Yes," Al said flatly.

"What? You mean that we all have to be as sincere and pure as *you* are?" Kemp snorted.

"Damned if I know," Al fired back. "But I do know that I've had two press conferences in the seven years I've been here, and you seem to have a press conference on every known form of human activity, across the board. So I guess that *is* what I am speaking about." He told Kemp he thought his activities in the Medvid situation were not at all helpful to the president.

Simpson returned to his office and asked his press secretary to check the records. She advised that he had conducted three formal press conferences and five personal visits to the Senate radio and television gallery during his seven years in office. "I think that is what burned Jack, since I end up going on all those programs like *MacNeil/Lehrer* and *Meet the Press* and *Nightline* and all the rest, at *their* request, while he cranks out one metric ton of press material a month trying to do that." Years later, Simpson recalled apologizing to Kemp. "Jack said he felt badly [about his comments] and I told him I had been a bit harsh too. Then I gave him the correct figures about my press conferences. He seemed fascinated with that. He wanted to apologize, and said he had great respect and admiration for me, for taking on the tough issues that I did."

In the following weeks Simpson tried to avoid conducting his own Medvid hearings in the Immigration Subcommittee, but finally relented in order to avoid an even larger political circus.

Senator Gordon Humphrey has this one like a bulldog. I am having these hearings to see if we can assuage his anxiety. The issue obsesses Gordon and we are just going to keep plowing and try to keep it at the immigration subcommittee level without setting up a separate commission with a three hundred thousand dollar budget. . . .

The "far right" has made it their cause célèbre. I have never heard a more vaporous bit of questioning. When this [hearing] is done, so am I. If someone else wants to drag it around for years, as they did the deaths of John Kennedy and Martin Luther King, they can have a go at it, but on their own. I am going to drop out.

On January 30, 2001, sixteen years later, Medvid returned to the United States and revealed that he had long planned to jump ship and had joined the Soviet merchant marine solely for the opportunity to defect from the Soviet Union. He said he jumped near New Orleans because that was his ship's first American port. When the vessel departed with him aboard, it sailed into the Atlantic, where he was transferred to another ship and taken to the Baltic. He said he was placed in a mental hospital where criminals were shackled to their beds and where the KGB drugged him and tortured him with electric shocks. He was finally sent home to his parents and on December 30, 1990, became a priest.

When Senator Jesse Helms said he had done all he could to keep the twenty-four-year-old sailor on United States soil after his two swims to reach it, Medvid said he had never been advised of that effort.

THE ROYALS

It would be hard to fathom a less glorious arrival in America than Medvid's, or one more celebrated than that of Britain's Prince Charles and Princess Diana.

November 10, 1985: Seven o'clock, time for the big event. Off Ann and I went to the British Embassy for a rather private dinner with the Prince and Princess of Wales, Charles and Lady Di. We tooled right up to the embassy in our Chevy Cavalier and waded right into the middle of the most fascinating evening of our lives.

There was an extraordinary array of guests from all over the United States. As we came through the main entry, then to the top of the stairs of the second floor and onto the landing, the prince and princess were in the receiving line.

Al and Ann carefully noted not only what the royal couple said but also their demeanor and appearance.

> Diana is much slimmer than her pictures. She wore a beautiful diamond tiara with an elastic band, and said it was quite heavy. She was in a beautiful white dress that Ann could describe better. I was looking at her lovely features.
>
> When we were invited into the dining room, I was at table number two and Ann was at table twelve. Suddenly a gentleman came by and said, "If you will please stand by your seats . . . they are coming." I turned around and there was the prince, who took his seat. Next to him was Barbara Bush, and then your loyal correspondent, me. Don't ask me how we both got there, but I can tell you that we had a marvelous evening.

Dinner conversation turned to visiting Wyoming, and Al assured the prince that Wyoming people would respect the couple's privacy, just as they had respected that of his parents many years before. Prince Charles said they would enjoy such a visit.

At one point he asked Al how the American government deals with constituent questions and problems.

> I told him that when I get nasty letters, I sometimes write back and say, "If you continue to carry on like this you are going to burst a blood vessel in your neck and unravel your underwear."
>
> The prince got a hell of a bang out of that, and later told me he had written a letter to one of his nagging subjects. He said that when the person got quite irate, he, the prince, knew he had "twisted his knickers."
>
> I talked about his two fine sons, and how it was raising two sons in my own life. We talked about the coming summit conference and the vagaries of his job as the Prince of Wales. We shared a good story or two and I found that he has a delicious sense of humor.

Simpson especially loved knowing that the Prince too enjoyed authoring spirited letters. Simpson did that the entirety of his public service, and far beyond.[1]

At the conclusion of the dinner Prince Charles toasted those present and spoke about "ancient ties" between the two countries. He said he was in America to see the Treasures of Great Britain display at the National Gallery, and mentioned good-naturedly that most of that material had been "raided" by the United States. Although President Reagan was not present, the prince concluded with a toast to him. Vice President Bush eloquently returned it.

Then it was over. "I think it was the princess who gave 'the signal.' Suddenly people were up and ready to call it a day. Prince Charles said, 'Is it over? I was having a great time and I wish we could go on.'" The royals expressed appreciation for the evening and took their leave. Al and Ann lingered a few minutes. After most of the big black limousines had departed, they ducked into Ann's little gray Chevy and motored off, marveling over their good fortune. "I never saw Ann more lovely. She wore a beautiful long, black dress with scooped neckline and pearls. I have a picture of her. We got home and just sat around talking for an hour and a half about a most remarkable night in our lives. We got to bed about two in the morning and I was back up at six for a flight to Chicago, where I gave a speech."

Experiences like the one with the royal couple at the White House hint at Al's appreciation of a passage from Rudyard Kipling's poem, "If."

> If you can talk with crowds and keep your virtue,
> Or walk with kings—nor lose the common touch,
> If neither foes nor loving friends can hurt you;
> If all men count with you, but none too much.

The next day, after speaking to the National Association of Independent Insurers in the "windy city," Al hopped a plane back to Washington, went to his office to catch up on matters there, returned home to change into a tuxedo and, with Ann again on his arm, drove to the National Gallery of Art to meet up with the royal couple for a second time.

As the prince and princess emerged from a dinner with I. M. Pei, architect of the gallery, liveried footmen blew bannered silver trumpets. The royal couple descended the stairs into an area where guests had been asked to form in groups of ten to fifteen. As Princess Di went in another direction, Prince Charles approached Al, who was chatting with Congressman John Dingell. It was the perfect opportunity to flabbergast the man he called "the tough cookie from Michigan."

> I said, "Stick around, John. I'll introduce you to the prince— he's an old friend of mine." John chuckled to beat hell on that one, but in a few minutes, the prince came by. When he was close, I stuck out my hand.
>
> He said, "Senator Simpson, it is nice to see you. I enjoyed my time with you last night. That was great fun. We will be coming to Wyoming. We are going to plan on it. I would love to have you tell me some more of those stories."
>
> I said, "Well, I loved it too, and we will see you in Wyoming. Now let me introduce you to Congressman John Dingell, chairman of the Committee on Energy and Commerce in the House."
>
> He said, "Oh, yes, I have heard of Mr. Dingell. It is nice to see you."
>
> Within a few minutes, he was spirited away. I said to a surprised Dingell, "Stick with me, John, and this is the way it will be."

Months later Prince Charles wrote Simpson to say, "I remember with great pleasure your marvelous jokes during the course of the evening. I would willingly come to Wyoming just for more of those. . . . I will certainly be in touch the moment it looks as though we could make it. Thank you so much for a thoroughly tempting suggestion!"

COLLEAGUES

Al Simpson early in his career learned that some senators and government officials were leaders and others were "back benchers." His highest respect was reserved for those who "got into the fray and mixed it up in an honest, straightforward way," even when he disagreed with them.

Byrd

If one were to make a list of senators with whom it would have been wise to avoid locking horns, Robert Byrd, especially while serving as majority leader and later as chair of the Appropriations Committee, would likely top it. A number of senators on both sides of the aisle learned the hard way to be wary and respectful of the wily West Virginian.

On one occasion Simpson feared he had offended Byrd during a debate. He sought the first opportunity to speak privately with him.

> He shared much of himself, and much about his goals, dreams and fears about the Senate. I told him he was an awesome personality and that I regretted "coming on strong" before him.
>
> He shared insights with me about the positions we all have in the Senate, and what would happen to any of us when we leave—how easy it is to fill our shoes and how quickly people forget the fine senators of the past. . . . He is a most fascinating, complex and enigmatic man. I do enjoy him. He gives off a powerful, kinetic energy.

Over the years Byrd vexed, frustrated, and impressed Simpson, sometimes in a single day. Because Byrd conducted himself in an almost regal manner and took himself extremely seriously, Al took care not to share off-color jokes with him.

President Reagan had no such reservations. According to Simpson, Reagan once laughingly relayed a particularly ribald joke to Byrd and several other senators: "The Lone Ranger had been captured. They were going to kill him at the stake. They gave him one wish. He asked for Tonto, whispered something to him, and Tonto took off. Twenty minutes later Tonto rode up with twenty naked women on horseback. The Lone Ranger cried out, 'No, no, Tonto! I said *posse.*' "

Byrd seemed a bit confused, but then chuckled. That afternoon he motioned Simpson over to his desk and whispered that he didn't much like such jokes but had one to share. It was a mildly colorful tale about two preachers, one of whom said, "oh shit!" during a church service. The story ended: "It took two weeks to clean the church!" When Byrd added that he didn't know if he should have told a joke like that, Al jumped to assuage his concern. "Robert, it was marvelous, and well told!" Al considered this exchange an important step in his developing relationship with Byrd.

Thurmond

On March 10, 1993, Al Simpson joined a tribute to Senator Strom Thurmond, whom he revered as a second father. During the event Al's mind drifted back to a bizarre incident that occurred while his real father was in the Senate.

> Thurmond wanted to keep the Democrats from making a committee quorum, so he grabbed Senator Ralph Yarborough of Texas outside the hearing room and *sat on him*. He just took Yarborough down and sat on him, to prevent him from going in.
>
> Dad was walking down the hall and saw what was happening. Strom said, "Now Milward, you just go right back to your office. I can handle this."
>
> Pop couldn't believe it. There Thurmond was, *sitting* on a fellow United States senator.

In the Capitol Building Al now had a chance to share his own special moment with Thurmond. In the vice president's ceremonial room he and Thurmond found Senator Carol Moseley-Braun of Illinois sitting next to a famous desk. Al decided to give her a history lesson. "Do you know that this is the desk where Nixon taped his activities during Watergate? Get down here and I will show you where the microphones were stationed on the underside of the desk, where the clips were that held them." That inspired Thurmond to stand in the middle of the room and ask, "Do you want me to tell you more about that desk? President McKinley sat there on the very day he was *assassinated*."

Ninety-year-old Thurmond leaped into the air and tapped the chandelier's crystals with his hand. Then he explained that the wood in the room had come from the *U.S.S. Constitution*. "Old Ironsides is *right here*," he said excitedly. Al glanced admiringly at his friend and thought to himself, "Indeed he is."

Udall

Another person Simpson likened to his father was Representative Morris "Mo" Udall of Arizona. The Democrat was first elected to the U.S. House in 1961 in a special election. He ran unsuccessfully for president in 1976 and became a well-liked member of Congress. Like Milward, he was diagnosed with Parkinson's disease but continued to represent the people of Arizona until 1991. In 1985 Simpson joined Senator Pete Domenici and Congressman Bill Richardson in Udall's office. Although the discussion focused on taxes, Al's notes focused on Udall.

> Had a great visit with Mo in his comfortable office. Lots of good stories, too. He reminds me so much of my Dad in his early stages of Parkinson's disease. He still has a great sense of humor and is very alert. He is a bit bent over, and the mask-like expression is there, but the twinkle in the eye is just like Pop's. Even if it weren't, I would enjoy him so much anyway. He is a great guy.

In 1993, ten months after Udall's December 1992 death, Simpson was interviewed at Harvard University as a participant in the Morris K. Udall Oral History Project. "I guess the influence that Mo had on my life was how to do things with fairness and patience and kindness—and with good humor, no matter how knotty or puzzling the issue was. That's what he taught me."

Gore

In spring 1985 Simpson formed his first impression of a senator new to the national spotlight, Al Gore, Jr., of Tennessee. He considered Democrat Gore "a very impressive young man . . . thoughtful, articulate, and seemingly sincere. He gave a great talk." Gore's father had been a member of the Senate from 1953 to 1971.

Over time, Simpson's opinion evolved downward to the point that in 1988, after Gore delivered a speech on the Senate floor, Simpson accused him of duplicitous behavior.

> Gore put on a real show. He got up and attained the floor at exactly seven in the evening, prime time television, and put on a dog and pony show about satellite dish owners and how they should not have to pay for descrambling programs. It was a real populist thing. Of course, it was the position of people who contributed to his campaign. He had spread the word throughout America that, at that hour, he would be making his pitch, and they should then call their congressmen.
>
> When Gore finished his prancing and dancing, he went over and assumed the chair [under normal circumstances, only senators of the majority party preside over the Senate], and he was there two *hours*, so viewers could see that he was a pretty big cheese. That was bad, and I told him so.

Senator Goldwater approached Gore at the height of their exchange and angrily shook his cane. "You're not like your dad!" Goldwater scolded.

On NBC's *Meet the Press* the next morning, Simpson fired a few shots at Gore, who was also on the program. "I talked about people who just watch the camera lens and just seem enamored by that, but don't ever say anything." He was talking about many politicians, but looking at Gore.

During the time Gore was vice president, Simpson alluded to another characteristic he found annoying. "Al Gore gave his updated report on reinventing government. He started to talk and none of us thought he would ever end. I'll be damned if I know why he does that, but he ruins his effectiveness by doing it. He kept saying, 'Now, finally' this, and 'now, finally' that, and finally you just *pass out*."

Jackson

Simpson had occasion to observe another scene-stealer in 1990, at a dinner event honoring Nelson Mandela, who had been held in a South African prison more than twenty-seven years for advocating violence and sabotage in protest of apartheid. As Simpson took it all in, he found himself distracted by a fellow audience member, Jesse Jackson: "Every time a camera light would go on, he would leap for it like a giant moth. Somebody said that Jackson had been at eleven functions that day with Mandela. Wherever Mandela was, there was Jesse. He is quite a cat, but he will never be president. Jesse Jackson wants to be the eternal commentator and criticizer, but never wants to do any heavy lifting."

Three years later Simpson participated in a Larry King program with Jackson. He came away with the same impression and explained it similarly: "I suppose I could get to like Jesse. The only thing about him that is so remarkably bizarre is that if you are talking with him—and he is a pleasant conversationalist—and a television light flicks on, or someone with a microphone enters the room, he heads for it like a moth to light. It is so obvious that even his friends chuckle when they see it happen."

Biden

Simpson had a much different relationship with a senator destined to become vice president. In spring 1987 Judiciary Committee Chair Joe Biden was accused of plagiarizing portions of speeches given by Robert Kennedy and by Neil Kinnock of the Labor Party in England. Twenty years earlier, it was also charged, Biden received a failing grade in a law school course for plagiarizing a legal article.

These were especially volatile allegations, since Biden was running for president.

Biden called Judiciary Committee members together to ask whether he should relinquish his chairmanship in light of these revelations. With no staff present, Al and a handful of others spoke with Biden. Simpson spoke first.

> You know, I do exaggerate, Joe. I tend to weave a tale. But let me tell you something. I was in deep crap in my earlier life. I was on federal probation for shooting mailboxes. I was charged with battery assault at the University of Wyoming, and with disturbing the peace. I am not proud of that, but it happened. . . .
>
> Put it on the table, Joe. People understand that. I am not proud of the stuff I did either, but that was me at that time of my life, not now. Anyone can understand that.

Simpson mentioned the indiscretions of several other prominent people and pointed to public acceptance of those who "'fessed up, paid up, and moved on."

Later Simpson publicly lauded Biden for having had the "guts to run for president," unlike some of his "fainthearted detractors who would try to pull him down." Biden should "get on with it," he said, since nobody is granted a "certificate of protection" in this world.

> Biden came to me privately the next day with tears in his eyes. He said, "I can't tell you how much I appreciate your coming to my defense. Anything I can ever do for you, Al, I will."
>
> I said, "There is no need for that. I did that because I wanted to do it."
>
> Biden repeated, "I just can't thank you enough. I feel that I owe you more than I can ever repay."
>
> I said, "Just do your job, Joe, and do it well and fairly."
>
> Biden persisted. "This is the second most painful thing that has ever happened to me in my life. First is the death of my first wife and daughter."

Four years later, in early January 1991, after Simpson was sworn in for his third six-year term, he popped into a reception for Senator Biden. The man destined to become vice president of the United States had not forgotten Al's friendship and support in the wake of his plagiarism scandal. Spotting Al, he jumped up, blew a whistle for attention, and addressed the group: "Here is a guy that I greatly enjoy and admire. When things were toughest for me, he stuck by me, stuck up for my integrity and my honesty. I appreciated that so much. And what I really appreciate is that he is a lovely friend who keeps me on my toes—because he is one ornery son of a bitch."

Biden's mother, father, sister, brother-in-law, and son came up. His mother said, "I never forgot what you did for my son. You are one of the finest men I have ever known." Al later wrote: "I just basked in it all, and was stunned by it. All the in-laws, outlaws, and everybody else in the Biden family came up. It was a lovely thing."

Coelho and Wright

Simpson found Congressman Tony Coelho, then majority (Democratic Party) whip in the House of Representatives, "impossible . . . absolutely the most partisan man in the United States Congress—on either ticket." He held similar feelings for Congressman Jim Wright, who was House majority leader until 1987, and then speaker of the House. "Jim Wright is more partisan, more contriving and more devious than anyone in the scheme over there except Tony Coelho—who, as far as he is concerned, would die and go to heaven if he could just assure that every single member of the House of Representatives had a 'D' behind his or her name instead of an 'R.' That would not solve the problems of the country, but I don't think Tony gives a crap about that."

Coelho later resigned his leadership job in the face of questions about the propriety of his personal finances. A month after that he resigned his seat in the House of Representatives. Wright too was destined to resign in an ethics scandal, in 1989.

Helms

Early in Simpson's career he mixed it up with Republican Jesse Helms. In a late-night session just before a December holiday recess, Helms was filibustering a nickel-per-gallon federal gas tax increase by demanding roll call votes on a seemingly endless series of minor amendments. It was a stalling tactic, since the lopsided outcome of each vote was obvious to everyone.

Finally, in the middle of the night, Al rose to his feet, drew himself to his full height, faced Helms, and said pointedly, "Seldom have I seen a more obdurate, more obnoxious performance. I guess it's called hardball. In my neck of the woods, we call it stickball. *Children* play it." Simpson said that when the time came for Helms to request continued federal support of North Carolina tobacco farmers and other programs he favored, senators would well remember the night he kept them from adjourning to go home for Christmas. The threat was clear and unprecedented.

There was an extended explosion in the press, but the two eventually made their peace. Years later Simpson appeared on Helms's behalf at a North Carolina campaign event. Reporters were quick to remind the two of their highly publicized exchange.

> The reporters said, "Senator, nice of you to come down here for Senator Helms. Let me quote what you said about him . . ."
>
> Jesse was sitting right there. I looked at one reporter, stretched my arms and said, "Here, drive a nail in each hand. Get a couple for the feet, too!"
>
> I said, "Look, that was then, this is now. I don't carry any grudges and neither does Jesse. I was tired, I was young, and I wanted to go home for Christmas. So now drive the nail." I put my hands against a huge wall. God, it was fun. I loved that.

Stevens

One day when Simpson was particularly tired and testy, he scrapped, and not for the first time, with blustery Alaska Republican Senator Ted Stevens.

He was raising hell with Bob Packwood for putting "secret stuff" into the tax reform bill. Hell, nobody puts more "secret stuff" into any appropriations bill than does Ted Stevens.

I allowed as to how he was the envy of all of us at that game, but said I didn't want to get into it with him, because he is a feisty guy. I did say that we sure ought to be aware that he hauls "pork" out of here by the metric ton.

I have seen him place condition upon condition and project upon project and waiver upon waiver, all having to do with Alaska. He said that perhaps I owed him an apology. I stated that I did not.

Simpson told Stevens that he would produce evidence of the huge amount of "pork" he had tucked into appropriations bills over the years. "I have no problem with that kind of funding, if it is all done up front," he told the Alaskan. "But yours isn't."

Metzenbaum and Kennedy

One of Simpson's most intensive bouts came in late 1986, when Senators Ted Kennedy and Howard Metzenbaum were engaged in a quest to derail Supreme Court Justice William Rehnquist's elevation to chief justice. "I never mind seeing people wade into the fray and fight the fight, but the hypocrisy of Metzenbaum and Kennedy is just too much, especially when you get into areas of right and wrong."

Metzenbaum had himself been in public disgrace two years before and had returned a $250,000 finder's fee he received in the sale of the Hay Adams Hotel (see chapter 4). Simpson's irritation with the Ohio senator ranked nearly as high as his disdain for the tactics deployed by his friend from Massachusetts. "Ted Kennedy, with *his* past capers—some of which match my own—can ill be seen making those kinds of judgments about Rehnquist. That is the galling part."

As the hearing began, Simpson made what he termed a " rather powerful" statement, warning the committee what to expect from Metzenbaum and Kennedy. "Everyone ought to hang on tight, because they are going to try to prove that he [Rehnquist] is all of the following: a racist, a sexist, an extremist, an assassin of the First Amendment, and that he had been a crazed young law clerk who was about two tacos short of a combination plate." Kennedy actually said, "Justice Rehnquist might have made a brilliant nine-teenth-century chief justice, but brilliance of judicial intellect in the service of racism and injustice is no virtue in our times."[2] Senator Metzenbaum also extensively questioned Rehnquist's candor, honesty, and judicial ethics.

Completely irritated, Simpson said he thought of Kennedy and Metzenbaum as resembling a certain bird of prey—the "bug-eyed zealot, with ruffled feathers and pinched bill, a bird that spends time scratching around in dirt, then emitting a continuing whine whenever the president submits an appointee for confirmation." The hearings were broadcast live on C-SPAN and were covered heavily by the mainstream media.

Among those viewing was President Reagan, who phoned the next morning. "I had a very gracious call from the 'prexy' himself. He said that he had watched the proceedings and that my remarks were just about the best he had heard. He commended me on them." Reagan especially enjoyed Simpson's use of the phrase "bug-eyed zealots" and mentioned that Kennedy and Metzenbaum had problems in their own backgrounds.

Simpson was surprised to see Metzenbaum working so hard to keep Justice Rehnquist from becoming chief justice, since he would remain on the court as an associate justice in any case.

> Metz came back to complain about something Rehnquist had done in some election. Finally I just said, "You know, Metz, you might beat him for chief justice, but he's still going to be on the court. You are going to wander in there someday when you finish this, and he's going to nail your ass."
>
> He said, "You know, you are really a smart ass."
>
> I said, "Well, *you* are a horse cock!"
>
> He asked, "What's a horse cock?"
>
> I said, "It's a term of opprobrium and ridicule."

Now recognizing the expression as a gross insult, Metzenbaum stared coldly at Simpson and said, "Well, well—fuck you!"

Simpson-Kennedy

Simpson's staff and many of his constituents understood his occasional blowouts with Senator Metzenbaum but remained puzzled that one of his closest friends was Ted Kennedy. As early as 1980 Simpson was saying of Kennedy, "He's a charming person whose philosophy is at the opposite end of the pike from mine . . . he can take a lot of stuff on the chin that would drag a lesser person down."

In 1988 Simpson and Kennedy entered an invigorating sparring partnership. The radio show *Face Off*, broadcast every weekday on nearly three hundred Mutual Network radio stations around the country, allowed each fifty seconds to expound on an issue of interest. Simpson's former press secretary Mary Kay Hill described the arrangement. "*Face Off* was a grand adventure. It included commercial breaks, a brief intro, a promo for the next issue and the guts of the debate of the day. Alternating every day, one of them [Simpson or Kennedy] would pick a topic and take his best shot at the other. The one responding got a bit more time, and always won. We would wait for Kennedy to pick a topic, just so Al could win it. It was a very popular program." Over the years, Simpson and Kennedy disagreed about almost everything, except their friendship.

> Look, Ted and I were the same age. We liked the same horrible, earthy humor. We laughed a lot. We did that radio program together for eight years, you know. The strengthening of our bond was five days a week, when for two minutes at a time we would beat each other up. He would see me on the floor and say, "You bastard, you stuck it in me yesterday." I would say, "I know, and you deserved it." Then he would hammer one into me . . .
>
> I was a pure legislator. I had no ability to administer or to manage human beings. But as a legislator, you want to find a

legislator to work with, not some guy who is just going to give speeches and screw you up. Kennedy was a master legislator. Occasionally he got up and started ranting, and I would look over and stop him.

One day he launched off and I said, "Well for heaven's sakes, we've already discussed this. What in the world is going on?" Boy, I really nailed his ass.

Later, he saw Ann in the gallery. He went up and said, "He's really pissed at me, isn't he?" Ann said, "Yes, he is." He said, "Oh God," and never did that again.

Simpson's willingness to give Kennedy advice extended to personal matters, such as Kennedy's approach to losing weight. In 1991 Al logged a note about Kennedy and milkshakes. "He looked gaunt and spooky. He has lost about twenty-four pounds on that damn *milkshake* diet. He is just *crazy*. I told him he was nuts, that if he just quit eating so much other stuff he could 'get there,' but over a longer period of time."

For his part, Kennedy openly professed admiration of Simpson. He was quoted in an *American Politics* article titled "The Gentleman from Wyoming" as saying, "He works harder (at listening) than anyone I know. We may not always agree, but he knows how to narrow the differences and get things done." In 2008, one week before he was diagnosed with cancer, Senator Kennedy spoke with Wyoming Public Television's Geoff O'Gara.

I developed a very warm relationship with Al right from the beginning. I still consider him to be a very true and important friend in my life. He had a delightful way of pulling my chain frequently. Sometimes when I'd get excited on the floor of the Senate, he'd just lean over and whisper to me, "Now Ted, calm down a little bit." If somebody else did that . . . but I just couldn't resist smiling and laughing and enjoying it.

In the final days and weeks of Senator Kennedy's life, the two spoke frequently. Simpson was profoundly saddened when the end came.

BUSH, REAGAN, AND NIXON

Over the years, the friendship between Al Simpson and Vice President George H. W. Bush grew steadily. One day in early November 1985, Bush telephoned an unlisted number to see if his friend Al was available for lunch. Hearing someone answer, he said, "Hey, big Al! This is George. Are you available for lunch?"

He had inadvertently dialed my private number. After explaining, and without checking my boss's schedule, I made their luncheon arrangements. That evening Al added to his diary: "It was a great visit. He is such a special person. Just the two of us were there for about forty-five minutes, lunching together and covering aspects of the Senate's relationship with the Administration right now, and how tough that has been."

Not long afterward, Ann and Pete Simpson hosted a fundraising luncheon for the University of Wyoming, in the U.S. Capitol. As the university's vice president of development, Pete was particularly eager for the attendees, most of whom were lobbyists, to recognize an opportunity to support a good cause. The group was preparing to view a video extolling the virtues of the university when Al, in another part of the Capitol building, mentioned the event to Vice President Bush.

"Where are they?" he asked.

"They're in room 120," Al said. "They're putting on a little show for the University of Wyoming, shaking the tin cup."

Bush brightened. "I'll go down there."

Off we hustled, with the Secret Service looking rather inquisitive. We went down to room 120 and they were just starting the movie. They were sitting in darkness when I threw open the door and presented the vice president of the United States. It certainly startled those lobbyists.

When I said, "There's my brother, Pete," George went over and greeted him. Then I turned to the stunned group and said, "Now, this man has just offered to give his entire salary for the next year to this remarkable cause."

George never missed a beat. "Yes, I'm doing that because I heard that Ann Simpson is involved."

He reached over and gave Ann a big hug and kiss. Then he waved, told them all to support the university, and took off. He is a hell of a guy to have done that. It was a lot of fun, and they all seemed to love it. So did I.

The Summit

The next day Al went to the White House for a leadership meeting with President Reagan, who was preparing for his world-awaited summit with Soviet leaders in Geneva. "He was in good form. He said that for all these decades we have had 'old poops' running the Soviet Union. He thought, now that he was part of the 'senior guard,' he would say to Soviet leader Mikhail Gorbachev, who is fifty-four, 'Now, young fella, this is what we are going to do, and I want you to listen closely,' just like they used to do to us in years past."

Reagan flew to Switzerland in the third week of November 1985. After the historic session he returned to Andrews Air Force Base and from there, via helicopter, to the east front of the U.S. Capitol. Simpson and his fellow escort committee members watched *Marine One* settle gently onto the parking lot. "We were sitting around watching television coverage of the landing on the east front of the Capitol building, and pulling the curtains back to watch the same thing through the window. It was a fascinating observation point. Reagan looked good, given the recent pressures of the summit and his lack of sleep."

Inside, the group greeted Reagan, who mentioned that the frigid temperatures in Geneva reminded him of his frozen inaugural in Washington the previous January.

We escorted the president into the House Chamber, where, after not sleeping for twenty-one hours, he gave his speech about the summit to a joint session of Congress.

One of the great thrills was that Ann had been invited to sit with Nancy Reagan in the family gallery. There was

Nancy in her lovely red dress, and directly behind her was
Ann, looking smashing in a reddish silk dress—a couple of
nice looking chicks. It was a great thrill for me to be down on
the floor within an arm of the president, looking up to see the
two of them visiting.

The president's remarks were frequently interrupted by applause.
When it was over, Al congratulated the president, and then the first
lady. "I just walked over and said how proud I was of how she handled herself in Geneva, and how thrilling it was for me to look up
and see her and Ann together during the speech. I reached over,
gave her a bit of a kiss, and said, "You really are a great lady."

He walked to his office in the Capitol, where television crews had
set up satellite feeds to transmit his reaction to the president's report.
The interviews went well; much better than the special edition of
ABC's *Nightline* later that evening. "It turned rather spirited when
Bob Dornan, the loose cannon congressman from California, called
Robert McNamara [U.S. secretary of defense during the Vietnam
era] the 'keeper of the body count,' and the man who 'led us into the
tragedy' of Vietnam. He really laid it on." As the situation grew intol-
erably uncomfortable, Simpson was saved by the bell announcing that
a fifteen-minute vote was commencing on the Senate floor. He was
grateful for a chance to escape the "grandstanding pontificator."

Nixon

The following week, with the Senate in its Thanksgiving holiday
recess, Al and Ann flew to New York City. They prowled museums
and attended a Broadway play—then set off to visit a former president.

We arranged to see President Richard Nixon at the Federal
Plaza, but then messed around out in the street for forty-
five minutes trying to find a cab. I finally called his staff and
said that I was deeply disappointed and embarrassed, but we
just couldn't make it, there was no way to get there at the
appointed hour.

A few minutes later, a guy called back and said that Nixon was disappointed too. He suggested that we change our plans and come instead to his daughter's apartment, Trisha Nixon Cox's home. He planned to meet us there, so we hustled right on down there, walking.

They found the apartment decorated in pinks and reds and a new Christmas tree glinting brightly. After a few minutes the former president emerged from a bedroom. "He looked taller than I had remembered him, and he looked well. We were ushered into a side room. While we spoke, Ann and Trisha and Ed Cox had a nice visit. Occasionally we 'mixed it up,' so that each of us could speak with the others. It was a fascinating visit of forty-five minutes."

After the two men discussed congressional deficit reduction efforts and related matters, Simpson suggested that Nixon meet with members of the Senate leadership. "He thought that was an excellent idea. I'll make the final arrangements. It was just absolutely a most remarkable visit. Ann and I enjoyed it thoroughly." Later Nixon wrote to Simpson about their New York conversation: "Al, as I have often said, there is only one thing worse for a politician than being wrong; that is to be dull. You are *never* dull."

Dinner for Six

Before Congress went out of session in late December 1985, Al and Ann hosted a dinner party at their home. It stemmed from their evening at the British Embassy with the Prince and Princess of Wales, when Barbara Bush mentioned that she had just read and loved David McCullough's 1981 book *Mornings on Horseback*, a biography of the young Theodore Roosevelt. As the dinner hour approached, the Simpsons, joined by David and Rosalee McCullough, eagerly anticipated the arrival of their special guests. Al described the scene: "We had a young man helping us at the house. He didn't know who the principal guest was until George [and Barbara Bush] came up the walk—with eight Secret Service men. There were two black vans filled with armaments and two police cars out front. I think the neighbors thought Ann and I had been in a domestic fight and that we would be carried out the door in bags."

That evening the six discovered they had a number of friends in common, by virtue of both George Bush and David McCullough having attended Yale. The conversation developed into what Al called "a spirited view from the moderate Democrat from Massachusetts, McCullough, and the moderate Republican from Connecticut-Texas, Mr. Bush. Barbara, Ann and Rosalee fully interjected their thoughts into it all."

Vice President and Mrs. Bush departed at 11:15. "George is usually a nine or ten o'clocker," Al later said. It seemed clear evidence that the Simpson-Bush bond was growing tighter yet. Ann held special affection for Barbara. Of all the high-ranking women she had come to know in Washington, she felt closest to Mrs. Bush. Looking back in 2007, she said, "Barbara Bush is very down to earth. We have done a lot with them, and stayed with them. I consider her a close personal friend."

The next morning Al and Ann attended a brunch at the vice president's residence. After rehashing the previous evening's revelry, the Simpsons set off for what Al described as the "perilous experience" of Christmas shopping.

Soon the Capitol's corridors fell silent. Hearing rooms went dark and a warm cloak of peace encased the Senate Chamber. Revelers departed the last receptions, and thousands of staffers headed to homes throughout the country to reacquaint themselves with loved ones. The first session of the 99th Congress had finally—and, for some of the combatants, mercifully—drawn to a close.

Chapter Six

CAMPAIGNS, COLUMNISTS, AND GAZOOS

~

AL SIMPSON'S BUSY first year as a Senate leader had been laced with heady new responsibilities and memorable experiences. An even broader array of challenges and opportunities awaited him in 1986, beginning with foreign diplomacy. In January the Simpsons departed for Asia with a delegation of six other senators and their wives. Headed by John Danforth of Missouri and aided by staff and military and medical personnel, they flew to South Korea and Japan to discuss international trade and defense issues. They continued to Hong Kong, touching down at Kai Tak Airport on January 14.

Their agenda included discussions with the American consulate and the consumption of numerous Peking ducks. They toured, shopped, and absorbed as much culture as time allowed before jetting back to America. Of the return trip, Al later said, "It was the longest day in the history of Al and Ann Simpson."

Their blue jet bannered with the words "United States of America" landed for fuel at Ellsworth Air Force Base near Rapid City, South Dakota, where Al and Ann left the group and set off for Casper, Wyoming in a chartered twin-engine propeller plane. They flew over Mount Rushmore National Monument, but saw little, since their craft was being rocked violently in winter turbulence. "When we got to Casper, I shaved and showered as if I were getting ready for breakfast, and then actually ate a breakfast. I delivered my speech about the First Amendment and responsibilities of the media, chatted with people for a while, and collapsed into bed. It was my first sleep in thirty-two hours."

The next day he addressed the Wyoming Press Association convention, met with representatives of the uranium industry, and visited with members of the Wyoming Education Association before flying on to Washington. "I lit up a fire. Ann and I sat there for the first time in a month. I didn't read the mail, didn't do any work. I just unpacked and read the newspaper and hit the sack at about a quarter to one—and slept until *noon* the next day."

Before departing for Asia, Al had written a heartfelt letter of condolence to former senator Barry Goldwater, whose wife Margaret, also known as Peggy, had died following the amputation of a leg. Goldwater's response had arrived.

> Dear Al:
>
> You haven't received an answer to your wonderful letter of December 15 because, frankly, I haven't known how to start. The whole Simpson family holds a special place in my heart, starting with your father and mother. . . .
>
> Losing one with whom you have lived for over fifty years is not easy, but I suppose as time goes its dusty way I, like others, will learn to live with it. The easiest thing in cases like this is to just say, "thank you." But, in your case, Alan, thank you is just a couple of words. What I want to say to you may be just a couple of words, but they come straight from the heart. I cherish our friendship and I look forward to a lifetime of enjoying it.

REAGAN RESOLVE

On Tuesday, January 21, Al made his first trip of the year to the White House. He found President Reagan in good shape and eager to talk about his colon, which had just been explored by doctors. "The president was in rare form, after having about forty-four centimeters of garden hose rammed in his gazoo. No problems there. He had a small growth removed from his face. He looks tremendous. Seventy-four years old and he looks forty-four. An amazing guy."

As the meeting began, Reagan warned everyone: "Beware, I have my hearing aid on." Then in a low, serious voice, he expressed concerns about tax reform. He was emphatic. "I *want* it. It is that simple. It is a top priority and we are going to get it. I want it to be separate from other legislation, and I want the Senate to work it over so I can sign it." He revealed a firm grasp of tax brackets and related aspects of the economy.

The group moved on to foreign affairs, which prompted Reagan to mention the story of an elderly woman who was in the Kremlin one day. As he told it, she spotted a ranking officer and fired off a question: "I just want to know, since you are one of our great heroes of this country, whether a politician or a scientist started communism." The officer said, "Why, it was started by a politician, of course." She looked him over and said, "Well! They should have tried it on *mice* first!" Everyone laughed at the president's joke, none more robustly than Reagan himself.

Later that day Al sat with Congressman Tom Foley for an interview on the *MacNeil/Lehrer News Hour* on PBS. The program was unlike any other.

> Foley was speaking from a studio in Spokane, Washington. Jim Lehrer asked him about the political ramifications of deficit reduction, and whether it would be painful for politicians to make those spending cuts. Foley said it surely would be—but as he began describing it, suddenly his image was replaced by the film *Exodus*, right at the scene where they were operating on some guy. Tom could not see that, but I looked at the clip and said, "That is *exactly* what we are doing in the Gramm-Rudman effort."
>
> Five minutes of film ran before technicians sorted out the gaffe. It was a riot. Luckily, the program was fixed before being aired. Jim, Tom and I busted a gut afterward.

Nobody in the White House was laughing a few days later, when Simpson addressed his colleagues with a perilous suggestion: "It seems obvious that we are going to have to find *some* form of

revenue enhancement—whether in the form of a one cent per gal-
lon increase in federal gasoline taxes or an oil import fee or a business transfer tax—*something*."

At that point, Reagan walked in. Seeing that Simpson had been
talking, he said, "Go ahead, Al." Keenly aware of how Reagan felt
about most forms of tax increase, Simpson smiled and said, "Maybe
it's just as well that *you* go ahead, Mr. President. It seems only right."

Tipping O'Neill

A subsequent White House meeting turned seriously contentious
when President Reagan said he felt that nobody should be counted
as "unemployed" until they had not worked for twenty-six weeks.
That propelled House Speaker Tip O'Neill into a fit.

> Tip said he wasn't going to be part of this kind of thing where
> we just weren't taking care of the poor. Even though unem-
> ployment was down in his area, there were plenty of people
> out of work around the country. He said there were no cheats
> or deadbeats—"well, maybe a few," he clarified.
>
> O'Neill told the president, "Your policies with all of your
> rich friends are giving us all the problems in our country. You
> are taking care of your friends at the expense of the poor."
>
> I finally jumped in and said, "I've been right here at this
> table and I have heard the two of you go at each other before.
> I have come to know you both, to some degree, and I find you
> warm and delightful human beings with great senses of humor.
> However, you do seem to get a great charge out of mashing
> each other around and whacking on each other. It makes our
> job three times as tough when you do that. It is just *not helpful*."
>
> At least I got that off my chest. The meeting went on from
> there and did settle down a bit. Tip said that he greatly respects
> the office of the president, and Reagan remarked that it is just
> the incumbent that he doesn't like. I said to the president on the
> way out that I regretted breaking that up, but I just had to do
> that under those circumstances. He said I did the right thing.

Simpson ran into O'Neill a day or two later and said, "You've always been fair with me, and I with you. It just seems that it doesn't make our labors easier to do this. When you are not whacking on the Administration, your press guy, Chris Matthews, is whacking on them. It just makes for a hell of a tough way to do our business." O'Neill said he was not going to listen to the president's "old stories" anymore, and if the president insisted on telling them, then he was going to get in his own licks. When it was all over, Simpson concluded that O'Neill's behavior did not raise his stature with any Republicans at the White House. Simpson acknowledged that he too had been "a bit heavy and judgmental—but it was something I had wanted to say for a long time and there couldn't have been a better two to say it in front of."

Soon afterward Simpson and O'Neill were together at a Ford's Theater charity auction, selling its uncomfortable but historic old chairs for five hundred dollars each. Throughout the event they laughed and joked together like lifelong friends. Still, O'Neill remained displeased with the president until a few days later, at the State of the Union Address. There, the retiring O'Neill received one of the highest-profile tributes of his life, which Simpson felt he had helped engineer.

> What particularly pleased me was that twice during his speech, the president paid deference to Tip O'Neill. When he started his speech, he said, "Tip, this is not part of my prepared remarks, but this is the tenth State of the Union address that you will have presided over as Speaker of the House, and it will be your last. I just want to thank you for the service you've given to America, and to say how much we all appreciate it."
>
> There was a standing ovation, and Tip was touched, visibly touched. I have come to know him and let me tell you, he nearly felt washed away with that one.

Later Simpson was present when Congressman Silvio Conte, a Republican from Massachusetts, told Reagan that O'Neill had been deeply moved by his remarks. As always, Al took notes.

The president seemed pleased about that. Silvio told me that he had dinner with Tip, who told him that he had been "out of bounds" two weeks earlier at the White House meeting with the president.

Silvio said to me, "The reason the president said what he did at the State of the Union message was because of you, Simpson."

I said I appreciated the kind words, and if I had a small part in it, I was pleased.

The Political Bug Bites Another Simpson

Out in Wyoming, Al's brother Pete was becoming interested in the governorship. Word spread east, appearing first in the *Washington Post*. Al assessed the situation: "He has a long, tough haul ahead of him. He is such a sensitive and dear man. I know that he will be prepared for the buffeting that will come with that. His good sense and kind nature will overcome the hard hammering that will begin to rain on him."

Pete was not the only person eyeing the governorship. A Democratic friend named Mike Sullivan was also interested. Of course, each man's immediate challenge was to win his party's primary election. On February 16, 1986, Al flew to Wyoming to talk with his brother about "shoes, and ships and sealing wax and kings." He often used the phrase, memorized from Lewis Carroll's *The Walrus and the Carpenter,* to describe discussions about anything and everything.

> "The time has come," the Walrus said,
> "To talk of many things:
> Of shoes—and ships—and sealing-wax—
> Of cabbages—and kings—
> And why the sea is boiling hot—
> And whether pigs have wings."

At a meeting of the Wyoming Republican Central Committee Al made it clear that while he loved his brother, he could not support one Republican over another in a primary election. "I told them about my rich relationship with brother Pete, and why I would not be able help him at all in the Republican primary election campaign. I said I would not be helping him with fundraising, bankrolling, or anything of that nature—and that all candidates for governor would have equal access to my office." After the primary election on August 20, 1986, things would be different, he promised.

Time Out

No matter the intensity of a day's business, Al could always set aside politics to revel in the physical scene. At a White House luncheon, he took a long look around.

> The west wing of the White House looked absolutely magnificent—bright sun was coming in through the window on a seventy-five-degree day with a crisp blue sky. Afterward, I walked to the veranda and looked across the fountain rimmed with red flowers, and then across the ellipse to the Jefferson Memorial and the Washington Monument. Senators Bob Dole, John Chafee and I just stood there and reflected about the fact that if you ever lose that feeling, you had better head out of this town.

Simpson could scrap with the best of them and would have plenty of opportunity in his second year of leadership. But part of his balance in life came—and continues to come—from knowing when it is time to take stock.

PRODDING AND PROBING

The public was awakening to a confusing and growing foreign relations issue that involved Iran, Nicaragua, key members of President Reagan's Administration, and perhaps Reagan himself. Al wanted to know what was going on. "Tuesday, February 18, 1986: I went to the White House for a GOP leadership meeting on Nicaragua. The president let Secretary of State George Shultz, Secretary of

Defense Cap Weinberger and the CIA's Bill Casey handle the issue. It was well presented. I don't know if the American people understand it, but they'll have to start realizing it is serious."

What could American hostages in Iran and "freedom fighters" in Nicaragua possibly have in common? While that question went unanswered for months, the president's aversion to communism remained patently clear: "The president was burned about the avowed communist that came on [American television] after his defense speech. He was angry that they gave the guy seven minutes of airtime to call him dishonest and generally raise hell with him. The president said, 'I'll be damned if I could believe it, to see a *communist* commentator come on [television] after I spoke.' "

Congressman Jim Wright, who had delivered the Democrats' official response to Reagan's speech, provoked laughter as he turned to the president and asked, "You aren't talking about *me*, are you?"

Focusing on Nicaragua a few days later, Simpson joined several other senators in a meeting with the Nicaraguan ambassador. He was not impressed. "Carlos Tunnermann, Nicaragua's ambassador to the United States, is one of the smoothest cats I have ever seen in diplomacy. He is wily—and really is a slick little lying bastard. There isn't anything you can trap him in. He is probably a shithouse rat, a rat that crawls around in that stuff all day long and never seems to get a single bit of it on any part of his body."

Something must have stuck to Ambassador Tunnermann, however, since he and seven other diplomats were soon expelled from the United States. As tensions between the countries rose further, more officials from both nations were forced to return home. After a top-secret briefing by Reagan Administration officials on March 25, 1986, Simpson dictated the following: "We reviewed the situation where the Sandinistas in Nicaragua actually made the 'incursion' into Honduras with about sixteen hundred to two thousand men. Now we have Black Hawk helicopters ferrying Hondurans back across their country to near the border. We stay away from the combat area, but we are involved. It is a troublesome situation in Nicaragua."

Tough on Terrorism

Meanwhile, international terrorism was becoming another increasingly serious issue. On April 15, while Simpson was being driven to an event in Georgetown, he received word of plans for a U.S. air strike against Libya.

> [The White House] told me they were going to make a military strike against Libya in retaliation for recent terrorist activities. The president was scheduled to be at the Georgetown Club, but when we sat down, he was not there. Then General P. X. Kelly of the Marine Corps told us that a successful strike had just taken place against five military targets in Libya.
>
> Afterward, we went down to the bar in the club and watched the president give a ten-minute address on television. It was a powerful statement. He said he took no pleasure whatsoever from the attack, but that we are not going to see our people terrorized anywhere on the earth.

Even though Washington was swirling with domestic and international challenges, the Simpsons found time to socialize. They had dinner one night at the home of Ted Kennedy and the next night with Supreme Court Justice Sandra Day O'Connor and her husband, John. Now on Washington's social A-list, Al began to question whether his popularity might become a problem: "People might wonder if it will lead to the curse of hubris."

During a congressional recess the two spent time in New York and Boston before returning to attend a gala dinner honoring Tip O'Neill. A famous entertainer was there. "Bob Hope asked me to do a three-minute skit with him in Carnegie Hall, but it was the very night the president of the United States was honoring the new Senate leadership. There was no way I could accept Hope's invitation, and it broke my heart." Simpson's schedule and appearances before a broad range of groups around the nation gave some observers the impression that he might be running for president. It was the last thing on his mind.

Chamber Performance

Senators had long debated whether to broadcast Senate proceedings on television. Al was concerned that it would lead to grandstanding before a nationwide television audience. At the same time, there could be benefits.

> I am glad America is tuned in, because now they will get to hear how we wade through great piles of emotion, fear, guilt and racism around here.
>
> I get tired of watching the military veterans in the chamber who were wounded in combat never really getting into the debate, while the guys getting everyone all juiced up are often the ones who never served at all, but just use the issue to grandstand. People will see that for what it is.

Noting that C-SPAN would be broadcasting Senate proceedings, President Reagan had some advice for Senate leaders: "Learn your lines. Don't bump into the furniture. And in the kissing scenes, keep your mouth closed."

Now it was time for the 1986 Washington Press Club Gridiron Dinner, the sole purpose of which was to lampoon well-known people—which many members considered themselves well qualified to do. While this might seem an unnecessary celebration of daily routine, presidents, diplomats, and members of Congress eagerly anticipated the evening each year because it afforded an opportunity to return fire. Simpson noted his favorite moment, which involved the First Lady, whose relationship with the media was not the warmest.

> The president and Nancy were superb. The president said, "Now Nancy, wouldn't you like to say something friendly and personal to the media? They are all here."
>
> She just stared and said nothing.
>
> He said, "Now Nancy, couldn't you just say something nice, just a friendly comment or something?"
>
> She stared, and she did it well.
>
> Reagan repeated, "Well surely, Nancy, if you could just say something nice to the media . . ."

Finally, she said, "I'm thinking, I'm *thinking*!" Then she just sat down with a big smile. People loved it.

Hoops and Heritage

One event that spring combined two of Al's greatest loves: New York City and the Wyoming Cowboys basketball team. With Wyoming pitted against Florida at the National Invitational Tournament in Madison Square Garden, the senator and seven hundred fellow Wyomingites cheered enthusiastically as the game began. The Cowboys fell behind at halftime but surged in the second half. "Boy did they get their act together for the next thirty minutes. They were down five at the half, but then scored three buckets and kept coming on. What a thrill it was. They won 67–58. I haven't been this excited for quite a spell."

Simpson returned to New York a few days later for the Cowboys' final game. It was against Ohio State, a potent opponent. "I thought Wyoming would have a tough time with Ohio State, and they did. They came out like a house afire and led 12–6. Then four fouls were called in forty seconds and they just seemed to go to pieces. They never did get cooking again, and lost 73–63. Still, they acquitted themselves well and I was very proud of them. I went into the dressing room afterwards and had a good visit with them."

Another contest was still developing. Al and Ann flew to Denver, drove to Laramie, and checked into room 31 at the Wyoming Motel. The "WYO" was not up to international standards, and never had been, but the Simpsons had routinely rented the same room for decades and were not about to change. While in Laramie they spoke with Pete about his campaign, which Al called the "Great Race." He felt that although his brother was in a tough primary fight with a more conservative Republican opponent named Bill Budd, he could prevail.

They drove on to the Wyoming Supreme Court in Cheyenne, where their son Colin was being sworn for admission to the Wyoming State Bar. Al was bursting with pride when he made a diary entry for the date. "It has been nearly a hundred years of Simpsons practicing law in Wyoming. My granddad, William L. Simpson, was admitted in 1892, and since then his son Milward L. Simpson, and then me, and now my two sons." His father and grandfather had both been admitted to the state Bar without completing law school.

A Medical Mystery

In the spring of 1986, Simpson made a discovery that would vex him and a small army of doctors for a long time. "I had an X-ray on Monday and was soon off to Bethesda [Naval Hospital] to have a lung examination. They want to follow up on a spot on my left lung that was not there last December. I could have something from eating uncooked or poorly cooked food in Japan or Korea. Or it could be an infection in the lung caused by a severe cold." Because he had coughed up a small amount of blood during a recent flight from Denver to Washington, Bethesda doctors put him on antibiotics. If the problem failed to clear up, they advised him, an examination with a bronchoscope would be performed.

On April 13 he returned to Bethesda for further investigation of the mysterious spot. New pictures showed it somewhat diminished but not gone. "I have taken my antibiotics faithfully for ten days, so even though the doctor is not alarmed, I'll have a bronchoscopy and see what is down in the 'tree trunk.' This is the same procedure Mom had when they diagnosed her with Valley Fever." The Mayo Clinic describes Valley fever as a fungal infection that causes fever, chest pain, and coughing. It is especially prevalent in the desert Southwest, where Milward and Lorna were spending their winters. Al returned to Bethesda on April 16 and checked into the pulmonary clinic for a new examination of his lungs.

I sucked about a pint of anesthetic through my nose and down my throat and then the good doctor performed a bronchoscopy with a light on a slender tube that goes right down into the "trees" of the lung. In the bottom of the fifth sac of my left lung is a small "infection." They just simply snipped a piece of it off for biopsy purposes.

There is no tumor in the area, but obviously some type of parasite or irritation. With all that information, they will begin to treat it. They also made up an auxiliary magnifying glass so I could look through the tube and examine my own innards, including the vocal cords as the tube came past them. It was quite a sensation.

He hoped the procedure would resolve the matter, but it did not. At least there was no malignancy. The medic recommended that he get extra rest.

Even with this uncertainty, Al's primary health concerns were not his own but his father's. Following a quick trip to Cody on Senate business, he ricocheted to Arizona where Milward was hospitalized. "He really was not too responsive. He had lost an eye to glaucoma and infection. It is the first time I had seen him not respond when Pete, Lynne, Ann, I, or one of the grandchildren came through the door. He is sluggish and dull. I stayed around about an hour and a half, and fed him some sherbet."

That evening Al took his mother to dinner. Afterward, he returned to his father's bedside. "He is still very dull, and is sleeping a great deal. I went back and visited again with Mom." Morning brought dramatic improvement. "Pop was bright and shining this morning," Al cheered. "He was smiling and had that great glittering face that still comes through at the age of eighty-eight." Doctors released Milward from the hospital and returned him to the family home in Phoenix.

Full Tilt

Grateful that his father had been alert while he was there, Al kissed his parents, boarded a plane to Chicago, and continued to Washington. He was home and in bed at midnight, ready for another breakfast meeting. In the Senate numerous important issues were spilling from the legislative plate. His few slack moments were consumed

by constituent visits, interviews with print and broadcast reporters, and receptions sponsored by every organization, individual, and
cause imaginable.

He found it odd to be engaged in a blazing whirlwind of activity
while, outwardly, the Senate was showing little progress. He was
running full tilt all day, hitting the books until well past midnight,
arising at the crack of dawn to rush to the Capitol and open up
the day's session, yet little was being resolved. In an April meeting
at the White House President Reagan was focusing on the Russians, Nicaragua, and a variety of foreign relations matters. Then he
turned to the budget—after a light moment involving a feathered
friend that Congressman Bob Michel had given him, a crocheted
duck. "It was made of strips of rag in a very attractive green and
gray combination," Al noted. "It was filled with jellybeans. As you
squeezed it, jellybeans popped right out of the butt of that duck.
That was quite a bizarre thing to witness, that duck crapping jellybeans. The president really split a gut laughing. Reagan picked up
the duck and whispered, 'Couldn't you just *spit* them out?'"

The conversation turned serious when Reagan made it clear
that he actually would veto a tax increase. Meanwhile, Senator
Domenici's budget proposal had passed the Budget Committee
and was ready for consideration by the full Senate. Simpson was
surprised and a touch irritated by Republican Congressman Jack
Kemp's views on the budget. "Jack Kemp really got into the fray.
He said everything was rosy and that we didn't need to touch anything and that the deficit was almost something 'contrived.' It was
fascinating to hear his pitch on it."

One issue, Superfund, had grown into a sweeping legislative initiative. It was being crafted to address the problem of toxic waste,
huge quantities of which had for many years been dumped inten-
tionally, and often secretly, at sites throughout the United States.
Al found the challenge difficult, even without having to deal with
a wily staffer who seemed bent on thwarting his every effort. "At
the Environment and Public Works Committee, I met with [chair]

Senator Bob Stafford and the Superfund bill conferees. I really came down heavy on the staff guy—maybe akin to bullying. I will have to watch that. He must have been injected with a toxic chemical when he was a one-year-old, and is going to take it out on somebody. He does too, pretty much."[1]

His feelings had not abated later in the year, when he said this: "That damn committee staff is in league with the devil. They have their own agenda. They will not listen to Pete [Domenici] or to Lee Thomas, administrator of the EPA, or to me. They are wily and crafty and tough—and just a touch dishonest."

In late April two of the Simpson's children, Sue and Colin, visited Washington for the weekend. As fate would have it, Al was scheduled to be in Wyoming. "Damn it. I head off for Wyoming tomorrow and will miss being with the two kids. So it goes in this crazy business." Although he regretted missing Colin and Sue by a few hours, he found an opportunity to spend time with one Simpson he considered particularly pleasant company. It came after he missed a flight from Denver to Laramie.

> I missed the Centennial Airlines flight. I was pooped, but rather than get a hotel room in Denver I just thought I would rent a car and turn the stereo up and visit with myself—a delightful companion.
>
> I drove to Laramie, on the Interstate all the way. I listened to a great FM selection of Anita O'Day and learned of her vocalist professional life with Stan Kenton and Gene Krupa. Actually, it was quite pleasant. In Laramie, I watched a little TV and hit the sack in room 31 at the WYO.

His musical musings and several-hour self-guided tour to Laramie had been his longest time alone in months. The next day included a flurry of meetings, dinner with friends, a fierce Wyoming snowstorm, and a flight back to Washington just in time for Sunday-night dinner at home.

Meltdown

April 26, 1986: Simpson stared at the normally concealed television in his office as reporters described a serious accident at the Soviet Union's Chernobyl nuclear power plant near Pripyat, Ukraine. Not only was it disastrous for the town of Chernobyl and the entire region; Simpson realized that fear of a similar disaster in America could seriously damage what was left of the nation's nuclear power industry. As chair of the Senate's Nuclear Regulation Subcommittee, he paid keen attention to the situation: "It is a bad accident in every way. We don't use a graphite-modified reactor here in the United States, so this type of accident would not have happened here. Furthermore, the damn Russian unit had no containment vessel whatsoever, and rather primitive piping. We have no knowledge yet as to the deaths and injuries from exposure to radiation."

While monitoring Chernobyl, senators finally passed a federal budget package, although it pleased neither party. Before the final vote, leaders made an unsuccessful attempt to contact President Reagan, who was in Japan. The package was designed to produce $25 billion in overall savings over the coming three years, much less than had been sought. "We voted on the package about one in the morning, rolled up shop, and called it a day. We sent it to the House of Representatives, where they can't duck it anymore. I went home, packed and hit the sack about 2:30, and slept until 7:30. That's progress."

Through all this, both the Iran-Contra matter enmeshing the president and the foreign matter enmeshing Simpson's left lung remained troublesome and unexplained.

SIMPSON AND THE PRESS

Al Simpson has an apt description of his lifelong relationship with the media: "One day you're the toast of the town, the next you're toast." Unlike senators who seek every opportunity to bleach their clothing in the klieg lights of fame, during his eighteen years in Washington, Simpson rarely called formal news conferences. Mastery of issues and the use of rich and sometimes ribald humor drew all the press coverage he could handle.

Year after year, while reporters were judging him, he was judging them. It became apparent that he held an unrestrained disdain for sloppy or biased reporting. After several major confrontations with "pontifical powdered poops," he began referring to the media as "an unelected and largely unelectable" force of society.

Letters to the *Star Tribune*

Simpson found the largest newspaper in his state, the *Casper Star Tribune,* a frequent source of irritation. His view of the *Star*'s editorial policy ricocheted between frustration and befuddlement.

The *Star* was known for dedicating generous amounts of space for letters to the editor. While he heartily endorsed free speech, he began realizing that some of the many letters addressing his actions in the Senate were factually incorrect. Because the paper would print no more than three letters per month from the same person, Simpson was unable to respond to everything written in error about him. He thought this ironic, since he was the Wyomingite in the best position to protect everyone's freedom of speech.

He was particularly aggrieved by numerous letters objecting to the 1985 increase in senators' salaries. He had voted against it, had stated publicly that he would not accept it, and was not accepting it. He was irritated that the *Star* continued to receive and publish readers' letters stating that he was. Al knew the paper's editors knew the truth, and he suspected they were disinclined to correct writers' misunderstanding on the matter in order to see him cast in an unfavorable light. In November 1987 he met with *Star Tribune* editor Dick High.

> I had an hour-and-fifteen-minute meeting with Dick High—
> just the two of us. Damnedest conversation of many a moon.
> All he wanted to talk about was "integrity." I said that as
> far as I was concerned, if he continued to print letters to the
> editor charging me with taking the salary [increase] when he

personally knew damn well it was false, then in my mind that reflected directly on *his* integrity.

High asked if Simpson's harsh comments were a threat to him. "Hell no," he responded. "But if you just keep running letters you know damn well are false, I'll just send my same response each time and expect it to be published too." He could "expect" all he wanted. The *Star* did not intend to publish more than three letters from anyone in a one-month period.

In late November 1989 Wyomingite Karl Gustafson sent a letter to the editor of the University of Wyoming *Branding Iron,* complaining bitterly about Simpson's acceptance of the salary increase.

> Hi, Al. It's me, one of those whiny taxpayers. . . . You had the brass to get on the news and lecture us on our lack of seriousness about the deficit. Way to go, but we're not the ones voting to raise the debt ceiling and give ourselves a pay raise. . . .
>
> I'll take a cut in my VA check without a whimper if you take the same cut in your paycheck. You can also freeze my benefit at its present level, if you don't give yourself a pay raise. Now the ball is in your court. What are you going to do about it?

Al had been waiting for just this kind of opportunity. He wrote to the paper, pointedly directing his comments at Gustafson.

> Been living in a cave? . . . I've been sending that extra money back to the Treasury. . . . My salary is $77,400, while the rest of the Senate has been earning $89,500. Now I've gone one better and refused the cost of living allowance, which was agreed to the other night, keeping my salary at its present level instead of $98,200. . . .
>
> Now the ball is in your court. . . . Please let me know where you'll be sending the extra money you will be cutting from your VA check, just as you pledged. . . . In your own words, "What are you going to do about it?" Awaiting word!!

Muckraking

Simpson was delighted by the opportunity to refute Gustafson right away. But it took twelve years to refute syndicated columnist Jack Anderson. In 1979 Anderson's column reported that Simpson accepted a campaign contribution from Babcock and Wilcox, corporate owner of the Three Mile Island nuclear power plant in Pennsylvania. The column asserted that the contribution had been offered and accepted shortly after the plant's accident, a clear implication that the company had tried to buy his favor during the investigation he would conduct as the top-ranking Republican on the Nuclear Regulation Subcommittee.

Indeed, the company had made a small campaign contribution, but it was received and deposited by Simpson *before* the accident, and thus could not have been an attempt to influence the investigation. Many weeks later Anderson responded to Simpson's demand for a correction and apology, but he wrote only that the date of a contribution to Simpson had been incorrectly stated. There was no attempt to explain the significance of the error.

The perfect opportunity to confront Anderson finally came in 1991, during a live television program in which Simpson was participating from Wyoming, and Anderson, via satellite, from Washington. Once they were on the air together, all hell broke loose.

> I was off the rail. He was stunned—I could see his face. I didn't even respond to the [reporter's] question, I just cut him up. He had dinged me on that contribution. He had also tried to savage Strom [Thurmond], and I was pissed off that he had done that. There was a lot of stuff in me about that guy.
>
> When he hurt people, and was proven wrong, he would finally retract it—but knowing that the human wreckage could never be put back together. I poured it on about Tom Eagleton, how Anderson tried to do him in, and what Anderson had done to others.
>
> Then I said that he had not served in the military, because

of "cowardice." Before he could react, I said, "How does it feel having *those things* exposed, Jack?"

Anderson was enraged. After he defended himself, Al harpooned him again. "There! You have had a chance to explain a very credible record of service to your country, Jack. Most people don't get that chance, when *you* take *their* words out of context."

Years later Simpson laughed heartily while recalling the incident. "Anderson was huffing and puffing, and if looks could kill . . . !" The incident surfaced again in 2006, when it was revealed to Simpson that Anderson had published but had not personally written the original article. "When I was in Washington earlier this year, a guy came up to me and said, 'I'm the guy who drafted that Anderson piece about you on the Babcock and Wilcox contribution. I feel very badly. I was wrong. I never got a chance to tell you personally, but here I am now.' He gave me a piece of paper about it. I still have that."

Buying Free Speech

In 1990 Simpson found a way around the *Casper Star Tribune*'s three-letter limit. It came in the wake of hostile letters to newspapers all over the state from Mildred Olsen of Lander, who had been lambasting him for months. Her primary complaint: he was not doing enough to help unemployed uranium miners. She was also bitter about what she saw as Simpson's lack of support for Social Security and Medicare.

After taking all the criticism he could stand, he drafted a lengthy article setting the record straight on numerous subjects and sent it to the *Star* for publication. When the paper refused to print it, he paid to have it printed. "Free speech is not free at the *Star*," he complained:

> My answers appear here as an "ad" because the *Casper Star* has a "policy" that limits me to three responses a month, even though a great many published letters ask for my response. . . .
> Yes, Mildred, I do remember our conversation when you mentioned "the Social Security thing." I have come to know

you pretty well. You also earnestly urged me to "do some-thing" with the Uranium Miners Compensation Bill, and I did just that. After meeting with you and that fine group of people many weeks ago, I went to work with my staff and hammered out a bill [that] passed the Senate and was then passed by the House of Representatives. . . .

[On] Social Security, you asked if I had "lost my mind" to even be addressing this "hot" issue. No, Mildred, I haven't. But I can tell you that our kids and grandkids are sure going to lose theirs in the year 2030—and not only their minds, but they will lose their butts as well—unless we have the courage to deal with Social Security in an honest, forthright fashion, without budget gimmicks or beneficiary hysteria. . . .

The "average retiree" gets back three dollars for every dol-lar he or she put in. Life expectancy is 10 to 13 years from the time of retirement. The "average" Social Security workers get their money back—plus interest!—within the first four and a half years of retirement. You can see that a system like that simply can't last. The problem deepens dramatically as the number of people receiving Social Security grows. . . .

We have never touched [limited or reduced] the benefits. We have never even "means tested" it for people who really do make big bucks and still draw full Social Security—a pro-gram originally conceived as a post-retirement "safety net," or "income supplement," and not a retirement program in its own right. . . .

Groups like Jim Roosevelt and his fellow alarmists at the National Committee to Preserve Social Security and Medicare are asking people just like you to send your hard-earned $10 to them, so they can "save you from Congressional meddling." What a money machine. Last year they picked up $34 million by terrorizing your fellow American citizens with emotional, hysterical and inaccurate mailings. But they spent only $4 million on "lobbying." The rest of it went to salaries for their board members and for buildings and the trappings of "success." It is so unfortunate if people believe their hysteria and ignore the solid facts available from true, unbiased experts— and then use that erroneous information to launch public attacks on people like me. That doesn't "alert" anyone to the "evils" of government. It just confuses and scares people.

As for reference to my salary, you know darn well that I never took the last two congressional pay raises, so that is a misfired shot. . . . Since 1985, I have returned more than $60,000 of my Senate salary to the Federal Treasury. . . .

To answer your closing question, I guess I am "dumb enough" to take this kind of heat on sensitive issues, because I figure that when I "hired on" for this job, people didn't expect me to duck the tough ones. . . . There are problems. Serious problems. And unless politicians and the public have the stomach to face up to them in a thoughtful, cooperative way, programs like Social Security won't be there! It makes a lot more honest sense to me to tell people the truth. I can't lie and just kind of josh them along. I'm just not built that way.

Simpson received a number of positive responses from the public, and Mildred Olsen's writing campaign slowed.

Too Charming?

Simpson found himself the object of a blistering assault by the conservative magazine *American Spectator* in early 1986. The article focused on his immigration reform efforts and his position on abortion. Al was incensed, not just by the article's content but that author Tom Bethell failed to speak with him before publishing his piece. Simpson's sharp response appeared in the magazine's April 1986 edition.

Well, if I might just take one moment to dig the hatchet out of my old bald dome, I will respond to the testy little attacks lobbed in my direction by Tom Bethell. Seldom in my twenty years of political life have I witnessed such a rapid-fire assault of drivel. . . .

Tom Bethell is a complete mystery to me. His grim visage and furtive shadow have never darkened my doorstep. He has never, at any time, attempted to communicate with me personally. . . . His deep-seated personal aversion for me must then be based on what he has read and heard second, third or maybe even fourth hand. Is that journalism? . . .

It is easy to be a critic—any fool can qualify. I often flunk the many litmus tests that are administered in this fascinating village by single-issue groups. I most surely flunked Bethell's test, since I don't seem to measure up on immigration reform, the abortion issue, or the Medvid case. . . . We're all entitled to our own opinions, but Bethell is not entitled to his own facts. The information he uses in the February and March issues is goofy. Maybe he is too.

He allowed that his pro-choice stand on abortion would never satisfy some, and he reviewed his rationale on immigration reform and other issues Bethell brought up. He closed by quoting British statesman Edmund Burke: "Those who would carry the great public schemes must be proof against the most fatiguing delays, the most mortifying disappointments, the most shocking insults, and worst of all—the presumptuous judgment of the ignorant beyond their design."[2]

In a published reply, Bethell said something illuminating about Simpson's personality and charm.

One issue the Senator raises is worth exploring. He says that I never contacted him or his office. True, but I just do not agree that journalists are obligated to abide by such rules of decorum. . . . Had I spent an hour with Simpson, I wonder if I would have written anything at all. I disagreed with him, and still do, about immigration, abortion, and the Medvid case, but I wonder how inclined I would have been to voice my disagreement after a friendly chat—perhaps even lunch. The Senator has a reputation for geniality which I'm sure is well deserved. Human nature (mine anyway) is such that the interaction of personalities is likely to prevail over misgivings about policy.

Simpson was dumbfounded: Bethell chose to publish his long article without meeting him personally, simply because he feared he might find Simpson too charismatic to be attacked in print.

In fact, Al could be disarmingly charming. In a *Washington Times* article on November 12, 1986, reporter Cathryn Donohoe noted that Congressman Romano Mazzoli, a Democrat and Simpson's House side counterpart in immigration reform, had taken note of the way he used humor and personality. "I've seen him disarm people in a second who were ready to hand his head to him on a plate, just by saying the right thing at the right time. They kind of rolled over to have their stomachs scratched."

Insiders knew that Simpson actually enjoyed many journalists and broadcast officials. In March 1986, he described to his diary meeting the top officials at NBC television: "I had dinner with Grant Tinker and all of the Executive Committee of NBC. It was informal, delightful and earthy—a pleasant and delightful evening with some remarkable men at the top of one of America's principal networks." He returned from New York to Washington and went straight to the ABC studios to appear on Ted Koppel's *Nightline* program. "I've done that show about five times. It is a good one. Later, I had a good visit with Koppel." After one *Nightline* program Al spent forty-five minutes with Koppel, talking about philosophy and life. Afterward he wrote, "He is a delightful guy. I have come to know that over the years."

The Gazoo "Blowout"

On the other hand, in 1987, when reporters were "frenzy-feeding" on the Iran-Contra situation, Simpson objected to the increasingly discourteous way they were treating the president. On March 18 he was sitting at the White House with President Reagan and several congressional leaders. As they discussed issues of the day, reporters and photographers were allowed to step in briefly to take a few photos—but not to ask questions. Several ignored the prohibition and began shouting inquiries about Iran-Contra.

After the meeting Simpson walked up to the bank of microphones on the White House lawn. A reporter eyed him and asked, "Why are you Republican senators trying to protect the president? We had many serious questions to ask." Simpson stared coldly down at the throng of excited faces, narrowed his eyes, and cut loose. "Oh what a bunch of *crap!*" Things went downhill from there, as he conceded to his diary that night. "I said to those reporters, 'You are doing a sadistic little disservice to your country as you continue to ask the president about the Iran situation, when we have people going to the root of it all. We have an Independent Counsel and a Special Counsel pursuing it.' "

The reporters appeared neither dissuaded nor diminished. Instead, some seemed exasperated by Simpson's rebuff. Now additionally irritated by their irritation, he launched a counterattack that included a word new to them: "You are asking him things because you know he is off balance—and you would like to stick it in his *gazoo!*" As he angrily spat out the words, he raised his hand as if to mimic and ridicule the reporters' frantic questioning. A tortured, mocking expression contorted his face, one he later called "an extraordinary grimace." At that instant, someone snapped a photo, catching the unfortunate pose that will forever remain a part of Simpson's public image.

> My God! I looked like a sex-crazed knife slayer from Lower Slabovia. After I had made enough faces to outdo a contortionist, one guy said he was offended by my conduct. I said, "Really? I'm offended by *yours!*" There were several more remarkable exchanges before I went back to my office to dig out of the rubble.
>
> I'm sure my mother almost collapsed when she saw it. It was grotesque, a photo so extraordinarily bizarre that the ombudsman of the *Washington Post* called me and said he had

received many calls from people who were offended by it. He
said some people who saw the picture didn't know me, but
thought it was a terrible thing for me to do.

Simpson told the paper that yes, perhaps he could have expressed
himself differently. He recognized that he had crossed the line separating "good humor from smart ass" and agreed that he had been
caught in a "rather remarkable" pose.

About two hundred phone calls came into his office that day and
the next. Most callers said they were *pleased* by what he had said to
the media, and many were upset by the disrespectful way reporters had been treating the president. One caller the following day
proved a significant exception.

A receptionist entered Al's office and said, "Senator, I have a call
that you really must take." He lifted the receiver and recognized
the voice of an eighty-seven-year-old woman. As she spoke, he felt
the impact of her message sharpening as it worked its way inward.

"Alan! I thought I told you a long time ago *not to make faces!*" The
"velvet hammer" was not pleased. As she lectured her son softly but
sternly, Alibi Al, for one of the few times in his life, offered no
defense. In the months that followed, Al occasionally conceded to
his audiences that he would not be utilizing his full intensity and
range of vocabulary, since he was determined to avoid another such
call from his mother.

Gazoo Mania

Within two days of the incident, "gazoo" buttons depicting Simpson's grimace began flooding Washington. Throughout Capitol
Hill, staffers and even a few members of Congress could be seen
wearing them. A *Washington Post* reporter wrote that he had con-
sulted the dictionary and found the word *kazoo*, but was unable to
learn the definition of *gazoo*. Sensing a marketing opportunity, a
kazoo manufacturer in Tonawanda, New York, called me to say
the company would be sending boxes of kazoos to the office. They
would be easier to use than gazoos, the spokesman laughed.

That weekend, Simpson ran into Hugh Sidey, senior White House correspondent for *Time* magazine. "He had been reporting on the White House through six presidents, and he told me he was absolutely thrilled about what I had said to the Washington press corps. He expressed that with feeling. It was a splendid time with a man for whom I have the greatest admiration and respect."

By happenstance, Sidey was scheduled along with Simpson on that evening's *Nightline* program. During the broadcast participants were shown a clip of the president answering a question at the end of a recent press conference. Helen Thomas had asked if Vice President Bush had tried to dissuade the president from supporting the Contras. The president said, "No."

Moderator Ted Koppel thought that significant and proclaimed it a devastating admission. Simpson was galled, as he later noted in his diary: "I called Ted on that one and said, 'You've added a lot of high drama to that, and it really doesn't deserve it. You used the word "devastating."'"

Koppel denied it.

"I said, 'Yes, you just did.'"

Koppel responded, "Well, then, I guess I'm *judging* the news content—and I *shouldn't?*" Simpson and several others suggested that if he intended to report rather than editorialize, it might be good to avoid that kind of comment.

A day or two later Simpson was told that presidential spokesman Marlin Fitzwater had opened his morning White House press conference with: "We have a new deputy press secretary—Al Simpson." A reporter got up and buzzed a tune on a kazoo. Goodhearted laughter filled the room.

Simpsonizing the Press Corps

NBC reporter Andrea Mitchell felt that media questioning of the president in the wake Simpson's explosion had been muted, and she suggested that the White House press corps had been "Simpsonized." When Al saw her a few days later, he said, "Boy, Andrea, you mean to tell me that some old cowboy from Wyoming can Simpsonize the nation's crack press corps? That's a laugh."

One of the many people contacting Simpson regarding his raucous encounter with White House reporters was former President Richard Nixon. "He wanted to commend me, to tell me how proud he was of what I was doing and what I had said. He said my exchange with the reporters had softened the tone of their questioning of Reagan the next day." Nixon said that instead of responding to questions shouted by reporters, President Eisenhower would simply walk away from the microphones. He suggested that Al extend that advice to Reagan.

On March 24, one week after the gazoo incident, the lanky senator once again came face to face with his reporter buddies while exiting the White House.

> There they were, the White House press corps. They were calling, "Senator, senator, come over and see us, come visit with us." Of course, I went through my usual grimacing and walked their way rather slowly. There was a great deal of hoorah as I stepped up to the bank of microphones and said, "Well! I have learned several things since I saw you last."
>
> Reporters strained to hear. I said, "I've learned that 'gazoo sticking' is a team sport, and that maybe I wish I had said some things differently. Possibly, I could have. But I don't have regrets—well, if I do have a regret it's that I didn't go down to the *Washington Post* and help that guy pick out the right photograph."

At a GOP policy luncheon later in the day, everyone was talking—not about gazoos but kazoos, since the promised box of shiny new musical instruments had arrived. Simpson had discouraged the company from providing them, but since they arrived anyway, he sent one to each of his ninety-nine Senate colleagues. He penned a note explaining that he simply wanted everyone to be aware of the difference between kazoos and gazoos. He did not provide an example of the latter.

Grudging Respect

Simpson noted in his diary that he once said to Helen Thomas, commonly regarded as the first lady of the press: "What we need to do, Helen, is to have you people in the media and the politicians all join in a 'town meeting.' Let's let the public come in and raise hell with both of us. We are both held in pretty low esteem—and the reasons, I think, are obvious."

Washington Post reporter Charles Trueheart reviewed Simpson's press strategy, if such it could be called, in October 1987: "Reportedly against the advice of staff, he unburdened himself of a vituperative 4,000 word jeremiad against 'a very clever trio of cats' at the biggest newspaper in his state, the *Casper Star Tribune.* . . . He seems gentle and kindly, but when he is agitated, he can turn sour," Trueheart wrote.

Dick High, former editor of the Casper *Star Tribune,* whose relationship with Al remained adversarial throughout their association, spoke admiringly of him to me in 2007: "He was his own person. He said what he thought. You could like it or not. He was a great example of how I think a Wyoming leader should be. He had a very sharp wit and was very effective."

High commented about the paper's 1986 editorial cartoon depicting Simpson wearing the button that said: "Never Give an Hispanic an Even Break." Even though he had been the paper's editor and intimately involved in its editorial policy, High claimed no control over or understanding of his political cartoonist: "The paper's cartoonist had the freedom to say whatever he wanted. His opinions were not necessarily the paper's editorial policy. I didn't understand what he was saying about a third of the time. I didn't have a clue what he was talking about."

During his phone interview with me, High also yielded on the issue of immigration reform. A vital element stripped from Simpson's 1986 bill was a secure identification system for all people legally in America. High had vehemently opposed the idea of an identifier and repeatedly mocked the "Simpson Card" as a dangerous and

unacceptable invasion of American freedom and privacy. In 2007
High conceded that Simpson might have been right.

> In retrospect, I might end up agreeing with him. It is a tricky
> thing. It can represent a loss of personal freedoms and it
> increases the capacity of the government to follow or control
> what you are doing. But privacy is pretty much dead at this
> point. He may have been right about that—but we were, at
> the time, opposed to it.
>
> His approach was pretty good, I think. He was reason-
> able—treating the people already here [in the country] fairly.
> Al is a civilized person. He is not somebody who is going to
> run amok over people. He will try to stay within the balance
> of good policy. I think he was more right than not, at the
> time.

In retirement, High summarized his view of the senator he had
frequently challenged in print and in person: "I think from the long
perspective, Simpson will be remembered as one of the great senators—because he's his own person. He was effective on lots of legislation. He was a leader. He had his foibles and his issues, but he was
a person who could work with the other side of the aisle and get
things done. He was, and is, charming, personable and effective."

Bill Simpson, looking back on his father's spats with the media,
said in 2008: "Freedom of the press is a great and glorious thing
in America, but Dad was never afraid to take on the press—and
believe me, there were a lot of politicians, in fact most politicians,
who would never cross the press. For him, it is just another act of
courage. He has political courage. He has intellectual courage. He
has independent courage. You don't find that in society anymore."

Chapter Seven

LAND OF HIGH ALTITUDE AND LOW MULTITUDE

~

THE POLICE WERE shadowing Al Simpson, but now they were not protecting a town from a young rebel. They were protecting a U.S. senator from a resident who had written threatening letters to Simpson in advance of the 1986 Wyoming Republican state convention in Riverton. This was not the first threat. Simpson occasionally received menacing notes from around the country. It was usually determined that although the writers were somewhat radical or eccentric, they were not dangerous. Other than time spent pondering the ignominy of being murdered by a deranged fanatic, Al found the Republican convention enjoyable.

For the most part, once in Wyoming, Al was among friends. Of all the Simpson family members ever interested in politics, he remains unchallenged in his ability to remember the names of those he meets. One day, as we were driving on a road north of Laramie, he claimed that he could name 10 percent of all the people in the state, on sight. I challenged him to prove it.

"Okay, just stop at the next town and follow me around," he said confidently. The small town of Powder River was just ahead, so I parked on the main street and we walked into the first business we saw. To my amazement, he addressed the owner and more than half of the customers he encountered by name. It was a remarkable feat, especially since he had met some of them only once before, during his first Senate campaign six years earlier. He remained deeply engaged with Wyoming people, even long after "retirement."

THE TRUTHS OF LIFE

At the crack of dawn on May 18, 1986, Al Simpson departed Washington for Wyoming to address the Big Horn High School graduating class of twenty-four students. He spoke about the things he learned over time, often the hard way. That gave him the credibility, he said, to offer some advice.

> [At] Cody High School, Cranbrook Schools, the University of Wyoming, Fort Benning, Law School at Laramie—I always thanked my dear parents for sending those checks to me. I worked too, and had an athletic scholarship. I weighed 260, had hair, and thought beer was *food*. Then, finally, I grew up.
> . . .
>
> Don't ever use the present condition of things as an excuse to "cop out." There are always those who say, "Oh, woe is me, life is a bummer, this is terrible." They are the critics of our time. They are persons who usually go on to emphasize proudly how actively "anti-establishment"' they are, and that nothing is right for them. Some of those people are already among the "dead unkilled."
> Let's deal with the real truths of life, truths that have never changed in all the years of human habitation on this old apple. Some are these: be kind to yourself—accept yourself—learn self-esteem—be who you are—and always be open to change and growth. If I had never been able to change, I would have graduated from a place down the road [the state reformatory for boys in Worland] instead of a high school.
> I was a mess, a big fat pimply-faced kid who weighed 185 pounds in the seventh grade. I was on two years of federal probation for shooting mailboxes. I even had a probation officer. I always seemed to be in trouble. It was a painful time, but a very important time in my life.

His consistent cornerstone, he told the graduates, was the concept of forgiveness, since at critical junctures of his own life someone had

always forgiven him. That was why he developed a deep and endur-
ing instinct to forgive others as well as himself.

> The real reason I made it in life is because there were other
> people who believed in me, even when I didn't believe in
> myself. They were people willing to give me a second chance.
> Those are the people I never forgot in life: parents, teachers,
> many people who took time with me, and for me. . . .
>
> I pulled off some great capers in high school and college
> because I thought I was very clever. I always, *always* had an
> excuse. I could usually get somebody to say, "Al, I forgive
> you." But what good did that do when I couldn't forgive
> myself? Not much.

On accuracy and perfection, Simpson spoke of not becoming
obsessed in the quest for perfection.

> Striving for perfection is a noble, slow effort—but don't get
> all tangled up in it. The real living of life is simply in being
> human. Some of the most driven and stressed people I have
> come to know are those who seem obsessed with the seeking
> of perfection. I know very little about my perfections, but I
> sure do know an awful lot about my imperfections. I do best
> with myself when I treat those imperfections without harsh-
> ness and with a spirit of good humor toward myself. That is
> very helpful.
>
> Here is an important thing to remember: For those who
> have integrity, nothing else matters. For those who don't have
> integrity, nothing else matters.

He had reached the crux of his message, but he circled back and
came at it again from a different angle. Of boredom, he said:

> If you are bored in life and you think there is "nothing to
> do," or you are thinking, "Boy, this place is absolutely dulls-
> ville," you might remember this: boredom is a strong signal
> coming from down inside of you to do something else.

So *do* something else. Read a book. Learn a new thing. Play a game. . . . Get off your fanny and do something. *Anything*. Boredom is the refuge of the cynical and dull-witted. Don't let it enter your life—but if it does, it is something you alone can control. For heaven's sake, be alive—*all* of your life.

About the importance of accepting difficult as well as pleasurable things in life, he said, "That is when boys become men and girls become women—and life fills up." Then he turned to the role of humor in his life.

[As I kid] I couldn't out-run anybody or out-think anybody, so I learned humor. That became my "sword and shield." . . . My dear mother had a phrase: "Humor is the universal solvent against the abrasive elements of life." And so it is—but not the humor of sarcasm, ridicule, or bringing another person down. Humor is an avenue toward self-esteem. The ultimate goal of humor, for me, is the rich ability to laugh at myself. When I think of myself as being overly wise, cleverly alert, the great intellectual and the great legislator, the all-seeing eye helps me to chuckle into the mirror and say, "Al, you are so full of it."

Yes, I take my work very seriously, even though I do best when I don't take myself too seriously. I try to work very hard, and not because I want to be a great statesman or a great legislator or president. No, I do that only because I don't want to make an ass of myself. I say again, it is nothing more profound than this. If you have integrity, nothing else matters. If you don't have integrity, nothing else matters.

ATTENTION WASHINGTON

Senate Republicans had twice as many incumbents running for reelection as did the Democrats in 1986, and thus twice the exposure to loss. At a meeting of his GOP colleagues, Al suggested they protect themselves by getting on with business. "Nobody wants to do anything that might risk the reelection chances of our twenty-two campaigning incumbents, but only sixty-three legislative days remain in the session. We'd better get off our asses and get moving, or we'll leave a lot of stuff on the table."

Dole took it further, aiming a verbal spear at Ted Stevens, who had been holding up Senate action because of a matter involving financial depreciation of fishing boats in Alaska. Now Stevens was threatening to filibuster. Al recalled Dole saying, "Well, if you are going to protect fishing boats in Alaska, or Eskimo Pies, or whatever else you're doing, we'll never get *anything* done around here."

"Stevens was *pissed!*" Simpson said later.

Intra-party tension continued to mount, as did the federal deficit. The Office of Management and Budget was now describing defense outlays as "uncontrolled," and yet most legislators were still unwilling to pull the reins on increases in defense and other popular big-ticket items such as Social Security. At a White House meeting, President Reagan demanded a "clean" debt limit ceiling, meaning there were to be no spending exceptions.

During the discussion, Al found himself focusing not on the numbers but on the president's style: "When you tell him those tough, hard things, he listens. He likes to confront. He likes to argue his position. The worst thing you can do is just nod your head and try to avoid controversy with him. He likes to mix it up a little, and does it in his own unique way, with great zeal and good humor." Afterward, Reagan took Simpson by the arm and held him back to tell a story. Departing senators saw the two doubling over in laughter.

What Other People Do

That weekend, Al and Ann finally had a chance "to do what other people do on weekends." He must have assumed they buy shoes, a process he found neither simple nor inexpensive.

> I went down to Chevy Chase and bought myself a pair of
> custom-made shoes to fit around these grotesque tootsies of
> mine. They cost a hell of a lot of money, but it is better than

buying golf clubs and sticking them in the closet and never
using them. I find that I use my feet every day. Had a mold
made of my beaten up and battered old size fifteen feet. Laid
out a chunk of money to get a set of black wingtips. Then I
did a little shopping, like the rest of the folks do on a Saturday.

His reference to what other people do reveals a long-held frustration. Whenever someone complained that he must live a life of
luxury, he was quick to say that while being a senator carried many
privileges, he had the same obligations in his personal life as everyone else. Although his time was often at a premium, he and Ann
did their own shopping, prepared most of their own meals at home,
and puttered around their house fixing things.

For most of their nearly two decades in Washington, they maintained the old Plymouth Horizon brought from Wyoming in late
1978. One morning Al peered at it through his kitchen window
and then phoned me with a question: "Don, did I ask you to have
my Plymouth serviced?"

"No, sir."

"Well, it is parked in front of the house, where I left it. I'm looking right at it. It appears to be on blocks. In fact, it looks like the
wheels are missing. What do you make of that?"

"Al, this is just a wild guess, but I think someone put your car
on blocks because that made it easier to steal the wheels. Nothing
else is worth taking." Indeed, all four wheels had been stolen in
the night. Simpson was comparatively lucky. Soon after Wyoming's
Craig Thomas was elected to the House of Representatives, both of
his cars were stolen—on the same day.

Al continued to be aggravated by assertions that he did not pay
for his own gasoline, food, and utilities, or that he didn't answer his
home telephone, the number of which had always been listed. Of
course, there were times when a Sunday caller heard someone who
sounded very much like the senator say, "You want Al Simpson?
Oh, he stepped away, but I'll sure give him your message."

Heading for the Bushes

Al and Ann flew to Kennebunkport, Maine to spend the weekend with their friends, Vice President and Mrs. Bush. That Sunday, services at the little town's First Congregational Church were impressive.

> A little old-time clock was on the wall, clicking audibly.
> There was a man playing a trombone in accompaniment to a
> woman playing the organ. A four-member choir of adults was
> sometimes "on stream" and sometimes not. The minister was
> a woman who was disarmingly candid, delightful, and very
> special.
>
> George spoke for about ten minutes about faith, and then
> [Secretary of Commerce] Mac Baldrige talked about war and
> his involvement in it, and some of his deep feelings. It was
> a very moving and beautiful talk about responsibility and
> God's will, and about violence and the need to control that in
> society.

The rest of their weekend involved competition, since the vice president was perhaps the most competitive person they knew. After playing golf in the rain, the four launched into an "adjective game," which Al prepared. Ann's role in the evening's entertainment had her standing on her head while reciting poetry. "George and Barbara still marvel at that," Al said in 2009.

Driving the Spike

Back in his office, Simpson met with Drew Lewis, the former U.S. secretary of transportation and current chair of Union Pacific Corporation. During their session he urged Al to be more supportive of the railroad. Lewis might as well have challenged him to a duel.

> Drew was surprised by the intensity of my remarks about
> Union Pacific. I described how they had undercut us on the
> two-year demonstration highway project. I talked about what

they had done to the Wyoming Legislature years ago. I filled
them in on House Bill 208 and all the dazzling array of intrigue
that went on behind that. I mentioned how they poured it
to the Wyoming coal industry, and how I was tired of that. I
talked about freight rates for trona. I was tired of that too.

They were not quite as hard-nosed when they left as they
were when they came in. I laid it on a bit heavy, but Drew
was very able to receive it that way. He is probably one of the
sharpest political people in the United States, a total realist.

The next order of business was at the Judiciary Committee,
which was still considering confirmation of Supreme Court Justice
William Rehnquist to succeed retiring Warren Burger as chief justice. Burger's impending departure resulted in President Reagan's
nomination of Rehnquist to be elevated and of Antonin Scalia to
become an associate justice. "Good choices all around," Simpson
felt, although he knew Democrats on the Judiciary Committee
were scheming to derail both nominations.

SEQUOIA AND THE LADY IN THE HARBOR

Some official duties were altogether less fraught. In an austerity
measure, President Jimmy Carter had disposed of the presidential
yacht *Sequoia*. Over the years the vessel passed through three private
owners before being acquired by the Presidential Yacht Trust, which
extensively renovated the historic craft. As an original sponsor of the
Senate resolution endorsing the trust's maintenance and operation of
Sequoia, Simpson was asked to preside over craft's rechristening in
Norfolk, Virginia. With Ann at his side he spoke for seven minutes,
explaining *Sequoia*'s service during eight United States presidencies.

President Roosevelt planned foreign and domestic strategy
here. President Truman held the first conference on nuclear
controls. President Eisenhower made the *Sequoia* available to
public groups. President Kennedy hosted gala social functions,
including the celebration of his forty-sixth birthday. President

Nixon negotiated with foreign leaders, including Soviet president Brezhnev. President Ford conducted ceremonial functions and hosted family gatherings—all aboard *Sequoia*.

The Presidential Yacht Trust was created in 1981 and the *Sequoia* was returned to Washington as an Historical Landmark at no cost to the taxpayer.

Ann went to the bow, where a large red ribbon was strung. As she ceremoniously cut it, three hundred balloons lifted from *Sequoia*'s top deck.

The vessel soon departed for New York City, where it was due to participate in the upcoming Statue of Liberty centennial celebration and to serve as an anchor location for ABC's Independence Day broadcast of the International Naval Review and Parade of Tall Ships. Simpson had one other use in mind. With the Senate in recess, Al, Ann, all three of their children, and a few friends prepared for a memorable Independence Day event in New York City centering on the one-hundredth birthday of the Statue of Liberty.

Joined by Senator Bill Bradley and his wife Ernestine, the group enjoyed a July 3 powerboat tour of New York Harbor before anchoring near Governor's Island. They were peering toward a nearby U.S. Navy vessel when President Reagan aimed a laser—a high-tech device at the time—and pushed a button. Suddenly the Statue of Liberty, which had been standing in darkness, was ablaze in light. A brief fireworks display exploded over the harbor. They found it spectacular, although it was but a preview of the monster array scheduled for the following evening.

Friday, July 4, 1986, was a day of unforgettable images. "We slept until 10:00 in the morning and had a big breakfast with the family. The *Sequoia* people sent a limousine and eight of us got aboard and headed over to 73rd Street, where we watched the tall ships coming up the Hudson. . . . At five-thirty, we all gathered in the lobby of the Mayflower Hotel and boarded a bus to Brooklyn and then the *Sequoia*." That evening, Senators Simpson and Bradley co-hosted an elegant event aboard the yacht for Senators John Chafee, Carl

Levin, Sam Nunn, author David McCullough, and their families and some two dozen other guests, including my wife and me. The *Sequoia* never looked better. With the finest food and drink eloquently presented by the elegantly appointed staff, the floating stage was set for a grand experience.

> [Don] said that nobody could board until I went first. When I did, they ran up a brand new Wyoming flag. It was a great thrill. Everyone had their picture taken with the flag. It truly was the "night of nights."

A harpist played in the main salon as champagne flowed freely. The *Sequoia* slipped its dock lines and the historic vessel eased gracefully into a beautiful dusk on New York Harbor.

> What a magnificent evening—beautiful temperature, pinkish orange sky, not a cloud. We went out into the East River and past the Manhattan Bridge and then under the Brooklyn Bridge, and you can imagine the thrill of hearing David McCullough relate the history of the Brooklyn Bridge. He wrote the definitive history of the structure, called *The Great Bridge*. It was thrilling. People were transfixed, as only David can transfix them.

Before the fireworks display, *Sequoia* was anchored, briefly. "We found ourselves anchored near the MTV ship, and the rock band ZZ Top was playing. It didn't take long for every boat anchored nearby to move on down the harbor. I never heard such a damn racket in my life. The MTV boat was sitting in solitary splendor when I last saw it, blaring away out in the harbor."

Once re-anchored, *Sequoia*'s passengers climbed to the top deck. A moment later President Reagan, still aboard his military vessel, ordered the lighting of the Statue of Liberty's torch. To Al, it appeared as "a beautiful gold leaf object filling the sky." As fireworks thundered deafeningly, Al's mind reverted to the excitement of his childhood. He dearly loved explosions, and this was the largest fireworks display in U.S. history. More than forty thousand fireworks effects from nine countries were being launched from forty barges around Manhattan, all in coordination.

> In all my life as a fire maniac and lover of pyrotechnics, I have never seen such a sight. It was thirty solid minutes of an absolute bombardment of beauty. Some of the mortar shells were being lobbed higher than the World Trade Center, over 1,500 feet.
>
> We watched the Statue of Liberty, where many of the shells detonated right behind the torch. It was as if the torch itself were lighted. It was dazzling. It was thrilling and I was goose-pimply. . . .
>
> A great silence came over us as we watched this array of splendor and patriotism for the birth of our country, and for a magnificent statue. We looked at it, and then at the skyline of New York and back at the fireworks. It was one of those days I shall never forget.

The ship's radio was describing the contribution of immigrants to the United States. Symphonic music wafted through *Sequoia* and through the minds and hearts of her passengers, each of whom was transfixed. Afterward *Sequoia* weighed anchor and slipped gently back to its dock and discharged its passengers. Everyone agreed that the event—not funded at government expense—had been memorable.

ATTENTION WYOMING

Two weeks before the celebration in New York, Al learned that his eighty-five-year-old mother had fallen in her home. She had not felt anything "snap" but was in pain. Al asked that, to avoid triggering the local rumor mill and upsetting his mother, the ambulance come to her house without lights or siren. He departed Washington on the next westbound flight and while en route learned that his mother had suffered a fractured femur. She was highly concerned—not about herself but about Milward, for whom she had been providing primary care.

That afternoon and evening, Al comforted his mother. The next morning, he addressed a gathering of independent insurance agents and quickly returned to the hospital to reassure her that all would be well after surgery. During the operation he chartered a plane to Riverton and spoke at a Veterans of Foreign Wars convention. Back in Cody, he was told that his mother's operation had been a success.

He lingered with her as long as possible before slipping away to address a convention of the Wyoming chapter of the Fraternal Order of Eagles, then returned to help arrange personal assistants for both parents. He missed his first Senate vote of the year but later told his diary, "I really didn't give a damn." Al flew to Washington and caught up on appointments but was soon back in Cody assuring his mother that she would be okay, even though still hospitalized. That evening he sat with his father. "He talks a lot, although some of it is not always quite topical. He always returns to the 'here and now' when we talk directly to him."

Al was thinking of his parents in particular when, during another June trip to Wyoming, he visited a tiny church at the base of the spectacular Teton Mountains: "I stopped by the Church of Transfiguration and saw that amazing little log church where so much of our family history has taken place. Many Simpsons have been married and buried there." He sat by himself, thinking about his involvement in a number of churches over the years. He and Ann, lifelong Episcopalians, had helped with every possible church social event and project back in Cody, although in Washington their hectic schedules often prevented attendance.

When they did go, they were relieved not to have extra responsibilities. "Ann and I [sometimes go] to Saint John's, a magnificent church, a good church for those who have been through 'Episcopal burnout' like Ann and I have. We both have been on the building committee, members of the vestry, ushers, on special committees, stewardship drives, etc. It is nice just to go to church."

"Head" Aches

August brought a happier reason to be in Wyoming. On August 2, 1986, the Simpsons joined friends and relatives from the far reaches of the country in Cody to attend the wedding of their eldest son Bill to Debra Ann Persin. Everything went well until Ann discovered that the portable toilets rented for the occasion were lacking chemical deodorant. Al laughed while telling the story. "Ann, in a magnificent pink silk dress, was galloping around the outdoor toilets in her *slippers* with this rich, blue deodorant elixir, which, if you spilled it, would probably eat through your epidermis. Quite a sight it was." Bill's sister Sue laughed: "That's the thing about my mother. *Nothing* could embarrass her."

Bill and Debbie also recall the unusual wedding music that rang out later. Bill explained.

> Our wedding was once again kind of an indication of Al and Ann Simpson's flexibility, because they had hired, with us, a traditional wedding band. The band never came. We were forced at the last minute to hire a good rock band that was free that very day. We didn't know what kind of "condition" they were in, but they were available, and we hired them. Mom and Dad gave us a little extra money to get that done, so the band came.
>
> The opening song was not the traditional wedding march. It was something like an Eric Clapton rock ballad. And from there on, let me tell you, the fuse was lit. I don't recommend it for everybody, but sometimes a rock and roll band at a relatively staid wedding can really liven things up—and it certainly did. They played until four in the morning and it was a *great* time.

Bill's brother Colin recalls that on June 20, 1998, thirteen years after Bill's wedding, their mother again encountered problems with portable toilets. Colin and Debbie Oakley were about to tie the knot when Ann noticed that someone had painted the name of the family law firm on the sides of the outhouses rented for the outdoor reception. "Mom was extremely upset. They had new port-a-pot-ties set up and a friend had written 'Simpson, Kepler & Edwards' on them. She did *not* like that," said Colin.

Ancestry

Traveling in Wyoming always made Al think about his ancestry. One day he made plans to join his son Colin in the tiny northern Wyoming town of Ranchester for a father-son visit to Kooi, the town founded by his grandfather, Peter Kooi. When the day came, Al jumped into his car and headed east across the Big Horn Basin and up the narrow road that crests the soaring Big Horn Moun-tains.

> I was driving up the mountain when the damned brown Ford got vapor locked. It choked out near a turnoff. I backed down in a big arc and let it cool a minute. When it wouldn't start, I just coasted down the mountain in neutral. I had brakes but no power, so I coasted all the way into the Wagon Wheel Lodge.
>
> The owner, Frank Murray, came out and said, "Hi, Al." [He] was the father of one of the kids I gave the Congressio-nal Award to in Cheyenne last spring. I called my Cody office to say that I sure needed transportation. Hearing that, Frank said, "Hell, take my van."

In March 2009, almost twenty-three years later, Murray laughed when asked about that day. "Sure, I let him use my van. He is a great guy, gave my son that award. I'm a Democrat, and Al is about the only Republican I've voted for."

After cresting the mountain range in the borrowed vehicle, Al found Colin and the two drove together to Kooi, now a ghost town. "We found the flagpole that was put in by my grandfather. His fin-gerprint was set in the concrete. He had written 7-2-1910. It was just two days before July 4, a day he loved and celebrated with gusto.

Colin and I went through the old site and looked at the foundations and bricks, finding walls still standing. We picked up some old barrel parts and some bricks to take home with us."

Years later, Colin spoke of that day: "It's an odd experience to be in a place where there was once a town that your great-grandfather started, and yet there is nothing left but a few foundations and an old rotten flagpole—and memories." After examining the remnants of Kooi, the two dined in Sheridan with Pete, who was now in the heart of his campaign for the governorship. Al asked Pete about his prospects. "I read his eyeballs to see that he is doing well and is enthused. He is going to do a magnificent job on August 19, in the primary election." Al drove himself back over the mountains to share the experience with his parents.

> We had candles and the works. It is tough for Mom, because she does not have her fifty-seven-year companion there at her side to talk things over. Pop is still troubling along and seems very concerned about things. He is articulate, but not on base. Mom is concerned about that. I had a lovely visit with her after Pop went to bed. What extraordinary grace and courage. What a lucky guy I am. I kissed them goodnight. It gave me a lump in my throat."

The next morning, Al drove to the Bobcat Ranch. Echoes of days long ago filled his mind as he filled the air with bullets.

> It was beautiful and clear, a crystal blue sky and cool wind. The mountains looked like they were right in the front yard. On some nearby trees sat about seven magpies. I went back to the shed, got my trusty rifle, came back, and drilled three of them. I have not done that since I was twenty-two years old. That will save a couple of pheasants come the fall. [Magpies eat the eggs and chicks of other birds.]
>
> I even threw a bottle into the sky and shot it out of the air, just like I did when I was a kid. I did some target practice, just "plinking" from the porch for a while. I didn't get to hike

Bobcat Creek like I had planned, but what the hell? It was an absolutely marvelous few hours.

It had been a meaningful weekend. Al had spent quality time with his parents and reveled in a few rare hours of reflection at his precious Bobcat Ranch. With his son at his side, he had investigated the remnants of his grandparents' home. Someone had loaned a vehicle when his broke down. Once again, the man under enormous pressures in the glare of Washington found himself emotionally restored in his Wyoming sanctuary.

Wyoming Primary

Al felt a similar sense of renewal when he chartered a plane and departed for Jackson. It was one of the most magnificent days he'd ever seen: "There was not a cloud, but there was snow on the high mountains. Ann and I flew right over Gannett Peak [13,804 feet], about a thousand feet over the summit. It was an absolutely still and magnificent day. Ahead, the Tetons loomed up sharply against the blue sky. It was superb."

After the function Al and Ann flew north-northeast toward Cody, over the remote southeast corner of Yellowstone National Park. This provided another opportunity for emotional renewal. "I saw an absolutely brilliant orange and red sun go down right behind the Teton Mountains as we hit an altitude of 13,000 feet. It was a dazzling, smooth and beautiful flight. We went right over the Bobcat Ranch and on into Cody. I got a car and went right over to see the folks. Mom was watching Pete's campaign like a hawk."

Late in the evening on August 19, 1986, Pete Simpson finally took his first deep breath in months. He had won the Wyoming Republican primary for governor on a 453-vote margin nail-biter. Pete was thrilled. So was Al. "I went out on the lawn and did my sage chicken dance in front of the full moon. Then I said to everyone, 'Pete has worked so hard. He is a marvelous brother and he deserves a boost.' He got one."

The next day Al joined his Wyoming staff and two employees from his Washington office at a ranch near Jackson. After their day-long annual meeting, the group mounted horses and set off on a nighttime horseback ride through the hills. Moonlight guided them between the trees as they sang, told ghost stories, and laughed. It was a revitalizing break for staff and emotional catharsis for their boss. Years later, Sue talked about her father's lifelong fascination with the night.

> I really believe that's where he finds peace, in the nighttime. He is a night owl. Look at how productive he is in the middle of the night. Other people find mornings great, but Dad was never a morning guy. The quiet of night is right for him. I think that he has a hard time shutting off the world—because he is so *of* the world. In the morning, the world would come awake and alive, too alive. In the nighttime, there is a peace and a solace that gives him strength. It always has.

Because Pete had won the Republican primary, Al was finally able to assist him. He flew back to Washington and phoned the president's chief of staff to request that President Reagan meet with Pete.

A few days later Pete had lunch with Al and Ann and Vice President George Bush. Afterward, he was driven to the White House to meet President Reagan.

> Reagan worked this in on a three-day notice. It was really quite extraordinary for him to do that. Pete and I went out onto the south White House lawn while the helicopter flew in with the president, who was just returning from his speech at the United Nations.
>
> That helicopter with the white roof came down and landed right on the spot. The old president bounded out of there amid the wind and the blowing of the first leaves of fall.
>
> I remember watching the presidential helicopter before, always with the same tingle as when you look down the south

White House lawn and across the Ellipse at the Washington Monument and the Jefferson Memorial. It still gives me goose pimples. Guess that is a good reason to stay on the job.

The Simpson brothers were escorted into the Diplomatic Room, where Al made the introduction. "This is my only brother, the guy running for the governorship of Wyoming," he proudly told the president. After handshakes, Al told a joke and a photographer came into the room to snap shots while Pete chatted with Reagan.

TAKE A DEEP BREATH

Several times over several months during 1986, Simpson needed to set aside his well-founded concerns about the Senate's funding activities and the balance of political power to focus briefly on the mysterious imbalance in his lungs. He met with Dr. Tom Walsh in the Capitol to talk about his most recent X-ray. "He said that little baby is still there in the lung. It has not grown, and there is no tuberculosis, no infection, no malignancy, no nothing—but it is still there. We'll just keep watching it, although there is no apparent cause for any alarm."

A later diary entry suggests he was growing weary of being probed. "I cancelled my meeting with Dr. Walsh—didn't want that bronchoscope rammed down my windpipe again. I will have to do it again anyway, after I finish my regimen of penicillin. I'm on a double dose for an unknown number of days to see if we can knock out our friend lurking down there in the fifth lower sac of the left lung." Other than Ann, nobody knew of his medical situation—nor would they, unless it came to surgery. Doctors again suggested that he get more rest. They may as well have saved their own breath.

Then a new health problem rudely presented itself. "I was exercising to beat hell in the house this morning and I worked up a lather before sitting too close to the air conditioning duct, which was blowing cold air. I got up, and whamo! The stab was like an ice pick in the kidney. It's a terrible muscle spasm and it hurts like hell." At the Senate he slipped into the physician's office to request something to relieve pain; "something light," he emphasized. "I told the doctor I'd be damned if I'd be taking anything like Valium. He did give me something light, but I am still in a lot of pain."

Cannons were shooting through his back the next evening while actual cannons were being fired at Wolf Trap, the outdoor center for the performing arts west of Washington. The National Symphony Orchestra performance the night of July 25, 1986, was an all-Tchaikovsky program that included the overture from the *Festival of 1812*. Simpson loved the piece, and since it included explosions, he dearly loved it. "Powerful? You bet. They had real cannons that were fired about ten feet from where I was sitting. I could actually feel the concussion in my head and body. It added a great touch to the music and made me tingle with excitement. It was the damnedest performance of the 1812 that I have ever witnessed. I had goose pimples big as hailstones."

The next day, a Saturday, Ann was out of town. This allowed Al a "monkish experience," in which he enjoyed performing the kinds of personal chores for which he seldom found time. "I went over to a store and picked up some pants. I came back home, cleaned up my den, did my laundry—socks and shirt—cleaned up some drawers, and then hit the books. I cleaned up old letters that had been here about three months, and worked until about two thirty in the morning before hitting the sack."

He worked on Sunday too, again well past midnight. "I got more damn stuff done this weekend than I have in three years. Ten belts [hours] of taped dictation. I will hide some of it from the staff." He was always concerned that if he showed up at the office with ten hours of dictation for transcription, recipients of the workload would feel overwhelmed and become discouraged. He always told me to "feed it to them gradually—don't dump it on them all at once." We went through this routine for eighteen years, proving again that he was a better legislator than administrator. The staff was on to him the entire time.

As summer advanced, doctors tried to decide whether to remove the mysterious dark spot from Simpson's left lung. He was not fond of the idea, especially after receiving conflicting medical counsel at Mount Sinai Hospital in New York. "They called it the 'Midas Syndrome.' If you go into a Midas Muffler shop, it is likely they will want to sell you a muffler, no matter the problem. Likewise, if you go to see the chief of surgery at a hospital, it is very likely that surgery will be recommended."

This time, it was not. Pulmonary specialists drew Simpson's blood for testing and conducted lung examinations not performed at Bethesda Naval Hospital. Afterward, the head of pulmonary medicine looked over his new X-rays, saw that the spot on Simpson's lung seemed reduced, and said, "I see no present need for surgery."

"Ann and I did a little jig in the presence of those august physicians," Al cheered later. Still, the persistent black hole was not gone. Doctors ran more tests, and a team of surgeons and specialists again attempted, unsuccessfully, to identify it definitively. Back in Washington, Al finally explained the situation to senior staff.

Later that summer, he visited a different doctor for a different problem. A small lump that had been on his chin for twenty-five years was suddenly changing and "getting glossy." It was also painful, since he had inadvertently sliced it several times while shaving. Within minutes, the lump was gone and in its place were eight stitches. His bout of health concerns in 1986 would make it seem that he was prone to physical ailments. From a broader perspective, that was not the case. Seldom truly ill during his eighteen years in the Senate, he worked through minor problems and avoided medications whenever possible. On one occasion, I entered his office as he was considering whether to take a baby aspirin for a headache. He finally decided to cut it in half. "I don't want to take too much of this stuff," the 195-pound, six-foot seven-inch man warned himself.

MISCELLANEOUS BUSINESS

The July 4 celebrations in New York had left many in Washington feeling a warm glow, President Reagan among them. "Ron Reagan was in top shape," Simpson noted. "He talked about the great

thrill he had in New York during 'liberty weekend.' When he finished relating it, he said, 'It gave me some great ideas for my *own*
one hundredth.' "

Congressman Silvio Conte of Massachusetts told the president
that he had attended the same event but from a distant vantage
point. "I ended up a long way back in the crowd," Conte lamented,
evoking his family's arrival in America: "It reminded me of how
my parents must have felt at Ellis Island." The president joked,
"They must have gotten further than *you* did."

Slugfest

There was no such humor in the Senate Veterans' Committee,
however. In early July 1986 the committee heard from a witness
who thought it might be good to punch Al in the face: "I tell you
something, Senator, I object to your statements, this personal attack.
. . . I'll tell you what, I would see anybody in the parking lot." That
was the final straw. Al was now more convinced than ever that the
two men sitting before him were "complete charlatans."

Mark Smith, a retired U.S. Army colonel, and Melvin McIntire,
a retired sergeant, had advised the committee months earlier that
a film made in Southeast Asia at Smith's request depicted the existence of American soldiers being held in Vietnam against their will
more than a decade after the war's end. Smith and McIntire had
promised to present video proof at a committee hearing, but they
failed to appear. Now before the committee under subpoena, they
still lacked the promised proof.

Smith did provide what he admitted was a fictitious name for
a person in Asia who, he claimed, was in possession of the filmed
"evidence." He also asserted that he and others had been working
with Vice President George Bush and other top federal officials to
obtain government money in exchange for the film.

The two told the committee they had arranged for Congressman
Bill Hendon of North Carolina, a POW/MIA activist, to deliver
a letter about the matter to President Reagan. That part was true.

Dated February 28, 1986, the letter said that Colonel Smith, Congressman Hendon, and Senator Dennis DeConcini of Arizona were prepared to fly to Asia in an airplane provided by the U.S. government, where they would view the mysterious video. The letter's key paragraph read: "After these three representatives have had the opportunity to view the film and are satisfied with the validity of the contents, they will be required to pay the sum of $4.2 million dollars in cash and take receipt of the original of the film and other evidence of live Americans and other allied POWs still being held in Southeast Asia."

Colonel Smith presented the committee with grainy copies of photographs purportedly of Americans in Asia, but he conceded that they were not necessarily being held against their will. They "might know something," he offered. The pictures were of such low quality that the individuals could not be identified, and not even Smith knew where they were taken or who these people were.

Simpson listened as Smith was questioned by other committee members, but finally could stand no more. The following is taken from the hearing record.

> I practiced law for 18 years, and I have never seen such lightweight stuff. So we have pictures. One of them looks like three guys, three GIs, where somebody took a picture of them on a lake. You don't know where it is. One in a stateroom, and a guy with a rifle, smiling yet. . . .
>
> The issue is, who is behind bars in Southeast Asia, and a prisoner of war or an MIA. The issue is, do you have tangible evidence of U.S. citizens who are incarcerated or held against their will in Southeast Asia? . . . I don't know what you are up to, but I can tell you, it is not savory. . . .
>
> I think there is a problem before the committee, and I think it is you. . . . How nuts. How stupid.

Simpson declined Smith's subsequent challenge to fight in a Senate parking lot, and that night mentioned the incident to his diary.

I am disgusted by the brazen and cynical phoniness of the pair. I never heard two dudes give less testimony after being sworn in than those two very reluctant witnesses. They didn't have a damn thing to share with us. They were just trying to revive the anguish and pain of those who think they have living relatives in Southeast Asia. It is a holdup in every way. They say they have a 234-minute video of actual "live sightings," but they want $4 million for it. These guys are a real pair of assholes.

Simpson eventually obtained the movie and had it carefully analyzed by professionals. "It was proven beyond any doubt whatsoever," he said afterward, "that those scenes were recorded in Hawaii."

In all, the Senate Veterans' Committee conducted seven hearings on the issue. No federal money was paid for video "evidence" of POWs, and no concrete proof of any kind was received by the committee. It was finally revealed that a mysterious individual allegedly in possession of "evidence" in Southeast Asia was not an American, and that he had served time in a Singapore jail for scamming tourists.

Drugs and Defense

President Reagan was becoming concerned about illegal drug trafficking into the United States. Predictably, Al approached the matter from an immigration perspective.

I told him that if they were going to talk about trying to cut off the flow of illegal drugs into the United States, it might be a good idea if we cut off the illegal flow of *people* into the United States. I said that [nearly two] million people cross into the United States *illegally* each year—and yet there are people in our country who are still goofy enough to talk about having an open border.

I said that when people who are poor are coming into the country illegally to seek work, and find they can make $20-30,000 carrying drugs on one entry, no *wonder* there is a problem.

The next morning, Simpson returned to the White House for another difficult session. Under discussion was the Strategic Defense Initiative (SDI), often mockingly referred to as "Star Wars," after the movie of that name. President Reagan was having more trouble with Republicans than Democrats, since conservatives did not want him working out compromises of *any* kind with communists.

The president complained that reporters were misrepresenting his efforts. He told the visiting senators, "That will drive you crazy—and damn I get tired of that! SDI *will* be deployed." Simpson decided it was time to calm the president: "Mr. President, you have heard some powerful things from some of your closest friends in Congress. They are on *your* side. These are *your* people, they are people who care about *you*."

When the meeting concluded, Reagan told a joke—his way of registering that he harbored no hard feelings over the blunt exchanges. However, for some participants, irritations of the day were too significant to be easily soothed. As the November elections loomed, internal discord among Republicans increased the likelihood of electoral disaster.

Guilty, Guilty, Guilty

While the Republican incumbents' reelection prospects were sliding into serious trouble, so was the career of federal judge Harry E. Claiborne, who became the object of an extraordinary Senate impeachment trial. It resulted from his court conviction for fraud and his failure to report $107,000 of income on his 1979 and 1980 tax returns. Simpson described the unusual scene in the Senate chamber: "In executive session, we did our deliberations. Then we 'switched on the lights' [resumed open session] and did the voting. It was really a remarkable thing to watch as the Senate worked its will in its truest form. I weighed in with about four minutes of debate."

The Senate found Claiborne guilty on three of four articles of impeachment, with only one needed to divest him of his job. Al found it a fascinating procedure, as Judge Claiborne sat in the Senate chamber with his lawyers.

> Each senator had to stand at his desk and announce his vote as guilty, not guilty, or present. It was rather dramatic. I wonder what Claiborne thought as we stood, one after another, looked at the clerk and said "guilty." It must have been like a surrealistic movie of people popping up by the gravestone, hooded figures with bony fingers, saying "guilty, guilty, and *guilty*!"
>
> When the order came down that he was to be removed from the federal bench, he handled it about as well as anybody could expect. The marshals took him from the Chamber and that was it. His salary stopped as of this day.

Simpson incorrectly predicted that the proceeding, which had not been used in the Senate in more than fifty years, would send a signal to others who might be inclined to misuse their federal powers. "I'll bet a buck that after the results of this one are known, there won't be another session like this for many more years. It really was quite an experience."

As we have seen, guilty also remained the watchword in Simpson's fuming perspective on Senator Metzenbaum's condemnation of recent Republican-appointed Supreme Court nominees: "Metz and I were going down the hall and had a few words. In fact, we had rich words. I dropped the whole load on that old cat, and he got his licks in too. I shall leave the actual words out of this missive, but I felt damn good about it." Simpson asked Metzenbaum how he could be quite so moral after the $250,000 finder's fee for the Hay Adams Hotel. Metzenbaum said he had given the money back after the *Cleveland Plain Dealer* published a front-page story about it, but Simpson considered this proof that he should not have accepted it in the first place.

"That doesn't have anything to do with *this* situation," Metzenbaum sputtered.

"The hell it doesn't," Simpson snapped back.

WINNING AND LOSING

Al Simpson's hard work paid off in key legislative victories during 1986: passage of his immigration bill, Superfund, and the Clean Water Act. While signing the Immigration Reform and Control Act, President Reagan praised the effort.

> The act I am signing today is the product of one of the longest and most difficult legislative undertakings of recent memory. It has truly been a bipartisan effort, with this administration and the allies of immigration reform in the Congress, of both parties, working together to accomplish these critically important reforms. Future generations of Americans will be thankful for our efforts to humanely regain control of our borders and thereby preserve the value of one of the most sacred possessions of our people: American citizenship.

As for Superfund, although senior staffers at the Environment and Public Works Committee had vexed Simpson continuously, he later identified that legislation as bringing him the most satisfaction, and the most concern about cost to taxpayers. "I ran into John Dingell, senior House Democrat and chair of the House conference. We practically squeezed each other's hands off, congratulating each other. Dingell is a hell of a guy to have on your side, and I think he feels that way about me. He is potent, powerful, opinionated and tough. When he knows you aren't trying to slip him a load, he is very fair."

Family Matters

Before Al set off to campaign on behalf of his brother against Mike Sullivan for Wyoming's governorship, he drove his parents to the Bobcat. "Pop was a bit out of touch, but I believe he loved it. I rolled him through the house in his wheelchair. As the sun was going down on the snowcapped mountains, I showed him the scene through the kitchen window. It was a place we used to stand while he did his pancakes and the artful cooking of hamburgers, potatoes, onions and stewed tomatoes. He said, 'Wow—fantastic.' Mom loved it, too."

The next day Al joined Pete, whose campaign schedule from then to the November election would be a blaze of travel, meetings, rallies, and interviews. Al spoke on his brother's behalf, offered political counsel, and crisscrossed the state repeatedly. The two had enthusiasm. They had name recognition. They had optimism. But they also had a problem.

On November 4, 1986, Mike Sullivan garnered 88,897 votes to Pete's 75,841. Bill Budd, whom Pete had defeated in the Republican primary, had not endorsed Pete against Sullivan in the general election. It was a key factor in Pete's loss to Sullivan. A week passed before Al committed his feelings to his diary.

> It was a sad day around the Simpson homestead. Brother Pete lost the race for governor by some 13,000 votes. It is tough to figure all the ramifications of that. There are many things that could have contributed to it, but one was that I was serving as a United States senator. People may have figured there was some kind of "dynasty" in the making—or a "power grab." I think those things were latent down there, even though people were not expressing them, because of their affection.

Pete, Lynne, Al, Ann, other family members, a paid campaign staff, and hundreds of volunteers had given it everything they had—for naught. "We were out there with them on the road, on the 'victory blitz' the last eight days of the campaign, working hard. It seemed like there was a good reception—but so it goes. Polls showed deterioration in normally Republican areas. Apparently, about twenty to twenty-five thousand Republicans just didn't vote." Pete had lost, but Al seemed to feel the blow as sharply. In 2007 Ann spoke of the days after the votes were counted. "It was very, very painful for Al. For about a year, we hashed that over— what could have been done differently, who did this and who did that? Finally, one day I said to him, 'Let's stop this. This is ridiculous. It is doing nothing but negative things to us, and there is no way to redo it.'"

Pete was not the only person suffering voter rejection. Several Republican U.S. senators had been swept out of office, transforming the GOP's 53–47 majority into a 55–45 minority. In the Capitol, Simpson met with Senator Dole to review the damage. "The two of us sat around for about forty-five minutes and discussed where we were going legislatively. We reviewed some of the new problems that would confront us as members of the minority—and, perhaps, some of the new opportunities. Dole was a bit discouraged, so I tried to buoy him up. I said, 'Bob, it's your optimism that makes you what you are. That is the very touchstone of your existence.'"

Al flew to Billings, where he joined Ann, Pete, and Lynne for dinner at the Northern Hotel. They reviewed Pete's loss and the challenges of politics, then faced the challenge of a major winter storm during their hundred-mile drive to Cody.

Hell Freezes Over

Whether it was emotional catharsis, temporary insanity, or a long overdue opportunity to spend time with his sons, Al decided to hunt elk with Colin, Bill, Pete's son Milward, and several other men in a remote area near the southeast corner of Yellowstone National Park. His Washington staff questioned his undertaking a strenuous high-mountain hunting trip in winterlike weather, after suffering weeks of debilitating fatigue. But he was determined. "I watched them pack the horses and finally slung my fanny onto my new saddle and headed up into the hills. The weather was blustery and cold. It had already begun to snow nearby."

The likelihood of dangerously severe weather was so obvious that Ann warned her husband not to go. Colin remembers how she felt: "Mom told him, 'Al, if you insist on going, if you are going to be stupid enough to do it, I want you to get more life insurance.'" Al shrugged her off, joined the group, and rode over the rims high above the deep valley southwest of Cody. That afternoon they descended into a hunting camp, where they enjoyed a hearty dinner accompanied by wine. The group played cards before retiring to their tents.

The temperature dropped through the night and warmed little the next day, as Colin recalls. "We were lucky if it ever got above zero. And the nights! It was so damn cold you had to stoke the fire all night long." The half-frozen group of intrepid hunters arose at 4:00 the next morning and saddled their horses. With dawn approaching, they rode off in search of the mighty wapiti. What they found as the stark sun crested the horizon was extraordinarily cold air—and that was before it started to move.

"The wind began to blow and it never quit for *two days*," Al later wrote. "I had a wool cap and it felt about as warm as a doily spread over my bald dome. I didn't really have proper boots, either. The boys had insulated boots—but not their old man." Colin remembers his father's discomfort. "Dad didn't bring much gear, and he wasn't a cold weather guy anyway. But he was a good sport. You couldn't have much skin showing. Whatever was showing was going to freeze." The party returned for breakfast at nine o'clock that morning. They departed again and remained out through the afternoon and past sunset. "We came back in the dark, along a trail about one foot wide and with a pretty good drop of about four hundred feet on one side. There was a half moon and the horses needed it to see. Whether or not they did, I sure as hell did."

That night, conditions turned truly bitter—"like the Yukon of Robert Service," chimed the freezing but still optimistic senator. The words of *The Cremation of Sam McGee* came to mind, and Al quoted them.

> The Northern Lights have seen queer sights,
> But the queerest they ever did see
> Was that night on the Marge of Lake Lebarge
> When I cremated Sam McGee.

He continued the famous poem while the temperature dropped further and the wind chill made it feel colder yet. Although it was now dangerously cold, the senior Simpson made the best of things. "I got up to take a leak about four on the morning of November 10. I thought the stars were sitting on the edge of the tent. I have never seen such a crisp, clear and absolutely extraordinary night. The morning was just as magnificent—a rich, pure, blue sky of great density, cold and crispness."

The temperature hovered at nearly thirty below zero. Nonetheless, Colin set off at five and returned at midmorning. "Got one!" he shouted. Encouraged, Al and the others headed out and hunted until midafternoon, when the wind, which had lessened during the morning, picked up again.

> It was a real howler. We were up on the rims, riding on either side, where the elk might be. It was cold as hell and the wind was really blowing. We couldn't see a damn thing. There were two guys with me and one of them began to get frostbite on his nose. I had a silk scarf over my face. My feet were cold as hell. The hat I borrowed from Colin may have saved me.

The wind was so strong that when one of the other hunters dropped his reins, the wind blew them straight out, parallel to the snow-drifted ground. At the storm's height, with the wind and snow howling violently, Al suddenly found that he and his horse were being blown toward a cliff. "I almost couldn't stop! When I started to swing off the horse, a gust of wind took me as I lifted my leg, throwing me into the rocks. I thought that if I had hit my head, I'd have been out of business."

The nearly frozen senator decided that was enough. "I turned to the guide and said, 'Look, pal, I'm not the great Olympic hunter. Let's get the hell out of here and back to camp.'" They spotted several elk but let the opportunity pass. "If you had shot them, you'd have had to take a knife and fork up there to eat them on the spot. You never would have been able to haul them out." In camp, instead of huddling over a dead elk with knives and forks, the hunters whipped up a meal that included blueberry pie and the sip of cabernet not frozen. Playing cards with his boys warmed and cheered the elder Simpson until they all fell asleep in their tents.

The next morning two hunters set off to retrieve Colin's elk. The rest headed toward civilization. Writing about the trip later, Al said, "The wind had blown drifts in the mountain pass. It was so deep that the packhorses bogged down and broke their ropes. It was quite exciting." Snowdrifts on portions of the trail were so high that the hunters walked alongside their horses rather than risking tumbling into a deep ravine. When they reached base camp at midday, Al said, "Next time, I'll get myself a hell of a good state-of-the-art hat or cap, and some state-of-the-art boots." More than twenty years later, Al's son Bill observed:

> Dad has never quite mastered the fine art of Patagonia clothing and lining, and down clothes. His idea is that if you put on five Pendleton shirts and a silk scarf, you can weather anything. It doesn't always work that way, and these were arctic conditions.
>
> If you're not a Christian before you get to the mountain in conditions like that, you will be when you get down off it, because you really don't know if you're going to make it. It was that cold and that brutal. If you didn't have shelter and you didn't have clothing, you would have died very quickly.

Looking back on the adventure, Al sat comfortably in his Cody home and called it a "great experience, one that we'll get a kick out of relating in years to come."

For Al, the year 1986 was a time of emotional and physical extremes. He relied on core qualities for survival. He reveled in legislative victories, agonized in his brother's electoral loss, prayed daily for the health of his parents, and was able to laugh about nearly freezing to death on a remote mountain. More extremes were just ahead.

Chapter Eight

MERCENARIES, EMISSARIES, AND EMINENT DEMEAN

LATE IN 1986 President Reagan held a news conference. It did not go well. "He was halting and ill at ease. There is much repair work to be done," Al told his diary. The situation was poised to worsen. Within a few days the sale of arms to Iran was revealed. Newspapers splashed the news, since it appeared to be an attempt to pay hostage demands for the release of Americans held in Iran. Worse, it seemed that someone had inflated the price of the arms sold, depositing the extra money into a Swiss bank account for use in funding the Contras' totally unrelated fight against the Sandinistas in Nicaragua. The Contras were armed opponents of the Sandinista government, which itself, in 1979, had overthrown the Somoza family's forty-three-year rule of the country. It was the leading edge of great consternation for America's president.

The following weekend Al received a telephone call from White House Chief of Staff Don Regan, who was aboard *Air Force One*. It was about Iran-Contra. "Regan told me to gather the top Republican leadership to discuss the matter. On Tuesday, December 2, 1986, the meeting occurred. It was a very small group, involving Bob Dole, myself, Trent Lott, Bob Michel, Dick Cheney, George Bush, and Don Regan. Once they were in the Cabinet Room with the president, we ran off the staff."

Simpson recorded that Senator Dole was circumspect during the session. Acknowledging that Americans were becoming concerned, he recommended a special legislative overview of the situation in both the House and Senate. During Dole's recent appearance on CNN's *Larry King Show,* hundreds of people had phoned in. Not one was supportive of the president on the Iran arms sales situation. It had every appearance of being an arms-for-hostages deal. Simpson's diary reads: "I told the president that I thought it a very grave mistake to continue blaming the press in this situation. I said the people of America were looking at him and wondering how that sale could have taken place without his knowledge. I reminded him that people think a president has to know everything going on."

WHAT DID HAPPEN?

Even the president's strongest supporters were turning down opportunities to speak publicly on the matter, since they simply did not know the truth—even after speaking with their president. "Reagan went through the chronology of it quite capably, and with some irritation. Time was an issue because he had to go on national television at noon and say that he was appointing Frank Carlucci as national security adviser—and that the attorney general was putting the machinery in place to appoint an independent counsel, both very important steps toward getting answers on Iran-Contra."

Dick Cheney said he knew the president would not like the suggestion, but he should simply tell the American people he had made a mistake. The group was ushered out of the Cabinet Room and into Don Regan's office. Two minutes later the president was on national television, showing no sign of the irritation he had exhibited moments before. Simpson was impressed: "I don't think I could have done that. I would have stepped up to the tube and said, 'I've just been in the Cabinet Room with some of these ornery bastards, and they have been less than supportive.' He handled it well and with great class."

After the televised statement, Don Regan told the senators his side of the story, describing his role and how little he knew about the arms sale. He said he thought it would be important that the president retain his services as chief of staff in order to get through preparation of the State of Union message. He acknowledged that he should keep a lower profile. Simpson later recorded what he said to Regan.

I told Regan that enough damage had been done. The president should just gather the American people around him and say, "Look, I'm a man of compassion and care and love. I read all the stories about the hostages and I have even had their families in the Oval Office. I finally determined that the way to handle this was to deal with Iran. It was a mistake. I should not have sold them a single fifty-caliber bullet. I thought it would work out, but it was something I did out of my own compassion and my longing for the return of those people. It was a mistake.

Back in Al's office the phone was ringing off the hook with reporters clamoring and pleading for information. He let the requests stack up, but for one. Ted Koppel of ABC's *Nightline* spent fifteen minutes trying to persuade him to appear that night. Simpson finally said, "Look, Ted, the reason I'm dabbling with you here on the phone is because I don't want to come in and dabble with you on your program tonight."

He instructed his press secretary to turn down other requests as well. Until he had all the facts, he was not going to wade in. When he finally did meet with some of the nation's top journalists, he expressed frustration. "It is tough to really come out with everything on this Iran-Contra National Security Council–CIA caper. I am a person who loves and lives on facts, but there still aren't enough facts to really decide what the hell *did* happen."

That afternoon he spent time on the phone with Regan, Bush, and Reagan. At day's end he dictated his thoughts—not about Iran-Contra but about the differences between Reagan and his predecessor, Jimmy Carter. "Reagan mixes it up with us, but does that with good temper and a hell of a lot of good spirit. I like that. Carter used to just sit and watch and smile, and then plead. Reagan sits, watches, smiles, and then argues. He does it with gusto and lots of action. He is a most competent president."

A later meeting between the president and top congressional leaders occurred in the Oval Office, again without staff. "We get a hell of a lot more done without staff," Simpson emphasized. Although the stated purpose of the session, Iran-Contra, was serious business, the meeting began with a joke. Simpson told Reagan about a man who went to the doctor: "The doctor said, 'You are going to have to cut out quite a lot of things,' and gave the guy a list. He said, 'And you are going to have to cut your sex life in half.' The guy looked at the doctor and asked, 'Which half—thinking about it, or talking about it?'"

When the session turned serious, Senator Dole summarized what Congress would be doing in coming days. He applauded the appointment of a special counsel to review the Iran-Contra matter. Congressman Cheney told Reagan that he could expect "a disclosure a day" on the Contra situation until he got it out of the way. He advised the president to "put it all out there, give some kind of indication that a mistake was made." This did not have to include the decision to sell arms to Iran, but the president could certainly admit to having erred in not overseeing more closely the activities of Colonel Oliver North and John Poindexter.

Marine Corps Lieutenant Colonel North was a member of the National Security Council, and naval officer John Poindexter was the council's deputy advisor. Both were central players in the growing controversy. Simpson said he believed that if North and Poindexter continued to take the Fifth Amendment—which he described as their right and even something he would advise, were he their lawyer—scrutiny of the matter would finally come up the line to CIA Director Bill Casey, and then to President Reagan.

> I told the president I thought the people of America really didn't care how many divisions were perched on the northern border of Iran, or how many arms Iran got versus what Iraq got. I said the only thing they really want to know was how we could have sold a single fifty-caliber round of ammunition to those bastards that took fifty-three of our American citizens hostage and held them for 444 days.

He later logged these additional notes:

> I suggested to the president that he say [our government's]
> contact with Iran was an "approach" to them, but not a
> "trade." I also said that although this was done with the best
> of motives and for the most compassionate of reasons, it might
> not have been the most appropriate thing to do. I told him
> that obviously things went awry with regard to North and
> Poindexter, and he should make it clear that he found this his
> responsibility, and that he turned the matter over to the inves-
> tigating arms of the executive and legislative bodies. I said
> that if it were found that people had violated the law, "their
> heads should be lopped off."

Simpson suggested that Reagan have "a little photocopied stack
of resignation forms" to be used by people found to have been disloyal. Everyone in the room agreed that while it was not yet a crisis of monumental proportion, it would grow incrementally until
dealt with to the public's satisfaction. Congressman Trent Lott said,
"Either somebody is awfully screwed up out there, or some dumb
bastard ought to be fired." Simpson took careful note of the president's reaction: "I think Reagan heard us. We will know in the
days to come. I think we finally rocked the Model T's oil pan off
the rocks. It will begin to move forward now. Some people ought
to resign. Get them out. Let's move on with it."

In the days ahead, a number of Simpson's Senate colleagues
shared his view that the president ought to admit mistakes and
move on. Others disagreed. "The president appeared to accept that
it made no sense for him to continue talking publicly about Iranian
arms on the Iraqi border or the overall politics of that region. The
public only wanted to know who screwed up."

Christmas Greetings

Al's concerns about political scandals abated temporarily a few days
later, as he and Ann arrived for the annual White House Christmas

Ball. "The White House was absolutely a sea of splendor. The tree, holly, mistletoe, poinsettias and candles were just dazzling. Lionel Hampton and his orchestra were there. Lionel and I were two of the six people who ushered George Bush onto the platform in Dallas when he accepted the nomination for the vice presidency in 1984."

Mrs. Reagan told Al that she appreciated his support of her husband "in these present circumstances." Al said he thought it was the right thing to do, and turned to the president: "You know, you are a very patient guy to sit in a room like you have in the past several days and have people say to you, 'I want to tell you something for your own good,' or, 'I have some advice for you.' I know how tough it is to receive that kind of commentary."

A few days later Al followed up with a phone call to the first lady. "I just wanted to contact Nancy and share with her some of the things that were on my bosom with regard to the president and Iran and the entire situation. We spoke for about forty minutes and covered the whole spectrum of things." He said he thought the president had not been well served by certain members of his administration—but that the president should issue "some sort of apology" about the Iran–Contra situation.

"She did not go for the apology business, and talked about there being no tie between the hostages and the sale of arms [to Iran]. She said the president was always overwhelmed with compassion about the hostages, and always tried to get them out." The two discussed various White House staffing problems and touched on a range of other topics. Later he described their talk as "enjoyable, a chance to share things that had been on my heart for some time."

McFarlane

Also weighing on Al's heart was former national security advisor Robert Carl "Bud" McFarlane. Two weeks earlier, an intentional overdose of Valium had nearly taken his life. During a dinner party at the apartment of Commerce Secretary Mac Baldrige and his wife

Midge, the Simpsons emphasized to McFarlane that he was not the only person in the high echelons of government to fall into deep depression. Al described his army days, including the moments when he considered suicide.

"I shared with him our experience in Germany—mine in particular, where I lay for thirty days in the Eleventh Field Hospital with a black sheet over my head." The word *help*, noted Simpson, "is sometimes the dirtiest four letter word in the dictionary—when obsequiously used."

Picking through the Wreckage

After spending Christmas in Cody with his family, Al declined an invitation for an overseas trip with fellow senators. He thought it wiser to tour Wyoming, where he found people engaging in hot debates over contentious public policy issues. Also raging were Wyoming's winter blizzards, making travel between events difficult and uncomfortable.

Back in the Senate, Republican senators were now in minority status. The impact of that became painfully clear to Simpson when he witnessed Montana Democratic senator John Melcher presiding over the Senate; a function permitted only to members of the majority party. "The reality of *that* really settled in on me," he groaned into his recorder. Senators Simpson and Dole discussed the challenges of minority status and quickly agreed that to have any chance against the Democrats, Republicans would have to be better organized and more cohesive. Al was put in charge of coordinating and solidifying tactics.

Meanwhile, they would have to suffer political indignities large and small at the hands of the Democrats. "We've had our GOP meetings in the Mansfield Room for fourteen years. Losing that room will be the final—well, probably not really the final—indignity. There will be more. These are little and niggling things, but they do injure the relationship between the majority and the minority." It was the first time in many years that Republican senators found themselves barred by the Democrats from conducting their policy luncheons in the prestigious room located conveniently close to the Senate floor. Some Republicans pledged that when they someday regained majority status, they would be thrilled to return the insult.

Anti-bullshit

After a meeting at the White House in mid-January 1987, Vice President George Bush invited Al and Ann to dinner in the Capitol building's Senate dining room, a prelude to the president's State of the Union speech. Al said he thought Reagan looked well despite having just undergone prostate surgery. The president's medical problems did not preclude some members of Congress from trying to embarrass him, which Al found galling. "They applauded Reagan in a cynical way when he discussed the deficit, and applauded even more when he talked about the Contras. I was embarrassed. Republicans and Democrats were both at fault, but some goofy congressman, a Republican from somewhere, was leading the cheers. It was juvenile stuff."

Simpson's account of the evening included his description of what he called an "appalling television stunt: They were showing the Ku Klux Klan in Georgia, while a sepulchral voice in the background said, 'Is this too perhaps a legacy of the Reagan Administration?' Blame him for things that are legitimate, but for God's sake, the Ku Klux Klan?" Al was pleased when an NBC reporter later revealed that the network had received a flood of negative public reaction.

Now Simpson was beginning to have his own problems with the president, who had decided to veto the Clean Water Bill—or the Highway Bill. "It seemed nuts to me. I told him not to do that, but he will. Then I told Don Regan it was a bad mistake." Al had worked long and hard on the Senate's Clean Water legislation and, as a conference committee member, had helped resolve differences between the House and Senate versions. "The bill does the job. It phases out the grants, takes care of non-point-source pollution issues and various other things. We will never get a better bill."

Al felt the president's advisors were insensitive to the reality that the Republicans were now a minority in both houses of Congress. Reagan needed to be reminded that he would surely find any substitute bill initiated in a Senate controlled by the Democrats markedly less acceptable. "I also said that we are going to have to establish better relationships with Senator Bob Byrd if we are going to get through these next two years." Predictably, starchy Democrat Byrd was busy reveling in his newfound power as majority leader: "He is flushed with the success of the new majority. He looks somewhat like Count Dracula after having just found five bodies in an alley."

That same day, Simpson took special note of something that President Reagan said about himself: "The president said, 'I do tend to repeat myself.' I have never heard him say that before."

TENSIONS MOUNT

During a White House meeting, after Secretary of Defense Caspar Weinberger discussed the defense budget, Congressman Jim Wright, newly anointed as speaker of the House in the wake of Tip O'Neill's retirement, tore into Weinberger.

> Jim Wright really ripped into Cap, talking about his "phony figures." He really laid it on. Then he laid into the president about his domestic cuts and other things. The president's old nostrils were widening and he was trying to interrupt, but Jim just kept right on going until I finally interjected.
>
> I said, "Boy, you really brought the whole load in here, didn't you, Jim? You dropped it all over the table. But *you* are among the people who keep us from dealing responsibly with the entitlement programs and Social Security and Medicare and Medicaid. What a bunch of *shit*."

Al was pleased that after Wright finally relented, the president "really got cooking—he quoted some good figures and brought up some stuff about the defense budget and defended himself very adroitly and with a lot of passion."

When Reagan finished, Wright said, "You may feel I was a bit intemperate. If so, I apologize." It was a typical Washington apology. Wright wasn't admitting outright to being intemperate, but he was sorry if Reagan happened to take it that way. Al himself was no stranger to apologies. His brother once made this observation: "Al is quick to make amends, politically and personally. He can really take a shot at somebody, and then find a way to restore some equanimity."

As for Weinberger, Simpson was beginning to admire the way the man could take a punch: "He is tough, dedicated, strong-minded, and he has a hell of a sense of humor. He can take an awful lot of crap. He is tough as nails and never takes things personally." The senator who had sometimes spoken of the need to "break Cap's knuckles" concerning the Pentagon budget was amending his view.

Before departing the White House that morning, Al cornered the president—and not to share a joke, as was typical. He wanted to make a recommendation concerning the Russians and Cold War relations.

I suggested that the president invite the Soviet Politburo here to the United States. It is the only group in Russia that is accountable. I said, "Bring the 'big boys' over here—or at least extend the invitation. It will rattle the hell out of Gorbachev just knowing they were invited."

The president cocked his head at the suggestion, in the way that he does, and said he liked that idea, that it sounded good to him. Then I thought I had better cover myself with George Bush, so I went into his office. He was gracious and kicked a couple of guys out into the hall so we could visit.

I said, "George, now don't laugh at this one, but I just told the president he should invite the Politburo over here to the United States. Gorbachev would go goofy . . . it would shift all the emphasis back on the Soviet Union. I don't think they would come, but they sure would wriggle around in that one."

Near the end of February 1987, Al met not with the Politburo but with a group of visiting Soviet journalists. He had no idea whether any of them had the independence or language skills to report or understand what he said, but he stated things as clearly as he could: "I just said, 'Why don't we cut the bullshit and find out how to keep from blowing each other's asses off? Who gives a shit about throw weights and megatons? Let's just get to a person-to-person relationship where neither of us wants to do this—and get to the point where we have weapons verification.'"

The senator from the state into which the U.S. government had burrowed the most deadly missile on earth, the MX "Peacekeeper," repeatedly emphasized the difference between first strike and defensive systems: "If we were building a first strike weapon, we would simply hide it in a clump of sagebrush and let the jackrabbits run around it, and then push the button when the time came."

He stressed that America's missiles were not hidden, nor were they intended as first strike weapons. He admitted great conflict—personally, professionally and philosophically—about all weapons of mass destruction. "I said that I represent a state where, in its southeast corner, is the most awesome destructive power on the face of the earth. In the northwest corner of the same state are some of the most magnificent vistas and scenery that God ever planted on earth, in Yellowstone National Park. I said that I found that a terrible irony."

The journalists may have been confused by Simpson's cacophony of imagery. Still, he pressed on, revealing the depth of American familiarity with Russian military facilities outside Novosibirsk. He revealed that America's military satellites had recorded the removal of trees and the construction of rail lines there, and that America knew the exact moment eighteen months later when "out came a missile, or some similar awesomely destructive thing." One Russian journalist asked him if he really believed that. "If you believe your eyes, you'll believe it," he responded. "We have our people on the ground in the Soviet Union to verify it. We have our spies there, just as you have here and at our test site in Nevada."

If the KGB was at all uncertain about the location of America's most destructive missiles, or its test site, or America's capacity for spying on the Soviet Union, this presentation cleared things right up.

MONEY MATTERS

As mentioned earlier, Simpson gave up a significant salary increase. This is how that happened. During a February visit to his home state, a single question from a lone constituent cost Al and Ann Simpson a great deal of money. The query came during a town hall meeting in Lander and concerned the Senate's recent vote to raise members' salaries.

> One old boy stood up and said, "You voted against the pay raise—twice—didn't you, Simpson?"
>
> I eagerly said, "You bet I did."
>
> The questioner responded, "But the raise passed, and you're going to *take* it, aren't you, you son of a bitch!"

A political dictionary once passed around Simpson's office defined the word *klong* as a major political problem striking without warning—one producing "a sudden rush of shit to the heart." Simpson had just been klonged.

He knew that virtually every senator who had voted against the pay raise would nevertheless accept the increase, and that many of those voting against it did so only because they were the next to face reelection. He also knew that many people in his state would view his accepting the raise he had voted against as pure hypocrisy. They tended to hate hypocrisy. "I told him I would *not* accept the raise. The audience was immediately pleased, although Ann was not very damn pleased. Still, considering these hard times in Wyoming—well, if times were better, I would take it, but not while the pain is so evident."

Twenty years later, Ann remained irritated: "I sold real estate for seventeen years, paying for all our children's college tuitions and enabling us to not rent our Cody house and making it available for us when we were in Cody. This was partly in response to Al impulsively giving up his Senate raise."

Each year Al rejected his pay increase, until eventually a change of rules banned senators' receipt of honoraria for speeches and performances. Until then, each year he wrote a check to the United States Treasury equal to the net increase in his salary, plus interest. He found it easier to face town meeting crowds armed with the reality of his own concession. In all, he returned nearly $100,000 of his personal salary to the U.S. Treasury.

Money was an issue in Washington when he addressed the Board of Directors of the Paralyzed Veterans of America. The organization had publicly distributed untrue information about federal funding for veterans. It was as if they were begging for a dose of Simpson admonishment. "They did a fundraising letter that was just hysterical. It was harsh, and a damned lie. I waded right into them and told them they lost a lot of respect from me. I told them what we have been doing for veterans, and especially for disabled veterans. I laid it out—book, page and hymn number. I ended up saying that I am not anti-veteran, but I sure am anti-bullshit." Afterward several members of the organization said they actually enjoyed the session. That night he told his diary, "Whether they did or not, I sure as hell did."

PERSISTENCE AND DETERMINATION

An employment guillotine awaited those responsible for the Iran-Contra scandal, and the nation eagerly awaited the rolling of heads. Anticipation and apprehension built as two separate investigations continued.

Public speculation had been in overdrive since December 1986, when President Reagan appointed a Special Review Board. Former senator John Tower of Texas headed the commission. It hired a staff of twenty-four people and interviewed fifty named individuals and three unnamed CIA officials. Colonel Oliver North and National Security Advisor John Poindexter declined to testify. The panel produced its findings in February 1987. A parallel congressional report, which required the efforts of a hundred lawyers, investigators, accountants, and auditors from both the House and Senate, was released nearly eleven months later.

The Tower Report was widely expected to be a whitewash but proved surprisingly critical of President Reagan's management style. It also provided the first official confirmation of the National Security Council's arms-for-hostages policy. Internal memos and e-mails that had circulated among the scandal's major players were quoted in detail, and Colonel North's private funding network for the Contras in Central America was exposed.

On February 27, 1987, one day after the Tower Report was released, Al Simpson, Dick Cheney, Bob Michel, and Bob Dole were ushered into the Oval Office. Already present was Frank Carlucci, assistant to the president for national security affairs. He was soon to become secretary of defense. Simpson wasted no time offering the president his recommendation: "As we used to say on the school ground, it is time to kick ass and take names. It shouldn't just be a new face, it should be plural new faces. . . . These changes ought to be made now, because these damn congressional hearings are going to consume America. It will be a lot less fun for Congress if they have *former* high officials of government testifying instead of *present* high officials."

He also suggested the replacement of "certain Cabinet officers" but did not name them in his diary. He told the president, "The American people are saddened to see the presidency get involved in this. It is the ideologues who got you here, and they caused you pain. Now it is going to be up to Republican pragmatists to get us all out of it. People do not want to see you fail. They believe in their president and want you to remain strong." This may have been an overstatement, since at that moment, political opponents across the country were reveling in the president's problem. Reagan knew it, and that it was time to set things straight.

"Suddenly the president said, 'I think you'll all be pleased at who the successor chief of staff will be.' It was the first time anyone had heard of the decision to replace Don Regan. It was a shock." The four members of Congress left the meeting enthused that Howard Baker, former majority and minority leader of the Senate, was to become chief of staff to the president. It was not their news to release, of course, which led to an interesting exchange with reporters outside the White House when one asked, "Has anyone been fired?" Al recorded how he answered: "I said, look, we have a country to run. We need the Administration to establish a solid relationship with Congress so we can get about our business. Since there are 244 million people in America, surely it is possible to pick one or two good ones to serve the president."

That evening, Al reflected on his session with President Reagan:

It was an interesting visit. He was not defensive, and he was listening. He did not try to talk about issues of Soviet or geopolitical relationships involving Iran, and he didn't try to name the dates when he had done this or that. He just said he did not know of the diversion of the funds, although he surely did know about the arms sale.

When it was all done, we asked about his health and those peculiar and strange rumors about his age and possible senility. He didn't respond to the latter, but did say that his prostate operation had been a dandy—and that he could now "hit a fly on the back of the urinal."

To lighten the atmosphere further, the president asked, "Has anyone had heard the good news and the bad news about Iran's Ayatollah Khomeini?" They hadn't, so he told them: "The good news is that his sister died. The bad news is that she was a 156 years old." The president followed that with a story about hierarchy within the Russian military.

Two Russian generals were toasting each other after the revolution. One said, "I am the son of a peasant, you the son of a duke. I was educated in a small school in the Ukraine, you in Paris and London. Yet, we are equal. Here's to Stalin."

They toasted each other and got drunk on vodka.

Later, as they were taking a leak, the second one said, "I can hear myself pissing, but I don't hear you. Why is that?"

The first one responded, "It is because I'm pissing on your coat—you peasant son of a bitch!"

Excisions

Back in the Senate, references to urinary function continued as doctors who had earlier noticed a slight abnormality in Simpson's prostate performed a biopsy to excise samples. He found the procedure uncomfortable, but not as painful as the political excision being experienced by Donald Regan. He was having his entire body excised—from the White House. Officially, he resigned, but only after learning from a television broadcast that he was leaving.

A few days after things settled down, Al phoned him. "He didn't seem bitter, even though his aide had told me—and it was later proven correct—that Regan first learned about his resignation by seeing it on CNN. That would be devastating for a guy who had served as secretary of the treasury and then chief of staff to the president. A sad exit." Regan told Simpson that he planned to go to Florida, where he had two homes, to sort it all out. Simpson said, "You'll need them both." Regan later wrote a pleasant note, and the two never again communicated.

During Simpson's next meeting at the White House, he found the president's new chief of staff, Howard Baker, seated at the end of the table. Regan had seldom participated in the president's meetings with congressional leaders, and Simpson loved having Baker there. When it was time for lunch, Nancy Reagan asked Al to sit next to her. They discussed the Baker appointment and the president's decision to name the FBI's William Webster to replace William Casey as director of the Central Intelligence Agency.

Eye of the Storm

As the days of spring continued, so did partisan bickering. Simpson dropped by a Judiciary Committee session. "I witnessed Senator Metzenbaum trying to tear Attorney General Ed Meese to pieces— so everything was normal there. On the Senate floor, Majority Leader Byrd was sternly scolding and lecturing a Republican sena- tor." Nothing new there, either. Simpson escaped the clamor by phoning his friend Mo Udall. "We were talking about the fact that we had been selected the most popular members in our respective houses of Congress, in a Capitol Hill poll. We were laughing like hell about that. Mo is a special person. As I watch him battle Par- kinson's disease, I think of my own dear Dad. Mo contracted it at about the same age."

Although Udall was one of the most powerful Democrats in the House, Simpson felt no partisanship barriers. His solid relationship with the Arizonan was akin to one he enjoyed with the Senate's Democratic whip, Al Cranston. Not long afterward, Simpson and Cranston appeared together on Daniel Schorr's National Public Radio program. The topic was aid to the Contras. "I think Dan Schorr was expecting some kind of blowout between Cranston and me, but our relationship is such that while we have fought the good, hard battles, we have always done it with great stability. I have the highest regard and respect for Al. We enjoy each other thoroughly."

$1.1 Trillion Is $1,100 Billion

Simpson's agenda that spring was packed with more items than could be printed on the schedule cards he carried in his shirt pocket and occasionally misplaced. Among his many public appearances, he spoke before 2,500 people gathered at the Washington Hilton Hotel for the Annual Legislative Conference of the National Association of Counties. Knowing of their enthusiasm for federal grants, he cut them off at the pass. "I gave them a hard, tough shot. I said that rather than asking for things, they are going to have to help out, to help us reduce the $1.1 trillion budget. I said, 'We can't do that if everybody just gets up and says what they would like to have. That's absolutely absurd.' I'll be damned if I didn't get a standing ovation."

He hustled back to his office and worked a few minutes before speeding to the airport for a flight to Boston. There he was driven to the John F. Kennedy School of Government at Harvard, where he engaged students in political discussions. He found them "a splendid group of people—a bit liberally minded, but splendid." He concluded: "Idealism is not dead in America—and certainly not in those young people. Pragmatism escapes them, but common sense will eventually come to them. Isn't that what education is all about?" The dormitory room where he spent the night had been occupied by John Kennedy in his 1939–40 academic year. Its guest record read like a who's who of the famous and powerful. Al picked up the book *John Fitzgerald Kennedy—As We Remember Him* and read until 2:30 in the morning.

Just over three hours later he jumped up, ate breakfast, and departed for the airport. On the way he saw people dressed in green and realized it was Saint Patrick's Day. "It looks like they are already gearing up," he chuckled.

Full Court Press

The next few days were jammed with appointments, interviews, and legislative activities. His immigration bill was not being universally well received by the public, and as he arrived at the Capitol Hilton Hotel to receive an award from the Center for Migration Studies, he encountered picketers. Inside, many participants applauded his courage in just showing up.

During his address, he said the protests made one of his long-held beliefs even more obvious. "Anyone making tough choices in the halls of Congress is likely to draw some opposition." From memory, he cited two poems that his mother had shared with him as a child. Both fit the occasion.

No Enemies

You have no enemies, you say?
Alas, my friend, the boast is poor;
He who has mingled in the fray
Of duty, that the brave endure,
Must have made foes! If you have none,
Small is the work that you have done.
You've hit no traitor on the hip,
You've dashed no cup from perjured lip,
You've never turned the wrong to right,
You've been a coward in the fight.

Charles MacKay (1814–89)

Press On

Nothing in the world can take the place of persistence.
Talent will not; nothing is more common than unsuccessful
    people with talent.
Genius will not; unrewarded genius is almost a proverb.
Education will not;
The world is full of educated derelicts.
Persistence and determination alone are omnipotent.

*Attributed to a Calvin Coolidge speech
in Washington, D.C., on January 17, 1925*

PAINFUL POLITICAL LESSONS

Two things were being made painfully clear to Al Simpson: judicial brilliance does not assure confirmation of Supreme Court nominees, and holding a leadership position can be detrimental to one's political health.

The $88 billion 1987 federal highway funding bill was in the national spotlight because it would also lift the national fifty-five-miles-per-hour speed limit. The so-called "double nickel" had been mandated in 1974 by the Emergency Highway Energy

Conservation Act. It was unpopular, especially in large, sparsely populated states—like Wyoming.

After the bill raising the speed was approved by both houses of Congress, it was vetoed by President Reagan, who felt it contained too much pork. That threw Simpson, an aggressive champion of the bill, into a particularly uncomfortable position. As a Republican leader he felt obligated to protect the president's veto—in other words, to assure death of the very bill he had helped give life. "This will be the toughest vote in all my eight years here," he predicted as the veto override debate began. "I want to do anything I can to help this fine president, but his veto sure hurts my state."

Reagan was riled that "demonstration projects" would inflate the bill's cost by $10 billion. Many members of Congress could not resist earmarking additional funding for projects in their home districts—whether or not they had much to do with highways—as a way of demonstrating their ability to secure federal pork for constituents, most of whom were not expressing concern over excess spending. The president told reporters, "I haven't seen this much lard since I handed out blue ribbons at the Iowa State Fair." Having been damaged politically by the Iran-Contra controversy, Reagan intended his veto to show that he would be more than a caretaker during his final twenty-one months in office.

As things played out on April 1, 1987, Terry Sanford, a sixty-nine-year-old Senate freshman from North Carolina, ended up in the hot seat—which became his political electric chair. When the veto override effort came to a vote, Sanford stood on the Senate floor, unsure what to do. He was surrounded by fellow Democrats urging him to overturn the Republican president's veto. One Republican among them, Al Simpson, was pulling him the other way. Adding an unusual complication, Sanford told his colleagues that he agreed with the president: the bill should be killed—not because it contained too much pork but because there was not *enough*.

With Democrats urging Sanford to help override the veto, and Simpson arguing that he should support the president's veto since he had voted against the bill in the first place, Sanford was in a particularly confusing and ugly fix. If he remained consistent with his original opposition, he would be the only Democrat supporting the president. At that point, nobody imagined an even more anguishing scenario, but Sanford encountered it.

Appearing confused by the rules and much conflicting advice, he voted "present." He felt that this would mean the veto would be sustained without his having to vote against the will of his own party leaders. But then he changed his vote to nay. This caused the veto to be sustained, and the bill to be killed—by a single vote.

Deft parliamentary maneuvering by Majority Leader Byrd forced another veto override effort the next day. As this second vote neared, Sanford's Democratic colleagues pleaded with him to change positions one more time and vote in favor of the override. He did. His yea vote caused the veto to be overridden after all and the bill to become law. It was a legislative nightmare. Because he had been on every side of a high-profile bill and cast the deciding vote, twice, political opponents began calling Sanford "Turnaround Terry."

Simpson had his own problems. Having supported and voted for the highway bill in the first place, and having urged the president not to veto it, he was, because of his leadership position, obligated to support the veto. Irritated and befuddled constituents began calling and writing to question his loyalties.

As for President Reagan, when the voting neared that second day, he needed to change the mind of only one of the thirteen Republicans working to overturn his veto. He took the unprecedented step of going to the Capitol to lobby them personally. *Time* reported that he uttered six words not often heard from a commander in chief: "I beg you for your vote." Not a single senator budged.

Back home in Wyoming, Simpson quickly found that most of his constituents were more interested in a higher speed limit and an infusion of federal highway money than in the intrigue and conflicting loyalties of the situation. They were flummoxed that their powerful senator, the number two ranking Republican, had used his influence to help kill a bill that Simpson himself had helped create. In his diary, Simpson noted the *Casper Star Tribune's* biting editorial commentary: "It was a powerful blast against Malcolm [Wallop] and me by Dick High of the *Casper Star.* He noted that when we voted to sustain the president's veto on the highway bill, we could have doomed it. That did not happen, of course, but Malcolm and I are taking a ton of flak."

The Simpsons escaped to New York City for dinner at the Explorer's Club. Immediately they noticed that a young man had an owl on his arm. Another had a Burmese python looped around his neck. The hors d'oeuvres included Burmese chicken feet, moray eel tongue, sambusa (lentils and beef) from Island of the Moon, and tidbits of Patagonian rodent, which Al found "quite tasty, all white meat." Then they witnessed something quite singular. "When an explorer removed the hood of a peregrine falcon, it took off and soared about the Waldorf Astoria's ballroom until it attacked a lady's feathered hat." They found their dining experience fascinating, but the evening much too long. Al later told his diary, "By the end, the only thing I was exploring was how to get the hell out of the building before dawn."

Confrontations

In Washington the following day, after Simpson made scheduled remarks to the Domestic Policy Association, he encountered new opposition to his immigration bill—and to him, personally. A woman in the audience angrily charged that his presentation had been "patronizing," since he did not appear to think those present understood the difference between immigrants and refugees. Taken aback, he said, "I thought you represented people throughout the United States. Many people throughout the United States do not understand it, so I assumed that many of you did not."

That propelled the woman into a full verbal assault. When she stopped to take a breath, Simpson interjected, "I suppose now you are going to call me a *sexist*." He told his diary: "That really blew the bun off the back of her hair. As she was storming off, I said, 'Don't walk away—come back and talk.' She *did*! Then she spirited away again."

Simpson came under a different kind of assault, at least indirectly, on his status as a 33rd degree Mason, the highest Freemasonry degree. Senator Patrick Leahy was claiming that since a federal judgeship nominee standing before the Judiciary Committee was a Mason—a member of a "men only" organization—he was not acceptable.

> Strom Thurmond and I really came out of the woods on that one. It was the most absurd thing I had seen in all my eight years in Washington. Strom read off all of the people in government who had been Master Masons in the past—from George Washington on down through seven presidents, fourteen present members of the Senate, and fifty-eight members of the House of Representatives.
>
> I think Pat Leahy was embarrassed, even though he brought it up. He should have been. It was the nuttiest, most asinine and puerile thing I have ever seen.

The Judiciary Committee's next order of business was confirmation of Federal District Judge William Sessions to become director of the Federal Bureau of Investigation (FBI). As the hearing began, Simpson was confused. Where was the overt partisan wrangling, the posturing, the pontificating, the grandstanding, the red-faced condemnation, the subterfuge? "I've never seen such a love fest," he puzzled. "The only thing they didn't do was hug and kiss him." He wanted to believe that Sessions's smooth confirmation signaled an end to disproportionate partisan scrapping over judgeship nominees. His optimism was about to be crimped by an extraordinary debate over Robert Bork's nomination to the Supreme Court.

Bork had been a federal judge on the United States Court of Appeals for the District of Columbia Circuit since 1982. Because he was conservative, Republicans knew that Democrats would do everything possible to deny confirmation. The president's chief of staff Howard Baker and a small group of Republicans, including Simpson, conducted a dry run of the anticipated questions. "We asked a lot of tough questions. Howard Baker was right on target about how Judge Bork should handle them. 'Let him be himself,' he suggested. 'Don't change him, and he will do well.'" The group failed to anticipate either how Bork would be perceived by the public or the tactics being planned by several key Democrats.

Shevardnadze

Meanwhile, the Reagan Administration was trying to hammer out a tentative arms control agreement with the Soviet Union. At Senator Ted Kennedy's home on the evening of September 17, 1987, Soviet Foreign Minister Eduard Shevardnadze joined a group of politicians, Al Simpson among them. "It was very special. Shevardnadze was open and frank, and very pleased about what he and [Secretary of State] Shultz had put together in recent days. They have made a superb start toward reducing tension in the world. He was excited about it."

During their discussion Al mentioned the importance of continuing to work with people, even those on opposite sides of an issue. "I told Shevardnadze that Ted and I didn't vote together but maybe five percent of the time, but that I enjoyed him very much and had high regard for him. I said that although I have been accused of being naïve in my political life, that doesn't bother me." Then he suggested a visit by the Politburo.

Fifty-one United States senators have been to the Soviet Union at one time or another, but you send political figures over here who have no teeth, no ability to make decisions. Why don't you send over the twelve members of the Politburo and their seven backup people and let *them* see the United States? We will let them see what a massive and extraordinary country this is. We'll make progress because we'll be visiting with people who really do make decisions, rather than with functionaries.

As the interpreter related Simpson's words, the Soviet foreign minister peered back, expressionless. After a pause, he responded that members of the Politburo were probably the busiest people in Russia. Many of them were quite old, and often tired, he said. They had difficulty keeping up with their many duties and were too worn out to come to the United States. That night, Al recorded a diary entry: "I'm just going to keep romping around on that with everyone. I have already said it to the president, and I hope he will extend the invitation. It would really be a ten-strike if we could get that done." Simpson described Shevardnadze as candid, open, and sober. "Only one shot of vodka was distributed to each person."

Denunciation of Robert Bork

On Monday, September 21, 1987, Simpson was back in the Bork Supreme Court confirmation hearings, astonished that a man universally conceded to be brilliant could be so heavily condemned.

> They agree that here is a man of soaring intellect and extraordinary brilliance, a man of absolute honesty and absolute integrity, but one who opponents think would sterilize his fellow man and woman—and is anti-black, anti-Semitic, anti-woman and anti-right-of-privacy.
>
> This is the most extraordinary stuff I have ever seen. It will be tough to break through the emotion of it. It will be a long haul, but I still think we can get him confirmed by one or two votes. We will see.

Simpson slipped away to participate in a C-SPAN broadcast, where he could say how unfairly he thought Bork was being treated. He favored C-SPAN because he knew his comments would be broadcast unedited.

The following week he learned that fellow Republican Senator Arlen Specter had changed positions and was now planning to vote against Bork. At a White House meeting to discuss the development, Simpson, Thurmond, and Dole found the president discouraged. Simpson told him, "I think it was a very poor and misguided mistake on Arlen's part."

Years later, in 2004, Specter was in line to chair the Judiciary Committee when he found that thousands of people had not forgotten his reversal on Bork. Many—prominent among them, Robert Bork—publicly opposed the moderate Republican's ascension to the chairmanship. Specter did become chairman, in 2005. In 2009 he became a Democrat, and in 2010 he ran for reelection in the Pennsylvania Democratic Party primary and lost.

A Homecoming Break

With the Bork nomination in shambles and partisan shrapnel raining all over the Capitol, Simpson flew home for a series of public meetings and to participate in homecoming activities at the University of Wyoming. Scheduled to be in the parade, he eagerly anticipated waving to the crowds from a convertible. No such vehicle materialized.

The state's lankiest politician was displeased to be wadded into a Saab, not solely because his knees were necessarily tucked up against his chest but because he wanted to be seen in an American-made car. That was a key reason he still owned his ancient and heavily weathered Plymouth Horizon. "I looked like a monkey riding a football. Occasionally, I stuck my head through the sunroof and hollered, 'When it's warm like this, they give me a sedan. When it is twenty degrees below zero—*then* they give me a convertible.'" His frame of mind improved during the Cowboys' thrashing of San Diego State 52–10.

Back in Washington, Senator Kennedy made this comment about Bork: "Robert Bork's America is a land in which women would be forced into back-alley abortions, blacks would sit at segregated lunch counters, rogue police could break down citizens' doors in midnight raids, and children could not be taught about evolution." In 2006 Simpson recalled his subsequent conversation with Kennedy.

> I walked up to him a day or two after that and said, "I want to tell you, that was just savage. There is no call for that. You didn't have to do that. That was just dramatic bullshit, and you know it. This is not just some jerk. This is a law professor at Yale. You never even *met* a professor like this guy—this sharp, bright guy."
>
> He said, "Well, we're scared to death of him."
>
> I said, "You might be, but you didn't have to do *that*."
>
> Ted didn't say he was sorry or anything, he just said, "We've got to bring him down."

At the time Simpson and Kennedy were sparring over the Bork nomination, Al realized it was in serious trouble. Everyone seemed to concede Bork's brilliance, but it was painfully clear that his opponents would stop at nothing to preclude his confirmation. On October 6, 1987, President Reagan told Simpson and other Senate leaders that he wanted a roll call vote, not a withdrawal, to conclude the process. He wanted Bork's opponents clearly and publicly on record.

Meanwhile, Bork and his family were feeling the effects of the campaign against him. They began calling Simpson to ask whether the fight should be continued. "I told them, and him, that he ought to hang in there, that he ought to get the vote onto the Senate floor where forty or forty-five senators could speak on his behalf and clear up those terrible inconsistencies." Mary Ellen Bork, Robert's wife, phoned to say that she and the children had been talking about it and agreed that he should not withdraw. They were concerned that if he pulled out, people would believe the charges against him.

> I said I thought it was important for his wife and three children to resist seeing their husband and father portrayed as a

gargoyle and the personification of evil, that it was important that he get in there and clean up the record. I had a ten-minute conversation with him. Later that day he went to the White House and said that he was going to hang in there, that it was a matter of principle.

After weeks of wrangling, the Senate rejected Robert Bork, 58–42. Before long his name became a verb. Individuals publicly vilified were now considered to have been "Borked," as defined by *Webster's New Millennium Dictionary of American English*: "Bork. Part of speech: verb. Definition: to seek to obstruct a political appointment or selection; also, to attack a political opponent viciously. Etymology: from the incident involving Robert Bork, United States Supreme Court candidate in 1987. Usage: politics."

BEYOND BORK

The postmortem of Robert Bork's failed nomination included the conclusion that since he was a respected judge and admired legal scholar, White House aides assumed it would not be a difficult confirmation. A key lesson learned was the importance of personality and appearance in public life. *Washington Post* staff writer Tom Shales summed it up. "Bork came across on television as coldhearted and condescending." Shales saved his sharpest criticism for Simpson: "You'd think Simpson had been suffering through 40 years of bloody congressional skirmishes instead of a mere nine. He's always playing Marc Antony to some imagined slain Caesar. The nomination of Bork by Ronald Reagan was a plainly political move; why was it then so heinous to attack it on plainly political grounds?"

Although the Bork confirmation fight had largely—but not totally—fallen along partisan lines, Bork himself had little interest in party labels. Much later, when Republican President George W. Bush nominated Harriet Myers to the Supreme Court, her political stripes proved unimportant to Bork. A vocal opponent of her nomination, he called her "a disaster on *every* level" since she had "*no* experience with constitutional law whatever."

After watching the Bork hearings on television, former President Nixon wrote to Simpson: "Pat and I agree you have been superb in the Bork hearings. What a tragedy. In such a gut-fight, you can't win playing by Marquis of Queensbury rules when the other guy is kicking you in the balls. Keep fighting. Sincerely, R.N." Retired Senator Barry Goldwater viewed the hearings at his home in Scottsdale. He too wrote to Simpson.

Dear Al:

I want to congratulate you for the superb job you did, putting the finger on several Senators who have done more to disgrace the Senate, in the last several weeks, than any Senators have done before.

The defamation of Bob Bork by Metzenbaum, Kennedy, and Biden, not to mention our own Republicans, was despicable. At no time did they represent, what I recall, as the prestige and honor of the Senate. . . . I cannot believe that the body I served in for 30 years has so suddenly become the harbor of rascality that it has. . . . I believe everyone who voted against Bork should have the extreme pleasure of being defeated the next time they run. Anyway, I just wanted you to know that you did one heck of a job, and I thank you for it.

Barry

Then Robert Bork wrote.

Dear Al:

Though I said a few words of appreciation about you at the Crawfords' party the other night, I wanted to write to tell you how much your support meant to me, to Mary Ellen, and to my children throughout the whole nomination process.

You helped keep our spirits up even when we knew the cause was lost. As I have told you, I particularly am grateful for your advice to stay in and make the matter go to a debate and vote. Not only is there a record that sets the matter straight but I feel a lot better about myself than I would have had I withdrawn. You have my gratitude forever.

> All the best,
> sincerely,
> Bob

Senator Kennedy wrote this note to Simpson: "I understand the posturing going back and forth in the post-mortems, but I continue to believe 100 percent that Bork got a fair shake by the Judiciary Committee. . . . He was his own worst witness before the committee. Liberals did not beat Bork, and they certainly did not beat him unfairly. Bork beat Bork."

In the wake of Bork's rejection, the White House announced the nomination of Judge Douglas Ginsburg. Simpson was impressed. "This is a hell of a good stroke for the president. Ginsburg is very conservative, probably more so than Bork. He has no public record of any type. I think we can get him to a vote and get him confirmed." Ginsburg's nomination was never fully debated. His name was put forward at the height of Nancy Reagan's widely recognized "Just Say No" anti-drug campaign, and the moment he admitted to the use of marijuana—not only as a student but also as a Harvard Law School professor—his quest was doomed.

Later that fall Al met with President Reagan's subsequent nominee, Anthony Kennedy. "He is a very impressive man with a great sense of humor. I think we finally have one who will cut the mustard. Of course, Bork would have really cut the mustard, but that was not to be. And poor Doug Ginsburg got caught in the buzz saw. Funny how we do this game. We savage the first one and kiss the next one. Fascinating business."

Relationships

It was an exhausting and somewhat lonely time for Al, since Ann was often busy in Wyoming. One night he dictated this: "I went to a reception for Jim and Sarah Brady and I stopped by several other events. But the best news is that Ann is coming back. She hasn't been here in Washington for several weeks—although we've met together in Detroit, Minneapolis, and other ports. It'll be great to have her home."

Over the years Al never failed to demonstrate love and admiration for his wife, both publicly and privately. He frequently mentioned her in speeches and referred to her in correspondence to others. He once said to me that a number of his colleagues had been divorced or were involved in ugly personal and even public conflicts with their spouses. "That," he said emphatically, "is not going to happen to me. I get myself into enough trouble of various kinds without having relationship problems."

I examined his diaries two decades after he began their creation. Numerous entries confirmed with certainty the staff's theory about Ann's role in his life. If private diaries are among the more intimate and honest forms of expression, it can only be true that his loyalty to the former high school cheerleader from Greybull, Wyoming, was and remains absolute.

At the White House on November 3, 1987, President Reagan was also thinking about relationships: "An Idaho potato and a Maine potato had a child they named Sweet Potato. She grew up and said she wanted to marry Walter Cronkite. Her father said, 'Oh, you can't do that—he's just a Common Tater.'" Simpson thought it interesting that Reagan was able to carry on as if nothing were amiss, even during contentious court nomination hearings in the Senate and revelations about Iran-Contra. "That's the way he is. He is in the midst of all kinds of stuff flying around, but is courageous and unthreatened. I really, honestly feel that the only time he gets a little confused is when guys are talking from both ends of the table and both of his hearing aids are vibrating away."

Back at the Capitol a few weeks later, a group of senators met to discuss the challenge of paying for everything everybody in Congress wanted. "I just said there isn't any way we are going to get a reduction in the deficit until we deal with the entitlement programs.

We must freeze them, or at least cut back the increases. We do not have to take one penny away from anybody. We should tell people that they will get their same benefits, but we are going to have to do something with the cost of living increases." It was a familiar theme, one he would promote throughout his Senate service and beyond.

By late 1987 Simpson's involvement in many high profile issues and his frequent access to the president were producing numerous speech invitations. Since they provided an opportunity to spread his views widely on many topics and to contribute his speech honoraria to charities, he accepted as many offers as he could squeeze in. He found it possible to meet with the president in the morning, conduct Senate business on a dozen matters through the middle of the day, hop a flight to New York, Chicago, or any number of other destinations, give a speech, and fly home in time for a late dinner at home with Ann—and catch up on paperwork in his den into the wee hours.

Law School Drama

In November Simpson had a "spirited"—that is to say, extremely testy—encounter with members of the faculty at the University of Wyoming College of Law. Long before the hearings on Robert Bork, they had drafted a strongly worded letter opposing his confirmation. "I told them how disappointed I had been to see the law school faculty sending out a letter rejecting Robert Bork before the hearings even started. I told them that the University of Wyoming had taught me fairness and to listen to another person's opinion. I said it might have been best for *them* to do that." Several professors were not at all appreciative of his sentiments, but since he was now a member of the United States Senate rather than a law school student, he felt perfectly comfortable, and even enthusiastic, about critiquing them.

Not able to fly to Cody because of adverse weather, he remained in Laramie. His disposition brightened the moment he flipped on the television to find the UW Cowboys football team defeating

Utah, 31–7, in Utah. After the game he picked up his recorder and said excitedly, "If they win one of the next two games, they will be off to the Holiday Bowl in San Diego December 30—and I'll be there!"

The weather finally allowed his flight to Cody, where he shared time with his parents before driving to the Bobcat Ranch with his son Colin.

> It was one of those crystal clear, blue-sky days. Lots of snow.
> We stopped at the pond. I'll be damned if the trout weren't
> feeding on some kind of little flies—on November 15.
>   I just stood and bathed in the beauty of it all, before hiking
> back to the ranch. I saw more mule deer than I could count.
> It was amazing. We were going to get some wood, but didn't.
> We just stood around and looked at the beauty all around us.

In Cody that evening the family gathered with Milward and Lorna to watch their old home movies. For months Milward had been in and out of awareness, but the films seemed to perk him up. His family wanted nothing more. They huddled together as precious memories flickered into the night.

Chapter Nine

COLD WAR MELTDOWN

IN LATE 1987 the Reagan Administration was negotiating arms reduction treaties with the Soviet Union. The goal: elimination by June 1, 1991, of all American and Soviet missiles with a 3,500-mile strike range, and deactivation of shorter-range missiles within eighteen months. If all went well, 2,692 missiles would be eliminated and the Intermediate-range Nuclear Forces (INF) treaty would be the first nuclear arms control agreement to reduce nuclear arms rather than merely setting limits.

Senators Bob Dole and Al Simpson felt that Congress should have a role in crafting the actual treaty language and that Soviet leader Mikhail Gorbachev should be invited to address a joint session of Congress during his coming visit to Washington. When a number of other senators objected, the idea of inviting Gorbachev to speak to Congress was dropped. The Soviet leader was disappointed. So was Simpson.

> In his country, Gorbachev spent many hours with fifty-four United States senators and a couple of hundred House members in the last three years. I can understand his pain. The Library of Congress has all of Lenin's materials and books from when he was in exile in Siberia. We almost have more material than they have in Russia, and we have some great maps that are unable to be duplicated in Russia. We should show all this to Gorbachev.

THE GORBACHEV VISIT

The Soviet leader flew to Washington in early December 1987. At the Soviet Embassy he met with nine American lawmakers, five from the House and four from the Senate. "It was one of the most fascinating days of my life in Washington—or at any time. I was up early and off to the Soviet Embassy with invitation in hand. We were ushered into a sitting room off the conference room in the embassy, where we met with former ambassador Anatoly Dobrynin. While we awaited the arrival of the secretary general, Dobrynin asked about Wyoming."

Dobrynin, who was appointed ambassador to the United States in 1962 by Nikita Khrushchev, knew America well. He especially enjoyed the western part of the country. Simpson was impressed that the Russian was familiar with the Wyoming license plate, which depicts a cowboy riding a bucking horse.

As the two discussed things they knew in common, Al mentioned that the center's board sent western art from the Buffalo Bill Historical Center in Cody to the Soviet Union, via industrialist Armand Hammer. They were chatting agreeably when Gorbachev entered the room. He met each guest individually before inviting the group to make themselves comfortable in a conference room. Simpson's diary says: "It was beautiful, with large amounts of gilding. There were two large mirrors, one on each side of the room. Nine Russians were sitting on one side of the table and the nine of us took the other. On their side, Gorbachev was in the middle. There were scores of reporters and cameras. No questions were being shouted out, like they do to our prexy."

After the reporters departed, Gorbachev said, "Well, we can get down to work now, as soon as the press leaves us alone." As the Soviet leader spoke, Simpson penned notes.

Gorbachev started off saying, in essence, that he didn't like to beat around the bush, that it was very important for his country to reach out to other nations. He said they were going to do all they could toward that end.

Why am I here? Am I here because I need the United States to agree with me because of problems at home? Is that

why I am here? No, I am here because we are in the rut of
the arms race, and we must stop. This is only one small step,
because we are only reducing five percent of our nuclear arms
in the INF treaty.

Gorbachev spoke about perestroika, a restructuring of the Soviet
economy. "Soviet people are becoming bolder," he said, "raising
their heads. They are asking questions they never asked before, questioning their past and future." He revealed that he and his colleagues
were aware of the immense burden being shouldered by the Soviet
people and government. He spoke of the willingness of the people
of the Soviet Union to live modestly—"but not *that* modestly."

He explained that people in his communist-ruled country
were used to a "certain order" and found any change disturbing. Yet change must take place, he said, and not just at the
leadership level. There must be a change in philosophy "at the
work bench."

He said change was inevitable and that the process was
"irreversible." He described glasnost openness as important.
His country would not "jump over" various stages, as it had
in the past. It was certain to take time, but the changes he
foresaw now would warm his country's relations with the
United States.

Gorbachev cautioned that various "ultimatums" placed on
the Soviets by the American Congress were "painful" and
pointedly asked how Americans would feel if his country did
the same to the United States. "What if we were to do that to
you? You write us petitions and demand that we 'behave.' It is
almost as if you are telling us to be good boys. We do not like
that."

After scolding us, he spoke of the changes he was seeing in
his country. "I can tell you that we are giving up the traits of
forty years ago. These are new times with new leaders. We
want you to know that we are sincere. The past is the past.
We are ready to go forward without destroying ourselves."

He concluded by saying, "I know you are going into your elections [eleven months hence] and perhaps you will find my remarks very timely."

Simpson's diary says House majority leader Jim Wright brought up the issue of Soviet military activity in Afghanistan, likening the situation to America's Vietnam quagmire. In a protracted conflict, the Soviet Union was supporting Afghanistan's Marxist government against Islamist mujahedeen resistance. The United States supported the resistance. Gorbachev told the visiting senators that his military wanted to leave Afghanistan. At the same time, he stressed, they did not want to see the vacuum of their departure filled by forces destructive to his country, since they share a two-thousand-kilometer border. He said it was "in our common interest" to see that a "bad government" not take root there. He promised that his country had no plans for socialism in Afghanistan, and "no intent to injure."

Gorbachev then said he was most disturbed by the "dynamite situation" building in the Persian Gulf. This, he said, could threaten the United States: "If too much pressure is put on those fanatics, they might do anything."

Senator Byrd drew the conversation back to Afghanistan, opining that the Soviet invasion had caused the failure of previous Soviet-U.S. arms treaties. He pressed for a withdrawal timetable, stressing that it could help assure completion of the pending INF treaty. Byrd suggested that with cooperation, the treaty could be before the U.S. Senate for approval within a few months.

Senator Dole thanked Gorbachev for his comments and commitments, and agreed that the Persian Gulf was a "powder keg." He asked that the Soviet Union join the United States in assuring that no arms would be sold to those who would not pledge peace in that part of the world.

A revealing moment came when Congressman Bob Michel asked, "What do you want your country to be in fifteen or twenty years?" Gorbachev said, "We have come out of our cold war thinking that we cannot easily cast off the burdens of past years, just like that. But we have to rid ourselves of old anxieties." He left no question that reforms of global significance were taking place in the Soviet Union.

When he paused, Ambassador Dobrynin addressed the Americans.

You must help. You must get rid of old habits and reservations and you must not do things in the old ways, as you deal with issues like the environment and poverty and people who are in backward conditions. We must not take a confrontational attitude with each other.

We have made our choice in our country, and we will go forward. We do not want to end up, and I do not think you do either, playing the role of fireman all over the world, putting out fires all over the world. We need to do better than that, and that is what this treaty will begin to develop.

Gorbachev emphasized the importance of the treaties. "The INF treaty is a start. We must continue to accelerate the process. We must not lose pace. We are here to send you some good vibrations. You need to send some too. You have heard us engage in openness and candor and self-criticism and we are ready to do business. We are here seeking peace."

Simpson was impressed by the presentation and noted approvingly that Gorbachev repeatedly used western phrases like "beating around the bush" and "taking the bull by the horns." He decided that since Gorbachev seemed to enjoy a good story, he would mention the time when American general Ulysses Grant sent General Philip Sheridan to explore America's West. Months later, Sheridan reported his findings: "All this country needs is good people and water." Grant responded, "That's all *hell* needs!"

Then Simpson turned serious: "What we all need is control on the arms race, and that's why what you are doing is so critically important. We like meeting with people who can make decisions. Why don't you send the members of the Politburo to the United

States so we can visit with them here? Or, we can go there. The important thing is that we visit with them."

Gorbachev "seemed quite fascinated by the idea," but made no firm commitment. Participants on both sides turned to a discussion on human rights, drawing a further commitment from Gorbachev: "I assure you that we will have a seminar or joint session on human rights in the Soviet Union. It will consist of the Secretariat and the Politburo, and your congresspersons. We will discuss human rights, both sides, honestly, and not just these things that you continue to bring up. We will talk about the fact that in our country the standards of life are lower." Simpson found that fascinating. "He said it and I wrote it down. He said that the standard of life was lower in his country and that we [in America] give better protection to the citizens of our country."

Referencing Simpson's immigration bill, Gorbachev said he was interested in American restrictions on who can enter the United States. "I noted you passed a new law recently and that you have people in your country who almost want to shoot other people when they come across your border illegally." He held his hand in the shape of a gun, and laughed. Everyone turned to Al, who said, "What kind of nut would pass a law like *that?*" Gorbachev went on to compare the penal codes. "There are stronger and more vile laws in West Germany and France and the United States than in the Soviet Union," he emphasized.

The session ran nearly ninety minutes before Gorbachev said, "I thank you. It has been very good. I have enjoyed it. It was very important to me." As the Americans headed for the door, the Soviet leader said, "I want to shake your hands." With that, he made his way down the row. Gorbachev stopped in front of Simpson, who said, "We have a feeling about people out in the West, one I feel about you. You seem like a *no bullshit guy.*"

"I smiled as I said it. He smiled too, and when the interpreter repeated the phrase, Gorbachev reached up with both hands and kind of gave a little slap with his fist and thumb and put his head back and laughed like hell. He said, 'I *know* what that is, and that *is* the way I am.'" Al had first used the "no bullshit guy" phrase on Ronald Reagan. Now he had worked it into conversation with the leader of the U.S.S.R., arguably the world's second most powerful person of the day. Both considered it a compliment.

Round Two

During Al's ride back to the Capitol, he thought about Afghanistan. What *would* happen there, if the Russian military pulled out? His concerns were valid. The Soviets did pull out of Afghanistan two years later. During their occupation, approximately fifteen thousand Soviets and one million Afghans died in military action. Among those resisting was a twenty-seven-year-old Saudi Arabian, Osama bin Laden.

At midday Al joined Ann and the two headed to a State Department luncheon hosted by Secretary George Shultz in honor of the Gorbachevs. Newscasters from the three major broadcast television networks were there, as were the heads of the nation's print media and scores of other reporters.

As everyone took his seat, it became obvious that Simpson was the highest-ranking leadership member of Congress in the room. At his table were Mikhail Gorbachev, Secretary Shultz's wife Obie, and a corporate farmer from Iowa who had met Gorbachev when he was Soviet secretary of agriculture. Also present were President Eisenhower's granddaughter Susan, and Donald Kendall, the president of Pepsi Corporation. Rounding out the group were Senator Sam Nunn, Meg Greenfield of the *Washington Post,* and the president's chief of staff, Howard Baker. Ann sat with Raisa Gorbachev.

Al later described the luncheon as "beautiful, featuring lobster, shrimp, crab, venison and desserts—all accompanied by two wines and champagne." He avoided the alcohol. "I didn't have a drop—keeping my old pact with my fine staff. There is to be no drinking at noon on my time." That did not preclude the participants from talking about drinking, with a particular focus on bootlegging in the Soviet Union. After the meal, Gorbachev discussed agriculture and human rights and then exchanged toasts with Secretary of State Shultz. Live music followed.

That night, Al worked late, recording key aspects of the historic session: "It is a quite fascinating time for a gal from Greybull and a fellow from Cody who linked up thirty-three years ago and never knew we would have such remarkable opportunities to meet world leaders, and to participate ourselves. We are both still sniffing [celebrity], but we're not inhaling."

Reagan's Take

Simpson's busy week included a flight to Houston to deliver a midday speech. He returned in time for the culmination of Gorbachev's visit to Washington. "Goose pimples came to me on that shimmering, hazy winter day as I watched the president of the United States and the leader of the 'Evil Empire' shaking hands. They were both searching for peace, so they don't bankrupt their own countries and lead them into destructive warfare."

The next bipartisan congressional leadership group assembly at the White House was one of President Reagan's most memorable. As he entered the Cabinet Room, congressional leaders of both houses and both parties stood and applauded. Simpson saw a quizzical look flash across the president's face as he said, "You must have seen one of my old movies last night."

When the laughter subsided, Reagan presented a complete review of his five private sessions with Gorbachev. Issue by issue, point by point, he explained every commitment and nuance, emphasizing that it was Gorbachev who had bought up the issue of reducing *conventional* forces. When Reagan was through, members of the leadership of both parties praised his efforts. Even Senate Majority Leader Robert Byrd was lavish in his compliments. "No one but you, Mr. President, no one at all could have done this, but you."

After the others had spoken, Reagan went on to say that he had

shared jokes with the Soviet Leader. He repeated one that Gorbachev particularly liked.

> There was a new directive from the Politburo that anyone
> caught speeding—anyone—would be fined, without excep-
> tion.
>
> One day Gorbachev had to return to the Kremlin quickly.
> He was late and anxious, so he decided to drive himself, tell-
> ing the chauffeur to get into the back seat.
>
> Sure enough, the police stopped the car for speeding and
> one of the two cops went to the driver's window. When he
> returned to his police car, the other cop asked if he issued a
> ticket. The first one said, "No, I didn't."
>
> When asked why, he replied, "It must have been someone
> very, very important."
>
> The second cop asked, "Who?"
>
> The first cop said, "I don't know, I didn't recognize him.
> But his driver was *Gorbachev*."

Simpson laughed and thanked the president for his service. Then
he spoke to his colleagues, Democratic and Republican alike: "My
friends, if those two fine national leaders could reach an accord on
serious issues like arms control, we should match it, especially in
this (holiday) season when we seek peace and try to live in peace.
. . . If our president and the head of the Evil Empire can begin to
ameliorate and stabilize their relationships, we can do the same with
ours."

WINDING DOWN, GEARING UP

A sense of peace and accord hung over Congress in the final days
of 1987, except when Democratic Senator Tom Harkin went to the
Senate floor at 2:30 one morning and started, according to Simpson, "the most damn insensitive debate and discussion and reading of papers." Other than that incident, which kept the Senate in

session until 4:30 in the morning, relative calm blanketed the Capitol as light snow dusted its dome. A sense of harmony spread to the Judiciary Committee as it approved and passed on to the full Senate the nomination of Anthony Kennedy for a seat on the Supreme Court.

For the White House, however, this period of good cheer was brief. As Christmas closed in, conservatives began criticizing the president for being too soft on the Russians. North Carolina senator Jesse Helms was the driving force behind an organization called the Conservative Caucus, based in Virginia. The group issued a statement calling the president a "useful idiot" for backing the INF treaty. It was a particularly pithy phrase, since it had first been used by Lenin in describing liberals.

Other than those whose fingertips were clinging to the fringe of the political right, Americans were having a difficult time thinking of Ronald Reagan as liberal, or considering his recent progress toward a warmer relationship with the Soviets as idiotic.

Three days before Christmas in 1987, the Senate adjourned. Al hit his pillow at 5:30 in the morning; four hours later he and Ann were aboard a westbound airplane. During the holiday he conducted contentious town meetings in Jackson, Pinedale, Sheridan, Rawlins, Jeffrey City, Saratoga, and Casper. Many of the people he encountered were unhappy, and seriously so. "I sensed unrest and irritation out there. There were tough questions and hostility on many issues, and I got a bit argumentative with two guys. One was simply off the wall. Finally, members of the crowd said to the guy, 'Sit down and shut up.'"

The mood lightened during a meeting in one small town. "I was telling them how special Glenrock was to me, and that my car had broken down there when I was a sophomore in college. I said that a guy at the Ford garage put me up for the night and fixed the car. A guy in the back stood up and said, 'Hey, that was *me!*'"

As Congress resumed its work in late January 1988, Republican senators began to question who would be leading them while

Senator Dole was running for president. During an organizational session, Al said, "I'll be in charge of the Republican activities on the floor, as acting leader. I'm ready for the transition." He repeated that he intended to do all he could. "I said I was expecting their good assistance, but that I was not running for later election to the position of majority leader."

On January 26, 1988, an impassioned debate erupted between President Reagan and congressional leaders concerning Central America policy in general and aid to the Contras of Nicaragua in particular. Simpson took special note of one key comment by the president: "There was a very interesting little aside, where one of the participants asked, 'Well, what if we don't approve Contra aid in the House or the Senate?' The president said, 'Then we'll go *private*.'" Al said other conversations partially obscured Reagan's remark, but he was certain about what he had heard. "That was a very interesting comment, and I heard it, without question." But what exactly did that mean?

Nasty and Harsh

Having developed close relationships with the leading candidates for the Republican Party nomination—Bob Dole and George Bush— Al Simpson was in a delicate situation. A couple of days later, he spoke with Bush: "George seems pleased about what he thinks will happen on 'Super Tuesday,' and how tough it is between him and Dole. They are going at each other hard. 'Nasty,' is the way he referred to it. He thinks it will get nastier, and is surprised by the harshness of Bob's tone."

Simpson too was surprised when Dole made a public comment about his "gazoo remark." Briefly, it became a matter of contention between them.

Some reporter asked Bob if he had heard what I said about the president—the "right in the old gazoo" thing. Bob asked, "What did he say?" They read it to him.

In his flip way, which gets misread, he said, "Maybe he's trying to out-Agnew Agnew" [Nixon's vice president Spiro Agnew had called the media "nattering nabobs of negativism"]. Somebody on my staff handed me the news clip of Dole's comment, as reported by the *Baltimore Sun*.

I went up to him the next day—I don't think I waited— and I said, "Bob, I'd like to see you." I went in and said, "I just want to tell you that I read your comment in the *Baltimore Sun*. I want you to know that really hurt me. Agnew and me in the same breath?" His jaw hit his tie.

He said, "Wait. I would never do anything to hurt you. You've been wonderful and loyal. I couldn't ask anything more from an assistant."

I said, "That's not the point. The point is that that hurt me. I didn't like it, and I found it very painful."

I never saw Bob in more of an abject apology mode. He just said, "Al, I just can't believe that you'd take it that way."

I said, "It isn't whether you thought I'd take it that way. I've been loyal and I was pained by it."

I tell you, he was stunned. He thought things were funny that sometimes pained the recipient. But [after our exchange] he was very sensitive. Our chat improved our relationship immensely. It made everything right again.

More Alfalfa

Six months later Simpson slipped into black tie attire and took three of his aides, including me, to the annual Alfalfa Club Dinner. He later wrote: "They were sitting right in the front row of the middle table, about ten feet from the president. You might imagine that they loved it." We did. Al passed a program around the head table, had everyone sign it, and handed it to me as a gift and memento. That night Al logged some of the stories told by others.

During the program, Senator Warner, referring to his famous former wife Elizabeth Taylor, turned to President Reagan and said, "You had some great luck in Hollywood. Wish I had had the same."

Senator Bentsen looked around and said, "We need some newer members in Alfalfa. As I look around here, I know that Alfalfans' idea of 'safe sex' is not to have a heart attack."

Another speaker mentioned that Henry Kissinger, who was present, was born in Germany but came to the United States when he was just a baby. He said, "Henry still has an accent. That's because he never listens to anybody."

Nicaragua

With Dole campaigning in Iowa, Simpson was a busy man, working out compromises on legislation and serving as traffic cop and negotiator both on and off the Senate floor.

The president, now more focused than ever on providing aid to the Contras in Nicaragua, felt the Sandinista government was moving toward Marxist-Leninist tendencies. He said America should continue to support Contra efforts, even as international human rights groups saw some Contra actions as brutal and indiscriminate. The situation remained complicated and ugly.

Daniel Ortega—referred to by Simpson as "Daffy Danny" at every opportunity—was continuing to lead the Sandinistas in takeovers of banking, mining, and other key industries. In what Reagan considered a dangerous move to the political left, Ortega had now announced opposition to free elections. Following the embarrassing exposure of the clandestine Iran-Contra operation, Reagan was asking Congress for special legislation to support the Contras openly.

At the same time, bigger issues were dominating the Senate's attention, such as reviewing the pending arms treaties with the Soviets and grappling with campaign finance reform. Since those matters fell more naturally along partisan lines, Simpson knew he would soon be nose to nose with Senator Byrd, a formidable and stubborn opponent. Even though Al came armed with the unified support of his Republican colleagues and twenty-four years of legislative experience, he recognized that he was up against the "Zen Master" of the Senate floor. This Zen Master knew the Senate rules like the back of his own hand and, making the challenge even more difficult, was easily offended.

That was not Simpson's only problem. In the tiny eastern Wyoming town of Moorcroft the following week, he ran into someone else who was offended: "A lady at the restaurant didn't like me at all. She said she had heard about my tricks to cut the Social Security program and freeze the benefits. She didn't like it one damn bit, and she let me know it. I thought she was going to pour hot coffee on my head. Ah, the perils of telling the truth in politics."

Fun and Games

Nobody envisioned that in early 1988, while Bob Dole was running for president and Al Simpson was leading the Republicans, Majority Leader Robert Byrd would order the arrest and physical manhandling of senators. At issue was a Democratic Party push for campaign finance reform. Byrd was determined to advance the issue, and Simpson was determined to stop him. At one point Al counseled his fellow Republicans to stay away from the chamber.

"Byrd could do only a couple of things in that situation," Al noted. "He could move to adjourn, or send the sergeant at arms to *arrest* the absent members. To the shock of many, that night at 10:30, Byrd exercised the latter option." This tactic elevated the skirmish into the realm of outright legislative warfare. As instructed by the majority leader, the sergeant at arms and several Capitol police officers fanned out through the Senate complex in search of the missing senators.

They . . . served a warrant on [Republican] Lowell Weicker. He told them to stuff it. The poor old sergeant at arms was beside himself and did not like his work just then, since Weicker was six-six, 260 pounds.

They said, "Senator Weicker, we're here to take you to the floor." He said, "Fuck you!" They told him, "Very well then, sir, we'll come back tomorrow." When asked by the majority leader why Weicker was not to be seen, they responded, "Well, Senator, the reason is that he told us to go fuck ourselves!"

The officers soon reached Senator Bob Packwood's office. When Packwood refused to cooperate, they trooped in, picked him up, and carried him feet first through the halls of the Capitol building and into the Senate chamber.

The moment his feet came through the door, the presiding officer announced a quorum present and ordered the continuation of debate. However, Simpson found a way to be recognized and held the floor for ninety minutes. He was relieved by Republican Senator David Durenberger at 5:00 in the morning and was home in bed by 6:00. He returned at 9:00, ready for duty. It was a form of combat only truly understood by politicians.

Later that morning Simpson told Byrd he thought "calling out the troops" was a bit excessive. He pointed to news reports critical of the incident.

They made it look like he had overreacted—which he had. . . . I told Byrd there would be a lot more of that kind of coverage and that I had people on my side who were plenty pissed and ready to stay up all night for as long as it took.

We held tough and did a hell of a job of sticking together. We sent the message that we sure as hell will do that again if they get tough with us and try to ram a bunch of shit through. The rules of the Senate protect the minority. We used them beautifully.

When the Senate finally quieted down and ruffled senatorial feathers had been preened into place, Simpson brought up a new topic—Buffalo Bill's 143rd birthday. He was eager, as he always was on the famous showman's birthday, to describe Buffalo Bill Cody's life and death. He especially enjoyed noting that after Buffalo Bill was buried in Colorado, a Wyoming group went to the gravesite and tried to return Cody's body to the town bearing his name. Controversy lingers today as to their degree of success.

More Fun and Games

At the end of that contentious week in the Senate, Al flew to Alberta, Canada, to attend the Olympic Winter Games. He was especially eager to join his friend Peter Kriendler, who had flown in from New York City. Co-founder of the internationally known 21 Club restaurant in New York, Kriendler was an older-generation kindred spirit whom Al enjoyed, much as he enjoyed knowing Senator Strom Thurmond.

On the day of the seventy-meter ski jump, Al and Peter decided spontaneously to view it—even though they had no tickets. Al's diary tells the story.

> We had our driver take us out to the site of the seventy-meter ski jump. It was not an unpleasant day, a little warm with a Chinook wind blowing lightly. But up on the mountaintop the wind was blowing so hard—sixty-nine miles an hour— that they had to scrub the downhill and alpine skiing. All of the ticket holders who missed those events came on down to the seventy-meter ski jump. I tell you, the joint was packed.

About midway on the hillside was a large lodge called Fisher House, which was unknown to the two. Instructed to go to the ski jumping event, their driver let them out at a turnaround in the parking lot. They walked from there, about one hundred yards to the base of the hill and the admissions gate. Their tickets were to the Olympics opening event.

> It was then that Peter and I put together all the combined wiles and craft of an eighty-three-year-old native New Yorker and a fifty-six-year-old Wyomingite. It was here again proven that guile and craft will overcome youth and inexperience every day.

We started our work in almost a "sting-like" fashion at the admissions area, when I showed my official United States Senate identification card.

"I'm Senator Al Simpson of Wyoming, a guest of your government. I have here Peter Kriendler, the owner of the 21 Club and a member of the International Olympic Committee. We need some kind of transportation for Mr. Kriendler, who finds it very difficult to get up that slope to the ski jump area."

Well, they got on their radios and brought up some security people. Then came some courtesy people. Then a van showed up. A fellow asked, "Where to you wish to go?"

I said, "We wish to go up."

The fellow said, "Oh, you mean the Fisher House."

We said, "Yes, that is exactly where we are going."

We gave that driver a line of guff that would have choked a horse and he took us midway up the slope, to a gate where the security people came out. I said, "I would like to be sure we get Mr. Kriendler up to the Fisher House as soon as possible. It is difficult for him to get around."

Old Pete played the part beautifully. He had that great big Russian hat on, and he held tightly onto my arm and whispered, "I think I can look even paler than this."

I tell you, he bent himself over and stumbled along. I was holding him close with my arm and he was weaving along. People up front were saying, "Folks, please step aside and let these folks through." They cleared the path for Pete and me all the way up the slope.

Finally, we had some official people come up to us with badges (we had none) and we were taken to the door of the Fisher House. Some big guard who looked like Hulk Hogan said, "Yes, what can I do for you?"

I said, "I'm Senator Simpson of the United States, a guest of your government, with my friend Pete Kriendler of the

Olympic Committee and owner of the 21 Club in New York." Pete filled him up too.

The guard said, "Oh, yes, come in."

In they went, into a beautiful lodge with fireplaces and comfortable chairs. When they climbed the stairs they encountered the chairman of International Olympics, a parliamentarian from the Calgary area, and the head of the Olympic ski jumping events.

Peter and I just waded right into the middle of them as if we knew all of them from "way back." We greeted them one and all, and Peter had a hot brandy as the fire crackled.

We then went out and watched the seventy-meter jumps right from the broad vista of the porch. We could not have missed anything. We had an unobstructed view.

We continued our visit with all of the officials, as Peter and I worked the crowd. We told them who we were, and up to Pete came the prince and princess of Sweden. She crushed Peter to her bosom and said she remembered him from when she was twenty-one years old and had come to the 21 Club. She was excited, although the prince was not too excited.

Pete met many members of the Olympic Committee. All asked Mr. Kriendler how he was feeling after his arduous climb. He allowed that he was doing pretty well—now that he was there by the crackling fire with an admiring throng, telling tales and hoisting a bit of brandy.

I tell you, the two of us were treated like kings. We had no official identification, nothing at all—no passes, no nothing. We were just a pair of spirited guys having a lot of exciting fun with vigor and vitality surging around in us.

Finally, Pete and I decided we would go. I said, "I wonder now if you would please call for transportation for Mr. Kriendler?" God, they ran out of the door and rustled a vehicle and Peter and I hustled back downstairs. We both picked up a nice souvenir hat or two in the process.

Then we were out into the cold again, and down the slope. I was helping Peter and he was hanging on and "trying to look pale," so we could make better headway as people cleared the way for us. Down from Fisher House we went and out through the gate, and here was a car, waiting.

After the two returned to family and friends, they couldn't stop talking about their grand adventure. "I tell you, we gut-laughed all the way back to the hotel. We laughed all the way through dinner together, just the two of us. I am still chuckling as I dictate about it. It was an absolutely special day with my special friend, Pete."

MIDNIGHT IN MOSCOW

On March 6, 1988, with President Reagan focused on the Soviet Union and international weapons treaties, Senators Simpson, Nunn, Levin, Cohen, and Cranston launched a mission to Moscow. Knowing this was an extraordinary opportunity, Simpson recorded detailed notes on a small handheld tape recorder.

We had flown in through a great, gray overcast into a great gray airport. . . . It was a lonely and stark looking place.

We headed to the hotel. . . . My room has great high ceilings and a big old chandelier with six lights and a large blue kind of egg-like thing hanging from it. Crazy wallpaper, high drapes. . . . There was one television and an old refrigerator that didn't work. I had a felt-covered couch and a bed that was about a foot and a half off the floor. . . . This will be my home for a week.

We had dinner at the hotel, the third time we had caviar today. I was ready to go to bed, but we began talking about the subway system. My pal Carl Levin, about the most curious guy in the world besides me, asked why we didn't take the subway and go into Red Square while there was a little skiff of snow.

We left the building and found an old subway stop built in

the 1930s. . . . The cars are old, but the subway runs beautifully. Not a bit of graffiti, nothing on the walls. We came up right next to the Bolshoi Ballet and walked around the corner to Red Square and Lenin's tomb. There were searchlights. Light snow falling. Very cold, crisp—startling, unforgettable.

Decided to take the subway back, but they had closed the station. We walked about twenty minutes, about a mile. A cold, crisp, lovely night for talking and visiting, and just keeping warm. . . .

Tired, well exercised, ruddy of cheek, ready to go. This is going to be a great adventure. We can all sense that. Read a bit and hit the sack. So it goes in my first night ever in Russia.

On March 8 the group visited the American ambassador's residence:

The ambassador told us about the country. He said there is a resistance to what Gorbachev is doing, a real debate going on. Factory workers are told that shoddy work will not be accepted, or there will be no bonuses if it is. No more drinking on the job. No more vodka—or when there is, it is more expensive. New and dazzling products are not overflowing the stores.

There are eight million people in the Soviet bureaucracy. There is widespread resistance to government, but not open opposition. More resistance by various nationalities. Each wants its own glasnost.

We asked how the military fares here. They messed up in Afghanistan and lost lots of hardware there, and they will lose lots of hardware in the INF treaty. The military is not displeased, because they know the domestic overhaul of the economy will help them, help their salaries.

Afghanistan. Boy, the Soviets really know they have to get out of that country.

Intense fighting behind the scenes on human rights.

People understand now that they have rights. The Soviets are reviewing their legal code, and are having some real scraps reviewing their religious rights.

Later that day they met with a group of "Refuseniks," a title given people, mostly Jews, who were refused certain human rights, most notably the right to emigrate from the Soviet Union.

Met some of these people in an apartment. A marvelous group, but they smoke incessantly, and smoke some of the foulest cigarettes I have ever inhaled or smelled. Some spent time in prison camps. Obviously, the boredom and strain of that led to smoking. Half of them looked like the damn cigarettes might have killed them before the confinement could have.

I reminded them that they had a revolution in Russia only seventy years ago, and that on the seventieth anniversary of our own revolution, about the year 1850, we were not exactly a model country. We had slavery, child labor, and a tremendous imbalance of wealth. People worked like dogs. The Russians freed the serfs before we freed the slaves, something to remember in the course of history.

The sun broke through the gray for the first time. You don't see much sun around this place. Gray city, gray sky. However, the people are not as gray as I imagine they once were. They cannot be, if they are sniffing freedom and capitalism, and they are.

Then the delegation visited Andrei Dmitrievich Sakharov, in his small apartment. An eminent Soviet nuclear physicist who spent two decades designing nuclear weapons, Sakharov was regarded as the father of the Soviet nuclear bomb, contributing perhaps more than anyone else to the military might of his country. Over time, he became a political dissident and human rights activist. Sakharov had been awarded the Nobel Peace Prize in 1975. He died eighteen months after Simpson met him.

Sakharov was in exile in the closed city of Gorky and returned to Moscow December 8, 1986. No phone. Living starkly. Said that one day a man came to install a phone. The next day Gorbachev called him and said, "You are free."

Wife is Yelena Bonner [born Elena Georgievna Alikhanov in 1923], a very activist lady. Their apartment is on the seventh floor. Rickety old elevator. We walked up, and were told this was an average apartment. It was really beat up, scuffmarks and chipped concrete. A lot of mileage on that old baby. You could tell that many people had beaten a path to that door.

We all sat there that gray day while he said they were looking toward progress. He thinks America's development of SDI [Space Defense Initiative] is very dangerous. I think the old gentleman might be a philosopher. He is a man rather fearful of the world's future. Who isn't? He said in matters like this we can only go "all the way" toward peace.

On a snow bank across from the door of the apartment [building] was a burly looking guy with a huge boxer dog on a leash. He was just staring right at the door. Gave me the creeps.

The next three days were filled with meetings on issues ranging from refugee problems to the INF treaty, and entertainment that included a performance at the Moscow Circus and a visit to a cooperative restaurant:

> [It's] an example of free enterprise starting up. Their government is making it difficult. There is no owned property in the Soviet Union. People can run a restaurant, but they can't buy any food from the State. Tough for them to operate. They have to give five percent of their profit to the State, but have to find somewhere else to buy their food. Moreover, they cannot sell wine or beer. They have dried up the joint. Might be okay. The stuff I tried tasted like goat piss.

A visit to the Space Research Institute was particularly revealing—and getting there was exhilarating and frightening.

Caught one of the official cars that had been furnished to us with drivers. I can tell you that I now believe in reincarnation. Barney Oldfield [a pioneering race car driver who once held the world speed record of 60 mph on an oval track] is alive and well in the person of the driver of car number two. . . . He is a steely-jawed, serious guy who drives like a madman. He really is nuts.

The Space Research Institute of the U.S.S.R. Academy of Sciences. Technical things about arms and arms control and verification. . . . They do a lot of military planning in this shabby building. It really is just beat to hell. This crew put Sputnik into space in 1957 and changed the course of history.

Saw a replica of Sputnik. . . . Little bigger than an oversized basketball—but wow, when they put that baby up it made us wonder, in our high-powered nation, where the hell we had been. We went on a technological surge and have been racing for the moon ever since—both countries.

You see the building where these scientists work, all the things in a gray atmosphere with heaters just lying around and debris inside, and the snow and cold and ice outside, and chipped tiles and plaster falling and holes in the walls and toilets that are forty-five years old. . . . Shitty looking area, but marvelous people—solid, tough, resilient people with great good humor and very brilliant. Remember where all the great chess players in the world are from. You know why, after spending five days here. . . .

One scientist said, "We make five times more tractors, so if we are talking about balance and symmetry between our countries, here it is. You produce five times more grain." They like black humor and get a big bang out of it. . . .

They have a huge nation of 270 million people across twelve time zones. With everything they have, they still see little countries like Singapore and South Korea producing more and making more. They see Japan, a country that spends hardly a nickel on defense or hardware, and it is a rich nation. This is where they are turning the corner with perestroika and glasnost.

Talking about openness, one said, "Now that we have glasnost, we have the right to show that we have stupid people on our side. We have long known about yours." He said that in a kindly way. . . .

Now that glasnost has come about, people are finally willing to talk. Papers are carrying things about Stalin. What he did must have been grotesque.

Over to the fusion research laboratory, where they are working on a superconductor. This will put them up to the hundreds of millions of degrees inside—and yet the outer cavern would be about four degrees, all within a space of 18 inches. With that kind of temperature change, a guy could catch a cold.

Asked many questions about Chernobyl. Asked why they didn't drop the control rods down into the critical core. The reason was that they were manually controlled and they didn't dream the thing would explode. They said they didn't know much about "fallout." The international community has been tough as hell on them. They didn't need much criticism from us. They just said that everything that happened there was "surprising."

There is no way to describe this day, seeing these amazingly bright people, the kind who shape history and move nations, working in conditions where if OSHA ever walked into the building they would crap a brick. Wires hanging out of the wall, toilets looking like something out of the nineteenth century. They were just old piss pots in the corner, practically. All the stuff around them, the plastic, wire, paper, windows, everything was coarse, harsh, and tough. . . .

Driving back through the suburbs, the grayness of it all. The whiter the snow, the grayer the buildings. Low-slung people standing in queues to buy groceries, standing on the street patiently. People walking everywhere with those heavy boots and those great fur hats and scarves and gloves, and women out with their prams and babies, and life goes on. . . .

Light snow falling. I remembered they didn't turn the lights off along the beautiful little walkway along the street down to the metro station, so I walked out the door by myself and walked a half hour on the streets of Moscow. Walked along a path lighted with old lamps. Fascinating. A bit romantic, but not in the glandular way. Just a lovely walk in the light snow, in the gray-black night of Moscow. . . .

The Kremlin

We got into our cars and headed into the Kremlin, the inner sanctum. The rooms were the most opulent I have seen in any country. I wonder what Lenin and his ragged band would have thought of that in 1917. A magnificent hall.

Gorbachev visited with each one of us for a moment. He recognized me and said it was nice to see me again. He looked very fit—quite ruddy and even almost tanned. Very bright eyes. He seemed quite relaxed and was wearing a dark brown suit and a striped gray brown muted-orange tie, a tan shirt, silver and large horn-rimmed glasses. He looked quite confident.

Al Cranston opened on our side with excellent remarks, and asked a few questions. Gorbachev was not too responsive. He told a joke that I did not get at all. He did say, "Thank God we have debate and discussion in our country." He used the phrase "thank God" three times. We had a very extensive conversation about arms and nuclear treaties. All spoke, then I spoke. They wanted me to be last.

I told him that I saw him as a man of great good humor. I also said I felt a certain kinship because we were the same age. I said how much Ann and I had enjoyed his wife, Raisa, and that there was a phrase in the U.S.A. suggesting that we had both "over married." He smiled at that.

I said that I admired him as a spirited person who came at things head on. I said I wanted him to know that I represent Wyoming—the state that houses the MX missile. There are twenty-one missiles with 210 warheads. . . .

War would create the destruction of my state. All of those instruments in my state are aimed right here, and yours are aimed right at Wyoming." There were several nods at that. I said:

> We have another issue here that confronts us, and as you like to talk about things, let's talk about Central America. We cannot ignore the interests of Central America any more than you can ignore the interests of Europeans. Daffy Danny Ortega is bad business for us. He wants a six-hundred-thousand-man army. That disturbs us greatly. It does not make things any easier for us when you support Ortega.
>
> We can be ornery and you can be ornery, but the important thing is that at least when we are arguing, we are communicating. The worst thing would be to give each other the ice treatment. It doesn't work in relationships, and it doesn't work for countries.

I said that if he had a screwball like Ortega that close to him, he would be alarmed and irritated.

I said that we have signed the INF treaty, but it does not mean anything until it is ratified. I said that two things can make the progress start on all these other issues. "We'll get the INF treaty ratified . . . and you get out of Afghanistan."

Later, I asked if he is going to get out of Nicaragua. He said, "Well, yes, of course, but we would also be there to be sure that we help them with just enough arms to police their country, and if they had rifles they would be using them only for defensive purposes."

I said, "Hey, pal! Those are not for defensive purposes. I come from Wyoming. In our in our part of the country, 'gun control' is just how steady you can hold your rifle."

Later I spoke about other countries, advising him to let

the Afghans form their own government. Then he really got sarcastic. This is what he said.

> Don't tell us about your shining temple on the hill. That one does not sound good. We know what really goes on in your country, and we know that the turmoil that is springing up around the world is often created by *you*. You have your own problems. You look at us, but it is you burning fires in the west that keeps us concerned, all in the guise of human rights. You are always talking about human rights, but you are fanning those fires.

When Senator Levin [who is Jewish] spoke about the Refuseniks and anti-Semitism, Gorbachev had this response: "Those are the kind of people who stay in this country so they can linger and make more problems. That is so very transparent. We know who they are. They are the same people who for centuries held control over our economy and other fields."

I said to Gorbachev, "Well, since we are talking about refugees, I have a question. Why did you release the Armenians? There are nine thousand of them in the pipeline [to come to the United States], one thousand a month, overwhelming our systems. Why?"

That triggered him too. He said that people are always trying to make Russia look bad, and that we have plenty of problems ourselves, and he was tired of [the discussion]. He said, "It was you and your Congress that erected economic barriers that make it difficult for us—you people in the shining temple on the hill."

About the only thing he didn't say was "Bah, and to hell with you." It was fascinating. Then he got down to some pretty excitable stuff, as we talked about Afghanistan. This is what he said.

> What is *your* policy there? You have given us more problems, and now you want *us* to do it differently. We are trying to do

it, and you do not want to keep your part of the bargain. You said originally you did not care what form of government was left there if we withdrew. Now we are ready to withdraw and you are asking what form of government will be left.

Our position [on Afghanistan] is cloudy and it does not come through clearly. I really did want to assure him that we would not withdraw our aid to the Afghan resistance unless the Soviets get the hell out of there. We are not going to let them do it piece by piece. We both leave simultaneously.

It was a spirited exchange all around. Other people spoke, and then Gorbachev responded: "We have serious business to do here. But I am optimistic. I have a new feeling of realism. The path is not an easy one. We are only taking the very first small steps. We have many problems on the path. Great reserves of patience are needed. We are different, we are not alike. Our interests may vary. I receive letters from America, from young people."

It sounded like Reagan. He said, "One letter from America said, 'You have lived. Let us live a little bit too. Make our world free of peril.'"

Before the meeting was over, Gorbachev said this: "It is the right of every nation to have its own choice. If it is socialism, then let them live it. If it is capitalism, then let them do that. Do not try to impose your standards and form of government on others. . . . But we can interact and borrow from each other—technology, exchange, challenges—and share with each other about environmental threats."

That was the first time I heard him talk about environmental anything. Moscow is one great mass of pollution. . . .

Al Cranston thanked Gorbachev and said it had been a most extraordinary visit. Indeed, it had—three hours and fifteen minutes' worth. He came around the table and met each one of us personally. When he came to me, he said, "I much appreciated what you said, and the way you said it.

The leaders of our countries must have frank discussions like this—and I did not recall you were from Wyoming, where the MX Missile is."

The next day, the group was ready to go home.

March 12, 1988: I will see Ann, and relate the extraordinary adventure. Indeed, it was very, very lovely—invigorating, spirited, hopeful. I feel very hopeful that we can get the job done so we don't blast our asses to kingdom come, with Wyoming contributing the hardware to do it and ending up as the "nuclear sponge" in the process. That would not be great for the state my father has always called "the land of high altitude and low multitude."

I will bust my ass the rest of my days to see that that does not take place.

Chapter Ten

THE VP THING

~

AL SIMPSON WAS flattered by a growing wave of speculation that if George Bush won the Republican nomination for president, he might become Bush's vice presidential running mate—and he was eager to kill the idea in its tracks. He had just delivered a speech when reporter Marianne Means, who had recently published a syndicated piece suggesting that he should be on the ticket, approached. "Marianne," he told her, "I wouldn't worry about that. Remember, I have spent the past nine years punching brands on just about every sacred cow in America!"

It was true. His personal mission had consistently been to drag one powerful special interest group after another away from the federal trough. No presidential candidate would benefit from a running mate who made a point of telling people what government should not be doing for them; he never dreamed that more than two decades later a Democratic president would appoint him co-chair of a commission empowered to do just that as part of its proposal to reduce ballooning federal debt.

The latest example involved veterans. At the Government Affairs Committee, Simpson spoke in opposition to a Cabinet position for veterans' affairs. "I think it is just wrong," he said. "What is next, a Cabinet position for women, for aging, for youth, for the disadvantaged? Bah!"

As a former military serviceman and former chair of the Senate Veterans' Affairs Committee, he was well aware that the budget for veterans' programs was $30 billion. He considered this a sizeable sum for 27 million veterans. "They'll chop my shorts off, but I'll keep steady on the course," he said after the 1988 hearing. (The

Obama Administration's 2010 budget request for veterans was $113 billion. According to the Bureau of Labor Statistics, the 1988 equivalent of this would be approximately $62 billion. Thus, in "constant dollars," the cost of veterans' programs more than doubled during that period. A significant portion of this increase is attributable to the increased number of veterans qualifying for benefits.)

At a town hall meeting in Wyoming, a man noted the size of the federal debt and condescendingly asked what was so difficult about budgeting. Simpson spoke a few moments about the American culture of "entitlement" and then cut loose on his inquisitor.

> I said, "It is when somebody gets up in the back of a senior citizens center and raises hell about the deficit—and they are paying only a dollar and a quarter for [a subsidized] lunch, even though they have a cabin in the Snowy Range and a home in Sun City and could easily be paying five dollars. *That* is what's so damn difficult about the federal budget."
>
> Two people walked out of the meeting and drove right to the senior citizens center—to rat on me.

LIFE IN THE FAST LANE

The next morning, time got away from Simpson at a breakfast meeting while President Reagan and a group of congressional leaders sat around a table at the White House awaiting his arrival. "I was fifteen minutes late for the president. I felt like an idiot. My chair, the one on the president's immediate right, was empty. I leaned over to the president while someone else was talking and said, 'I'm a wretched bastard. I'm sorry I'm late.'" Reagan turned and said, "I know it." It was not clear which part of Simpson's comment he was referencing.

Later in the meeting Al joked that he was not quite sure why he was again late, but it reminded him of one night when the Senate was holding a vote open, pending the arrival of an absent Republican senator. "The wayward one called Dole and said, 'I'm on my way, I'm at Ninth and Constitution.' Later he called back and said, 'I'm coming. Now I'm at Thirteenth and Constitution.' Robert Byrd asked,

'Where is your colleague now?' Dole said, 'Lost, but he is making good time.'" Since the president laughed, Al knew all was well.

> It was one of the funniest meetings we have had in a long time. Maybe it was spring in the air. The temperature was about sixty-five. It was a lovely morning with a beautiful blue sky. There were crocuses and plantings outside the Cabinet Room window.
>
> I think how remarkably fortunate I am to have been in that room dozens of times, sitting one or two seats from the president of the United States for an hour or two. Ann and I ate dinner and I didn't even mention my fascinating morning with the president. I'm not jaded, just busy.

Dole Returns

The next day, Al arrived at the Capitol to find Senate Republican Leader Bob Dole back from the campaign trail.

> Sheila Burke [Dole's senior staffer] came in about 12:15 and said that Bob would like to talk with me. When I went back into his private quarters, he spoke to me about his campaign. This is what he said.

>> I appreciate what you have done. You have done a great job as acting leader. I am not going to Policy Lunch, and I'm not going to stay very active in things during the rest of this week. But at three o'clock, I am going over to the Dirksen Caucus Room and pull the plug on my presidential candidacy.

> He seemed very direct and matter of fact. I said, "Well, I understand. I am sure it is tough for you, I'm sure it is painful."

>> Yeah, but I've given it a lot of thought and it is what I need to do. Please tell them [the GOP senators] that at three o'clock I would like them to drop by, if they want to. I hope a lot of them would.
>> I realize fully that there could have been a "palace coup" while I was out on the road, but you held everything together and I really appreciate it.

I told him we got a lot done and that I am ready to do a lot more. [I said] it was nice to have him back in the bosom of his Senate family.

Far from anything resembling a palace coup—Simpson undermining Dole in his own quest for the top leadership position—Simpson told the Republican senators at lunch that serving as their acting leader had been a great experience. He thanked them for their help and said it had been a "hell of a lot of fun." He again pledged loyalty to Dole, and asked everyone to show up at three o'clock. "I sat down and they clapped for quite a lengthy time. I loved it. Then dear old Strom Thurmond said, 'Alan, you have had a lot of good practice. The next time that job [Republican leader] comes open, you'll be it.'"

Russian Treasures

Al's presence in government's inner circle would soon provide additional rewarding moments. Not long after Dole's announcement, Simpson learned that ten senators were planning an official trip to the Soviet Union. Even though he had just returned from Moscow, he asked delegation leader Bennett Johnston if he and Ann could join the group. "I said, 'Got room?' He said, 'Yes, another senator dropped out.' Ann has never been to the Soviet Union and, of course, I am an old hand there, having just returned two weeks ago. So, here we go. We'll go to Leningrad, Kiev, and then to Moscow."

The Simpsons were especially enthusiastic about touring the Hermitage Museum in Leningrad (now St. Petersburg). "I've been waiting a lifetime to see that. We are so excited," Al said. It was a long flight on a military plane, but finally they were there.

[We] headed off to the Hermitage and were stunned by what we saw. There is no possible way to describe that museum. We saw just a small part of it. We hardly had time to look at the French Impressionists, the items I had wanted so long to see.

We were on official business and scheduled for another stop, so we said we would come back tomorrow—and tomorrow didn't get done. I really feel rather cheated, and I did it to myself. I did see a great deal, the beautiful rooms, the clocks, and the treasures that abound. There are fifteen miles there—that's right, fifteen *miles*—of galleries in four separate buildings. No way to describe it, really no way.

The next morning the delegation flew to Kiev and spent the rest of the day in meetings. Then they flew to Moscow, where they were advised that the government's top officials, with whom they were most eager to meet, were not available. Mikhail Gorbachev had flown to Afghanistan. Some Politburo members, the people who were "too busy and old" to visit America, had accompanied him. As a result, the American delegation met with knowledgeable but lower ranking officials.

Nixon's Suggestion

After nine days in the Soviet Union the delegation flew home. Their plane touched down at Andrews Air Force Base on Sunday morning, April 10, 1988. Al and Ann went home, where they turned on the television just in time to see former president Richard Nixon on NBC's *Meet the Press*. He was telling the nation that if George Bush became the Republican presidential nominee, he might find Al Simpson a good choice for vice president.

I was standing in the kitchen in my exercise clothes and must admit that I got a big bang out of that. I even slapped my thigh and let out a little whoop, as you do at a basketball game. Ann was watching it on the other set downstairs and shouted up, "Did you see *that?*"

We talked—for not more than three minutes—about how that kind of thing [serving as vice president] would change your life in ways you would not want to happen. Besides, it would never happen anyway. I am a legislator and I love my work. It was a hell of a nice honor, though, to have that mentioned by the former president.

Al and Ann slept for nine hours and were just up and running the next morning when the phone rang. Vice President Bush told the latest joke and asked Al to join him and a small group of friends on a fishing trip to Florida in two weeks' time. When Bush mentioned that legendary baseball star Ted Williams would be joining them, Al was thrilled. "I said, 'George, that is a convincer right there—not you, but *Ted Williams!*'" He set off for his office to clear the date.

Before that trip, five Simpsons—Al, Ann, Colin, Bill and Bill's wife Debbie—flew to New York, where they all chatted with former President Nixon. After the others took their leave, the two principals conversed for an hour about the future of the Soviet Union in general and leader Mikhail Gorbachev in particular.

Nixon was fascinated that I had spent about eight and a half hours with Gorbachev in the past five months. He was interested in my impressions, and listened carefully. I listened to him, too.

Nixon and I spoke about the need to keep the lines of communication open, and agreed that perestroika will work. I related what Gorbachev had said about Afghanistan.

Turning to domestic politics, Nixon suggested that even though Simpson was not interested in the vice presidency, he should not publicly reject the suggestion. "Having your name in the mix would create more public interest in the campaign, right up to the nominating convention in New Orleans," he said. Simpson understood, but emphasized that he had no interest in the job.

In 2008 Al's son Bill described his own experience with Nixon that day: "He was friendly and jovial. We took photographs and he sprinkled the conversations with some 'God damns' and 'What is this crap?' and so forth. He was truly a political presence. No matter how anybody felt about Richard Nixon, he got in the arena and he fought the fight, and he kept fighting right up until the final days. He was, pro or con, a fascinating guy. Meeting him was an amazing opportunity."

Fun in the Sun

Al's trip to Florida with Vice President Bush and friends was one of the personal highlights of his career. Afterward, he logged the experience.

> Met [in Miami] by a Bush Secret Service agent and an advance person. We drove to Islamorada and up to a private condominium complex on the Florida Keys, about midway down.
>
> In one condominium was Nick Brady, the former senator from New Jersey. His room was across the hall from me. George's was upstairs. In the other condominium units were George's friends Fred Zeder and Fonsie O'Brien. O'Brien is from Shannon, Ireland. Also, there was Burt Lee, White House doctor and famed chemotherapy specialist. He is chairing the AIDS commission.
>
> We had a nice wine and ate stone crabs and shrimp balls that were beautifully prepared. We sat around and talked. I finally said, "I can't hit the sack after eating like that. I'm going to go take a walk."
>
> George said, "I'll go with you."

Secret service agents formed a protective phalanx front and rear as the two walked down the main highway at 10:30 at night.

> We walked about a half mile, to an old war memorial along the side of the highway. During our return, George decided he would campaign a little. We knocked on the door of one house, then went into the rear of an old restaurant and chatted with the help there. We went back and hit the sack about 11:30.
>
> Up early, we took a forty-five-minute trip out into the Gulf of Mexico. You think you are way out there in the high seas. But when you stop, the mud is about eighteen inches below the boat. Damnedest thing I have ever seen. Those are the flats where the bonefish frolic. I fished that morning with Fonsie O'Brien. Did more storytelling than fishing, but I did lay into some smaller game fish of various varieties.

We all rendezvoused out on the high seas, on the big boat. We had a marvelous box lunch, told some war stories, and drank a lot of soft drinks, no booze. . . .

The guide said to be careful, because those damn tarpon could come out of the water and knock you down. . . . By God, a tarpon surfaced about seven yards away from me and practically went right over the top of the boat in a whirling, splashing dive. Made a believer out of me—and Bush and all the rest of us.

Headed back at four in the afternoon and George played tennis with Ted Williams—yes, *Ted Williams*! He is the greatest baseball player who ever lived, in my mind. He batted 406 in one season, with a lifetime batting average around 344. He missed three years due to the Korean War and never bitched a bit. What a guy. What a special privilege and pleasure it was to meet him, a boyhood dream come true.

Simpson made a special point of logging what he and Bush did not mention.

The next morning, we talked about a lot of things, but never the vice presidency. It does not come up. I do not aspire to it. Our friendship is such that it just is not something to talk about. It is absurd. I do not want to do it. He couldn't afford to have me on the ticket. If he did, people would go back into the *Congressional Record* where I had punched the lights out of veterans, the notch babies, the crybabies, and the Social Security babies.[1]

They swam and then packed their gear. With other traffic blocked in order to clear their way, the group was driven to a military airfield about thirty miles away.

We smuggled some key lime pies, hopped aboard *Air Force Two* and headed for Andrews Air Force Base. We had a nice dinner on the aircraft and visited with each other. George finished his book about Lyndon Johnson. He gave me the copy and said it was the damnedest, most fascinating thing he ever read.

He is now ready to head out on the road again. We demand a tough and awesome job out of people who seek the presidency. He is up for it and is not at all spooked by it. He even said that if he lost, it would not change his life. He seems competent, calm and ready to go. He is behind in the polls now but seems to be calling his own shots.

It was such fun in every way. My gut aches from the good, ribald laughter.

VP? ME?

Back in Washington, Simpson found himself increasingly frustrated over the treatment Nancy Reagan was receiving at the hands of former White House chief of staff Don Regan, who had written a book about his experiences. It focused on his undignified departure from his job and characterized Mrs. Reagan as an overly protective and manipulative woman. Al was told that two people who shared lunch with the first lady the day Regan's book came out described her as "devastated."

Simpson, a man with a propensity to defend those he considered unfairly attacked, drafted the outline of a newspaper opinion article about Nancy Reagan. He phoned Meg Greenfield, editorial page editor at the *Washington Post*—who had earlier urged him to write a piece in defense of Nancy—to gauge whether the timing was right. Encouraged by her response, he fine-tuned it and sent it to her. On May 13, 1988, his article ran in a prime location on the editorial page. It read, in part:

> Nancy Reagan always seems to get a bum rap in the "tattle-tale" book business. She deserves a hell of a lot better. . . .
>
> She took on a tough job that has no definitions but many demands. She has fulfilled her obligations and her duties to her country and to her husband with great grace, class and distinction. . . .
>
> The bottom line of the latest catty little revelation is that she is protective of her husband, who just happens to be the

president. She is accused of unquestioned devotion and loyalty to Ronald Reagan. Egad, what will people think?

But the issue is not now "Don Regan's book," it is apparently Nancy Reagan's activities. How ironic to see two fine men whom I have known—Larry Speakes and Don Regan—bring themselves down to a lesser level by spewing out these rather vengeful portrayals. Their luster leaves their personalities as the bluster leaves their pens. . . .

Nancy didn't drive Don Regan out. There were a lot of people lined up in the batter's box to do just that. . . .

In this goldfish bowl of Washington (and it's odd how many sharks can get into a goldfish bowl), Nancy Reagan has put her own distinctive and unique trademark on the role of the first lady. . . .

How sad that anyone would be titillated by what is really a vengeful portrayal of a beautiful lady.

The president phoned at 11:00 that morning. "We spoke for seven or eight minutes about the article and he said how much he appreciated it. We talked about Nancy, and the president spoke about Don Regan, how vindictive he was. He couldn't believe how Regan had turned on Nancy." Three hours later Nancy called. "Boy, I needed that," she said. The first lady described how difficult it had been to face Regan's onslaught and emphasized again that she had never participated in any attempt to "get him." During their ten-minute chat, Al noted the depth of her pain. "She really is a very fragile and lovely lady. I told her it was a rich pleasure to have done that piece in the *Post*, and that it had come from the bosom. It was a good visit."

Whatever Suits Reagan

The next day at a White House meeting, Al noted that while the president was in good form, "he was wearing a ghastly *brown* suit—and Al Cranston was wearing the same."

The president told the story about Soviet Foreign Minister
Andrei Gromyko, who had died and gone to heaven. Saint
Peter said, "Well, you can't come in here, but I'll give you a
choice down in Hell. You can go to the Communist Hell or
the Capitalist Hell."

Gromyko said, "I'll go to the Communist Hell."

Saint Peter said, "Fine, but I'll frankly tell you, the Capitalist's Hell is a little better, and it's more comfortable."

Gromyko said, "I'll still take the Communist Hell. The
heating system there can't last that long."

Al enjoyed his frequent meetings with the president and regretted that Reagan's second and last term would soon end. His diaries indicate that if he was critical of anything about the president, it
was Reagan's propensity to wear brown suits. After another meeting
he wrote, "The president was fitted in a *mocha* suit—the damnedest
brown color. He *loves* those." After yet another, he recorded, "The
president was perched up there again in one of those brown suits. He
looked washed out."

Reagan was anything but washed out as he spoke of his upcoming trip to finalize the defense treaties. He was doing it over opposition from an aggressive anti-communist member of his own party,
Senator Jesse Helms. Senator Dole suggested to Reagan that perhaps
Helms could go with him.

Reagan laughed and said, "Maybe he will ride along—on the
wing!"

"The *right* wing," suggested Chief of Staff Baker.

Al noted later that Reagan was "gnawing on his fingernail, and
I hadn't seen him do that before." He speculated that the president
was apprehensive about the trip.

Guessing Game

At a conference for journalists and members of Congress, NBC television anchor Tom Brokaw speculated about who the Republicans

might select as their vice presidential candidate. "It might come down to Bush just picking Dole," he said. "But if he doesn't pick Dole, he might go for Lamar Alexander. Or he might well go for that man sitting right there on the edge of the room, Al Simpson."

Al smiled at the recognition but shook his head in the negative and gave a "thumbs down" to the suggestion. "I can't imagine changing my life to accommodate that kind of schedule," he told his diary that night. He had no trouble imagining how his assaults on sacred cows would go over in a presidential campaign. Veterans provided a case in point: out in Wyoming, he had the feeling that those gathered to meet with him in an American Legion hall thought him evil, since he was opposed to the creation of a Cabinet-level position for veterans' affairs.

> They were waiting for me—lying in wait. I just threw away my notes and said, "Look, we are a very generous nation. I am not trying to be defensive, but I don't have to take a lot of guff about my role for American veterans."
>
> I told them that while I was trying to kill off the Cabinet position bill, I was also trying to pass a Judicial Review bill for veterans' claims. I said it seemed to me that most veterans, although perhaps not the "professional veterans," would like to have a review of their claims and ratings, and they could have that through a judicial review.

Still, he knew it would be hard to stop the movement toward a Cabinet position for veterans. Once that ball was rolling, anyone opposing it would be seen as anti-veteran, perhaps even anti-American. The radical increase in funding for veterans' programs under Simpson's reign as a member and chair of the Veterans' Committee apparently meant little to his audience.

> One man in the back of the room said he thought the thing that was wrong with Washington was that there were too many guys who are assholes—guys like *me*. I said, "Yes, *I'm* the asshole who got you the $750,000 veterans' cemetery. *I'm*

the asshole responsible for the $14 million expansion at the VA hospital in Cheyenne. *I'm* the asshole who got the changes at the Sheridan Veterans' Hospital—all things you people *wanted!*"

Others in the room hooted the heckler into silence. In an about-face, one conventioneer said, "We want to express appreciation for your coming here. We admire the way you represent Wyoming."

Diversions

The following Saturday included a refreshing and rare change. Having no official business to conduct, Al worked on piles of paperwork in his office and home and took a break in the afternoon to play basketball. "I cleaned up some of that damn crap in my office and even cleaned my desk. Then I went over to a sporting goods store and bought myself a basketball. There is a court near my house. I worked up a hell of a sweat. It was ninety degrees. I came back and plowed through a ton of stuff and feel I have a better handle on the crap in the den than I've had in many years."

On July 1, 1988, as other Republicans and Democrats across the nation were enthusiastically demeaning and berating one another in advance of the coming elections, the Simpsons were spending time with Democratic senator Bill Bradley and his wife Ernestine at Barnegat Light, New Jersey. "The Fish and Wildlife Service took us over to some of the estuaries and nesting grounds. Fascinating, the terns and some other kind of gull. It was quite a thrill. There are great nests not far from shore. There were people all over the place, and yet here was this gentle sanctuary for birds."

That evening, partisanship was nowhere in sight as the four sat around the dinner table for nearly three hours, dining on swordfish steaks prepared by the other tall senator. Bradley was not quite as tall as Simpson—although the matter was not settled until some-time later in a Senate hearing room, when I asked them to stand back to back for a measurement.

Harkin

Simpson was soon back in the Senate locking horns, this time with Tom Harkin of Iowa. "Harkin kept us up late last night with his antics. He gummed up everything so badly that I don't think he could untangle it. He grinds my rump," Al groused. At one point Democrat Harkin let loose with what Simpson felt was a "blatant display of nastiness." The Wyoming senator gained his attention a few minutes later, out of microphone range, and the two had it out.

"You haven't learned *anything* here, as far as I have observed," Simpson told Harkin. "You don't know about comity or even cooperation with your own leader. You moved to table *him* two times. Then you called Barry Goldwater a poop. And you labor in conflict of interest. I want to tell you something very clearly—you are an *asshole*."

Simpson thought Harkin might come at him physically. Instead, the Iowan said he felt Simpson too might be an asshole. In fact, he was quite sure of it.

Senator Byrd observed the exchange with bemusement before suggesting that the two refrain from addressing each other in so undignified a manner. Al later described the exchange to his diary. "I unloaded a lot of old stuff on Harkin, and I haven't the slightest regret. Old Harkin's eyes were spouting fire. He mumbled and smirked and laid a couple of good verbal shots on me and left the chamber. I'll have to visit with him sometime and find out why I allow myself to be so pissed off at that dude."

Later, he did just that. "I met with him with regard to the blowout the two of us had on the Senate floor a few days ago. It was a good visit. I went to Tom's office, and I feel much better about him. I noted that I had called him an asshole. A man ought to apologize for something like that—at least every once in a while." Long after his retirement from the Senate, Simpson attended a dinner for retiring senators.

It was fascinating. Harkin was at the retirement dinner in Washington. I went up and said, "Tom, remember how you and I just thought we were a couple of horses' asses, and one night it was late and we were debating and I said, 'You are really a prick!'"

He said, "Yes, and I remember that you were a smart ass."

That ended whatever it was between us. I think we were too much alike—smooth, passionate—and you learn in life that if you see some trait in somebody else that really, really pisses you off, it is something you do yourself but don't deal with. That is life.

Sparring with Spence

The three members of the Wyoming congressional delegation met occasionally with nationally recognized attorney Gerry Spence of Jackson, Wyoming. During one session, Spence, not one to lose an argument without a scrap—or at all—came nose to nose with Senator Malcolm Wallop, who was not hesitant to characterize Spence's position and attitude as "horseshit." Afterward, Simpson described the scene.

> Malcolm was magnificent, as Spence laid it on about how powerful this delegation is, and how skilled, and how he knew we could cut the mustard [on this request], and the whole works. Malcolm said, "That's not what you said about me last year, or about us, when you called us the 'three stooges.' You said that I was one of the most inept and irresponsible senators we have ever had."
>
> Old Gerry loves a good scrap. He just put his head back and laughed—but he knew he had been hammered.

On another occasion Spence, wearing his trademark fringed western coat and hat, came to Simpson's office. Behind closed doors the two fell into a raucous and angry-sounding exchange. Staffers gathered outside the door, eager to hear the increasingly loud and profane discussion between two legal titans. Years later, just after his seventy-fifth birthday, Simpson laughed while describing their skirmish but was concerned that people unfamiliar with their unique relationship might not perceive the depth of their mutual respect.

He came in and I said, "Are you going to take off your big hat and big coat and talk about the 'little people?'"

He said, "No, Al, I came in to talk about how you sold your soul to a bunch of fuckin' corporate toadies—how you have become, instead of the defender of the Wyoming life we love, you have become a slave to the boardrooms of America."

I said, "Really? Tell me more about all the 'little people' who have paid you money so you can fly around in your Aero Commander!"

It just built. We were both chuckling inside, because it was "theater," it just was. It must have been ten minutes of that heavy battering and sarcastic commentary before he jumped up and hit the table and said, "God damn you, you son of a bitch! Do you know what I'm going to do right now?"

I said, "What could you possibly do that would be more offensive than the chickenshit I've been listening to?"

He said, "I'm going to take a God damned quarter and I'm going to go down to that God damned candy machine and I'm going to buy a candy bar! And then I'm going to cut it in half—and you, you chickenshit, are going to eat half of it and I'm going to eat the other half!"

He got up and left. It was just bizarre. There is no way to describe it. Nobody who witnessed it would ever understand it.

Spence left, returned, closed the door on Simpson's stunned staff, and resumed the debate. The eavesdroppers were appalled, unable to perceive the respect the two lawyers hold for each other to this day.

On one occasion, Spence kissed Simpson.

He *kissed* me on the forehead. People said, "God, did you see *that*?"

Spence said, "I just wanted to kiss the crowning head of a man with an intellect."

I said, "Just get out of here, for God's sake. Take your big coat and your big hat and *go*."

In 1962 Spence, then a Republican, had run unsuccessfully against incumbent William Henry Harrison for Wyoming's sole seat in Congress. He lost decisively but remained interested in elective office. When another possibility presented itself, he phoned Al.

> Gerry called me at home one night and said, "Al, I want the honest, no bullshit answer. How would I do in the Senate?"
>
> I said, "You'd die here. You would die. You would get up, thinking you were talking to a jury of twelve, and you would be talking to a jury of ninety-nine people who wouldn't give one shit what you were talking about, because you would be using high drama. And the workload is beyond anything."

Spence scoffed that it could not be beyond trial work. Al had a ready reply.

> You love trial work. I love this work. You wouldn't like this work any more than I like doing trial work all day long. So let me get the romance out of it for you. Do you know what I am doing right now, Gerry? Ann is in Wyoming and I am here at home. I just got here and I am going to go up to my den and work until about two-fuckin'-o-clock in the morning. I will be piecing shit together for a staff that feeds me that stuff all day long. When I go home on the plane, I get a hernia from hauling these fucking papers.
>
> Gerry, your ego is as big as mine, but you are used to seeing results and human responses—at the moment. You will never get that here. You will go crazy. You will be one of a hundred. You can be flamboyant, you can be you, but that won't get you where you are going. It won't work.

Long after Spence dropped the idea and Simpson retired from the Senate, the two met with former Wyoming governor Mike Sullivan, whom Spence had also once asked for political advice. Spence put his arms around his friends and said, "These two bastards saved my life. They sobered me up. I got sober when I quit the booze, then these guys got me off the booze of politics." The Simpson-Spence relationship demonstrates an ability to disagree forcefully without ever severing a relationship.

Continued Speculation

The cloud of partisan wrangling grew ever denser as the political conventions drew near. The funnel swirling closest to Al was a perception that regardless of his private and public denials, he might be named George Bush's running mate. On the morning of July 24, 1988, the Simpsons' home phone rang. "Up early, a call at home from George Bush. He said that a man was going to contact me about "this vice presidential thing." I said I would visit with him. I assumed that we would be discussing those various persons who would be considered for vice president—and that I would be helping in the process. I found out that I was wrong."

Simpson was visited by the vice president's assistant, who asked his authorization for a complete background check, just in case Bush selected him as the GOP vice presidential candidate. Initially, Simpson balked. Yet he did not want to refuse Bush's personal request that he at least be "in the mix," since it would build public interest in the coming Republican convention in New Orleans.

Vexed, Al sought counsel from his Wyoming congressional colleagues Malcolm Wallop and Dick Cheney. Both felt he should provide the requested documentation. Then he spoke with Bob Dole. "I told Bob I was not interested in being vice president, but that I was interested in seeing him, Dole, become the vice presidential candidate. I expressed my total support to Bob and told him about Bush's request that I fill out the forms. He thought it was important and necessary that I do so." Senator Nancy Kassebaum was also on the Bush list. Dole thought she too should grant permission for a complete background check. That evening Simpson spoke again with Bush.

George called about seven in the evening. I told him I did
not want to be vice president. I said I felt free in expressing
that, although I intended to fill out the forms. George said he
hoped I would do that.

I said I was flatly and openly recommending that he select
Bob Dole. I thought Bob would do a hell of a job as vice president. George was very high on Bob, but said that for now he
was going to leave it open. I told him that was fine, but also
that I did not see any possibility of my being on the ticket.

Al did concede to Bush, "It would be fun to ride the same horse
together." Still, he emphasized, his participation as the candidate for
vice president could only hurt his friend's chance of being elected
president. He told his diary that if his friends George Bush and Bob
Dole were elected president and vice president, the Senate Republican leadership post would open up, and he would seek it: "That
would make for a powerful combination. I could carry the lum-
ber for the Republicans in the Senate, and with Bush and Dole in
the White House, we could make progress in this country in seven
league boots. That is the only part that gets my excitement going."

Simpson completed the forms, but when it came to signing them
before a notary in his office the next day, he was again torn. He
turned to the vice president's assistant in charge of background checks
and said, "What is it about the word *no* that you don't understand?"

The aide replied, "If George Bush, the night before the convention, should say he wants you, this will have been done."

"But I do not aspire to *be* vice president," Simpson protested for
the umpteenth time.

That night he told his diary, "I have determined not to sign the
statement or allow the [background check] to proceed. Ann and
I do not want our lives changed in the fashion required." Then,
reconsidering again, he said, "But I guess that just putting my name
in the hat would not lead to that." On the third hand, "If word got
out that I had refused a background check, people would wonder
what I didn't want discovered."

Back in his office, he continued to twist in turmoil about the "VP thing." After meeting with me and other top aides, he made a final decision: "I've determined to go ahead with the forms, even though passion is still totally lacking in my bosom." At a White House event, he approached his friend Jim Baker, the former treasury secretary and currently Bush's campaign manager. "Jim, this vice presidency thing is getting out of hand, for me at least."

Baker noted that NBC commentator John Chancellor had recently suggested Simpson should be considered for the vice presidential nomination. There was also great speculation on Capitol Hill, with debates raging over whether the media wanted a vice president like Simpson so they could get into a good scrap now and then.

"This crap building up is not anything I have encouraged," Simpson pleaded to Baker. "I have never written a note or letter or anything about it to anybody." He wanted to make certain Baker understood he was serious about the matter.

Jim, I just do not want the job. I have seen what it is. It is administrative; it is jumping out of cars and airplanes and giving speeches. That is not what I want to do. It is very limiting and confining, no matter what you want to make of it. I am a legislator, I enjoy doing my current work and I do it damn well.

There are nine years of collected mutterings in the *Congressional Record*, where I have taken on every sacred cow in America. They would wrap those things around George Bush and me in thirty-second television spots. They would be dandy: "Here's what Simpson said about the REA—he said that they didn't electrify America so much as they electrified the taxpayers." Or, "Here's what Simpson said about the AARP," and, "Here's what Simpson said about the Disabled American Veterans." It would put a lot of heat on George.

Baker said, "You do need to tell George directly."

On Sunday, August 7, 1988, Simpson did that. "I told him, 'George, I'm just not interested in this vice presidency job. I do not want to be considered. The thing has gone further than I intended for it to go.' He said, 'Wait a minute, you should see the article in the *Boston Globe* this morning. It is very high on you.'"

Frustrations

As things were gearing up for the national Republican convention, Simpson was advised that because he was pro-choice on abortion, a considerable number of GOP convention delegates were prepared to disrupt the convention seriously in the event that Bush tapped him as running mate. That proved his point about the danger of his being on the ticket, but he was furious anyway. "About the attack of the far right upon me—and on Dole and Kassebaum—I said that if that's the way they wanted to be, and if their efforts ended up getting Michael Dukakis elected, they had best not come hanging around my door in 1989 like a bunch of poor relatives trying to get me to deal on their behalf with Dukakis as president!"

In a phone conversation with right-wing activist Paul Weyrich, Simpson said he thought it "crazy" for his followers to consider disrupting the convention. "It would be a juvenile exercise," he told Weyrich.

He spoke next with Republican senator Gordon Humphrey to stress that conservatives ought to be focusing on Michael Dukakis. If they wanted to assure his election by fighting within the Republican Party over abortion, they could "have fun dealing with Dukakis as president on *every* issue in the coming four years." If that happened, Simpson told Humphrey, "When the hardliners come to me for help on *anything*, I'll throw their asses out into the street."

In March 1989 a *New York Times* article had called Humphrey the most conservative voice in the Senate. The claim was of significance, since Jesse Helms was still a member. Ted Koppel repeatedly asked Al to talk about it on *Nightline* that night, but he resisted. After the fifth request, Al asked who else would be there. Senator Humphrey was scheduled. That changed everything. Al accepted the invitation and during the program shared his thoughts about the

Republican hardliners: "Republicans don't need to know who the vice presidential candidate is going to be, in order to get energized. They can get energized thinking about a guy with the philosophy of Michael Dukakis. That ought to give them a jump-start."

He went home, packed his bags and hit the books until 3:30 in the morning. He was ready for whatever might happen in New Orleans. Or so he thought.

EXHILARATION, FRUSTRATION, FATIGUE

The 1988 Republican National Convention in New Orleans—the "big easy"—was big but not easy for Al Simpson. There was no suspense in the selection of a presidential nominee. George Bush had that locked up. His VP choice was another matter, and thousands of reporters were hyperventilating with speculation. Simpson's repeated public denials of any interest in the job only seemed to fuel their guesswork.

Al, Ann, all three Simpson children, and several staffers—myself included—survived the first day and were given invitations to the best after-hours parties and receptions. They were not hard to come by, since sponsors were vying for ranking guests, especially those with even the slightest influence or inside information about Bush's pending VP decision. The Simpson group held forth in the French Quarter until after midnight.

The next day innovative reporters intercepted Al at every stop, even as Wyoming delegates were asking him for assistance with schedules, logistics, and political advice. Before long the variety of questions and problems being fielded by Simpson and his staff soared out of control. As the days turned to nights, no sooner had everyone fallen asleep than predawn alarms began ringing and the scramble to attend events began anew. On Sunday, August 14, these included Al's appearance on NBC's *Meet the Press*.

Simpson told John Chancellor, Tom Brokaw, and David Brinkley that he had no interest in the vice presidency and would not be on the ticket. His assertion was accepted, but skeptically. Frustrated, he finally repeated what he had said to Bush's assistant: "I don't know how else to say it. What is it about the word *no* that you don't understand?"

At one point he arrived at a large reception where the only other senator present was Dan Quayle. The Indiana senator had little idea that his life, not Al's, was about to change dramatically.

Simpson maintained a generally cheerful demeanor until shortly before he was to be introduced on television from the center platform in the convention hall. All would have gone well had the car scheduled to bring him from a downtown event to the Superdome arrived. With the designated moment nearing, he set off afoot in the blazing heat and humidity, and twenty minutes later burst into the Dome's staging area noticeably aggravated and dripping in sweat. Stage assistants had difficulty powdering his moist face for the cameras, something he resisted in the best of circumstances. After his speech, he demanded, "Why the *hell* was it so hard to have a car available when I need it most?"

The Call

Tuesday, August 16, 1988: The wildest day of all began well enough for Al, who submitted to a morning CNN interview and returned to his room to prepare for a meeting at the City Club with senior officials from *Time* magazine. "It was a very remarkable luncheon, and a lot of fun. I stayed until ten minutes after 1:00, although it was supposed to end at 1:00. Don Hardy came up to me and said that it was time to go. He was in charge of me then."

I aroused a flash of Simpson irritation by insisting with more than my usual intensity that it really was time to leave. After being brushed off, I waited less than two minutes before trying again. I grabbed Al's arm and squeezed it hard, while suggesting calmly but even more forcefully that it really was time to go. He remembers it well. "Don finally said, 'You have to go—you have to go *now*.' I got the message and got up." I ushered my boss through a nearby doorway. As soon as we were beyond the earshot of curious *Time* people, I whispered, "I have George Bush on the phone in that small room, right over there."

Everyone knew that Bush would begin calling his vice presidential possibilities in the order they were being struck from his list—meaning that the last person called would be the nominee. One *Time* official, noting that a surprisingly aggressive staffer had just dragged Simpson away and that he was now in a hushed telephone conversation, walked over to ask about it.

I planted myself directly in his path and said what seemed right under those circumstances: "This is a personal call. Al's wife Ann might be on the phone and she might be standing on the street in a phone booth wondering why he is late, and since it is nearly one hundred degrees outside she might be dripping in sweat—and she might be in a particularly unpleasant mood. Let's give Al some privacy."

The *Time* executive walked off while Vice President Bush was speaking with Simpson. The conversation's content was not revealed to anyone, including me, until I came across it in Al's diary seventeen years later.

The first thing George said was, "Hi, Al. I took you at your word. I want to get with you and I want to ask some questions about my guy. I haven't told the guy yet."

I said, "Who is it?"

He said, "I can't tell you yet, but I want to visit with you about it. I hope I haven't put heat or pressure on you. I feel badly about that. I know it hasn't been easy, and I know that Senator [Gordon] Humphrey has caused you some pain about the pro-choice stand, that they were going to walk out if you were selected."

I said, "Well, yeah, thanks, George. So it is Gordon that you are going to put on the ticket, eh?"

George chuckled. I said, "This takes the heat off me fully."

I told him that I was very proud of him and that I was looking forward to his speech. He said, "I want you and Ann to have a drink with Bar (he always calls her Bar) and me, tonight at the Doubletree, and I'll tell you who I've picked." I said, "We will do that."

Then he said, "I am going to start calling everyone [on the list]."

It was a good visit, and it was interesting that the *Time* people never knew who that call was from.

That did not mean Simpson had escaped the interest of other inquisitive reporters, such as his friend Phil Jones of CBS, who was staked out at his next stop. As Al's car door opened, Jones asked, "Have you been called by the vice president?"

Al laughed, "Now, Phil, I don't want to talk about that."

Jones responded, "Well, Dole has been called, Domenici has been called, Kassebaum has been called—there aren't many left."

After thinking about that a moment, Simpson escaped the CBS eye and whispered to his press secretary that either she or I should call the Bush staff and suggest that he stop making calls, lest his selection become known to the public via the process of elimination.

Too late. Within half an hour, the media had it figured it out. Moments later, Senator Dan Quayle was located by the secret service and whisked off to meet with Bush.

In my motel command post I learned that an official announcement from the Bush campaign was moments away. The two telephones in my room had been ringing constantly. I took the next call. It was CBS reporter Connie Chung, pleading to know if Simpson was off the list. Since the game was nearly up, I hinted that she might be wise to look for someone other than my boss to be selected.

Moments later she appeared on television, breathlessly breaking the news that an "unnamed source" had implied Simpson was off the list. I later received a handwritten note from Chung expressing appreciation for the hint; when checking a draft of this book, Simpson penned a note: "I never knew about this."

Quayle

On the last day of the convention, August 18, 1988, Al appeared on NBC *Nightly News* to defend Senator Quayle's National Guard service and to attack his media inquisitors. "It is hypocrisy to watch some pontifical powdered poop asking Dan Quayle questions about his guard service, knowing that that reporter was hiding out during the Vietnam War and carrying a Viet Cong flag."

Next, he wanted people to know how offended he was that because of his pro-choice position on abortion, a considerable number of conservatives had threatened to walk out of the convention. He vented his annoyance during dozens of rapid-fire impromptu interviews and scheduled remarks to groups of delegates.

> I said to the delegates that it would be a damn shame if they
> came this far in the political game, since many of them had
> never been in politics before, to work so hard to capture their
> precincts and counties and states, to then let a single issue
> divert their attention from Michael Dukakis, who didn't share
> a single one of their philosophies. I said that walking out of
> the convention would have been a flight from sanity.

Al had no deep insight into how a Dan Quayle vice presidency would fare but was convinced that his friend George Bush, whom Al felt he had served best by his refusal to be on the ticket, would become a fine president.

Although he was exhausted from days on the run, Al's mood held up most of the day. It collapsed entirely during a live interview on CNN's *Crossfire*. "I just barely made it to *Crossfire*, and boy was I pooped—and tired and hungry. I came down hard on [co-host] Tom Braden and kind of ripped around in it. I am glad my mother didn't see *that* one."

Crescendo

Now the convention was running full tilt, with balloons and bands and screaming delegates contributing to the bedlam. Because Al accepted almost every request, his meetings, luncheons, interviews, and racing back and forth became a disjointed logistical nightmare. Only one thing was predictable: everywhere he went, reporters were asking him to respond to the latest "revelation" about Dan Quayle. "It was the damnedest thing I ever saw. You could almost hear it in the air, like a forest fire, or a 747. Poor Dan wasn't ready for that baptism under fire."

That night Quayle was officially nominated as the vice presidential candidate. From the convention podium, Simpson gave him a three-minute "seconding" speech. The highlight of the evening, and of the convention, was George Bush's acceptance speech. Near its conclusion, he said:

> I say it without boast or bravado, I've fought for my country, I've served, I've built—and I will go from the hills to the hollows, from the cities to the suburbs to the loneliest town on the quietest street to take our message of hope and growth for every American to every American.
>
> I will keep America moving forward, always forward—for a better America, for an endless enduring dream and a thousand points of light.
>
> That is my mission. And I will complete it.

Al was impressed. "I tell you, it was just damn powerful. It was splendid. I was right down there with the Wyoming delegation in front of the podium, and it was special."

This time, when the conventioneers spilled into the French Quarter, they let it all hang out—what little was left. The Simpson group took Bourbon Street by storm. At Pat O'Brien's restaurant we sang and made requests of the piano player until 4:15 in the morning. Before departing New Orleans a few hours later, the Simpsons darted around their motel rooms scooping up clothes, briefing books, and all manner of gear and equipment while I dashed to the airline office and changed their flight schedule.

Days later, Al was in a reflective frame of mind.

> Wow, what a time. It was beautifully done. Everyone worked as hard as they possibly could. When I got tired, I got ugly and took out some heavy frustration on Don and Laurie [his scheduling assistant], and one in particular, Mary Kay [his press secretary]. I was certainly unfair to her. . . .

It will not happen again. I should never do that to people who work so beautifully and so hard and so loyally for me. Next time we will bring the whole damn staff. It is too much for even three, four, or five people. It was a real crusher. They all handled it with great grace under real pressure.

Once the Simpsons were on their way to the airport, I fell into a sleep of the dead. For the first time ever, wherever Al was going and whatever he planned to do when he got there did not much matter. I recovered soon enough but found less enthusiasm for the next national nominating convention.

Press Secretary Mary Kay Hill—who at one point during the convention did not know whether she had been fired, had quit, or both—recovered more slowly but returned to work. Others came away with their own stories of exhilarating moments, burning frustration, and crushing fatigue.

Years later Bill Simpson gave his explanation of how the family felt about the possibility that his father would become the VP candidate.

It was just kind of a surreal experience. I never knew what Bush's thoughts were, but I do think it would have been a wonderful ticket. It would have been an amazing ticket—it would have changed the country.

Dad was a lightning rod, no question about it, and I think in some ways the Bush people were a little hesitant, a little spooked. They didn't know what he would do or say at certain times. He'd speak from the heart. He'd speak the truth. But it wouldn't be politically nuanced and massaged for the audience, and that's a big time stage, the vice presidency of the United States. The decision was probably the right one at the time, but it was very close and it's interesting to think about.

Mom was disappointed. I think she saw what a remarkable opportunity and chance it would have been. I think, at that point in America's history, it really would have helped to have had someone who was direct, who was open, who was frank, who was honest, and who didn't have any further political aspirations. It would have helped the president. Bush could have taken the high road, and Al could have carried the load on many issues.

Colin Simpson said he would have loved having his father serve as vice president: "Oh yeah. I think he'd have been great at it. I think Mom would have gone along for the ride. I thought he should have done it." Daughter Sue Simpson Gallagher had her own thoughts: "I remember when he received 'the call' from G.H.W.B. We couldn't believe Dad had turned him down. Dad said to us, "Sure, it would be fun for *you*. You would all be sitting around the porch of the vice president's house sipping mint juleps and I'd be traveling the globe attending funerals of dignitaries I don't know."

Ann Simpson said that no vice president liked being vice president—that the only reason anyone wants the job is to try to become president. "Al did not want to be president, and I did not want to be married to someone who did not like what he was doing. It was such a joy to be married to someone who loved to go to work and loved what he was doing, even if he worked into the night." She admitted that if her husband had wanted the job, it might have been a good thing for her.

> My feeling about the VP thing was that it could have been a good experience for me. It gives one a bully pulpit. It would have benefited me more than Al. However, I would not have benefited by having someone in my life that didn't like what he was doing, so I had pros and cons about it. It would have been a nice house to live in—a cook, laundress, the kids would have fun visiting us—but I didn't see it as much for Al.

The night following the convention, at a friend's home in Jackson, Wyoming, Al and Ann had their first decent sleep in a week.

Simpson family forebears, Jackson, Wyoming, circa 1921. *Front, left to right:*
Virginia Simpson Brady Barker (Al's father's sister), with Margaret Brady on
her lap (daughter of Virginia and Clayton Brady, not depicted); Margaret
Sullivan Simpson and John P. Simpson (Al's father's father's parents),
John with William Simpson Brady on his lap (son of Al's father's sister's
daughter Virginia). *Back, left to right:* Margaret Louise Burnett Simpson
and William L. "Billy" Simpson (Al's father's parents); the boy in uniform
between them is unknown. Billy Simpson, sometimes called "Broken Ass
Bill" because he walked with a limp, was a man of accomplishment and
volatility. He shot two men, killing one. Simpson family photo.

(*above*) Al was visiting his grandparents, Mary and Peter Kooi, in Sheridan, Wyoming, in September 1944 when New York governor Thomas E. Dewey's campaign tour came to town. Al, just having turned thirteen, is seen behind Dewey. On his right is his aunt Doris Kooi Reynolds, his mother's sister. Simpson family photo.

(*facing, top*) Al Simpson's parents, Milward and Lorna, lived into their nineties. Milward served as Wyoming's governor and U.S. senator. Lorna was considered the family's bedrock. Al came to think of her as the "velvet hammer." Simpson family photo.

(*facing, bottom*) Milward, Pete, Al, and Lorna ride bicycles at their Cody home in December 1941. On the back of this picture Al wrote: "Save gas for our troops." Photo courtesy Buffalo Bill Historical Center, Cody, Wyoming; Jack Richard Collection, PN.89.107.21020.02.3.

Al and Ann Simpson's 1954 wedding in Basin, Wyoming. Al often said, "It's the closest I ever came to passing out!" Photo courtesy Buffalo Bill Historical Center, Cody, Wyoming; Jack Richard Collection, PN.89.6.1191.01.

During World War II, Al Simpson visited the Heart Mountain internment camp near Cody and met a fellow Boy Scout, Norman Mineta. Mineta became a member of the U.S. House of Representatives and U.S. secretary of both the Transportation and Commerce departments, and both served as Smithsonian Institution regents. The two are seen here in support of the Heart Mountain Wyoming Foundation's Interpretive Learning Center. The Heart Mountain site is recognized by the Department of the Interior as a National Historic Landmark. Photo courtesy Justin Lessman, *Powell Tribune*.

For two years Lieutenant Al Simpson served his country in the army. He was assigned to duty in Germany as an assistant adjutant in the Tenth Infantry Regiment of the Fifth Infantry Division and the Twelfth Armored Infantry Battalion of the Second Armored Division, "Hell on Wheels." Simpson family photo.

Simpson Blasts Union Pacific
For Opposition to Mining Bill

C/ST
2/7
1967

CHEYENNE (Special) — Rep. Alan K. Simpson (R-Park) slashed out at the Union Pacific railroad in one of the most bitter attacks ever heard on the floor of the House as House Bill 208 came before the Committee of the Whole Monday.

He is one of the co-sponsors of the bill designed to allow nine operators to establish underground connections between two sections of land cornering each other.

He was joined in introducing the bill by Reps. Ed Herschler (D-Lincoln) and Harold Hellbaum (R-Platte.)

Herschler pointed out that this is one of the most important pieces of legislation to the future of Wyoming. He discussed the economic factors involved and the importance to Sweetwater County in ad valorem taxes, property taxes and other related benefits.

Simpson said he could not understand why the UP was attempting to prevent the development of Wyoming's trona industry.

He said: "I'll tell you why. It's just that the Union Pacific wants part of the action.

"They presently own 49 per cent of the action in Stauffer Chemical and they want, very simply, half of the action of Allied Chemical."

Hellbaum spoke on the underground rights-of-ways and barrier pillars. He said there is no problem with barrier pillars in the proposed new mines at 1,200 feet underground. He pointed out that the UP has been using barrier pillars spaced at 50-foot intervals with no problem of cave-ins at that depth in its own mines.

The galleries were crowded with mining engineers and top executives of the major firms involved. Wives of legislators knitted and listened. The audience was intent on what appears to be one of the most important pieces of legislation to be head to date.

Legislative discussion of the bill, introduced by Herschler, Simpson and Hellbaum, was preceded by a press conference in Cheyenne Friday called to state their case by companies interested in processing Wyoming's trona. Union Pacific's case was presented to the public over the weekend before the bill was ever brought to the floor of the House.

Allied Chemical Co. has asked the Wyoming legislature to give it the right of eminent domain across corners of Union Pacific land in southwestern Wyoming for trona mining.

Allied has announced results of the legislation will determine whether or not a $20 million trona plant employing more than 230 persons a year will be built.

Gov. Stan Hathaway announced Saturday he would act as a mediator in the dispute between Union Pacific and Allied.

UP officials have asked legislators not to be "rushed" into making "harsh" mining laws.

Allied said it must have the right to run mining tunnels under corners of the checkerboard land holdings that UP has in southwest Wyoming because without the right to tunnel, Allied would have to sink additional surface shafts at a cost of millions of dollars, in order to mine trona for the manufacture of soda ash.

ALAN K. SIMPSON

LEADS THE FIGHT: State Rep. Alan K. Simpson (R-Park), one of the leaders in the House against the Union Pacific Railroad in its fight with Allied Chemical Co. over House Bill 208, is shown with his family. Others who introduced the bill with Simpson are Ed Herschler (D-Lincoln) and Harold Hellbaum (R-Platt).

(*above*) At John Gardiner's Tennis Ranch in 1985 Al and Ann won the "Senator's Cup" dancing contest. When they first met, Ann shunned Al because he could not dance. She gave him lessons and later said, "He shaped up." Photo by Conley Photography, Scottsdale, Arizona.

(*facing*) This February 2, 1967, *Casper Star Tribune* story reported that junior Wyoming House member Al Simpson "slashed out at the Union Pacific railroad in one of the most bitter attacks ever heard on the floor of the House." The issue involved easements for trona mining along the railroad's right of way. Simpson and his legislative colleagues were particularly proud of having prevailed over the corporation's out-of-state lawyers. Depicted are Al and Ann and their three children, Colin, Susan, and Bill. Photo courtesy *Casper Star Tribune*.

Al — As always you are absolutely right. Warmest Regard Ron

Senator Simpson explains to President Reagan why he was late for their meeting on March 26, 1988. Reagan wrote on the photo, "Dear Al—As always you are absolutely right." On the reverse Simpson penned, "I was sharing a dandy tale with the president as to why I was late for the meeting. I don't think he was believing it!" White House photo.

"Dear Al—I'm always happy when I see you. Warmest friendship," wrote Reagan on the front of this photo on June 23, 1988. On the back Simpson penned that he was telling the president what a county agricultural agent might say when asked by a cabbie for a tip: "Have your soil tested before you plant." White House photo.

Simpson with Soviet leader Mikhail Gorbachev, May 1992. Simpson later wrote, "He didn't know I was in the room and when he saw me he threw out his hand and arms and we gave each other a quick embrace." They first met in 1987. Uncredited photo.

Senator Simpson, Representative Dick Cheney, and President Ronald
Reagan at an event in Cheyenne, Wyoming, on behalf of Senator Malcolm
Wallop (not depicted). Reagan wrote, "You'll have to tell me what we were
looking at? Anyway it must have been fun." Cheney added, "Dear Al, A
classic shot of Wyoming's junior senator." Wallop penned, "Friend Al—
From the one whom the president obviously is greeting!" Uncredited photo.

Dear Al — I know you'll be glad to see your "Oscar" performance had been preserved for posterity. Warmest Regards Ron

Simpson demonstrates to Congressmen Bud Shuster (*left*) and John Paul Hammerschmidt the gesture he used in mocking the White House press corps' questioning of President Reagan, March 18, 1987. Reagan wrote on the photo, "Dear Al—I know you'll be glad to see your 'Oscar' performance has been preserved for posterity. Warmest regards, Ron." White House photo.

Hey, Al, some great words by you ~ Bob
Gratefully Gz Bush

Senator Bob Dole presents a Senate vote tally on January 25, 1990,
upholding President George H. W. Bush's veto of the Chinese Student
Exclusion bill. In the wake of China's Tiananmen Square incident, Bush
vetoed the bill in favor of his executive order accomplishing much the same
result in more diplomatic terms. White House photo.

Hey, Al, watch it! Don't step on the puppies — Gep Bush

While chatting with President George H. W. Bush on the White House lawn on April 14, 1989, Simpson got a nip on the ankle from one of "first dog" Millie's puppies. The president wrote, "Hey, Al, watch it! Don't step on the puppies." White House photo.

(*facing*) President Bush and Al Simpson are sharing stories about the one that got away, July 20, 1990. The president wrote: "Trout, big wily trout, tough-to-catch trout, fighting trout, gigantic mean trout. Let's eat." White House photo.

Al — Trout, big wily trout, tough-to-catch trout, fighting trout, gigantic mean trout. Let's eat. Gz Bush

On February 13, 1991, after Senator Simpson publicly denounced CNN reporter Peter Arnett's Iraqi-censured broadcasts from Baghdad during the first Gulf War, *USA Today* ran this sketch by David Seavey. Photo courtesy *USA Today.*

Senators Kennedy and Simpson staged this photo in promotion of their eight-year daily radio debate. Kennedy wrote, "To Al, who makes my day on *Face Off.* With friendship, Ted Kennedy 1988." Photo courtesy Del Ankers archives.

Although Al Simpson and Ted Kennedy were often on opposite sides of key issues, they became close friends. On this photo, Kennedy wrote, "To Al. Who telegraphs his punches with a smile. Your black and blue punching bag, Ted. Jan 90." Uncredited photo.

Chapter Eleven

THE BEAT GOES ON

~

AL SIMPSON WAS on his way to work on September 13, 1988, when the car phone rang. It was Ann, calling from Wyoming to report that their son Bill's wife Debbie had gone into labor in the night. While plowing through meetings on nuclear power, refugees, and Republican politics, Al eagerly awaited further word from Cody. He was speaking with Senators Dole and Byrd when the second call came. "While I was sitting there, about fifteen minutes into the meeting, they brought in a note. It said, 'It's a girl! Eight pounds, twenty inches. Call Bill as soon as possible!' A thrill came over me, one I am quite unable to describe. My first granddaughter."

He phoned Bill, who described his "new beautiful daughter," Elizabeth Lorna Ann Simpson. The new grandfather was so beside himself with joy that he logged every nuance of their conversation. Tears welled in his eyes as Debbie came on the line. "It is surely one of God's miracles," he told her, voice aquiver. He went to the Senate floor to announce the birth into the *Congressional Record*, speaking so emotionally that several of his colleagues were left with lumps in their throats.

A few days later, in Wyoming, Simpson peered deeply into a tiny girl's eyes. "Suddenly, I was just overcome with emotion, and cried. Holding that beautiful little thing, feeling my own hot tears going right down onto her tiny head—wow. Don't ask me what that was all about, but it is surely something I have never felt before. I sat there with her, hummed, whistled, made faces, sang lullabies, and did a little poetry." Elizabeth's proud father witnessed the scene: "Dad came shortly after Beth was born. We were there in the basement of the house on 1201 Sunshine. Dad came in and held her, and just cried. It was a tender and unforgettable moment."

Several months later, the Simpson family gathered in D.C. to witness Elizabeth's baptism at the National Cathedral. "Elizabeth was quiet during the entire thing. When Bishop John Walker finished, he held her high above his head, her little rump in his hands, and said, 'Now, let's have some applause.'" Al felt there was something special about Elizabeth, and time proved him right. In spring 2008 her proud father gave this update: "Beth is at Notre Dame studying theology and economics. She's just a wonderful, vibrant, incredible child, as is her brother." Eric was born on October 14, 1993.

After grandfather Al held little Beth in his arms, his thoughts shifted from the sunrise of life to its sunset. Struck with a powerful feeling of the inexorable passage of generations, he visited his father. The two were together a long time, as Al read aloud one account after another of Milward's days of acclaim. Next, he visited Ann's mother to express sympathy for her recent loss of one eye and her multitude of other medical woes. Then he sat with his own mother and found her quite depressed about Milward's condition. Later that day, Al and Pete arranged for their father to be moved into a nursing home.

In the course of a few days Al Simpson had ranged deeper than usual into the extremes of his emotions. At the Republican convention he demonstrated enthusiasm, optimism, joy, fatigue, frustration, and the purest of raging anger—followed by sincere regret. In Cody his eyes moistened and his voice trembled with love and concern for his parents. In awe, he held his precious new granddaughter to his chest, and wept.

REFLECTIONS

On October 4, 1988, Al attended his final leadership meeting at the Reagan White House. He thought about his many meetings there as a member of the leadership since early 1985. "The president seemed in good spirits. Reporters came in and asked a few things and he handled them all well. Then he went through a list of 'musts' and 'must-nots,' concerning remaining legislation." When someone told Reagan that Congressman Jim Wright was leaving town soon, he laughed: "Well, we could provide him with the rail." Simpson took that to mean Reagan felt Wright's departure might be hastened if he were ridden out of town on a rail. Near the end of the session, Simpson offered a few thoughts.

> I joked about the highs and lows I shared with Reagan, and said, "I remember all the advice I gave you—and the very little that you took." Reagan laughed about that.
>
> I said there had been some exciting and thrilling times and some that were most disappointing—but all the while, we were watching the essence of this remarkable man. I said it was a great honor for me to be at the table for nearly four years, and that I enjoyed the give and take and watching him in action. . . .
>
> I also said that it was my greatest delight getting to know him as a person and a friend—my greatest personal pleasure. I thanked him for his stewardship in the job of governing our country with compassion, caring and general good humor.

Simpson concluded his final meeting with Reagan by predicting that history would treat him kindly. The president seemed touched. "With all these accolades, I'm going to be tough to live with all day." he grinned.

Later, after a dinner honoring the president, Al again reflected on the Reagans.

> They leave their mark. No one will ever come along with the stylus of history and scratch away a single line about the fact that that these two people are very special human beings.
>
> Ron is absolutely undaunted and unthreatened. He talked about those things that he loves, especially about the ranch and its vista and the trees and the things he has there. He was almost teary-eyed.

A year after his return to California, President Reagan wrote this note:

Dear Al:

It was great to get your letter. Thank you for your generous words. Believe me, Nancy and I miss you all very much. We don't miss the place now that we're back in Calif., but believe me we miss all of you who were such great friends.

As for my health, your prayers have been answered, I feel great. My only beef is a schedule that keeps me from going to the ranch as often as I like. And yes, I'm ready and eager to get in the saddle again. And yes, I miss a certain Senator's stories—now I wonder who that could be?

Nancy and I send our love to you and Ann. We miss you.

Sincerely,
Ron

Simpson knew that threads of his memorable times with Reagan would be forever woven into his own life. He was dramatically reminded of that nearly sixteen years later. On June 4, 2004, Ann slept peacefully at the Bobcat Ranch while Al pitched and turned. His mind raced through the fitful night. In the morning he told his wife about his mysterious and emotional dream. Two and a half months later, he described it in a letter to a friend in California.

August 19, 2004

Dear Nancy:

I have waited to write, because words cannot seem to sum it up well enough. So I waited until the captains and the kings and all the proud and wonderful citizens of this great Country had departed to tell you that you were magnificent. Truly magnificent. But we've known that for a long time. You were the epitome of courage, style, class, stamina, determination, patience, and you were the maestro conductor of a stirring concert of pageantry and tradition that this country needed desperately. "Wow!" would be a Ron Reagan commentary.

What fun I had with him. When you would slip off to see your dad in Scottsdale, he would call me and Howell Heflin, and Dale Bumpers, and Gene Taylor of Missouri, and Bob Michel, and say, "Come on over for drinks and dinner, and we'll just tell stories." And boy, we did. I was privileged to be at three of those, and I shall have them forever recorded in the eye of my mind.

Then when I was honored to serve as assistant Republican leader under Bob Dole for a ten-year period—four of them while Ron was president—I was privileged to be there in the White House a half a dozen times a month or so, always greeted with the comment, "Have you got any new ones Al?" And I always did. And I'd say, "How 'bout you?" And he always did.

When I shepherded a major immigration bill through the House and Senate and finally onto his desk, there were many points along the way when some in his administration were not in favor of what I was up to, and hearing of that I would just call and say, "Are you still with me?" And he'd say, "What's up? Tell me about it." I'd tell him and he'd say, "I'm with you all the way."

He backed me to the hilt—always. He was always there for me. In my campaigns, in my legislative activities, in my leadership activities—always there. Warm, wise, witty, loyal, courageous, dedicated, patriotic—never one to abuse or misuse power, but fully aware that he had plenty of it. And when he did unglove the closed fist, there wasn't a soul observing that didn't know what was up. He also had that extraordinary gift of being able to love and be loved. Often folks flunk one—or both—of those tests.

Let me share with you a most clairvoyant moment of mine near the time he left us. Ann and I were at the Bobcat Ranch with our family that Saturday with no contact with radio or television.

I woke that morning to tell Ann of a most remarkable dream. I told Ann that it was so clear and I was visiting with Ron, in the Oval Office—just the two of us—and I was having trouble understanding what he was saying. I remember feeling very sad, as I did when my own dear dad labored in similar fashion in life—and then a few minutes later (in dream time) he looked up at me and said, "How are you, Al? What's up in your life?" And his eyes were sparkling, and his speech was clear and lucid, and we talked—and joked—and laughed—and then the dream tailed off. I told Ann I had surely enjoyed it.

Later, our youngest son Colin came to the ranch and told us he had died that day. I choked up, and cried, and told the assembled family about my dream, tears streaming down my face. I know these things are stupid, corny, silly, banal—but that one was for real—in dream language.

Though he passes from us, his legacy is eternal, not just in the annals of history, but in the hearts and minds of all of us who knew him and had the rich privilege to share his loving life. He was all the man there is.

We're thinking of you, our thoughts and prayers go winging out to you for strength and solace and comfort.

Ann joins in sending our love and sympathy to you and all of your dear ones whom America has clasped to its collective bosom.

                                        Love,
                                        Friend Al

Five weeks later he received this response, with its handwritten postscript.

September 27, 2004
Office of Nancy Reagan

Dear Al,

Thank you so much for your beautiful letter. As you suspected, we have received thousands of cards, letters, and telephone calls, and I am so touched by all the love and expressions of sympathy. But amid all this outpouring of emotions and condolences, your letter stands out and I just had to write to tell you how much it meant to me.

I loved reading your stories about Ronnie—you have such wonderful memories of him. Thank you for sharing them with me. Please give my love to Ann.

Fondly,
Nancy

The story of your dream is amazing! Certainly not crazy, corny, stupid, banal, etc.—I believe in those things, Alan. And I'm so glad it happened to you—wish it would happen to me! I'd give a lot to "see" his face and eyes again. I miss him terribly.

CHANGING OF THE GUARD

Ronald Reagan was succeeded by his vice president, George H. W. Bush—but not before Bush battled Democratic Governor Michael Dukakis of Massachusetts for the job. After their first debate on September 25, 1988, in Winston-Salem, North Carolina, supporters of both candidates were paraded before the cameras to claim victory. Al Simpson disliked the process but knew the Bush campaign was counting on him. "It's kind of phony," Al said afterward. "But if everyone is playing that game, I'll play it too."

After the October 5 debate for vice president in Omaha, Nebraska, Simpson said he thought Senator Dan Quayle "looked scared to death" as he faced his opponent Senator Lloyd Bentsen. Again, Simpson questioned the debate process: "If you want to raise the level of the debate—I don't know why the hell [they] waste so much time asking what a guy did in his summer job in college. That was actually one of the questions. I really don't know the worth of 'debates' anymore, since the candidates can't go 'one on one' on each other and box each other around a little."

Al may have thought the debate lacked punch, but it is doubtful that Dan Quayle agreed.

Quayle: I have far more experience than many others that sought the office of vice president of this country. I have as much experience in the Congress as Jack Kennedy did when he sought the presidency. I will be prepared to deal with the people in the Bush Administration, if that unfortunate event would ever occur.

Bentsen: Senator, I served with Jack Kennedy, I knew Jack Kennedy, Jack Kennedy was a friend of mine. Senator, you're no Jack Kennedy.

A second presidential debate was scheduled for October 13, in Los Angeles, and a few days before that, Vice President and Barbara Bush invited the Simpsons to their residence at the U.S. Naval Observatory. Al was surprised to find that Bush had erected a mock debate setup in his dining room. "Here were two podiums and two light systems with the green, yellow, and red, for timing the two-minute answers. There were questioners' seats and every damn thing you can imagine, including crowd noise. Old George said he was going to be ready for the next one. 'Loaded for bear' was his understatement."

Al remembers that the four were discussing politics when Bush suddenly said, "Oh Ann, I just remembered that you don't like Perrier in your wine, you like good old American water." He jumped up, went into the kitchen, and "rattled around in the cabinets until he found a brown bottle of Saratoga water and used it to fix drinks for himself and Ann," Al noted in his diary. "He is amazing, a sprightly and loving man. He is ready for the final thirty days. I will be out on the road too. I'm really going to hump for that guy. I will be in Detroit, Chicago, Cincinnati, Indianapolis, Philadelphia, Milwaukee, and Lord knows where else—and I am going to have some fun in the process."

Bush's performance in Los Angeles was much improved, and interviewers asked for Al's take on the exchange. He gave his spin and noted that while only one other Republican senator was interviewed, eight Democrats were questioned by reporters. Beyond the coverage imbalance, Simpson noticed that none of the Democrats was a moderate: "The moderates don't want to be seen with Dukakis. I don't think they will want to be on the platform with him. His views are too extreme."

On the Road

In the final days leading up to the November election Simpson crisscrossed the nation on the vice president's behalf. He spoke in so many forums that he found himself consulting his schedule card to double check his current location. All went well until a stop in North Dakota. He landed in Grand Forks in subzero weather to promote not only George Bush's election but elderly Senator Quentin Burdick's defeat. At a rally he was tough on the frail eighty-year-old Democrat.

> I really laid the wood on Quentin Burdick. I said, "If he really is all these things that his campaign staff says, then why didn't he take a better chairmanship and bring real credit to his state as the chairman of a major committee? He didn't do that, he declined. He rejected that each time it was extended to him. Is that a leader?"
>
> I also said he was a very kind man, but they won't remember that I said that.

While it was undeniably true that Burdick was in tough shape physically, his campaign and Senate employees went ballistic when they heard Simpson's attack. From their perspective, the Wyoming senator had come to North Dakota simply to hammer cruelly a frail old man loved by many.

Some months later Simpson visited with a senior staff member of the Environment and Public Works Committee who was still angry that Simpson had spoken against Burdick's reelection. The staff person, who declined comment for this book, seemed determined to thwart the Al's legislative efforts at every opportunity. Al tried to smooth the waters. "I told him that I was pained and embarrassed if my comments had caused Quentin that much of a problem, and that I did have a tendency sometimes to get my foot in my mouth. I said I did not intend to have an ugly relationship with Quentin Burdick, who has been very kind to me."

Senator Burdick was reelected on November 1, 1988. He died of heart failure September 8, 1992, two years short of completing his term, and after thirty-two years of Senate service.

Time Out

In the midst of the campaign season and his exhausting legislative schedule, Al had little time for rest. Still, nothing could keep him from attending homecoming at the University of Wyoming. He arrived in Laramie, joined Ann, and hopped into the back seat of a *convertible*. Finally, after years of his complaining about being crammed into a closed vehicle, the university had come up with a convertible. "We felt a real responsiveness of the people along the parade route. You get that sense as you ride in an open vehicle and watch their faces and listen to their comments. It was very pleasing. It was also good that Malcolm and French [Wallop] were there. He needs to do a lot of that in the coming five weeks."

Al was sky high emotionally as the Cowboys football team took on Colorado State. He soared higher when Wyoming won, 35–16. The school's homecoming theme that year was "Beat 'Em Goofy." It would be many years before Wyoming would beat any other teams goofy.

Later that year Al traveled to San Diego to watch the Cowboys battle Oklahoma State in the Holiday Bowl. Taking his seat at the game, he was ready. He was pumped. He was confident. He was four quarters of action away from being—deflated. "It was one of the most embarrassing athletic events I have ever watched the Cowboys participate in. Oklahoma State had an all-American player named Barry Sanders, who was in top form that day, racking up 222 yards and setting a Bowl record of five touchdowns—even though he didn't even play in the fourth quarter." The final score was 62–14.

Back on the Trail

During the months before the 1988 elections Simpson campaigned for his colleague Senator Wallop, who was running for reelection. Since Al did not think things were going well, he gave Wallop's campaign staff some unsolicited advice: "I said that certain things need to be done, that I didn't come out here to serve with Wallop's *opponent*. I told Malcolm's folks that people in Wyoming have to be told how badly he wants to be re-elected, that he has to be out there in Wyoming shaking hands and banging on doors and walking those precincts. If people don't think he wants it, they won't give it to him."

Shortly before Election Day Simpson's efforts on Wallop's behalf hit a snag. During a meeting with reporters in Casper, one inquisitor asked Al if he realized that an old photograph of himself with John Vinich, Wallop's opponent, was on display at the Union Bar in the tiny town of Hudson. When Simpson said he recalled a photo being taken with Vinich when they served together in the state legislature, the reporter asked if he remembered what he had written on it. He said he remembered thanking Vinich for his hard work, just as he had thanked numerous other Democrats and Republicans.

It suddenly became apparent that the reporter was attempting to make the case that because Simpson had once written a cordial note to Vinich, he might rather serve in the Senate with him than with Wallop. "That was then, and this is now," Simpson stressed, adding that since those early days, he had come to see Malcolm as the "superior legislator." Al added, "I now agree with *Democrat* Ed Herschler that John Vinich is ineffective." Herschler was a former Wyoming governor.

Next question: If Vinich defeated Wallop, and took his seat in the Senate, could Simpson work with him? "Of course," Al said without hesitation. "I could work with *anyone*."

The headline in the following day's *Casper Star Tribune* read: "Simpson Could Work with Vinich." The story implied that Simpson was readying for Wallop's defeat. The Wallop campaign was not pleased. Al phoned Malcolm to explain that he was certainly not suggesting Vinich should or even might be elected. He was simply saying that he could work with anyone, since it was hardly in his nature to refuse to work with people of any political or philosophical bent.

Wallop accepted Al's explanation, although his staff continued to grumble. One disgruntled senior Wallop campaign official called the incident "Simpson's gaffe" even though Simpson had been campaigning tirelessly on his fellow senator's behalf. Wallop defeated Vinich by the thin margin of 1,322 votes. In my 2007 telephone interview with former *Casper Star Tribune* editor Dick High, he had this take on the final weeks of Wallop's 1988 campaign:

> Vinich is a colorful guy, but there was no way he was going
> to be a United States senator, I would have thought. But
> he just damn near did it. Simpson and Congressman Dick
> Cheney went on the campaign trail and saved Wallop.
>
> My sense of what happened there was that they pulled
> Wallop off the campaign trail and put him in the safest venues
> possible, kept him out of trouble. Then Al went out and campaigned almost as if he *were* Wallop.

Simpson was relieved by Wallop's victory and ecstatic that George Bush had defeated Michael Dukakis by an electoral vote margin of more than three to one to become the nation's forty-first president. Three weeks after the election, Republican senators gathered to reelect Senators Dole and Simpson as their leader and assistant leader for another two years. Shortly after that, Al began to realize that he had an unofficial new title.

First Friend

"Everybody in Washington must think I am George Bush's *brother!* They want jobs. I tell them I will try to present something on their behalf, but I can't always deliver." Al's close relationship with the new president was reaching a broad audience. Suddenly it seemed that everyone desiring to work in government was attempting to slip a resume into Bush's hands, via the Wyoming senator.

On January 13, 1989, the two set off for Florida for another round of fishing in the Keys. On that hot day they learned a lesson about the news media's determination and innovation: "George and I took our shirts off and we were standing there. At one point, we took a leak off the end of the boat—which is all you can do when you are out there for that many hours." Al later discovered that a CBS television crew, so far away they could not be seen, was in possession of a long-range telephoto lens. CBS News did not air pictures of the two peeing into the ocean but did show them sitting around with their shirts off. "That PO'd George, and it PO'd me too. What the hell that has to do with the public's 'right to know' sure beats the hell out of me. I'll have a chance to get in some licks on that one with those in the Fourth Estate in the coming months."

Otherwise, Simpson's second trip to Florida with Bush was even better than the first. The two chatted privately about many things, including possible Cabinet selections. That evening, they gathered for dinner. Al remembers their "jolly and ribald time" telling tall tales, and that when the laughter subsided, Bush decided they should go outside and play horseshoes. To his surprise, Bush lost. He demanded another game and was perplexed to lose again, 15–14—his first post-election defeat.

He spotted a young boy who had been watching the game from behind a secret service barrier and went over to give him a lesson in sportsmanship. Simpson heard what he said: "Son, I want you to know that this is true sportsmanship. You can see that we had a marvelously competitive game, and yet my side lost. You can see that we handled that with great grace, even though we were playing against opponents as lucky as they are unconscious."

Speaking to his diary that night, Simpson said of Bush, "He loves to win. That is why he will be a damn good president."

Numerous reporters had hung around during Al's previous fishing adventure with Bush, but now there were even more. Armies of people bearing cameras, lights, and notebooks were constantly straining to get as close as possible to the president-elect. When a reporter asked Simpson about the day, he cheerfully reported catching the largest redfish ever snagged. He thought they would see it as a joke, but the next morning he was astonished. "My God, they printed it in the paper as if it were true. That is absolutely nuts. I think the record fish must be sixty pounds."

During their flight home aboard *Air Force Two*, Bush picked up the *New York Times* and spotted an article containing compliments by Ann Simpson about Barbara Bush. Also on the front page was a photo of the men fishing together. They laughed about the heady times they were living. Bush turned to Simpson and said, "You are going to *love* Camp David."

THE INAUGURAL

The multiday Bush presidential inaugural celebration in Washington was shaping up better than the inauguration of Ronald Reagan, when snow and subzero temperatures forced cancelation of some events. This year too, the streets were clogged, but not with snow and ice. Vehicle traffic was so heavy that Al found it difficult to get to work.

During the inaugural ceremony on the west front of the United States Capitol on January 20, 1989, Al watched his friend being sworn into office. It provided one his most cherished moments— even though both before and after the event, reporters repeatedly asked if he, rather than Dan Quayle, should be the new vice president. He told them, "I have not a twinge about it. But I do have a twinge of deep satisfaction that I worked so hard to help get these two guys elected."

It was a remarkable and thrilling time. Ann was on the platform near the back, amid other senators and one or two other

Senate wives. She had an extraordinary seat. The president and Nancy came in. It was just hard to believe, as I saw it happen. Ronald Reagan, in just a few minutes, would no longer be the president. He would be on a helicopter headed for Andrews [Air Force Base], and then into private life.

Congressman Tom Foley leaned over to Al during the ceremony and whispered, "You know something? We are temporarily without a president. There is no president of the United States right now!" Sure enough, it was just past the stroke of noon. By law, Ronald Reagan's presidency had ended precisely at noon, and yet it would be another five minutes before George Bush was sworn into office. No constitutional calamity beset the country before Senator Wendell Ford introduced Chief Justice Rehnquist, who administered the oath of office to George Herbert Walker Bush as the forty-first president of the United States.

Simpson mentally noted that the new president was a twenty-seven-year friend of his family. After Milward was elected to the Senate in 1962, he moved into the office suite being vacated by the retiring Prescott Bush, George's father. Al met the Bush family when Milward and Lorna sold their Washington house to George Bush.

During the swearing-in ceremony Al also mused about the time in 1980 when the Republicans had taken control of the Senate and Bush had just been elected vice president. As the motorcade passed the east front of the Capitol, where Al and Ann were standing, Bush grabbed a microphone and through the car's loudspeaker shouted, "Oh look, there's Al and Ann Simpson—I see you and the Wyoming crew over there." To the consternation of the Secret Service, Barbara rolled down the bulletproof window and waved.

Al was awash in memories of the two families' relationship and their many times together. It gave him a chill to think that one of their number had just become president of the United States.

George gave a magnificent inaugural address of maybe fifteen minutes. It was powerful stuff, beautifully done. When he said, "The American people don't expect us to bicker. They expect us to get something done," there was a big roar from the crowd. They heard that one.

I looked out over the balcony. I was just three seats from the edge and I saw the Washington Monument and the Lincoln Memorial and the clouds—and the sun that broke through right at the end. There really is no way to describe it, but it is recorded in my head.

Check with a Lawyer

After the ceremony Al and Ann remained outside chatting with people, until a security officer rushed up to say they were needed in the President's Room in the Capitol—"right now." They handed me their coats and broke for the elevator. Emerging on a higher floor, they bounded into the President's Room. The new chief executive was seated at the green felt table where previous presidents had signed their first official documents. The papers before him were the nominations for his new Cabinet. Al hustled over and said, "Wait! Don't sign that, not until you check with a lawyer!"

Bush chuckled. "Oh, there's Simpson giving me the business." He mentioned something about their recent fishing trip, but Al could not hear what he said. In a room filled with the highest-ranking people in the government of the United States, Bush signed the documents and handed his friend the first pen he used.

"Here, keep that one," he said.

"Boy, don't think I won't." Al said appreciatively.

When the ceremony concluded, Simpson said to Bush, "I can't tell you what a thrill it is for me to call you 'Mr. President.'" Bush smiled, gave his tall friend a slap on the back, then headed to Statuary Hall for the next activity. Now the Simpsons were becoming uneasy over the whereabouts of their twenty-seven Wyoming guests—friends and supporters they had invited to attend the inaugural events. Al never expected to find them where he did.

Senior members of my staff talked Capitol officials into letting my guests observe events from a special vantage point. I've never seen the private dining room opened to anybody but a senator. That was the damnedest coup. From that particular dining room, you could see out toward the Senate Library door, where I usually come in from the east plaza, and where Bush would go out. All of my guests would be able to see them as they set off in the Inaugural Parade.

Mr. President

Before the parade, Bush admitted that when the Senate sergeant at arms first addressed him as "Mr. President," he had just stood there, waiting for Ronald Reagan to respond. "With a gentle jab to the ribs, I got the message," Bush laughed.

The inaugural parade commenced, and hundreds of thousands of people along its route waved their greetings and approval. At its conclusion, restaurants, pubs, and meeting rooms across the city swarmed with inaugural celebrants. Traffic crawled as the Simpsons made their way across the Potomac River to their home in McLean, where they quickly changed clothes and drove back across the river into Georgetown. At the City Tavern Club, eight hundred people had gathered in their honor. The event's sponsor was George Koch, an old friend of the Simpson family and father-in-law of Doro Bush, George Bush's daughter.

The guest list included Supreme Court Justice Sandra Day O'Connor and her husband John and dozens of well-known politicians, media representatives, and corporate giants. Even top Democrats dropped by, including Senators Ted Kennedy and Howell Heflin. The event concluded just after 10:00 in the evening, when celebrants headed to the inaugural balls. At the Pension Building, Al and Ann wasted no time hitting the dance floor.

The party eventually wound down, but Al did not. He offered to pass the hat if the band would play for one more hour, but it was too late. "Gosh, that works in Meeteetse," the senator from Wyoming said dejectedly.

Down to Business

The next Tuesday, Simpson attended his first leadership meeting at the White House, under the new president. "You can imagine the thrill for me. Here was the guy I fished with, camped with, and spent time with on special Memorial Day weekends at Kennebunkport. It is going to be an interesting couple of years until I run again for reelection, and hopefully even after that." Bush addressed the attendees, Republicans and Democrats alike, by their first names—with one exception. He walked up to the tallest one and said, "Hi, big Al."

The president reported having called Soviet leader Gorbachev in Moscow to tell him all was well and that he looked forward to working with him. Then he reviewed his priorities for the Congress in the coming four years. When House Speaker Jim Wright presented him with a bottle of Texas Hot Pepper Sauce, Bush asked, "If that's Texas hot pepper sauce, how come it's made in Louisiana?" Wright responded, "It's similar to a guy from Kennebunkport saying he is from Texas."

Al noted how good it was that both the president and vice president had served in Congress, making it easier for them to deal with the legislative branch of government. He said, "The toughest part of my job in the past was to watch Ronald Reagan and Tip O'Neill smack each other around. That made it tough for all of us."

At the conclusion of a White House social event that evening, the president invited Al, Ann, and several other guests to tour their private quarters upstairs. "They took us up there and showed us through nearly every room in the White House. It was spectacular—closets, bathrooms, the Lincoln bedroom, their bedroom, the whole works. There are people who have been in Congress twenty years who have never been up those stairs." During the tour Simpson and Bush conducted a running debate about the works of art adorning the White House—laughing and joking more than debating. Both thought it a delightful way to conclude a special day.

Prayer Breakfast

On February 2, 1989, Al delivered the message at Washington's National Prayer Breakfast. In attendance were four thousand people, including the president and vice president, the Reverend Billy Graham, scores of governmental and corporate officials, and religious leaders of all faiths. Simpson spoke to his "fellow seekers" about life in Washington and repeated one of his favorite lines. "Those who travel the high road of humility in Washington, D.C., are not really troubled by heavy traffic." He went on to reveal not only his successes in life but also his failures. He was especially frank about his personal crisis while in the army.

> It was the first time in my life where other people were telling me what to do—and the very real consequences if I didn't do it. The humor, the charm, the old stuff, the B.S., none of it worked anymore. I was miserable. I couldn't do what I wanted to do. It tore me up. I had ulcers, gas, heartburn, blood pressure of about 220, depression—it was as if somebody had pulled "the great black sheet" over my head.

He revealed that in his thirties he had "grappled with jealousy and possessiveness . . . and the distortion of love." He spoke about his marriage, law school, jobs, and politics and quoted his mother's admonition never to lose his sense of humor. He spoke at length about the role of religion and God in his life, adding that he felt a responsibility to act on the gifts God had given him and entrusted to him on earth.

> As stewards, we must properly care for the things that He has given us, to be rid of the pain and the pity and the hate and the anxiety and the conflict down inside.
> Listen very carefully. [It] comes up in the east with the sun. One word. Only one. It is, "*Start!*" This is the only yard marker on the playing field of life. Today. Right here. This instant. This flash of time: February 2, 1989, 9:15 on a bright

Thursday morning. Start! It's not too profound, is it? But yet, it sure is.

Continuing to concede his mistakes and errors in life, he revealed the thing he found most difficult.

I couldn't love others until I learned to love myself. Teachers could forgive me. Principals in school would forgive me. My buddies would forgive. Other parents would forgive me, as I often led their sons astray. But boy! It was so tough to do that for myself, to be able to look in that mirror and say, "Al, I forgive you."

That was when things began to fall together for me, with God's help. When I learned God's grace of forgiveness, the boy became a man.

When it was President Bush's turn, he smiled and said, "The Lord works in very mysterious ways—but I wonder why it is that under the protocol sense of things, I always have to follow my friend Al Simpson."

Chapter Twelve

FRIEND TO
THE PRESIDENT

~

AL SIMPSON'S CODY office assistant watched in disbelief as a dozen radical environmentalists rushed into his office and began plastering Earth First stickers on everything in sight. Arriving a few minutes later, Al glanced at their handiwork and said to them, "What kind of chickenshit way is *this* to express yourselves?" Actually, he did not mind that much. "I enjoy those spirited little encounters, but I think their slogan ought to be 'Earth First—Bathe Last.' They really do give off an aroma. They are all very excitable and dedicated, and they think their cause is the only one in the world."

Later that day, in Green River, Wyoming, Al was again assaulted—this time humorously. He had just begun to address a gathering when several people suddenly leaped to their feet and said, "You have spoken too long." They conducted a mock trial and swiftly sentenced him to death by hanging. "This 'Hole in the Wall Gang' came out, had a trial, and *sentenced* me. They actually put a rope around my neck. It was somewhat ghastly—but fun." Instead of dangling their senator by his neck, the gallows attendants underwent a change of heart and presented him with a clock mounted on a block of locally mined trona. Al didn't know trona clocks existed, but under the circumstances he accepted it with great interest and enthusiasm.

WAY DOWN UNDER

In early March 1989, Al, Ann, a military escort, and I departed for Australia on a journey different from most Senate missions. In most cases the government arranges events and provides a military plane, a doctor, Senate staffers, and people to manage luggage and provide logistical assistance. In this case we were on our own.

One issue up for discussion in Australia involved an American policy requiring drug companies to import most of their crystalline morphine—which is derived from poppies and used in the manufacture of prescription painkillers and related products—from companies in south Asia. In theory, buying up Asian morphine would leave less of the raw product to reach American streets as illegal narcotics. Australia, which held tight control over poppy resin processing, thought the U.S. policy unfair to its poppy farmers.

Terrible Billy of Port Fairy

After a series of meetings on other matters in Sydney, we flew to Melbourne. At our hotel we climbed out of our van and were surprised to encounter uniformed members of the hotel management and staff standing at rigid attention in the driveway. With great fanfare we were escorted through the lobby and up in the elevator to the hotel's grandest suite, which had been booked by the U.S. State Department. It was dazzling. Eyeing it with amazement and some suspicion, Al whispered to me, "What the hell will this *cost* us?" A discrete inquiry produced the unwelcome answer: just over $900 Australian per day, or approximately U.S.$700.

Al called the manager aside to explain that he had not made the reservation and was not aware of the room rate; his allowance would not cover such opulence. "If you want to accept the amount of my per diem, I would love it—but I am not going to pay any more than that." The formerly smiling manager blanched when told that the senator's allowance was well under half the quoted rate, but he decided to accept U.S. $210 per day. Following this negotiation, the staff departed less jubilantly than they had entered.

Simpson looked around. He loved what he saw but did feel he should not be there: "They could have herded *cattle* through that suite. It was the damnedest size I have ever seen. It really made me feel quite uncomfortable—too grandiose and pompous for my style." Further disquiet arose during his first full day in Melbourne. He was guest of honor at a luncheon with the board of directors of a large Australian corporation. Everyone but Al appeared to think the session went well, but afterward, in the hotel lobby, he sternly castigated me for not having briefed him properly in advance. I stood my ground, reminding him somewhat bluntly that during our flight from America I had presented him with a large tabbed and indexed briefing book, which he seemed not to have read.

Of great interest to Ann was the discovery that her great-great-grandfather, William "Terrible Billy" Rutledge, had been a co-founder of Port Fairy, a town west of Melbourne. By coincidence, it was on our itinerary because of a nearby facility that processed Tasmanian poppy resin. When we arrived, the townspeople hosted a grand welcoming dinner that ran into the night. City officials reviewed the town's history, explaining that the settlement had been informally started in the late 1820s, well before William Rutledge arrived from Ireland. They said that in 1841, Billy, then thirty-five years old, arrived and purchased eight square miles of land in the area at a price of one British pound per acre. On twenty acres he mapped out lots and dubbed the town Kilmore, after his home town in County Cavan, Ireland. Port Fairy, the community's original name, eventually stuck. It was not explained what Billy did to earn the nickname "Terrible." The next day, we nicknamed a man we met "Crazy."

Crazy Rudy

We toured the morphine plant of Glaxo Chemical (now Glaxo-SmithKline) before a company employee drove us to the old mining town of Ballarat, where we had the most bizarre dining experience of our lives. Al captured the highlights.

> We went down to Rudy's Bistro, an Italian restaurant with the most absolutely goofy, raving madman of a proprietor I

have seen in some time—even back in my bouncing, bartending, and drinking days. He shoehorned us into a table.

The people at one table across the very narrow restaurant got up and left. They said they had not been served, even though they had been there more than an hour. That drove Rudy crazy. He raised hell with the cook and all of the help. He had them nearly in tears. That did seem to accelerate our order, although for a long time everyone was just kind of sitting there, staring.

Then, as a very attractive man and two women were getting ready to leave, Rudy began to rant a little at them. The guy said to Rudy, "You know, I'm just tired of your shit." Then he pushed over a whole wine rack. The bottles smashed as they hit the floor. Glass flew and trays busted as the guy went out onto the street.

Then another guy was running around looking like Hulk Hogan. His jaw was slack and his fly open. He looked like he had just come in from Mars as he wandered around the restaurant soliciting some kind of activity that was difficult to discern.

A short time later people went out in the street to watch Rudy holler "Fuck you" and other remarkable epithets into the night air. The rest of us just sat in the restaurant staring at each other. We began to chuckle as Hardy said, "Boy, this is *really* worth the price of admission."

As we left, I guardedly asked Rudy if he had a book of matches with the name and address imprinted. Rudy was nearly screaming as he said, '*Matches*?! What the *hell* are you *talking* about? I have *lighters!*'

He grabbed a whole handful of them, stuffed them into our hands, and waved his arms like a windmill as we headed out into the street. It was the damnedest evening I have had anywhere—at any restaurant, at any time.

Next we drove to Canberra, the Australian capital, where Al and I joined American Senator Jesse Helms, who was traveling Australia independently, for a meeting with Prime Minister Robert Hawke. Helms used the opportunity to urge Australia's importation of smokeless tobacco. Hawke made it clear that chewing tobacco would not be welcomed in Australia. Helms was undeterred.

Simpson discussed American purchases of Australian opiates, U.S. subsidies of agricultural products, the Export Enhancement Program, the question of American nuclear-powered ships being allowed to port in Australia, and President Bush's resolve on taxes and international trade. Helms took another shot at promoting tobacco imports. Now clearly frustrated, Hawke responded even more curtly that chewing tobacco was *not* a part of the Australian culture and would not become one. He suggested that Helms come up with some other product to promote. Before the session ended, Helms again mentioned tobacco products.

On March 31, 1989, after concluding the trip in Sydney, we departed Australia for Washington via Los Angeles. For the most part Al and Ann had enjoyed their travels, the highlight being Port Fairy. For the military liaison and me, a highlight was crouching in the rear of the van as we motored down the highway north of Port Fairy, drinking beer we had sneaked aboard and clandestinely recording Al's tenor rendition of "Waltzing Matilda" as he belted it cheerfully from the front seat.

Al and Ann were still gripped by jet lag when they boarded a plane bound for Al's fortieth Cody High School reunion. The CHS class of '49 had decided upon their graduation to celebrate this reunion not in Cody but in Hawaii, nearly ten thousand round-trip miles from Washington. It could have been held in Bangladesh, and Al would not have missed it. In 2008, his son Bill explained:

> Dad was always so close to those high school classmates, the class of '49. . . . These were people who loved each other. As time went on, they knew they had seen it all. They'd seen divorce. They'd seen death. They'd seen children die. They'd seen tragedy. And yet they all pulled together and were always there to support one another. Talk is always cheap. People

will say, "Well, they're like family." But these people really
were family—very much so.

TULIPS, HORSESHOES, AND PUPPIES

Once back in the saddle in Washington, Al enjoyed a remarkable
morning at the White House. It was on April 14, 1989.

> I was up early and headed for the White House. We reviewed
> the budget negotiations that had been put together. It sure
> as hell ain't perfect, and it really isn't even adequate. But as
> Senator George Mitchell said, the most unique part is that we
> did it.
>
> We finished our meeting and went out into the Rose
> Garden. It was absolutely one of the most dazzling days I have
> seen in Washington. Tulips were blooming and there were
> blossoms on the dogwoods. There was a cool breeze with a
> temperature of about sixty-five degrees under a cloudless blue
> sky. It was very clear, like in Wyoming.

There was a bank of lights and cameras, and more than a hundred
reporters stood on a steel platform awaiting the outcome of the
budget deliberations. The congressional leaders accompanied the
president to their assigned spots, where nametags had been placed
on the ground. Al's spot was to the left of the president's, at the
extreme edge of the tulip garden.

> I said, "What the hell are you trying to do, push me off into
> the tulips?"
>
> He said, "Simpson, go further than the tulips. Go right out
> into that flower garden and over there, against the wall." Later
> I saw a picture in the *New York Times* showing Bush and me. I
> was pointing, like, "You want me to go over there?" There was
> a good bit of levity and fun. It was spring and I felt like a colt.
>
> The president spoke and introduced others. Finally I
> stepped up and said, "Thank you Mr. President. I wondered
> why you were trying to push me into the tulips. I have done

nothing wrong here and therefore, because you have treated me like that, I intend to give a forty-five-minute talk about the fate of the domestic uranium industry in Wyoming!"

As Al was speaking, the president rolled up his cuff, pointed to his watch, and said, "Oh, no you're not, Simpson!"

After several senators had spoken, they walked toward the White House to chat further with reporters. Simpson told them, "I'm not going to go in there—I'll leave it to you budget guys." Instead, he went back into the Cabinet Room with the president and told him a couple of jokes. Bush responded with two of three of his own and then asked, "What are you doing right now?"

"Well, I am supposed to be at a hearing," Al replied.

Bush said, "Come into the Oval Office for a minute."

We went in there, just the two of us. He shut the door and I stopped right there and said, "You know, George, we do fun around a lot, but I want to tell you how damn proud I am of you. You are so special. You are doing it your own way and I just bust a button seeing you do it, and knowing that the American people are going to come to know you as I do."

He said, "Thanks. Now look what I have done with the office." He has turned it into his own place now. He has the Remington bronzes and some of his own American art. He said, "I just wanted you to see the way I have fixed it up."

Then he said, "Let's go see the horseshoe pit. You haven't seen that, and since you laid it on [defeated] me down there in Florida, I want you to see it."

We went out of the Oval Office, past a side office where Don Regan used to hang out. Outside that door were a beautiful little walkway, a bench, and a swimming pool. Right at the side of the pool was the horseshoe pit.

George said, "Look at this. Isn't this great?" There was a kind of plastic placed around the pins to keep the horseshoes from flying out. He said, "Here, take some shots."

He gave me the shoes and grabbed another set. We threw them at the same time. They were bouncing out and over a little hedge. George said, "Hell, you're not even getting them near the peg."

I said, "Yes, but my coat is in the way."

We threw those kinds of remarks back and forth and had a lot of banter. The White House photographer got some good shots and I have a dandy that George signed for me.

We sat down next to the pool, just the two of us, for about fifteen minutes. I had a nice glass of grapefruit juice with lots of chunks. Then I said, "George, what are we going to do with the future of the entitlements? At some point in time, this 'read my lips' thing is going to eat our asses."

He said, "I know that, and I know too that it was one of my campaign promises and I am going to keep it."

We talked about how he felt about things. He is going at his own pace, totally confident and with that great twinkle in his eye. He shared a few stories and we had a serious talk. We talked about his relationships with Congress—the House and Senate. Then after about fifteen minutes he said, "Let's go see the puppies."

They left the pool and walked into the back door of the White House and into what looked like an old laundry room. Mrs. Bush was there in her slippers, sitting by a big box that contained shredded paper and six puppies.

They were the most darling puppies I've ever seen. Millie, their mother, was sitting just outside of the box. Those little guys would jump out of there and head on over and try to nurse. She was very patient.

I gave Barbara a big hug and the three of us just sat there a while. As we looked at the puppies and held them, she said, "How's the weather out there?" I said it was beautiful, absolutely spring-like and magnificent.

She said, "These puppies need to get out. Let's take them out and let them play on the grass."

George said, "Well, grab hold, Simpson. Start filling the sack."

We put the six puppies in a big old sack. Millie was watching very, very carefully! Then Barbara, George, and I headed out of the room, down the elevator and through the downstairs of the White House. I was holding my side of the sack, George the other. As we passed one room, I asked, "Whose place is that?"

He said, "That's the White House physician, the eminent Burt Lee." He was one of our fishing buddies in Florida. We swung the door open while we were hauling those pups and said, "What the hell are you doing in there, Bert? We have patients for you to examine!"

He gave a professional kind of laugh from his room and said, "Who is there?"

We responded, "It is us, the dog handlers."

Burt came out and was glad to see us, especially Barbara, who was behind us. She had just been diagnosed as needing treatment for a thyroid deficiency. She seems to be doing well, but has lost weight. She said she feels well and looks well, although she is a little tired.

We spent a few minutes there and then I said, "Lee, you can help us take these dogs out to the Rose Garden."

George and I swung on down the hall, through the whole White House and out the back, where we had been before. The media had departed, although the scaffolding was still there and the brilliance of the day was unalloyed.

We reached down, took those little guys out of that sack, and set them right on the grass, with the blades of grass tickling their little bellies. Boy did they frolic. There was one male with a mark on his face that would identify him. The other five were females. Millie was standing there, watching.

We set them out on the grass and George, Barbara, and I talked for about a half hour.

While they were talking, an aide brought a lawn chair for Barbara, who asked Al about his parents. Everything went well until Al was "violently attacked."

> George and I began to talk, now just the two of us standing there. The dogs were milling around us, the puppies. In fact, one of them stuck his sharp little teeth into my ankle. I told George about it and he said, "Hell, that's not so."
>
> I said, "Well, watch!" I'll be damned if the little guy didn't do it again. George got a hell of a kick out of that.
>
> I said, "You know, I came up here for a meeting and ended up hauling dogs—and now the little sons of bitches are tearing my clothes off! I missed a hearing, and meanwhile you're egging those dogs on!"
>
> We laughed about that, and then began to talk seriously about some things. We talked about personalities, and how tough it is to get certain things done with all the political "undercutting" that was taking place at times.
>
> We were talking about some person in the House and George said, "I don't know—what do I do with that guy? He has always been a thorn in my side."
>
> I said, "Yeah, George, but there's a difference now. You are the president of the whole United States."
>
> He said, "Yeah, that does make a bit of difference, doesn't it?"
>
> We reviewed the budget some more and talked about Dick Cheney's nomination [as secretary of defense] and how great that was. We talked about the Iran-Contra thing and how that had been put to bed. We talked about minimum wage, talked about family, friends, and my trip to Australia. We talked about Dan Quayle and many things. We were just standing there on this magnificent spring day. I figured I wouldn't leave until being thrown out.

Finally, at about a quarter till twelve—I had spent an hour with him by then—George said, "Well, I think I've caught up with my schedule. It has been fun. I'm glad that guy canceled out of the meeting this morning."

I said, "So am I, pal. What a great time."

We headed back to the Oval Office. There was a great big sign. It said "Beware of Dog." George said Reagan had put that out there to keep the squirrels away—and so that Millie would feel strong and vital.

I said, "This has been an absolutely marvelous treat for me. I love you both and just think you are doing a tremendous job."

As we went through the side door he said, "We love you too. Goodbye, my friend."

Out the door I went. I will not forget that one. It is clearly etched into my mind—very, very clearly.

IN DEFENSE

On numerous occasions Simpson came to the defense of people he thought were being unfairly attacked—Democrats and Republicans alike. One was Environmental Protection Administrator Anne Gorsuch, the first female administrator of the EPA and a native of Casper, Wyoming. In February 1983 Simpson authored an article in her defense for the *Washington Post*.

> Lord, here we go again! With the scent of the kill filling the flared and twitching nostrils of "the observers" in Washington, and with good old "high emotion" vaporizing all desire to seek reason and balance, the "pack" is circling in on the Environmental Protection Agency and its Administrator Anne Gorsuch. It reminds me of that old cartoon of the two buzzards in the tree, with one saying, "Patience my ass. I'm going to kill something!"

Gorsuch was eventually compelled to resign, along with twenty of her top employees, after being found in contempt of Congress on a

House vote of 259–105 for refusing to disclose documents related to a conflict of interest involving the Superfund program.

Craig Thomas

In early 1989 Simpson was not defending so much as promoting another person. His friend Craig Thomas was running for the Wyoming House seat being vacated by Dick Cheney, the incoming secretary of defense. On the campaign trail Simpson and Thomas stopped at the Amoco oil refinery in Casper and were not warmly received. "They did everything but hock goobers at us! In fact, they handed Craig a yellow piece of paper from the AFL-CIO, explaining why people should vote for his *opponent*. We looked at each other and said, 'Why the hell hang around *here?*'"

That uncomfortable moment was followed by another, in the eastern Wyoming town of Guernsey.

> I looked into the back of the room and saw my old friend Jim Gibson standing there. He was making a motion with his hands, up and down. I just stared at him and then looked around behind me. Then he made the motion again. Finally, I realized that my fly was open. Others realized it too!
>
> My face was red and after zipping up, and I said, "Now I understand why you people in the front were all facing the other direction. Don't worry about a little thing like that." That brought down the house.
>
> Then I told them the story about how Churchill once came before the podium. As he spoke, people were laughing at the wrong times. Finally realizing his fly was open, he said, "Never fear—a dead horse will never bolt the barn."

On Election Day Thomas defeated Malcolm Wallop's former rival John Vinich by 13,500 votes. On April 26, 1989, he was sworn in as Wyoming's sole member of the United States House of Representatives.

President Bush

In the wake of China's April 1989 Tiananmen Square massacre, President Bush issued an executive order permitting all Chinese people in the United States to adjust their immigration status, so that they could not be forced to return to China. He vetoed legislation from Congress intended to accomplish much the same thing. That was a problem for House member Nancy Pelosi, sponsor of the vetoed bill and destined to become speaker of the House. Simpson sided with the president: "The administrative order does more for Chinese people in America than the vetoed bill would have. The bill only helped Chinese students. George's administrative action helped *all* Chinese people in our country."

When congressional opponents set out to override the president's veto, Simpson set out to protect it. He was soon distressed that something he said about the situation during an Immigration Subcommittee meeting was interpreted as conceding the president's defeat. Referring to the prospect of the House overriding the veto, Al said: "Before this thing passes like a dose of salts, and before we get about five votes, I would like to weigh in here." The media then reported that the Republican whip of the Senate was counting only five votes in support of the president. That was not what Al had meant, but it was too late to clarify. "It made me look like a boob," he sighed. "But it's not the first time that particular thing has happened."

At the White House, the president, who had served as ambassador to China, was irritated: "How did we ever get into a situation where I'm supposed to be less in favor of human rights than the Democrats—or that I am interested in seeing Chinese students returned to their destruction in China? I lived there for a year and a half and I know the cast of characters. This veto override effort is an attempt to embarrass me badly. . . . I don't appreciate it one damn bit." Senator Dole began making calls to senators, urging their support of the president's veto.

That afternoon former president Nixon phoned Simpson: "How did we ever get into this situation? Do we really only have five

votes? What can I do?" he asked. "Well, you can call a few senators," Al suggested. "I'll get back to you on that." Simpson and
Dole decided to have Nixon call Senators Humphrey, Symms, Hatfield, and Roth. Then Simpson convened a meeting of the "deputy
whips," an unofficial group interested in assisting the leadership. By
that evening they appeared to have the thirty-four votes necessary
to protect the president's veto.

Simpson visited with Congresswoman Pelosi. "I told her that
we had the votes to protect the veto and she seemed genuinely
shocked. I told her that it was an exercise we really didn't have
to go through. That steamed her up a bit." With the veto override vote pending, Al found one senator particularly agitated. "Ted
[Kennedy] was speaking—huffing and puffing all over the issue. He
went into one of his rants, ripping off a few minutes on patriotism,
the Statue of Liberty, freedom, democracy, human rights and civil
rights. He finally calmed down."

The Senate voted to sustain the president's veto, with three votes
to spare. It pleased Simpson to have defended his friend, the president. "Everybody did a hell of a lot of good work. The deputy
whip system worked well. The president worked superbly, he was
marvelous. It was his day to carry. Richard Nixon did his job too."
Al phoned the former president, who said, "Boy, we kicked their
asses." Simpson told his diary that Nixon used additional expressions that were "much more pungent."

Al soon encountered reporters who seemed disappointed by the
president's victory: "I answered some press calls from the *New York
Times* and the *Washington Post*. The poor old souls were very disappointed that we came up with the votes. The press, in their magnificent arrogance, had portrayed in gasping voices the night before
that the president was going to lose his first contest with the Congress. It tickled my fanny more than anything to ram it back on
them."

Barbara Bush was first to express appreciation. At a White House
event, she said, "Al, that was marvelous, what you did." She gave

him a hug, kissed his cheek, and said, "I know how important that was for George, to set a tone. It was just a beautiful thing for you to do. You're my favorite." As Simpson and Dole presented the president with the official roll call tally, Al joked, "You are a pretty poor fisherman, George, but you're a hell of a president."

The Conciliator

This victory did not keep a number of Al's Republican colleagues from being unhappy with him about other matters.

> They were dropping rocks all over George Bush. I took notes and vowed I would call him. I haven't done that before, but there is enough stuff brewing that I decided to.
>
> I spent about twenty minutes with the president, telling him in rather lucid fashion what had occurred with regard to the ranking members. I communicated my colleagues' irritation with the slowness of judgeship nominations and the lack of Administration consensus on numerous contentious issues. A particular annoyance was that the liaison officers at various agencies, and at the Republican White House, had been making deals with Democrats, while leaving Republicans out of the loop.

The next day Al met with White House Chief of Staff John Sununu. The two decided there should be periodic meetings between Sununu and the ranking Senate Republicans. "They will start when the Republican leadership meets with Sununu next week. They can bitch and whine and snort and tell him exactly what is up." During their first session, the president and vice president walked in. Simpson was pleased to have engineered the exchange, and especially gratified that the president recognized and appreciated his efforts.

Al was also pleased to have worked with former president Nixon, and arranged to again speak with him in person. At a Washington hotel, Nixon said President Bush needed more "fighters" in his

Cabinet. "You have to have that. I had political people, real fighters. There are very few in this Cabinet, almost none." The two discussed several other matters, leaving Simpson with the feeling that
his work as an unofficial, unnamed, self-initializing intermediary
was of value and an example of good leadership.

The Hammer

A few days later Al engaged himself in the legal fate of ninety-
one-year-old industrialist Armand Hammer. Years earlier, it had
been good for President Nixon that Hammer had provided a total
of $54,000 in Republican presidential campaign contributions. It
was bad for Hammer that at least one donation was given illegally.
In the wake of a 1975 investigation stemming out of Watergate,
Hammer was charged. Appearing in court in a wheelchair, he pled
guilty but emphasized that he was admitting guilt only because of
his serious heart condition. He was fined and put on probation but
served no jail time.

Hammer later requested that President Reagan pardon him—
while simultaneously donating $1.3 million to Reagan's presiden-
tial library. On his pardon application, he listed the reason for his
request as "innocence." When Reagan's lawyers saw that Hammer
had initially admitted guilt, they found him, for that reason, ineli-
gible to be pardoned. Hammer then rescinded his donation to the
library—which sued unsuccessfully for the money.

At the end of George H. W. Bush's successful campaign for president, Hammer gave the Republican National Committee $110,000
and updated his pardon application, now listing his reason as "compassion." He wanted Simpson to approach the president on his
behalf. Hammer said, "The pardon would be a wonderful thing for
an old man to have, in his ninety-first year."

Simpson agreed to give it a shot. "He asked me to talk with
George Bush. I told him I would, so off to the White House I
went." His session with the president was actually a routine meeting
that included the ranking Senate Republicans. Before any business

was conducted, Simpson turned to Bush and asked, "George, what about Armand Hammer?"

Bush was familiar with the case and motioned his counsel over. According to Al's diary, the attorney said, "We have looked at everything, and it is going to be approved. It should be on your desk now." Bush turned to Simpson, winked, and said, "You can take credit for it." Al said he was not looking for credit but just hoped it would be done.

Back in his office, Simpson phoned Hammer, who said, "I have been sitting here just half sick, thinking that because you didn't call, it must be bad news. What happened?"

"Everything is right on course," Al assured him.

There was a long moment of silence before Hammer said, "I am just so thrilled that I can hardly speak. It is a wonderful thing for an old man, if they can do that." He repeated several times that he would forever be in Simpson's debt. "It hasn't happened yet," Al cautioned. A few days later, Hammer wrote.

> Dear Al:
>
> I shall ever be appreciative of your interest and assistance in my obtaining a Pardon from President bush [sic]. Frances and I send our affectionate wishes to you and Ann with the fond hope of meeting very soon again.
>
> Sincerely,
> Armand

Bush's first presidential pardon was to Hammer, on August 14, 1989. Hammer, who had told Simpson he wanted to use much of his wealth in support of cancer research, died of cancer on December 10, 1990.

Self-Defense

Although Simpson was popular, well liked, and a man who would generally accommodate the interests of others, he could strike like a cobra if treated discourteously, especially when exhausted.

In June 1989 he returned to Washington after a tiring trip to Taiwan. When he walked into the Senate chamber, the next item on the agenda was his latest immigration legislation. Fighting the fog of jet lag, he asked his colleagues to delay the debate a few minutes, until he could prepare. He was dumbfounded to hear resistance to his request. "I lost my marbles. I said, 'I have accommodated every son of a bitch in this place for ten years, and now they won't accommodate *me?*'" A "rich discussion" followed, resulting in a seventy-five-minute delay.

Later in the day he dropped by a Republican policy meeting. As if Al needed a reminder of his youthful antics, Senator Conrad Burns of Montana gleefully presented him with a photo of a man peering into his mailbox. It had been shot full of holes.

IMPERIOUS, CROOKED, INFLUENTIAL, PRESIDENTIAL

During a meeting on federal drug policy on September 15, 1989, Simpson was irritated that every senator participating seemed to have different estimates for the cost of enforcement. He turned to Robert Byrd and complained, "I've never seen any figures yet that were correct. You estimate $50 million a year, and when it turns out to be $500 million you will say, 'Sorry, that's just the way it is.'"

Byrd took the challenge even more personally than usual. "I have never seen him so bizarre, or acting stranger. He realizes that he has more power than anyone in this place, because he is chairman of the Appropriations Committee. Every one of us has a list of things we want out of that committee, and he is the guy running the list. He does it masterfully, not allowing *anyone* to forget that he has 'the list.'" It did seem to Simpson that Byrd was not coordinating his legislative activities with anyone, including his majority leader, George Mitchell. Not even George Bush, president of the United States, had been able to contact Byrd in recent days. "The president tried to reach him three times, tried to invite him to Camp David, all to no avail. What a strange, bizarre, lonely, vulnerable, and even frightened man . . . and yet, what an unbelievable success story he is."

Byrd's "imperious behavior" during consideration of the drug bill mobilized and angered Republicans. Several senators told Simpson they had taken all they could tolerate of the Democrat's overbearing manner. They gathered to plot against their nemesis. Al observed: "Boy, they are really out to strike terror into the heart of Robert Byrd, since he is doing it to us. It is the damnedest thing to watch. I have never seen him involved in more bizarre behavior patterns. He is in full array. He has every damn person in the place cowed, because he controls the purse strings in every state."

Two days later Al joined a group of congressional leaders at the White House to mull over their Byrd problem. Several people favored blocking approval of appropriations bills, the passage of which was Byrd's primary goal.

> It is the only way we are going to nail him, by holding up
> on those until we get some sense into him. The power of the
> imperious Byrd is something terrible. If you talk tough with
> him, you are going to lose your money.
>   His conduct is almost Queeg-like, as in Captain Philip
> Francis Queeg's role in the movie *Caine Mutiny*. He rambles
> on and terrorizes people. His is an unbelievable performance.

The authoritarian Queeg was removed from power due to mental instability, but Byrd remained on course and on point. On October 4, 1989, Senator Byrd hosted a "prayer breakfast." Most senators attended, some of them present out of unspoken fear that Byrd would otherwise be angered. "Old Robert was in rare form," Al noted. "He really brought down the hellfire and brimstone. Great deference was paid him. He has everybody in the whole building hanging by the yipper."

The next day President Bush arrived at the Capitol for a meeting. Senator Dole suggested that since Byrd was presiding over the

Senate, it would be a nice gesture for Bush to express his greetings. The president entered the chamber, walked up to Byrd, and politely paid his respects. Simpson was later told that at the moment Byrd realized Bush was entering the chamber, he checked with the parliamentarian to see if the rules allowed the president to be there.

An encounter a few days later illustrates the extent to which Byrd kept everyone walking on eggshells. Byrd was walking down a Capitol hallway when Simpson and I approached from the opposite direction. As we passed him Al looked up and said, "Hello, Bob." Moments later he turned to me and said, "That was a mistake. I just called him Bob. I shouldn't have done that. He prefers to be called Robert." Al briefly considered catching up with Byrd to apologize but decided that would only make matters worse.

Simpson once asked Byrd what he did for recreation.

> My recreation is the Senate. I have been to one movie in forty
> years, and I walked out on that. It was with Yul Brynner.
> I forgot the name of it. I have been to three baseball games
> in my life—two in one day, a double-header. I have been
> to one football game, and that was a game where I gave the
> queen her crown at halftime. It was between West Virginia
> and Maryland. I think that in athletics, if you have seen one
> game, you have seen them all. What do I have to show for
> three hours of watching something like that?

Byrd said that during a recent Senate recess he had read all thirty-eight Shakespeare plays, completed proofing his history of the Senate, and read Webster's dictionary cover to cover. Simpson recalls that Byrd once told him: "What we want to remember is that the Senate leaves its mark on us—we do not leave our mark on it."

Robert Byrd had served in the Senate fifty-one years, longer than anyone in congressional history, when he died on June 28, 2010, at age ninety-two. Later that day Simpson released this comment: "During one night session, he asked me a remarkable question: 'Alan, in my leadership responsibilities, do our colleagues respect me or fear me?' To me, the balance ran toward respect, but I hedged: 'It's just that they are in total awe of you'—as we all were."

Judging the Judge

Simpson's ability to judge character was put to use in the case of federal judge Alcee Hastings. On a 413–3 vote, the House of Representatives had impeached Hastings on charges of bribery and perjury. It was now up to the Senate to convict or acquit him. "We voted on seventeen articles of impeachment. It only took one to throw him out. The first vote was on the charge that he knowingly and willfully misled and misdirected evidence and committed perjury. He needed 31 votes on his side. He got 26. A read dud, that guy. I voted to convict him on all charges, except one that had to do with wiretapping. He was a real smoothie."

After his conviction Hastings conducted a news conference on the Capitol steps to announce his intention to run for governor of Florida. He did so, unsuccessfully, and then campaigned for a newly formed seat in the U.S. House of Representatives—even though his removal as a federal judge barred him from holding "any public office of honor, trust or profit."

Alcee Hastings was elected to the House, became a member of the House Rules Committee, and eventually became a senior member of the House Permanent Select Committee on Intelligence. In late 2006 the issue of his impeachment surfaced as he sought chairmanship of the House Intelligence Committee. He was denied.

The Man from Gdansk

On November 15, 1989, Al Simpson focused on Lech Walesa of Poland. He was the former trade union and human rights activist, 1983 winner of the Nobel Peace Prize, and future president of Poland. Speaking before a joint session of Congress, Walesa began with a reference known to most Americans.

Ladies and Gentlemen . . . "We the people" . . . With these
words, I wish to begin my address. I do not need to remind
anyone here where these words come from. And I do not
need to explain that I, an electrician from Gdansk, am also
entitled to invoke them.

I stand before you as the third foreign non-head of state
invited to address the joint Houses of Congress of the United
States . . . the Congress, which for many people in the world,
oppressed and stripped of their rights, is a beacon of freedom
and a bulwark of human rights.

Simpson was so moved by the speech that he placed a complete
copy of it into his private diary, the only speech thus honored. He
described it as one of the most moving events of his time in Washington: "He was most inspirational—a man small in stature, but
big in human spirit. He had a kindly and gentle face, and when he
went to the podium of the United States House of Representatives
in joint session assembled, the shouts just welled up over him. Great
tears formed in his eyes. I tell you, there was a lump in every throat
in that building. It was a beautiful talk, spectacular."

Later, while meeting with Simpson and nine other senators,
Walesa emphasized that the people of his country were not asking
for American money. They were asking for an investment of time,
attention, and understanding. Walesa's visit gave Simpson much to
ponder.

I looked at the Capitol Dome late that night and thought of
the privileges we have in this country, of how we fought for
our independence through our revolution. Then I thought of
that quiet gentle man with that lovely face and the great laugh
and genuine warmth, the man who brought his country from
communism to some form of democracy yet undefined—but
one based on freedom.

What an interesting and remarkable thing, freedom, and
what it drives people to do all over the world. There is the

living example in our speed-enthralled, computerized, zap your neighbor, shoot the works, next quarter's bottom line society. He is the living essence and epitome of the phrase "one man can change the world."

Renewal

President Bush decided to deliver a speech in support of the Clean Air Act, and do so at the base of the magnificent Teton Mountains in western Wyoming. The previous summer, 1988, had been the region's driest in history, contributing to a series of major forest fires that burned more than a million acres in the Yellowstone ecosystem and 36 percent of Yellowstone National Park. Since 1978, because of biological evidence that fires have always played a necessary role in renewing and invigorating forests, the National Park Service and U.S. Forest Service had allowed some fires started by lightning to continue. Senator Simpson had been a vocal critic of letting some lightning fires burn.

Now the president and his party, including Simpson, were touring burned areas by helicopter. They landed in a remote location to continue their inspection on foot, and were fascinated by the forest's renewal. "On one totally black area of ground, we kicked a charred log. Underneath were three tiny and beautiful emerald-green pine trees less than an inch high. Who would have believed it?"

Bush and Simpson spent the evening together in nearby Teton National Park. "George caught fish. We filleted them and had them at the cocktail hour. There was a full moon, or nearly full. That night, I just threw open the curtains of my room at the Jackson Hole Lodge and turned off the lights. The bed was bathed in moonlight and the Tetons were shimmering in the background. Wow. That restoreth one's soul."

Movie Night

Later that fall President Bush called Al to ask if he and Ann were available that evening for dinner and a movie. They were, of course, and at the appointed hour they carried a package of Wyoming Pine Bluff Potato Chips into the White House. "We promoted our Wyoming product, sat down, ordered our soft drinks and dug in for one rollercoaster of a movie. It was called *War of the Roses*. It gave me the heebie-jeebies. I think that movie will shock the public about marriage in the way the movie *Fatal Attraction* changed perceptions about adultery."

After the movie's disturbing conclusion, the president and first lady escorted Al and Ann around the White House. When the four sat before a roaring fire, Bush reached for a telephone and called his mother. He handed the phone to Al, who explained that he was the son of Milward and Lorna Simpson. Mrs. Bush recalled them with affection.

Next, they strolled into the president's study to see his "new toy." With the push of a button, a section of wall opened up to expose a bank of television sets that were all turned on and tuned to different networks. Bush proudly demonstrated how he could "freeze" any one of them, or watch all of them at the same time. Simpson found it a fascinating rig. "George was having fun with his 'flipper,' trying to get it all zeroed in."

As the group sat for dinner, Al was asked to give the blessing. He requested that they all hold hands. "God bless these special people in this special home. We are thankful that America has come to know them as we have: as people of gentleness and civility and good will, a truly remarkable and delicious pair." Also delicious were the soup and Florida stone crabs with accompanying chardonnay. After dinner the group wandered through the private quarters, examining, Simpson said later, "every nook and cranny." They noted that Nancy Reagan had renovated the entire area, leaving it in beautiful condition for the Bush family.

Near the evening's end they were treated to something experienced by very few people in the history of the nation: a visit to the roof of the White House. "It was a beautiful, crisp night. From the roof we looked right over at the Washington Monument. It was a magnificent view. I don't know what the Secret Service thought of our being up there." I asked Al the next day what kind of defense hardware he had witnessed atop the White House; he declined to describe anything in detail, saying only: "I'll tell you this, they are ready for *anything*."

They strolled through much of the White House that night, telling stories and laughing as they walked. When the time came to leave, Al and Ann folded themselves into their little car and drove to the southwest gate. As they exited the White House grounds, a familiar feeling swept over them: "The minute that old gate swung shut, there we were—just Joe Citizen and spouse. It was a feeling of great transition, of leaving that magnificent president and first lady's home. We went on down the road toward our own home, talking about the evening."

Chapter Thirteen

HIGHS AND LOWS

~

NOW AT THE zenith of his career, Senator Simpson was frequently being honored. In 1987 he had been awarded an honorary law degree at Notre Dame University. In May 1989 he was similarly acknowledged at American University's Bender Arena in Washington. After receiving his degree and addressing the students, he was given a standing ovation. University president Richard Berendzen turned to him and said, "I have never seen students respond like that." Ann concurred. It was one of his best public addresses ever.

A few weeks later the Western Stock Show Association in Denver gave Al its highest honor, the Citizen of the West award. He began his acceptance remarks predictably: "I remember years ago, there was a group called 'Cattlemen's Anonymous.' If you felt like going into the cattle business, you could call an unlisted phone number and someone would come over to drink with you until you got the idea out of your head." Near the end of his speech, he turned reflective. "I salute my dear mother and father, the central core and internal working parts of my life. They are the spark plugs in my engine of life."

His relationship with his parents surfaced publicly again, in Casper on October 28. He was being roasted by the Wyoming Boys Club when the master of ceremonies read a letter from a woman the MC said had been unable to attend.

Dear Alan:
. . . Did I ever have a difficult time trying to convince you boys to join the choir! Then, when I finally did coax you to join, you found out you had to wear robes in church and I nearly lost the entire bunch!

Then I nearly lost you all again, when you grew old enough to have girlfriends and decided you would rather spend your evenings with them than practicing hymns like "Onward Christian Soldiers." But I was sly! I changed it from a boys' choir to a youth choir and included the girls. That seemed the only way I was going to get you boys to come to practice. . . .

Please always remember to keep your sense of humor, and remember what your Dad and I taught you: a sense of humor is the irreplaceable solvent for the abrasive elements of life. It has been this family's saving grace so many times.

Late in the year Al and Ann attended a production of *Twelfth Night* at the Folger Shakespeare Library. As they strolled back to the Senate, they compared notes about the many special moments in their lives. "It was one of those magnificent nights—not too cold, but very clear. The Capitol was lighted so beautifully against a blue-black sky that it looked like a piece of bisque porcelain. I could almost reach out and touch the 'relief' of it. It was the kind of night when you would like to go out and neck with a beautiful woman— so I did. Those Greybull girls are more advanced than Cody girls."

Reading this assertion in 2008, Ann laughed and said, "I don't know about that! I'm pretty sure those Cody girls were pretty advanced too." Asked if she had ever had second thoughts about her marriage to Al, Ann said, "Well, yes! I had second thoughts—but not about divorce. *Murder*, maybe, but not divorce!"

OUT OF OPTIONS

By late November 1989, more than three years had passed since an X-ray had revealed the unidentified and mysterious dark spot in Al's left lung. At Mount Sinai Hospital in New York City, doctors continued to ponder the mystery. "I took the 'lung test,' the exhalation and inhalation to determine lung capacity. I expel 8.2 liters of air on one exhale. The average for my size and build and age would be 5.9 liters. Both ladies running the test said they had never seen a lung capacity like that in anybody my size."

Because lung capacity was the only thing determined with certainty, and doctors in several other medical facilities had also failed to explain the problem, invasive surgery was scheduled. Al let doctors take two pints of his blood for possible use during the operation, but he continued to search for ways to avoid it. "I tell you, I am just sick about it," he confided to his diary.

Before his check-in date, he and Ann flew to Jackson, Wyoming. During lunch with their daughter, they calmly explained what would happen ten days hence. "Sue cried, and Ann cried. Frankly, I had no faith at all in the navy or army doctors. I had seen enough. I had been in the army. I was active with the VA and had seen some of the butchery that had gone on in VA hospitals. I hate to say it that way, but that is exactly what it was. They were not the top doctors. I don't give a damn what you say."

At the last moment it was determined that sometime years before, most likely after falling asleep with a Thayer's Slippery Elm throat lozenge in his mouth, Simpson had unknowingly aspirated the tablet during a coughing fit. With no dissolving chemistry in his lung, it remained trapped in its new home and for years flummoxed a score of the nation's top medical specialists in several of the country's top medical facilities.

It was only while being interviewed for this book, seventeen years later, that Sue learned her father had long grappled with the problem. She was flabbergasted. "You mean that went on months and months before they found it was a cough drop, that he had aspirated a *cough drop*? I never knew that. I had no idea." Tears built in her eyes. Then suddenly she laughed. "Dad would be *happy* to tell you about his feet! Jeez, Louise! He could go on about that for *days*—but real life threatening problems . . . ! But then again, if I had Dad's feet, I'd probably talk about them too."

In early 1990 Sue wrote a special letter to her father. She gave permission for its reproduction.

Dear Dad:

What an amazing man you are. Sometimes I forget to tell you how proud I am of you and how grateful I am to you for the richness of my life. You have always been, and are, such a loving and understanding father and generous provider for your children.

I am filled with awe and admiration when I watch you with others. Your way with people and the openness with which you approach everyone you meet is amazing. You truly employ your God given gifts in your life to the fullest.

You are a great example to me. You give me much, a wonderful heritage, a sense of what is right, and an ability to see beyond myself to the Big Picture.

Life. Your approach to life, your love of life carries into everything you do and touches everyone who knows you.

Thanks for your pride in me. I treasure your belief in me, and hold your love tightly. Just wanted to let you know that you are the first one I remember. You will be the last one I forget. I love you so.

A COLLAGE OF EMOTIONS

As hundreds of dignitaries gathered for the formal annual banquet of the prestigious Alfalfa Club in Washington, Al Simpson was the man at the microphone. He greeted America's president, George Bush, with the words, "I greet you on behalf of your fellow Alfalfans."

"Oh, Lord, here you are giving me the business again," Bush laughed. "I suppose you have those same old corny jokes again."

Al proudly responded, "You bet—and for one reason: They *work*." As the program began, he related the history of the Alfalfa Club before declaring dinner with the traditional phrase, "Bring on the Lobster." The evening rocked with hilarity and camaraderie. Its highlight, Simpson's speech, had people gasping in laughter. "My remarks seemed to be well received. I worked like hell on them and they were delivered easily. People just seemed to lap them up.

Brother Pete said it was one of my best efforts—and he has heard a lot of them."

Congressman Dan Rostenkowski, a Democrat, was among the speakers joshing President Bush. As he was doing so, Bush slipped Al a note: "Al, have you got a one-liner I can use that would fit what Rosty is doing?" Simpson modified the line he had used on television reporter Sam Donaldson years earlier. Bush got up and said, "Danny is a self-made man—thus saving God from an awesome responsibility." The rebuke brought laughter so vigorous that Bush was surprised. He looked down from the podium and whispered to Al, "I'll be damned."

The Crushing

On January 28, 1990, the Simpson family perched excitedly in front of their television in Cody. They were hopeful that the Denver Broncos, the "Orange Crush," would crush the San Francisco 49ers in the Super Bowl. "Son Bill and I cheered one time, when the Broncos made a twenty-six-yard gain. From then on there wasn't a single peep out of anybody. Nothing. It was the most devastating loss I have ever seen in all of my years of athletics. The final score was 55–10. The Broncos got creamed, destroyed, humiliated, ridiculed and embarrassed." To date, the forty-five-point loss is the largest margin in Super Bowl history.

Al's emotions hit a different extreme three nights later, during the president's State of the Union address in Washington. "The real thrill was looking up at the gallery as the first lady came in with Marilyn Quayle—and Ann Simpson. Annie sat right there with them for the evening's event. Many times the networks zeroed in on her, as you might imagine. She was the dazzler of the evening."

Al was in for yet another emotional twist a few weeks later when Vaclav Havel, president of Czechoslovakia, addressed a joint session of Congress. Simpson was delighted to be seated next to America's ambassador to Czechoslovakia, Shirley Temple Black—until he realized something disturbing: "She is now sixty-three years old, and she told me she *smokes cigarettes*! What a stunning shock to the boy inside of me, to think that my little tousle-haired friend Shirley Temple, five years my senior and the jewel of my young life, smokes evil and putrid bits of vegetation."

"Pure Bullshit"

Although he scrapped often with the media, Simpson did try to cooperate, even with the most unusual requests. The oddest came from *Dossier* magazine. "It was goofy. They had me sitting on the *floor*, on a *pillow*! When Ann got there, they had some other goofy ideas. I'm sure we both looked pissed off. One guy asked me to cup my face with both hands and look into the camera. I said, 'Good God, pal, if they ever saw that in Wyoming, that would be the end of me.' Besides, I don't *ever* do that."

The lengthy April 1990 *Dossier* article was headlined "Alan Simpson Bares All" and subtitled "A Candid Conversation with the Most Popular Man in the Senate." It included photographs and covered numerous topics but focused particularly on Robert Bork's Supreme Court nomination hearings and Simpson's critical observations about Senator Ted Kennedy's tactics.

In reality, Simpson's most critical views, as committed to his diary, were of Senator Howard Metzenbaum. Now the Ohioan was trying to derail Senate confirmation of William F. Downes, a Democratic Wyoming lawyer nominated to the U.S. District Court for Wyoming. Metzenbaum's objection had to do with bra burning. Al remembers that Metzenbaum walked up to him and said, "I want to ask you about this Bill Downes. I understand that he and two other men, named Herschler and Sedar, watched a bra burning at the Democratic National Convention—and *laughed*!"

He stared at Metzenbaum and said, "Metz, you are talking about two dear friends of mine, 'Gov Ed' Herschler and 'Whiskey Dick' Sedar. I would be surprised if they *hadn't* laughed at a bra burning. So what's your problem?"

"Well, this is *disgusting*," Metzenbaum stammered. "I have an *eye witness* who said that Downes not only laughed but made some kind of *remark*. That's *wrong*, Al."

Now it was Al's turn to be steamed. "This is pure bullshit, Howard. It is like you saying the Elks Club is some commie organization. Or how about the one you brought up the other day about the *Masons*? Eighteen members of the Senate are Masons. Go talk to John Glenn or Sam Nunn about that. This is bullshit—and your staff is *insane*. So *what* if someone burned a bra, and these guys laughed? Don't you have other things to worry about?"

Metzenbaum finally said, "Okay, I'll tell you what—I just won't show up at the hearing." Simpson thought that a fine idea and advised Senator Kennedy not to count on Metzenbaum's vote in opposition to the Downes nomination. "That's the way it worked. Old Metz kept his word and never showed up, and Bill Downes is on the court doing a hell of a good job."

Happy Birthday, Wyoming

Al stood before a large machine at the Bureau of Printing and Engraving and watched as millions of Wyoming centennial stamps were produced. Responsible for the production was Jack Rosenthal of Casper, Wyoming, a close Simpson family friend and chair of the National Postal Services Citizens' Stamp Advisory Committee. Back at the Senate, Simpson went to the floor and sought recognition: "The U.S. Postal Service has issued a centennial commemorative stamp that is a real piece of work in itself. The scene on that stamp . . . is based on a Conrad Schwiering painting of Wyoming's magnificent Teton Mountains. . . . It represents the authentic quality of Wyoming life—the spirit—the sense of independence—the true freedom."

Al was eager to help Wyoming celebrate its one hundredth birthday, on July 10, 1990. A celebratory performance of the Cheyenne symphony had him pacing backstage in anticipation. He had agreed to narrate the "The Lincoln Portrait" in the concert's second half. He was excited. He was energized. He was a nervous wreck. He was familiar with the performance, having seen Walter Cronkite present it at the Bohemian Grove, but he knew he did not have the nationally acclaimed professional broadcaster's soothing, rich, fatherly voice. In fact, he found the whole idea of coordinating his dialogue with music intimidating.

"I was nervous as hell. I had never said *anything* on a stage in the midst of a symphony orchestra. I felt like a fighter in training," he said. He stood nervously in the wings as a stagehand walked out to raise his stool, music stand, and microphone to his height. The audience laughed and applauded appreciatively. Offstage, the conductor whispered. "Al, I'll be damned. You've got them in the palm of your hand *already*."

The auditorium grew dark. The audience applauded enthusiastically. Simpson swallowed hard, entered the stage and sat motionless on his stool.

> There was nothing to do but hide my knees when they started to knock—and boy, I'll tell you, they did. Those magnificent woodwinds and violins surrounded me. They just sucked the wind out of me. I had goose pimples all over.
>
> When [the conductor] nodded my way, I started narrating. When he gave me the cues, I paused. It all seemed to be working beautifully and powerfully—at least I sure thought it was.

As the minutes passed and the performance remained on track, he grew more confident. By the time the piece reached its conclusion, he was beaming. He bowed, turned, and was about to disappear backstage when someone grabbed his arm and said, "Look out there, look at the audience." He glanced toward the sea of beaming faces and realized they were giving him a standing ovation. He felt a wave of relief and joy as he returned to center stage, bowed low and whispered to the conductor, "You made a *folk hero* out of me."

Wyoming governor Mike Sullivan came to the microphone and said, "This performance is historical—it's the first time Simpson *ever* stuck completely to a prepared script!" The crowd roared its approval.

Simpson's admission of "great performance anxiety" is the only such reference in the more than two million words of his personal diary.

In 2007 his son Colin revealed that even though it was never obvious, his father was often apprehensive before a crowd. "Pop and I just had a discussion about this, about how uncomfortable he is in some circumstances. It's when he is out in a crowd, speaking without a podium. He just has that. I have it, granddad had it. I don't know what it is. He has learned to hide it. Just yesterday [April 22, 2007] he spoke about that. He said, "That's why I could never be an actor.""

Looking Down and Back

As November grew nearer, Al kicked his 1990 reelection campaign into gear and began zigzagging across Wyoming, attending campaign rallies and events. On one flight across northern Wyoming's Big Horn Mountains, he happened to glance out of the window. Suddenly, his future seemed less consequential than his past.

> We were flying a straight line westbound from Gillette to Cody. I realized that we were passing over—or within 75–100 miles of each wingtip—the history of both my family and Ann's.
>
> We flew over Sheridan and the old town of Kooi, where my dear grandfather Peter Kooi labored and I spent some great hours of pleasure as a kid.
>
> We flew right over the top of Fort Phil Kearny, where Finn Burnett, my great-grandfather, served as a "sutler" in the 1860s.
>
> We soared over Shell, Wyoming, where Ann's grandfather started the stone store and where her mother was born.
>
> We flew over Greybull, where Ann was born, and then on to Cody, where I was raised. It was fascinating, and very moving, too.

He was with Ann the next day as they boarded another chartered plane and flew to Lusk, near the Nebraska border. Eighty-year-old

Chamber of Commerce manager Mary Burke picked them up and drove them to the fairgrounds for cocktails and a chamber dinner. Some weeks later, I too met with Mrs. Burke. She wanted to know if she could obtain an old railroad caboose to use as an office for the Chamber. I phoned contacts at Union Pacific and a caboose was soon on its way.

A Cinderella Night

The day after Al and Ann enjoyed their time with Mrs. Burke, they joined the president and first lady for a private dinner at the White House. The conversation turned surprisingly emotional. President Bush, while describing sacrifices of war, spoke movingly about a soldier who had won the Silver Star, the Medal of Honor, and a Purple Heart. Al saw tears welling in the president's eyes as he spoke of the soldier's death and his sacrifice to his country.

> Bush is a macho guy, and he was a little embarrassed by that. I told him that my dad always said he was not embarrassed by his tears. I said how Pete and I used to bet on when the old man might get teary, as he gave a talk about the flag, country, and God. George was very touched by that.
>
> It makes you feel good to know he is the kind of guy you have as your president. He is not a "softy" in any way. He is a man of great moral fiber and courage—and emotion.

After dinner, the Simpsons rode with the president and first lady to the Kennedy Center.

> We hopped into the limo—Ann and I in the jump seats, George and Barbara in the back—and we headed for the Kennedy Center. We had a great conversation, just the four of us, as the whole entourage motored through the city of Washington.
>
> George said again that he was embarrassed over having cried, and spoke about character in men. It is something that bonds him tighter to the American public. Ann added her

views about that, and how the man she has been living with for thirty-six years has those rich, deep feelings very often.

Secret Service vehicles loaded with weaponry and communications equipment led and followed the limousine into a Kennedy Center side entrance. Escorted by heavy security, the four made their way to the president's box—where, at the door, Al and George fell into humorous and familiar banter. The object of their amusement was a vase positioned just outside the president's box.

"George said, 'Look at *that*, now that's an interesting work there. I think it is early Greco-Roman. It has a peculiar fluke in there that's familiar.' I thought he was looking at a rather surrealistic painting on the wall. I said, 'Oh, yes, that was done during his depressed period in Paris.' Of course, I was talking about the painting and George about the vase." Nearby, people held back by security personnel were straining to hear whether the two were true connoisseurs of the arts. Instead of witnessing the sophisticated dialogue one might expect between a president and Senate leader, they saw two men kidding each other and having a jolly and almost silly time.

With the performance about to begin, Barbara and Ann dragged their men to seats overlooking the theater. "People in the audience were thrilled. They didn't know George and Barbara would be there. As you might imagine, there was a great murmur in the theater. They applauded enthusiastically as we sat down to watch a very delightful light musical." During intermission they walked out of the box to stretch their legs. The president said, "Al, let's look at this vase again." This time they concentrated on the same object.

I allowed as to how I felt the object was Syrian, or that perhaps it had come from Eritrea, or urethra. Someone said, "Hey! That's part of the *anatomy*." We said, "We know that, of course."

George said he was thinking about the particular sand the vase was made from, and noted the lip of the base. It was a "cuspid," he felt. Then he described how the vase was fired. I said I thought the whole thing was actually alabaster.

Only then did either of them refer to the plaque revealing that the vase was from the Step Pyramid. "We both said that we knew that all along, right from the start of our conversation." They had found a way to laugh, play, and balance their lives in friendship, even under the enormous pressures of the day. "It was silly business, best described as one hell of a kick," Al told his diary that night. "It was goofy, but fun."

After the performance, the four greeted the cast before stepping back into the president's limousine. Traffic was held back as the multivehicle motorcade, sirens ablaze, sped back to the White House. "We entered through the back area and down below the north portico, an area that is completely secured. I got out of the jump seat and walked through the door into the basement of the White House. The doorway was about six feet three inches high. I said, 'You've got to get this fixed.' George and I stood on tiptoe in the doorway. He reached it. I overreached it."

First dog Millie scampered excitedly. Al and Ann, after hugs, kisses, and warm expressions, tucked into Ann's little Chevrolet and drove into the night. "Ann and I reflected on how fortunate we are to enjoy this special friendship . . . and to have that be just as much a part of our lives as being at the Chamber of Commerce dinner with Mary Burke in Lusk, Wyoming."

EYES ON THE MIDDLE EAST

On April 11, 1990, as tensions built in the Middle East, President Mubarak of Egypt learned that the five U.S. senators sitting in his Cairo office had been unable to schedule a meeting with Saddam Hussein. He reached for his phone and minutes later told the delegation—Senators Simpson, Dole, Metzenbaum, McClure, and Murkowski—that Iraqi president Hussein would meet with them in Baghdad the following day.

That evening they placed a conference call to President Bush in Washington, who helped craft a letter to be handed to Saddam. The next morning the group departed Cairo and soon landed in Baghdad.

Meeting Saddam

"Saddam was supposed to meet us," Al noted. "He wasn't there. We got into cars and drove thirty or forty minutes to a Sheraton hotel on the river. There was Saddam, with his silk suit and foulard and patent leather shoes, smelling like a daisy." After initial greetings, Senator Dole presented Hussein with the letter and told him that the world was gravely concerned about his actions.

The Iraqis confiscated Simpson's small recorder, but after the session he wrote extensive notes.

> Dole said, "You killed a British journalist, and you said you would turn Israel into a fireball . . ." Boy, Hussein was watching Dole like a Hawk.
>
> I said, "I just read *Newsweek* on the plane yesterday. You are called the Butcher of Baghdad." He was listening. Then I said, "What you say is a baby food factory, other people think is a chemical weapons plant. Why don't you let the media in and let them ramble around in your country? They all want to win the Pulitzer Prize and this would be a wonderful thing for them. They would come in here and disclose that these things being said about you aren't true."
>
> I don't remember if those were exactly the words, but they were close to that.
>
> Hussein glared at me. He said that if we wanted to see how loved he was, we should go with him to where the Kurds were. He had helicopters out there, ready to take us. He bristled at what we said about his wanting to turn Israel into a fireball. I told him those things would not get him anywhere. But I did make a crack about letting the media in, that they are all arrogant.

Saddam recorded the conversation, but when the Iraqis released out-of-context quotes from the transcript months later, Simpson suddenly had a problem: "The *Washington Post* did a savage piece about me, saying that I had been kissing Saddam's ass. I couldn't even equate how they came to that, but it was just because I had shot a hole in their profession. They said I was again ranting about the media. Boy, I got the whole load."

Read My Forehead

Meanwhile, the Bush Administration was trying to give Simpson another load: a "carbon content" fee that would disproportionately affect mineral production in public-lands states like Wyoming. During a White House meeting after his Mideast trip Al made his feelings clear: "I was not going to stand for any 'creativity' such as having a 'carbon tax,' which is just bizarre. I told them that they would sure lose this old cowboy on a lot of issues if they did that. I expressed that rather clearly!"

As the meeting progressed, John Sununu, the president's chief of staff, slipped a note across the table. It was a doodle of a man's face. Across his forehead were the words "No Carbon Tax." Underneath, it said, "Read My Forehead," a reference to the president's "read my lips" promise not to raise taxes. Budget Director Richard Darman passed a note proposing that any carbon tax law be written so as not affect "any political subdivision, state or township beginning with the letter *W*." Afterward, Simpson said, "I don't think we'll see any more of *that* turkey"—meaning the tax idea, not the budget director.

August 1, 1990: It seemed that President Bush was scrapping with Republicans as often as with Democrats. Noting this, Simpson met with the president's media consultant, Roger Ailes, who said, "I can see that he is getting tired and testy. He needs to get away and just be with the family." Al suggested the place for that would be Walker's Point at Kennebunkport, Maine. Ailes said he would urge the president to go there, "regardless of what else is happening."

In reality, they both knew that volatile events in Iraq could preclude any opportunity for the president to get away from Washington—and indeed, Iraq invaded Kuwait the next day. "Hussein just went in and took over this country of Kuwait. He put in a puppet government. He says he is going to withdraw. He is a damn liar! I don't think he will. This really puts the heat on George, and George is going through a tough time right now."

Meanwhile, Simpson had his own problems. Even though his opponent in his upcoming November reelection effort was largely unknown and had no money, Al's poll numbers were slipping. He had recently picked up $100,000 at a single fundraising event, while his Democratic Party challenger Kathy Helling, a thirty-two-year-old sociology major at Casper College, had raised almost no money and yet was gaining public support.

Simpson realized he was being badly hurt by his pro-choice position on abortion and his insistence that Social Security cost of living increases should be limited for wealthy Americans. "The polling data shows that I have dropped seventeen points—like a rock—while this budget crap goes on in the Senate. I can't get home. The issues are Social Security and my comments about annual cost of living adjustments—and irritation about the Senate's pay raise, which I didn't even take!"

When he finally had a chance to participate in a Wyoming campaign event via satellite, which was exotic technology at the time, his "presence" proved dramatic. While his diminutive opponent sat before the cameras in Wyoming, a screen several times her size displayed Simpson's dominating image from Washington. He did not meet Helling in person until a debate a few days before the election. Their exchanges were respectful and subdued, and Al took care not to trumpet excessively his superior understanding of government and legislative processes.

Social Security proved his most damaging campaign issue. He had never supported an overall cut in benefits, as was claimed by some, but he felt strongly that increases for the wealthiest recipients should be limited. He griped aloud whenever he heard of wealthy Social Security recipients using their monthly stipend to pay golf club dues. Senior members of his staff advised him to avoid using pithy phrases such as "greedy bastards." As usual, he kept his own counsel. "The wealthy senior citizens are a greedy bunch. They don't give a whit about their grandchildren in the year 2030. Their kids will someday be out picking grit with the chickens. Annie told me, 'You'd better be careful there, Al. You are getting into some hot stuff. It could be very destructive.'"

He got a taste of that while campaigning in the Senior Citizens Center in Thermopolis, Wyoming. Several people gave him the cold shoulder. A few openly expressed displeasure with the things he had been saying. That lit his fuse. "Look, I have a ninety-three-year-old dad and a ninety-year-old mother, and Ann's mom is ninety. You think I don't know about senior citizens? Whoever is spreading that vicious rumor—that I'm trying to *cut* benefits for those who need them—by gad, I won't stand for it!"

On November 7, 1990, Simpson was elected to a third six-year term, defeating Helling 100,784 to 56,848. His victory was not what it should have been, considering his comparatively massive campaign war chest, name recognition, and clout in Washington. Entitlement program pragmatism had proven damaging, but not deadly.

A few days before the balloting, doctors had determined that Milward's right leg was gangrenous and must be amputated. The matter was hushed until after Election Day, out of fear that voters might think the announcement a play for sympathy. The surgery went well. "He didn't even go into the Intensive Care Unit. He went directly to a hospital room. What a guy. Guts of a mule, heart of a lion. That marvelous heart continues to beat inside that troubled body. If he could speak—but that damn Parkinson's disease has robbed those vocal chords of sound. It is just tough, tough, tough—tough to see it. It must be tougher by a thousand-fold for him."

Leadership

Republican senators gathered in Washington in late November to elect their party leaders. Strom Thurmond moved that by acclamation, Bob Dole and Al Simpson should be elected their leader and assistant leader, and the others agreed. Al thanked his colleagues for their confidence in him and said he hoped the group could "pull together" on Iraq and other important issues.

Also in late November, Simpson went to the Pentagon for a private update from Secretary of Defense Dick Cheney, the man who knew more than anyone about the situation in Iraq. "It's serious business, Al," he said, "and here's why." Cheney laid out a map. "We talked about the Middle East, and our dependency on oil and gas. We discussed the issue of human life and the possibility of war, and the reality of Saddam Hussein. We discussed issues that were classified and unclassified, including weaponry and some of the stuff [weapons] Saddam has that are just awesome. We talked about ground war, air war, and about peace and the future of Israel and Egypt and many things."

For days, the United Nations had been debating the situation. President Bush, having repeatedly made it clear to Congress that he did not want to threaten force unless he would be able to use it as the military thought best, spoke with confidants. One of them, Al Simpson, thought it best to reveal as many facts as possible: "How do we scare Hussein and not scare the American people? It is a true balance, but I will tell you one way. Let's scare the hell out of the American people—the right way. Let's tell them what this silly son of a bitch is capable of, how he uses the instruments of war, and what he has over there."

Relying on information from confidential security briefings, he continued.

Forget trying to tell them whether he will have a nuclear capability in three days or three months or three years, or ten. That isn't the issue. Tell them what he does have. Tell them how he uses his material. Tell them he has canisters of chemical and biological warfare tied to the top of missiles that he can launch with special fuses, and lay them out over a city like Munich or Jeddah or anywhere else within the range of the missile, dropping the most extraordinary hail of death.

After the meeting, the first lady approached, Millie in tow. Mrs. Bush mentioned that the first dog had gained back the weight she had lost when nursing her puppies. Their cheerful conversation stood in stark contrast to the dark and somber overtones permeating Washington.

Art?

A completely new issue was presented when movie stars Morgan Freeman, Kevin Kline, and Kathleen Turner arrived in Simpson's office to discuss federal funding of the arts. At issue was a federally supported Robert Mapplethorpe exhibition that Simpson and many Americans considered grossly obscene.

Freeman impressed Simpson. "He was interested in the Buffalo Bill rifle on the wall and wanted to see it and hold it. He knew about Cody's exploits and the type of rifle he used." Kline was likewise impressive and interesting, and Simpson later filmed a cameo for a Kline movie titled *Dave*. Turner was a different story. Al had seen her movie *War of the Roses* at the White House and knew who she was. As they spoke, he came to realize that she lacked a command of the issues she was there to lobby.

The three actors, it seemed to Simpson, were suggesting their lives would never have been fulfilled were it not for grants from the National Endowment for the Arts (NEA). When specifically asked if that was the case, they were quick to say that while their personal careers would not be affected by reductions in NEA funding, the careers of others might be.

> I showed them photos of three items—Ten and a Half, Man in the Polyester Suit, and Buggy Whip in the Bung. I said I thought they were gross and sickening. I told them I was offended by their insistence that public funds should be expended in support of such exhibits.
>
> Kathleen looked pretty blasé as she saw them, but Morgan and Kevin's eyes popped. Actually, what the artistic and

theatrical communities should have done, when $45,000 was cut out of a $171 million budget, was simply to clam up and forget it. But no, they had to ring the bell about the First Amendment.

I said, "Hell, this doesn't have anything to do with the First Amendment. It has to do with whether the federal government should spend taxpayers' bucks to help exhibit that stuff. That is the question. It is the only question."

Also attending the meeting was Senator Nancy Kassebaum. She looked at the displays and said, "I think that you people are elitists. You don't understand how the people out in the real world feel about [these] exhibits. It doesn't have a thing to do with artistic expression or the things you are doing or promoting."

As Mapplethorpe's work gained national attention, the American Family Association lobbied Congress to enact a new statute specifying that "the NEA shall clearly indicate that obscenity is without artistic merit, is not protected speech, and shall not be funded." In 1995 the Newt Gingrich–led House of Representatives reduced the agency's annual budget from $162 million to $99 million, a 39 percent decrease that remained in effect for years.

Bohemians

Al was honored to have been asked to present a second Lakeside Lecture at the annual Bohemian Grove gathering in California. He accepted without hesitation and arrived on the appointed day, this time with his thirty-one-year-old son Colin in tow. When the time came for Simpson's remarks, scores of America's best known and most accomplished men packed the site.

I began with some jokes, and then got serious. On the issue of banning assault rifles, I said that these are the kind of guns the marauders of the world use to destroy us. . . . When you have something that shoots three to five hundred rounds a minute . . . what *is* the purpose of a weapon like that?

Social Security: "Notch babies" are those people born between 1917 and 1922 who were getting so much out of the Social Security system it was all out of whack. We corrected it in 1983 and now they think they were cheated. We should have called them "Windfall babies." Jim Roosevelt and his happy band of squirrels [the Committee to Preserve Social Security and Medicare] and some irresponsible members of the AARP galvanize them all.

Citizenship: You are *not* members of the AARP first, or the AFL-CIO first, or the United States Chamber first, or the American Farm Bureau first, or the NRA first. You are *citizens* first, citizens of this remarkable United States of America. . . . Start tearing up your mail. When somebody tells you to send ten bucks so they can save you from your government run amok—toss it.

Saddle Up and Shoot—Once

Back in Wyoming and determined to celebrate its centennial, Al asked to be driven a few miles from Cody, where he mounted a horse and joyfully joined the July 4, 1990, Centennial Wagon Train. Thousands of spectators watched as the historically accurate reenactment of the original wagon trains paraded through downtown Cody and to the Stampede arena west of town. Ann, an accomplished rider with a lifetime of experience, handled the ride without complication. The journey took its toll on Al. "I let myself down off the horse and sank slowly to the ground."

The wearying ride was only one piece of the Simpsons' busy pace of recent months, and President Bush thought Camp David might be a good place for them to recover. When he invited them to spend a weekend at the presidential retreat, Al was pained to decline. "You won't believe it, but I have commitments in Wyoming, and so does Ann. She is scheduled to speak to a mental health group, and I've got the One Shot Antelope Hunt with Cliff Hansen and Stan Hathaway. I wish I could accept your invitation, but I just can't."

The annual One Shot event in Lander typically attracted twenty-four celebrity sportsmen from across the state and nation who each made a single attempt to shoot a pronghorn antelope. Both Hansen and Hathaway were former governors, and Hansen had been a senator as well. Al was correct in fearing editorial condemnation. To be gallivanting around Camp David—which is the way some people would have seen it—rather than participating in this Wyoming tradition would have inspired assertions that he was beset with "Beltway Fever." Most Wyoming voters considered that a politically fatal ailment.

In west-central Wyoming, near where his great-grandfather Finn Burnett and outlaw Butch Cassidy once lived, Al prepared himself for the hunt. He fired three shots at a stationary target, hitting it perfectly each time. He retired for the day, confident about the following day's competition. Morning came brutally early— 3:30. As the first glow of sunlight began to show in the east, Al and his intrepid fellow hunters set off in search of prey. He spotted several large antelope but judged them too distant for a good shot.

They hiked another mile and came across a large herd. "I ran into two or three hundred antelope. I should have taken a shot at anything around 150 or 200 yards, but I waited and got too close. I dropped down on my belly when I couldn't have been more than seventy-five yards away. I pulled the trigger and the shot went right over the top of him." Taking a second shot, he hit the animal. Later, he guessed that his miss the first time resulted from being too close, but he knew that excuses did not count for much at the One Shot.

"I messed up in ways that I can't even describe—even to a nonhunter. Ghastly. But at least we took it in and had it made into some loins, chops, and salami." Because he failed to bag an antelope on the first shot, he departed Lander without scoring points among Wyoming's hunters. He knew, however, that he would have lost points had he spent the weekend playing horseshoes at Camp David.

Political Tears

On his second day back in Washington Al received a phone call from Senator Joe Biden concerning Molly Yard and Eleanor Smeal of the National Organization for Women (NOW). Biden reported that the two had been "near tears" over the way Senator Thurmond greeted them during the previous day's confirmation hearing for Supreme Court nominee David Souter. Biden relayed that Thurmond had said, "Ladies, nice to see you here. You are a lovely group."

The women had not responded well to being called "lovely." Only a brazen sexist, they seemed to feel, would say that. This fascinated Simpson, so he walked to the hearing room to join the current session's fray. When his turn to speak came, he said of NOW's opposition to Souter, "Yours is a lost cause. You ought to save your horses for somebody you can really take on, someone other than David Souter." The women "shrugged and rolled their eyeballs," which irked Simpson. "You love to dish it out, but you don't like to take it," he said sharply. "You retreat to what men most fear—*tears.*"

One of them responded, "Don't you understand what we've been talking about here, with women's reproductive rights and the right of control over our bodies?" Now he was getting irritated. "Of course I do. I am on *your* side on the issue of abortion. But I think you've just gone too far. You have lost your marbles. You act strong, tough and nasty—but then you retreat in tears and invectives. I get tired of it. I don't like your double standard."

He mentioned how their organization had rallied against Representative Pat Schroeder, when she cried while announcing withdrawal from her presidential campaign. He remembered that NOW leaders said her tears had set back their movement by decades. Since the women were now "something beyond irritated," he invited them to talk with him in his office.

Their private exchange did not go well: "They pissed me off as much as I pissed them off. They are tougher than boiled owls. They pretend at using femininity, when toughness fails. What a pain." As they left his office, he said, "Well, we'll just keep it up then, tit for tat." It may not have been the best choice of words to use on the leaders of NOW. They stormed off, and I overheard one of them hiss, "He is even more offensive in *private* than he is in *public!*"

Al has a reputation for eventually mending fences damaged in political debate. He knew this rift would obligate an especially difficult repair job. "My relations with that group and my patience and my usual ability to reconcile certainly fell on rocky shoals there. I will probably get an opportunity in the future to try to repair the breach. But I'll be damned if I am ever going to *apologize* to those two!"

Night Vigils

Shortly before Al was sworn in for a third Senate term, he and Ann were in Cody, glued to their television as the Wyoming Cowboys football team battled the California Golden Bears in the Copper Bowl. Suddenly Al excused himself, found his car keys, and drove to the nursing home. He needed to visit his father. "For a guy who captained the Wyoming Cowboys in football, basketball, and baseball—well, I know some sparks were going on inside him as he watched the game. A few times he said something unintelligible, but that one eye never left the TV. It was like the old times, except that he used to let out a whoop."

At home that night Al walked alone into his yard. Moonlight always seemed to ease the anguish he felt over his father's excruciating physical deterioration. Later he dictated his experience into his diary.

> It was one of those magnificent nights, those "once in a blue moon" nights. That is exactly what it was, the second full moon of the month. It last happened in December of 1971.
>
> The moon was directly south, above the front door of the house. There was a high cloud cover and a lower cloud cover, which consisted of the dust that accumulated in the atmosphere over the past few days of high winds. The lower cloud cover was like a great disk. The dust particles gave it

an extraordinary richness of brilliant greens and oranges, in rings. There were rivers of orange, blue, green and yellow.

He called Ann and Sue to join him. They did, briefly.

> They soon gave up on me. But, you know the moon and me. In fact, the beauty of it transfixed me because the snow on the ground, about an inch and a half, added a brilliance that you never see otherwise.
>
> I got on my coat and wool hat and sat on the patio. It was probably forty degrees, quite comfortable. I had a little sip of brandy. Colin's black and white cat Charlie and I waited until about a quarter to two in the morning, when the moon came out of a cloudbank and again brilliantly illuminated the earth.
>
> At that point, you could hear dogs out in the neighborhood. Charlie seemed to be energized and activated by that. He climbed a tree and went out on a limb and over to the roof. He sat at the very top and just looked around, while I was doing the same from the ground. It was quite moving and exciting.
>
> I pumped my arm a couple of times in the air and took it all in one more time. Then I went in and hit the sack. I was thankful for all the things that have come to me in my lifetime, especially all the loved ones around me.

Years later Ann commented on Al's fascination with the night and how it always helped him deal with emotional matters. "Yes, he does love it. It is spectacular, when you see that moon come up and suddenly the whole land is lit around you. It is not just the moon—especially, it's the moon at the ranch. Al truly is a night creature."

Their son Colin agrees. "Dad has always been a big fan of the seasons and the solstice—and if there is a full moon, he's out in it. I think it all goes back to the Bobcat, because it's such an incredible place in a full moon." Asked if the Bobcat somehow represents the core of his family's soul, he paused a moment and said, "Yes. Yes. I think so."

IRAQ FRONT AND CENTER

During a trip to Wyoming, Al injured his wrist while jump-starting a car battery as the air temperature hovered at thirty below zero. It was still bothering him January 10, 1991, as he and his fellow congressional leaders gathered at the White House.

President Bush greeted the group, mentioning the ongoing problem of Iraq's invasion of Kuwait the previous August, and before anyone could ask about the possibility of going to war, he addressed the matter. "Look, we do not want war with Iraq. But if that becomes necessary, I will need Congress to agree to my full use of the military. This will *not* be another Vietnam. It will not be a dragged out confrontation. Someone asked me how many casualties there will be. It's impossible to know."

Simpson spoke up. "Congress would love to give you the authority to use force. But some of them want to give it only if you don't use it."

After the meeting, several Republican senators met in the Capitol with their leader, Bob Dole, to craft a resolution authorizing Bush's full use of military force. "It was a strong and powerful meeting," Simpson told his diary. "Lots of emotions were expressed." The resolution's introduction on the Senate floor ignited a debate that bubbled and occasionally boiled through the evening and three hours beyond midnight. Passionate and emotional exchanges resumed the next morning, Saturday, January 12. The Senate finally voted to authorize the president's full use of America's military power against Iraq, if he found it necessary.

After the vote, Republican senators again gathered in Senator Dole's office, this time to talk privately with Iraqi ambassador Mohammed al-Mashat, who was distressed by the possibility of American military action against his country. Simpson knew his history.

He went to school at Berkeley and earned a degree. He also went to the University of Maryland and married a German-Catholic girl. They were divorced after about fifteen years.

He knows America. He knows Americans. He even knows our humor.

During our session, he kept going back through the old ritual about what happened in the past—why they did this to Kuwait, and why we did it in Panama and Grenada. Finally, I just said, "Look, this is bullshit! The issue is about what is right for *now*."

Not long afterward, Saddam Hussein recalled his ambassador. Mashat departed, but he did not arrive in his home country. On June 21, 2001, *Time* reported this:

> Recalled to Baghdad shortly before the fighting began in mid-January, Mashat stopped first in Vienna, supposedly to seek medical treatment for his wife, and was not heard from again. Until last week, that is, when authorities in Ottawa disclosed that . . . Mashat had arrived in Canada, where he was granted permanent residence as a financially independent retiree. As it turned out, according to British diplomats, Mashat differed privately with Saddam over the gulf crisis and thus never went back to Baghdad.

While the Nation Watches

On the day the United Nations and the United States established for Saddam Hussein to have removed his troops from Kuwait, Ann Simpson phoned Barbara Bush, who had been injured in a sledding accident at Camp David. She told Ann she had suffered a thin fracture of her left leg and would be using a crutch and wheelchair for a while. At the end of their conversation, the first lady said, "I'll see you later." A few minutes later she called back to say she had spoken with her husband, who was inviting them to dinner that evening.

As the Simpsons entered the White House complex in their little Chevrolet with Wyoming license plates, they saw that Pennsylvania Avenue and Lafayette Park were filled with hundreds of people standing quietly in an organized "vigil for peace." Each held a single lighted candle to express opposition to America's military involvement in Iraq.

Inside the presidential mansion an elevator whisked the Simpsons up to the president's private quarters. Barbara greeted them in a green blouse and black slacks, George in a sport coat. Al said later, "He was looking pretty relaxed—considering."

There were other guests—the president's son Marvin Bush and former Congressman Thomas "Lud" Ashley. When everyone was seated, the president asked Al for an update on congressional action. Then Barbara read a cable from the pope. It urged world peace and expressed hope there would be no war, even though it recognized the problem of Iraq's president. Al found it a "very classically drafted, very powerful message."

The president read from several pieces of paper that described how the American people had felt about the prospect of war in the past. Americans had been reluctant to become involved militarily in Europe. Even after Japan attacked Pearl Harbor, many Americans were hesitant about declaring war against Japan. It was clear that Bush was very seriously weighing his options in the wake of Iraq's invasion of Kuwait. When dinner was served, he asked Barbara to say grace. She deferred to Al.

> I said, "Okay, let's hold hands." We joined in prayer and I said, "God bless the people who inhabit this house. Give them continued strength and courage. Let the world know them as we do. Know that they are people with caring and compassion and love, and that love and understanding will serve them well. Bless them, that they may do what is right. That is the wish of the world on this night. God bless them."

Barbara turned to Al and said, "I love that, Al, but where did you get that 'they' stuff?" She was questioning his inference that she had a role in the critical decision about committing American troops to war.

Al said to her, "I watched how my parents lived together for sixty-one years. Ann and I have done it for thirty-six. You have done a few more. We know how these decisions are made. Couples share in the anguish of them." Barbara understood, but she emphasized that her husband alone would make the decision. "She said that in a very direct but easy way," Al later told his diary.

The phone rang. It was the president's brother, Jon, calling from New York. The two traded jokes and the president passed them on to the group. Everyone laughed, though in the back of their minds was the deadly serious reality that America was poised to launch a punishing assault on Iraq.

> We were all very well aware that right outside, behind George's chair and beyond that fence out on Pennsylvania Avenue, there was a march, a candlelight vigil for peace. George was very moved by it.
>
> As we finished dinner, we all looked out on the north portico, toward the people standing shoulder to shoulder with their candles. George said, "I know war. I've been in it. I don't wish it either."
>
> Then we went back into the private sitting room. It was early, but you could see that George and Barbara were ready to hit the sack early, which they do.
>
> After a quick review of current events, and hugs and kisses, Ann and I headed out the door. We took their dog Ranger with us, so he could get out and run around on the south lawn. Boy was he excited about that. [He didn't mention seeing Millie.]
>
> As we drove out the southwest gate of the White House, away from the home of the First Family, suddenly ours was just one of the cars out in that great mix. I guess that is what makes America so special. After we left, there were no guards, no sirens, and no limos. We were just citizens having an evening with our president and first lady, and then heading out on our own rounds of life.

Barbara's warm but serious last words rang in their ears. "Thanks for coming. That was *just* what George needed."

War

The next day, the world watched and waited for the American president's decision. Suddenly the news broke. "January 16, 1991: We are at war. The news came to me just as I walked into the National Theater to see the new Neil Simon play *Lost in Yonkers.* Neil and Diana Simon were standing at the back of the theater as I walked in." Al noticed a Secret Service agent speaking with Doro Bush, George and Barbara's daughter. She walked toward an exit and Al followed. When he caught up with her, she confirmed that the war had begun.

Just then, Simpson's chief counsel, Mike Tongour, rushed up with an Associated Press bulletin.

> Here is the text of a statement by President Bush Wednesday night on the attack against Iraq: "The liberation of Kuwait has begun. In conjunction with the forces of our coalition partners, the United States has moved under the code name Operation Desert Storm to enforce the mandates of the United Nations Security Council. As of 7 o'clock P.M. Operation Desert Storm forces were engaging targets in Iraq and Kuwait." ap-wx-01-16-91 1940 est.

The next morning the Senate was abuzz with briefings, interviews, and conferences about America's military actions. After a briefing by the defense secretary, Simpson made notes.

> It was one of the most stunning revelations of military prowess I have ever heard. Dick [Cheney, secretary of defense] spoke for about ten minutes. He said it was top secret and classified. Then a young colonel from the air force stepped up with a sheaf of papers. He said, "This mission started at 0245 on January 16, and went as follows . . ."
>
> With overlays on a map, he described minute by minute

what happened in the first hours of the battle. It was awesome, overpowering, almost crushing.

The briefing given to the seventy senators in the secured room revealed that while thirteen hundred sorties had been flown over Hanoi during a two-week pounding at the height of the Vietnam War, an equal number had been flown in the first fourteen hours of assault on Saddam Hussein's armies in Iraq and Kuwait. Simpson was excited, yet troubled. "I have a feeling of great sadness that this man [Saddam] would take his entire country to destruction, along with hundreds of thousands of men. This is one sick son of a bitch. Saddam's egoism overcame his brains."

In the wake of the military's successes early in the conflict, the Senate approved a resolution commending the president for his leadership and the military for its bravery, patriotism, and professionalism. After the vote Al said to a group of Republican colleagues, "Boy, the Democrats who voted *against* him last Saturday [to authorize military action] sure wanted to get aboard today."

That evening he phoned the president and reported, "We just passed the resolution 98–0." Bush, unaware that a resolution had been debated, was pleased. Simpson asked Bush if he had heard about the new national anthem of Israel—"Onward Christian Soldiers!" Bush laughed, prompting another joke. "Saddam flipped a coin before this started—and elected to receive."

> Because I know George so well, I know that one side of him is ready to say, "Take that, you son of a bitch," even though that would not be the thing to do. The other side of him is this steady, thoughtful man who was thinking of the young people committing themselves to this mission, and those who will die or be wounded. Indeed, that will happen. This is a terrible thing, but a very necessary thing. Our president could not be more presidential.

Growing optimism in the following days was tempered by the concern that Israel would become involved militarily, possibly inflaming and complicating matters. Simpson cautioned the media that if reporters did not stop speculating on the possibility, it could become a self-fulfilling prophesy. Al was also grappling with the suggestion that Israel would be more inclined to hold fire if the United States gave it additional financial support. He considered that a political problem, since Israel was already the largest recipient of American foreign aid and numerous other forms of support.

In the midst of the day's drama, he found himself seeking solitude and inspiration.

It was a beautiful day, so I thought I would visit the Lincoln Memorial. Not many people were there. I ogled the temple and read the language I have always loved. It is above the marvelous Daniel Chester French sculpture.

IN THIS TEMPLE
AS IN THE HEARTS OF THE PEOPLE
FOR WHOM HE SAVED THE UNION
THE MEMORY OF ABRAHAM LINCOLN
IS ENSHRINED FOREVER

Boy, that says it all. Then I read the Gettysburg Address once more. It is on the left wall as you go in.

I was getting my batteries charged by that marvelous sculpture. Then I looked toward the White House, and back on the Washington Monument and the Capitol, far away to the east. I needed to do that, especially in this time of war. *War.* Hard to believe, another in my lifetime.

I thought of Lincoln, and his trials and tribulations and feelings of pain. I thought of the anguish and the difficulties confronting my friend, George Bush. He will handle it well. He is a mature and steady man.

Chapter Fourteen

HAND-TO-HAND COMBAT

~

IT WAS JANUARY 27, 1991, and the nation had been at war for eleven days. Al Simpson gave me a priority memo about a television correspondent who was getting under his skin.

> I want to do a check on Peter Arnett of CNN fame. A former wire service bureau chief came up to me and said, "Do you know about Peter Arnett's background?" I said, "No, I don't, but I'm offended by what he is doing."
>
> He said, "So am I. When I was bureau chief, the wires he used to send back during the Vietnam War were almost too sickening to print."
>
> He said that Arnett married a Vietnamese woman whose brother was a member of the Viet Cong and was fully involved in the fighting against the United States. He said it is obvious now that the only reason Iraq is allowing Arnett to broadcast from that country is that he is a "sympathizer," just as he was with the Viet Cong.
>
> I am not involved in a witch-hunt or anything else, I just want the same degree of backgrounding that any reporter would ask about a politician.

CHALLENGING ARNETT

Before I could respond to Al's memo, another CNN report from Baghdad caught his eye, and ire. At home that night, he mentioned it to his diary: "I watched Peter Arnett on CNN from Baghdad. What a phony bastard he is. He was in the Vietnam War as a correspondent and married a Vietnamese woman whose brother was a member of the Viet Cong. He was what we knew in WWII as a 'sympathizer.' Now here he is, reporting from behind the lines in Baghdad. What *trash*." Simpson felt that Arnett was accepting at face value Iraqi claims that American bombs were killing innocent Iraqi civilians, including children. He expressed his irritation in an opinion piece for *USA Today*.

> Reporters in Baghdad must be cautious to neither offend nor criticize Saddam Hussein, since that would surely mean getting the big boot back over the border. . . .
>
> I feel that journalists who allow themselves to be "used" by the Iraqi government for propaganda purposes as a condition for staying in Baghdad, severely diminish their credibility and any ethical commitment to the truth. The public has been pompously advised that as long as a "disclaimer" runs along the bottom of our TV screens, Americans are "smart enough" to see reports as propaganda and judge accordingly. Yet, this compromise of journalistic ethics sets a new and frightening standard. It suggests that propaganda is completely acceptable and proper if there is an absence of real news. . . .
>
> It is ridiculous that millions of dollars were spent to bomb and sever Saddam's communication link to the outside world, only to have CNN restore it.

Lally Weymouth, a writer for *Vanity Fair* magazine, asked Al about his "love-hate relationship" with the media. She was sensitive to the topic, since her mother was *Washington Post* publisher Katharine Graham. Al told Lally how much he enjoyed her mother and repeated what Katharine had recently said to him: "I have seen things come over you with regard to your reaction to the press and to others in the past year. I really love you and Ann. You are very special people, and you know that. I never want to see anything happen to you in Washington that would hurt you. However, Al, you are pretty tough on the media."

Accusation

Graham's comments did not deter Simpson. During a press luncheon at the Monocle Restaurant on Capitol Hill a few days later, he again vented about Arnett.

> It might have been better if I had stayed home that day—in bed, with the covers up over my head. We were talking about coverage of the war in the Gulf when I said, "Well, in my mind Peter Arnett of CNN is a sympathizer. It is known that his ex-wife was Vietnamese, and that her brother was active in the Viet Cong. Arnett stayed in Vietnam after the war and, in the same light, I think what he is doing over there in Iraq now is appalling."

He had been saying this to colleagues and during meetings at the White House for several days. This venue was different. Now he was talking on the record to a group of reporters—astonished, slack-jawed reporters who seemed flabbergasted by his assertions. "I am telling you, there was a palpable sucking noise among the entire twenty print journalists who were sitting there. Thank God it wasn't on television. They would have been playing it every two minutes, as they like to do when you get your foot in your mouth. I wasn't back at my desk ten minutes when reporters began calling to ask, 'What in the world are you *doing*?'"

The *Washington Post* dispatched a reporter, and Simpson thought he did a good job of explaining his position to the newspaperman. The next morning he stared in disbelief at a *Post* editorial sharply condemning his comments.

On February 8 Simpson met with CNN's Washington bureau chief and a company attorney in a session he later characterized as "spirited." No staffers were present. "I said that if he [Arnett] had been on a hillside outside of Baghdad with his sidearm and binoculars, I would have thought he was a war hero. But when he was being put to bed at night by the enemy, and awakened in the morning to eat their food and consume their drink behind enemy lines, well then, by God, I felt very strongly about that."

His informant about Arnett's activities in Vietnam was becoming alarmed. What if the senator's long finger pointed to him as the source? He phoned me to ask that Al not reveal his name. "I could lose my *pension*," he pleaded. He stressed that the information he had relayed to Simpson was "a rumor to be checked out, not a fact to be blurted out."

Firefight

Later that month Al participated in a forum on the role of the media in the Gulf War. While many politicians are quick to duck into a bunker as the media drop cluster bombs, Simpson's instinct has always been to stand his ground and fire back, as he did that day. Fred Friendly, president of CBS News, moderated a panel that included former secretary of defense James Schlesinger, former United States ambassador to the United Nations Jeane Kirkpatrick, author David Halberstam, Bruce van Voorst of *Time* magazine, Congressman Bill Gray, Pentagon spokesman Pete Williams, and Michael Gartner, president of NBC News.

Simpson remained silent until someone asked Gartner, "How many times are you going to ask when the ground war will start, and where?" Gartner responded defensively: "I'm just going to keep asking that question until we get an answer, even if it takes all day." Simpson launched. "Boy, you people don't have any idea what you are up to," he hissed angrily. "Anyone who would continue to ask that question in a time of war is either ignorant or disloyal." Gartner responded sarcastically, "Thank you."

A few days later the *Washington Post* ran an editorial titled "Senator Simpson and Peter Arnett." Predictably, it was critical of Al, who, just as predictably, drafted a five-page response. Not written for public consumption, it was a personal letter to Meg Greenfield, editor of the *Post's* editorial page.

> Get into it with you newspaper and media folks and a guy can really get sprayed by adjectives like "bootlicky," "obsequious," "butter up Saddam," and even "beloved" of him. I saw some

pretty good verbs too; like "greased around" with Saddam, "kowtowing" to Saddam, and that if only we poor Senators had "decency and a sense of embarrassment." Not only that, but then throw in a few dashes of "sleazy" and "slime." So much for the objectivity of a free press. . . .

When reporters or editors go after politicians, calling their actions or conduct into serious question, it is always considered "the public's right to know." But when I chose to question the ethical and professional conduct of CNN's reporter Peter Arnett, somehow my expressions became a "cheap shot" equated with "McCarthyism," "viciousness," "sleaze," and "slime."

Retrenching

On March 13, 1991, the *New York Times* printed a letter from Andrew Arnett, Peter's son. It soundly thrashed Simpson for "smearing my father" and went on to accuse the senator of employing the same "unnamed source" tactics for which he frequently berated the media. "Mr. Simpson used guilt by association, tactics more in keeping with a dictatorship than a democracy," Arnett wrote pungently.

In a letter of response on March 20, 1991, Simpson strongly defended his position about the role of reporters behind enemy lines, but he expressed regret for his error about Arnett's family:

At a Washington luncheon during the height of the air war against Iraq, I told a group of reporters that I thought Peter Arnett of CNN was a sympathizer for staying in Baghdad and for allowing Saddam Hussein to use him for Iraqi propaganda.

I also repeated a rumor that seems to have followed Mr. Arnett for more than 20 years—a rumor that indicated that because of his marriage to a Vietnamese woman, who was reported to have a brother active in the Viet Cong, Mr. Arnett decided it was safe to stay in Saigon long after the evacuation of United States forces. It is a matter of record that he was granted permission by the communists to continue reporting for the Associated Press after the fall.

While I still strongly criticize him for his reporting from Baghdad during the Persian Gulf war, I do feel the deep personal need to apologize for repeating the rumors about Mr. Arnett's family connection to the Viet Cong. I said from the outset that if it couldn't be proven, I would apologize. In the absence of concrete evidence to corroborate the family situation, I wish to do so now. I greatly regret any hurt, pain or anguish that I have caused his family.

Furthermore, I admonish all who have engaged in this item of gossip over Mr. Arnett's past to put up or shut up. I regret being part of it. Just as Operation Desert Storm has healed many wounds left from Vietnam—it is also time to allow that wound to heal. So, I direct this expression particularly to Peter Arnett's son, Andrew, who wrote so eloquently and poignantly in "The Truth about My Family" (Op-Ed, March 13).

Then he restated his opposition to Arnett's reports from Baghdad.

I have not changed my opinion of Peter Arnett's presence in Baghdad. I felt the "bunker incident" reporting was repugnant. . . .

I happen to know firsthand of Saddam's obsession for propaganda and disinformation and how he manipulated and abridged the transcript of a meeting I had with him last April. All references to our [delegation's] criticism of his government, from the gassing of the Kurds, to the hanging of the British journalist, to possessing nuclear triggering devices . . . went unreported. . . .

Yet, it is my firm belief that if western reporters had not been in Baghdad—"behind enemy lines" if you will—Saddam might not have been tempted to indulge himself in the various "photo ops" which were presented to the world. Saddam knew devilishly well the consequences of his actions. Unfortunately, the media naïvely overlooked theirs.

Simpson had asked me to provide a first draft of his letter to the newspaper. When he looked it over, he made several small changes and struck the paragraph in which he apologizes. I incorporated his changes but restored the apology. When I gave it to him for final approval, he flashed in anger. "Don, which one of us was elected to the Senate, you or *me*?" I allowed that he was the senator, and I left the room. An hour later he phoned to say the piece was ready for transmission to the *Times*; he had penned "OK" beside the apology paragraph.[1]

After the *New York Times* published the letter, CBS newsman Dan Rather phoned Al and said, "That was quite a thing you did. I wish I could admit mistakes, but I have a lot of trouble doing that." Simpson replied, "So do I."

Battles Continue

In May 1991, at the invitation of Meredith Brokaw, wife of NBC broadcaster Tom Brokaw, Simpson participated in a New York charity dinner and panel discussion on topics of the day. The event was moderated by Leslie Stahl of CBS. Al's fellow panelists were Sam Donaldson of ABC and Bob Herbert of the *New York Times*. The discussion immediately turned to coverage of the war.

Simpson mentioned news reports that detailed Iraqi Scud missile impacts. He felt the Iraqis could use such reports to adjust their aim. "We used to call people like [you] 'forward observers,'" he challenged. He did not stop there. "Aren't you the same group that tore the wheels off the carriage of Geraldine Ferraro, and her son and husband—and who tore Kitty Dukakis to shreds—and who ripped up Jimmy Carter's brother and his sister and his mother— and who tore into Richard Nixon's brother? Come on now. *Hypocrisy* may be the original sin."

As the evening neared an end, Stahl said, "You *like* doing this to the press, don't you?"

"I love it," Al grinned.

Later in the evening Stahl revealed that their mini-debate had resulted in an informal poll among her friends. It was nearly unanimous, Simpson over Stahl. Two nights later General Norman Schwarzkopf, commander of Operation Desert Storm, addressed a joint session of Congress. Afterward, Al spoke with him. "Well, I am still digging the shrapnel out of my ass, after taking on Peter Arnett," Simpson told the general. Schwarzkopf responded, "Boy, don't think I didn't see that. I loved it. I was totally on your side."

Star *Wars*

Back in Wyoming, the *Casper Star Tribune* continued its damnation of Simpson's dealings with both Saddam Hussein and Peter Arnett. Simpson asked his press secretary, Mary Kay Hill, to let the paper know he was drafting a "significant response." They said it must not exceed seven hundred words. After further negotiation, the paper agreed to a longer piece. Simpson was pleased—but only until he found that *Star* editors had eliminated nearly two thirds of his text.

He turned to the tactic he had used years before to clear up the pay raise issue: "I *bought* a full-page 'advertisement.' I personally talked to the ad people and said, 'How much is a full page, right across from the op-ed page, on Sunday?' They said, 'It's thirteen hundred dollars.' I said, 'A check is coming.'" Simpson's ad contained his entire original article, with every word previously cut by the newspaper *italicized*. By denoting sections the *Star* had dropped from his original piece, he not only set the record straight about his exchanges with Hussein—he drew attention to the *Star*'s trimming of his initial explanation. One paragraph originally dropped by the *Star* read:

> The media is constantly—almost religiously—harping on the fact that no one in the public eye should be above scrutiny. However, they wish to apply a double standard that seeks to make them immune to criticism and accountability. That is not fair. When "the media" makes a mistake, they should simply admit it, not try to cover it up. However, that would be like pulling teeth. But in the very least, they should encourage criticism of their craft, and not attempt to demean

"the messenger" or reduce the message to triviality or something to be ridiculed and scoffed away.

He also said it appeared that the *Star* had edited his original letter in much the way the Iraqi government had edited the transcript of his conversation with Saddam Hussein.

That transcript, issued by this deceitful government who we are warring with, describes in 15 small pages approximately one hour of what was in reality a three-hour-and-fifteen-minute meeting. . . . We asked all the questions any thoughtful American would have asked.

We also carried with us a letter signed by the five of us, and cleared with the president, setting out the perils in Saddam's future if he were to continue his course of action. Obviously that released transcript, supplied (not "leaked") by Iraqi officials, perhaps the same ones "cleaning" Peter Arnett's reports, carefully avoids any form of criticism which we leveled in the face of Saddam Hussein. Our own tape recorders were confiscated by Saddam's guards in order that there be no other record of the meeting. . . .

My critical comments of some members of the press in that part of the world . . . that some were "haughty, pampered, cynical, and that many of them were trying to win the Pulitzer Prize," were correctly reported, and my colleagues have said that also . . . but the transcript had many omissions. The media failed to point out any of the realities of this pure propaganda piece and in many cases they simply believed all of it themselves.

Simpson suggested that perhaps the American media, which casts a critical eye on every statement by an American president, might be as suspicious of our nation's bitter enemies. His piece concluded thus: "[The media] lash out in hellish fashion at anyone who would dare to question media ethics and professionalism. You folks love to dish it out. You don't like to take it."

Shoot to Wound

After the full text of his article ran as a paid ad, Simpson phoned Charles Levendosky, editor of the paper's editorial page.

> [Charles] said, "Al, my God, I can't believe what you've done here. All you had to do was ask us."
>
> I said, "Ask you? For God's sake, my press secretary has been asking you for a month to let me respond—and then when you finally published it, you cut out two thirds of it!"
>
> Charles said, "Well, God, we just couldn't believe it."
>
> I said, "How did it feel?"
>
> He said, "That's not the point. We are just all sitting around over coffee and bagels, and we're all just stunned by what you've done."
>
> I said, "How did it *feel*, Charles?"
>
> He said, "I want to tell you, if you had only called . . ."
>
> I said, "Charles, answer the God damned *question*! How did it *feel*?"
>
> He said, "It hurt!"
>
> I said, "*Merry Christmas!!*"
>
> I will never forget it. Oh God, the joy of that. Even right now, all these years later [2009], it just makes my skin tingle.

Late in Levendosky's life, he sent Simpson a letter containing this comment. "I was genuinely sorry to learn that you aren't running for the Senate again. We have had our numerous disagreements on issues, but I have always considered you a worthy and respected opponent. I enjoy your obvious love of language and your witty displays when interviewed." Al wrote back to express that underneath it all, he greatly admired Levendosky. Knowing of the journalist's deadly illness, Al closed his letter with, "We will meet again in the cosmos."

Today Simpson often recalls the give and take of many scraps with scores of reporters and editors, including several at the *Washington Post*.

The media knew they had given me an easy pass too many times. When I tripped, those bastards were on me—especially the *Washington Post*'s Kay Graham. I said, "Jesus, Kay, what in the world was *that*?" She said, "You bastard!"

She talked that way. I loved her, and she remained a dear friend, but at that time she said, "We had to do *something* to you. You just can't get away with that."

I said, "There wasn't anything to get away with. I didn't kiss his [Saddam's] butt or anything else."

Arnett Redux

As mentioned earlier, Simpson often warned others not to scrap with people who buy printing ink by the barrel. He usually ignored his own advice but did occasionally get the last word. That was the case long after his battle over Peter Arnett's reports from Baghdad.

The *New York Times* and the *Washington Post* called me and told me that Arnett had been fired. They said that I must surely have something to say about that. I said, "You people are calling for me to throw a spade of dirt in this poor bastard's face, after you ragged my ass for dinging on him? You want me to say more about the guy you once toasted to the high heavens? What kind of chickenshit people are you?"

One guy hung up. It was marvelous. It gave me great pleasure.

Red, White, or Blue?

In early June 1991 the media was also watching the White House position on granting permanent most favored nation (MFN) trading status to China. Even though annual approval had become almost routine, the army massacre of students in China's Tiananmen Square in 1989 had inspired many members of the U.S. Congress to want to punish the Chinese government.

The Bush Administration, believing it best to keep America's trade and dialogue with China open, favored permanent MFN approval. Before a Senate vote on MFN for China could occur, the country would have to be accepted for entry into the World Trade Organization, something not likely to occur in the near future. Even though Bush had served as ambassador to China and felt confident in his position, during a meeting at the White House he asked Simpson's views on MFN. Al suggested conditioning approval on changes in China's internal policies. The president rejected the idea flatly.

As the meeting wound down, Simpson laughed and said, "Well, that was pretty nice of you. You bring me in here and then, when I propose a few conditions, you trash my ideas thoroughly. I don't think I'll ever come back." At home that night, he told his diary: "My idea went over like a turd in a punchbowl."

Before the meeting concluded, however, Al could not resist telling a joke about another aspect of commerce. A shy cowboy went to the general store and was a bit flummoxed when he encountered a female clerk. He preferred talking with a man about this particular topic.

She said, "Well, my father owns this store, but I know everything here. What can I do for you?"

The shy guy said, "I'm looking for one of those 'conundrums' that you use to prevent disease and pregnancy."

The woman replied, "Oh, yes. I know what you mean. We have those in three colors. Which would you like—red, white, or blue?"

The cowboy said, "I'll take one of each," and out the door he went.

Three months later, he was back. He said to the woman, "You got a maternity gown?" Not knowing the size he wanted, she asked, "What bust?"

He stared at her coldly for a moment and through clenched teeth hissed, "The *blue one*."

CLARENCE THOMAS

The mood in Washington was serious on September 10, 1991, as the Senate Judiciary Committee opened its first confirmation hearing on the president's nominee Clarence Thomas for a seat on the United States Supreme Court.

On the second day Professor Anita Hill, Thomas's former associate, rocked the committee and the nation by charging Thomas with subjecting her to inappropriate comments of a sexual nature. She did not specifically accuse him of sexual harassment. This ignited debates within Congress and across the country as to whether her assertions were true, false, or exaggerated. In subsequent confirmation hearing sessions, Hill was questioned extensively about her assertions. She said it had been a difficult decision not to say anything at the time of the offenses she alleged. For his part, Thomas flatly denied Hill's accusations.

As the hearing pressed on Simpson grew more focused, exhausted, and intense. Accepting no counsel but his own—not even listening to senior members of his staff—he put his defense of Thomas into overdrive. At one point he said, "I have got statements from her [Hill's] former law professors, statements from people that know her, statements from Tulsa, Oklahoma, saying, 'Watch out for this woman.'" Simpson said the information he had in hand would discredit Hill's character and reveal her "proclivities." When he was reluctant to make the documents public, all hell broke loose.

Washington and much of the nation was soon abuzz about Simpson's "scores of faxes and letters" challenging Hill's testimony and character. His refusal to offer proof led to a rash of editorials by leading newspapers across the country. A *New York Times* article by David Rosenbaum included the following: "Senator Alan K. Simpson declined today to make public any of the derogatory correspondence that he said he had received about Anita F. Hill. He also declined to be more specific about what the material included."

Andrea Mitchell of ABC Television News interviewed Simpson.

When he refused her request to describe the information he said was "pouring in," she said, "You've raised it at the hearings, and you've raised it just now on national television. Isn't this McCarthyism of the first order?" Simpson fired back: "Well, not in my mind. McCarthyism in the worst order is to have someone gather up everything on a man for 105 days [the time since Thomas's nomination] that has nothing to do with his ability to serve on the United States Supreme Court. Your people have done a magnificent job of that, going into his garage to see what the titles of his books are."

Jack Nelson, Washington bureau chief for the *Los Angeles Times,* wrote: "I've been in this town for 21 years, and they play a vicious brand of politics in Washington. Washington can be a mean town. This was as vicious a fight as I've ever seen, except it was totally one-sided. . . . When you had Alan Simpson standing up there like Joe McCarthy, reaching in his pockets and saying, 'I'm getting stuff through faxes, from all over the country,' he sounded just like Joe McCarthy."

Newsweek's Washington reporter Eleanor Clift was even tougher: "The days of Simpson Chic are over. Now he is more often compared to Red-baiter Joe McCarthy. The image of Simpson flinging open his jacket and declaring he had lots of 'stuff' against Anita Hill—while revealing nothing—was the lowest of many low points in the Clarence Thomas hearings. Any Senator with a sense of history should have said, as attorney Joseph Welch eventually did to McCarthy, 'Senator, have you no shame?' "

During the hearing sessions, Simpson became so exhausted, angry, and defensive that he was almost impossible to engage. With his wife in Wyoming tending to her seriously ill mother, there was nobody to stop him from whipping himself into a raging tornado in defense of a man he thought was being unfairly accused. About sexual harassment, Simpson later said, "I had a wife, mother and daughter—one of whom had been subjected to many degrees more of that kind of conduct than the professor. I was furious!"

Running on Empty

During and after the Thomas hearings, Simpson's diary entries increasingly referred to the fast pace of his life and his deepening fatigue. When he occasionally logged a decent night's sleep, he considered it notable rather than typical.

> People say I look pale and tired. Funny. When I get about five or six hours' sleep, they say I look great. When I get eight hours a night, they say I'm a pallid wreck.
>
> But I slept nine hours. Another few days and I will be back. When you let your damn self get run down, you get tired, fatigued, and irritable. When I get six hours of sleep, I take it out on everybody around me.

Years later Ann spoke of the days during and after the Thomas hearings, times when her husband was frequently in high dudgeon. "When people would talk about how I wasn't here to deal with him during those hearings, I would say, 'Well for heaven's sake, I'm not his *mother*. I am not responsible for tending him. He got into it all by himself.'" At one point during the hearings Ann called Al from Wyoming to ask pointedly, "What is going *on*? You look so nasty, all of you men." Later she said to Senator Arlen Specter, "You all look *terrible*. You look like male chauvinist pigs!"

The phone lines in Al's Senate offices were clogged. "The anti-Thomas forces are working in almost frenzied fashion," he complained. Indeed, not even he could get through to his unlisted office phone. Somehow, the number had been circulated, and his home phone had always been publicly listed. "I would be at home and the phone would ring. Some woman would say, 'Mr. Simpson, I want to tell you, thank you. What that woman [Anita Hill] needs to do is to fight or flee.' Somebody else would call and say, 'You asshole, you jerk!'"

For the Record

As Thomas's nomination was cleared by the committee and brought before the full Senate, Simpson repeated his comments about anti-Hill materials having arrived in his office. On October 15, 1991, on the Senate floor he said: "Let me say that since some have addressed the issue of me saying that there was 'stuff dumped over the transom,' let me now dump it over the transom into the *Congressional Record*. Because of those cowardly charged headlines and baiting, I want to put it in the *Record* at this point, letters and statements which our committee received over the transom."

There being no objection, the material was ordered to be printed in the *Record*.[2] Al mentioned in an interview for this book that during the Thomas hearings he conferred privately with Senator Kennedy about Anita Hill: "I remember going up to him and saying, 'Ted, what the hell happened between these two people? This is bizarre.' He said, 'I think they had a great love affair and something blew it up, and she's going to make him pay for it, or they're going to make each other pay for it, I don't know which.'"

Confirmation

On the day Al placed his "transom" documents into the *Congressional Record*, Clarence Thomas, on a 52–48 vote, became an associate justice of the United States Supreme Court. Simpson spoke with President Bush on the telephone: "You know, George, while you are sitting up there drinking a highball, I'm out here sloshing around in the swamps. Bush chuckled, 'I know. You deserve it.'" Later in the week, arriving at the White House for Thomas's swearing in ceremony, Simpson ran into Joe Biden. The senator from Delaware said, "I know I will take some flak for being here." Al agreed but was pleased by the Democrat's attendance.

Thomas introduced his mother, and then a man nobody expected to meet: "I'll be darned if his dad didn't show up. His dad abandoned him at the age of two—and yet, there he was. It was quite a thrill."

It was a festive occasion on the White House lawn and later inside the presidential mansion. On the street outside the fence, the mood was markedly less festive.

During the hearings Simpson referred to his wife as the "most important person and the brightest guiding light" in his life. Reminded of this in 2006, Ann commented on those lowest days in her husband's professional career.

> He was so defensive during the hearings that I finally said to him, "You've had such a great reputation here, and now you are destroying it by the way you are behaving. Why don't you just *shut up*?"
>
> He was stunned. "That's the first time you've ever told me to shut up."
>
> I said, "Well, you *need it*!"
>
> For a long time he talked about it a lot. Now he doesn't talk about it much. It is a black mark for him and he knows that. He has a temper, and he is not easy to cross. Sometimes I don't have the energy to.

Al was so drained by the Thomas ordeal that restoration of his native cheer and optimism came slowly. "I've got to learn to cut back. I cannot keep my schedule and a sense of balance if I am involved in so many activities. They become almost non-ceasing. Then I feel guilty for not having done the work the staff sends home with me. I get irritable and ringy and take it out on all around me. It is time to mend—and un-mend—my ways."

Reverberations from the hearings echoed everywhere Simpson went, including the International Women's Forum. His invitation to speak had come before the hearings were conducted, and it was not his nature to back out. "It was all set up before the Thomas hearings. There were about three hundred women in that room, and they were just plain hostile. I think I handled it pretty well. At least I didn't react as they hissed and booed." He reminded them that they had asked him to be there. That calmed them, so he continued. "I gave them my views on the Thomas hearings and on sexual harassment, and reviewed some of the things I had said. I also reviewed some of my activities [on behalf of] the women's movement, and so on. I said that we have to remember we are not just members of special interest groups, we are citizens first. If we don't understand that, we're in a heap of trouble."

That night he pondered his difficult days of late.

> I've had my old butt hammered flat by the media and activist feminist groups and radical feminist groups. I am taking my lumps—but as I always advise other people, I am "moving on." Often, it is so much easier to give advice than to take it. I am working through it because of that dazzling woman at my side. What an inspiration Ann is. She doesn't give me sympathy. She just says, "Own up and move on—you are too great a guy to muck around in that stuff."

In the weeks that followed, Simpson continued to challenge reporters and editors about their coverage of the hearings. "The media really opened all the guns on me," he groaned. "I appeared in [newspaper] 'personality' sections—they ran photos that made me look half goofy." It seemed to him that everything he said was being turned against him. During a birthday party for Ann he mentioned that when he was twenty years old, he never dreamed he would someday be living with a sixty-year-old woman. He said it in a loving way, to illustrate how one's perspective changes as time passes and relationships grow.

Someone at the party took offense and passed his comment to a reporter. When that isolated portion of his remarks—about never dreaming he would be living with a sixty-year-old woman—made its way into print, feminist leaders went into a rage. He had been happily married to his one and only wife for decades. He was pro-choice on abortion and supported many other issues promoted by feminist groups. Yet he had become their public enemy number one.

An Extraordinary Letter

President Bush, taking note of the assaults on his friend, was becoming concerned. On October 21, 1991, he hand-wrote this letter.

Dear Al:

After you left today I got to worrying. I don't like to see my friend burdened down by anything at all. You seemed a little low. . . .

I am concerned that the press bashing may have been weighing on you.

You were right on all this. You helped a decent man turn the tide.

You walked where angels feared to tread by zapping some groups and some press; and in the process, they climbed all over your ass—but dammit, you were right.

Besides, even though some are sore at you, they won't stay sore. They like you, they respect you and they know you to be fair.

Having said all this I'll confess—there are days when I just hate this job—not many, but some.

The attacks that demean one's character sometimes get to me, too. The ugly columns don't set very well when we're trying our hardest on some project or another—but then, always, the sun comes up.

Yesterday at Camp David I was a little down. I picked up 2 bright red leaves; and I did something I haven't done in the last 60 years. I put the leaves, pressed, into a heavy book in my little quiet office.

I felt better—strange, but I really did—

Don't let the bastards wear you down.

Your friends love you and this President depends on you and believes in you and is grateful to you.

Nothing you can do can change that—

Abortion, Immigration, Deficits, Judiciary Hearings, all those together pale in importance when up against friendship.

G

Today that three-page letter is carefully tucked away among Al's most cherished treasures.

Owning Up

That November, during a public event in Cheyenne, Simpson said he wanted to explain a few things about his participation in the Thomas hearings. He did not issue an apology, but he did want to "take responsibility." He said: "I have been riding high, a bit too cocky, arrogant—yeah, too smart by half sometimes. I think it is time for a little honest reassessment. The responsibility is mine, and I shall handle it—and handle it well." Whether he was apologizing, explaining, or simply taking responsibility, his remarks generally went down well.

Senators Ted Kennedy and Howard Metzenbaum also made public statements conceding mistakes during the Thomas hearings. The *New York Times* noted the remarks of all three and reported, "They have admitted varying degrees of guilt at mishandling the inquiry into sexual harassment accusations by Anita F. Hill. . . . Mr. Simpson traveled to Wyoming to offer by far the most self-damning apology of the three."

In 2007 Al's son Colin recalled some of the more dramatic moments of his father's career.

> I thought he always did the right thing, but sometimes maybe not the right way. That was Dad. He was going to say things the way he believed them. I think it is a good thing to have loyalty to that degree. Dad was very loyal to the presidents that he served under. That loyalty carried over to their appointees. He may have done some of those things out of loyalty to the president—even though he was taking it in the shorts.

Although Al continues to believe that "an attack unanswered is an attack believed," Colin thinks his father sometimes goes too far. "He never turned down an interview request, so that kept things going. They knew he would say something newsworthy. He admitted more than once that his smart-ass streak got him into trouble."

AL AND GEORGE

Late in 1991 the president and Mrs. Bush invited Al and Ann for dinner at the White House, followed by a musical performance at the National Theater. The two arrived at the president's private quarters and found the president in his den, watching five television screens simultaneously. Al reached into the sack he had carried into the White House and pulled out a mother-of-pearl Bible, a small cask, and several other small items.

"How did you get that past the people at the front gate?" Bush inquired.

"I just had it in my hand and walked in—I smuggled it in," Simpson laughed.

He turned to the first lady and asked, "What do you get if you play a country-western record backward." She had no idea. "You get your job back, your wife back, your dog back, and your pickup back."

After a few more such stories, Al and Ann realized they were the only dinner guests—dinner for four at the most historic residence in the country. "We went into the private dining quarters. The fire was going and George said, 'Ann, you can sit looking at the fire, or with the fire at your back.' She was impressed by his courtesy, and said, 'I like it at my back.'"

The president gave a blessing, and dinner began with consommé-dumpling soup and a glass of California chardonnay. The wine was superior to that served before dinner, and Al commented on it: "That was a pretty foul wine you served up earlier." The president laughed: "Only a connoisseur could have noticed that."

Dealing with Criticism

After the four enjoyed their soup, chardonnay, and a leisurely meal, Al spoke of the criticism he had been receiving in the wake of the Thomas hearings. "I've been donged on for the last four weeks in remarkable fashion, but that was nothing compared to what you two have been through in public life. How the hell do you handle it so gracefully?"

Barbara spoke up. "Just don't listen to it. Don't watch the television. Just ignore it and keep right on going." Al thought that good advice and repeated the question to the president.

"I don't handle it very well," he admitted. "In 1963, I had ulcers."

Barbara interjected, "It is still painful for him—always is." The president said, "Yeah, but I just have to ignore it and remember my friends and family, to keep it all in perspective." The conversation lapsed into an exchange of jokes until at precisely twelve minutes before eight o'clock, Bush glanced at his watch and said, "You have three minutes to go to the bathroom, and then we're all getting out of here."

Traveling with the Football

While the four were preparing to depart, the president's dogs, Millie and Ranger, were nearby. The president was very fond of Ranger. "I just love this dog," he said. "He is a great and lovely friend. Today, at Camp David, I wasn't going to go jogging. But old Ranger's eyes were all bugged and excited, so I went out and did a mile and a half." With that, the four got into the limousine, Al and Ann in the jump seats, as always. The fifteen-vehicle entourage sped through intersections blocked by the police and within minutes they arrived at the National Theater's rear entrance.

As they entered and took their seats in the president's box, Al realized that in an adjacent box was the person carrying the "football," the secret codes needed for launching nuclear war. The football was never far from the president. Also nearby was the president's doctor. In the lobby, and at all the exits and standing outside, were scores of armed Secret Service officers.

When the performance concluded, the four climbed back into the limousine and departed for the White House. Along the way Al mentioned a time when Bush, as vice president, had invited them to dinner. As they arrived at the residence, Bush had grabbed a loud speaker and issued a warning to the guests. "Folks, please watch Simpson. He may try to take some of the silverware out of the house. Be sure to check that carefully."

"George, that was a terrible thing for you to do," Al laughed.

The president said, "I know—and I loved it."

The Bewitching Hour

At the White House, Millie and Ranger bounded up excitedly as Al and Ann prepared to drive home in their own car. Al's diary describes their departure.

> George had just given Ann a big hug. I reached out and said, "George, it was a special night. Thanks so much." He came forward and the two of us gave each other big hugs and a clap on the back—just as I do with brother Pete.
>
> Then we headed out the door. There was a big line of limos and Secret Service and armored cars. We jumped into our little Chevy with the Wyoming license plates. What a night. How many couples come into the White House and spend the evening with the president and first lady—just the four people?
>
> As we got the car warmed up, the whole entourage of vehicles left the southwest gate. For us, it was almost like the coach was turning back into a pumpkin.

The Simpsons flew to Cody and shared Christmas with their family. Ann remained in Wyoming when Al returned to Washington to catch a flight to Texas with the president for a day of bird hunting. He was especially enthusiastic about sleeping in the Lincoln Bedroom at the White House before and after the trip.

A Friend Where It Counts

By late January 1992 Al was beginning to sense ominous political clouds forming over his friend. When a number of his Republican colleagues complained that Bush was failing on the domestic front,

Al was quick to relay the comments to Bush: "My fellow senators require more leadership, George. You have it, but somehow it has not been evident on domestic policy. That is the ground you will have to cover in your State of the Union speech."

"I'll just do the best I can," Bush replied. "That is all I can do— all I have ever done."

After a trip to Japan, the president met with the Republican leaders of both Houses. "George was looking pretty dapper, with a red tie and sharp blue suit—but he also looked a bit pale. We joshed a bit before sitting down, and he referred to 'tossing his cookies' in Asia. That embarrassed him greatly." This was the incident in which Bush vomited on Japan's prime minister and then briefly fainted. The problem was nothing more than dehydration and stomach flu, which could have happened to anyone. But since it struck the president of the United States at a formal televised dinner in a foreign country, America's late night TV comedians had a riotous time with it.

Assured that the president was healthy, the senators got down to business. When they finished, Simpson wasted no time sympathizing about the challenges of the presidency.

> You get plenty of advice from every source. It must drive you goofy. But people have the "high bar" set at twelve feet, and they just keep raising it. We are at a point where we can't even get people who earn over $100,000 a year to pay 75 percent of their Part B premiums on Medicare. There is no reason why "Joe Six-pack" should be paying 75 percent of the premiums for Paul Mellon. It is just absolutely absurd.

The president's State of the Union speech on January 28, 1992, was generally well received. "It was powerful and direct and touched on substance," Simpson said later. "He laid down the gauntlet on a few items, too." Whether Bush's remarks would enhance Republican cohesiveness remained questionable, since intra-party bonding was nowhere in sight. Republican presidential candidate Pat

Buchanan, in particular, was seizing every opportunity to berate the president.

On February 17, Simpson spoke with Bush. "We talked about the campaign in New Hampshire. George said, 'It is just so ugly and vicious.' He feels it is just the worst thing he has been in. Buchanan is vicious, mean, and nasty." Al advised the president to remind the American public what he had accomplished. Then he said, "Quit watching those five television screens in your office. Opponents just tear your butt off day after day. Maybe it would be better if you didn't see all that. George, this [campaign] will be the worst of your life."

"I damn well know it," Bush agreed.

MORE PRESS EXCITEMENT

As celebrities, politicians, and other newsmakers all know, once someone becomes a public figure, the press is always part of the equation, whether as friend or foe or both. Al Simpson's long public service, prominent political rank, and habit of delivering crisply stated perspectives inevitably kept him in the spotlight.

Totenberg

A few weeks after his campaign predictions to Bush, Al received an invitation from a media combatant, National Public Radio's Nina Totenberg. To his surprise, she was inviting him as her personal guest to the annual Radio and Television Correspondents' Dinner.

Their previous encounter had been adversarial. During a *Nightline* television broadcast in the wake of the Clarence Thomas hearings, Al had turned to Totenberg and said, "What politicians get tired of is bias in reporters. . . . Let's not pretend your reporting is objective. That would be absurd." She fired back, "All I do is report. I don't know who is telling the truth here. There are inconsistencies on all sides. But I do know that I do not appreciate being blamed just because I do my job and report the news."

After the broadcast, in the parking lot outside the studio, the two had it out. The *Washington Post* described it thus: "Totenberg shouted, 'You big [expletive]. . . . You are so full of [expletive]. You are an evil man . . . I don't have to listen to this [expletive]. You're a bitter and evil man and all your colleagues hate you.'" Simpson reached into his wallet and pulled out the Journalists' Code of Conduct. Holding it in front of her face, he hissed, "Bet you never read *this!*"

Now, five months later, Totenberg was extending the olive branch. Recalling his mother's admonition that "hatred corrodes the container it's carried in," Al eagerly accepted. On the evening of March 19, 1992, he picked up Nina in a rented limousine and presented her with a wrist corsage and a gift—the book *Living in Wyoming: Settling for More.* Their arrival at the event caused a stir.

> I quickly realized that people didn't know what to make of the situation. Reporters rushed up with microphones and photographers gathered, all wondering whether we had buried the hatchets, or might soon be wielding them.
>
> We stuck close together. People came up to her, people who were her friends. They were very suspicious of me, and just looked askance. Up came friends of mine who were very suspicious of her. They looked askance.
>
> Finally, it was time for the big presentation, the Joan Shorenstein Barone Award for excellence in broadcasting. Guess who won it? Yep. Nina Totenberg. As I assisted her from her chair, I said, "You didn't tell me you were going to win the grand award." "I didn't know a thing about it," she said.

During her acceptance remarks, Totenberg said, "I knew it was going to be a good evening—Al Simpson gave me a *corsage*." Laughter erupted. Afterward, the two chatted with broadcasting's top brass until midnight. "I finally said, 'Stay and enjoy; it's your night—and thanks.' I gave her a kiss on the cheek and left for home. This is an example of healing that is important in this town—for us, *and* for the observers," Al reflected.

The Racist Card

Briefly stemming the tide of Simpson's warming relationship with the Washington media, the *Casper Star Tribune* published an old photo. Taken during a performance of the annual Cody Rotary Club's Minstrel Show in the 1960s, it depicted him in blackface paint. Simpson's explanatory statement said the Cody show was like many others around the nation during that period. He stressed that years had passed since blackface paint had been used in the show and that, even in the "old days," the program had been laced with humor, not racism.

Other Wyoming newspapers were generally accepting of his explanation. This is how the Associated Press reported the story.

> The club sponsored musical and variety shows beginning in 1952 to raise money for charity. . . . Simpson said, "It is my view that to a very large extent, the success of the civil rights movement in the '60s and '70s was due to the education and sensitization process of white Americans of good will— Americans who had an inherent sense of justice, fairness, compassion, humanity and civility. I consider myself to be in that category as a beneficiary of that movement."

Al told reporters that he had been a director of Cody Rotary and that after the racial rioting and anguish in Selma, Alabama, in 1965, the board banned both blackface and the minstrel aspect of the show. The Casper paper had run the "blackface photo," he said, solely as an effort to embarrass him, to plant a suggestion that he might be or had been racist.

He phoned the newspaper's editor to complain. Ann McKinnon said the photo had been in the paper's possession for a year before they ran it. She told Simpson she admired what he had said in his statement. "Well, that's easy for *you* to say," he snapped. "If they published a twenty-five-year-old picture of you doing something not appropriate today, I don't think you would be quite so philosophical!"

The newspaper might have taken a different approach had its editor been aware of an incident that occurred during Simpson's college days, when he walked into a Cody bar with six black co-workers.

I had worked with blacks on road crews in 1952, for Read Construction. That summer, we worked in Cheyenne and Rawlins, and then came here to Cody. We worked on the town's curbs and gutters, and after work one night I took my friends down to the Log Cabin Bar. My friend "Red" was the bartender. I walked in with the guys. There were six of them, all bright guys.

I said to Red, "Give us seven Budweisers."

He told me, "Al, we don't serve niggers in here." He said it so they couldn't hear it over in the booth.

I weighed 250. I had been working as a tamper of dirt in concrete forms. I had muscles hanging out of my shirts. I was mad. I reached across the bar, grabbed him and lifted him up. I said, "We are going to *serve* these guys. These are guys I work with. They are part of my crew. They are *not niggers!*"

While I had him up in the air, he said, "Well, I guess we could . . . yes, we *could* serve them."

Every night we went there, and there was no more of that crap.

Al's son Bill spoke about his father's views on race relations.

They ran the photo of Pop at the Cody minstrel show, which was in the early sixties. It was a different time. Was it racially insensitive? Sure. Was it malice? No. Absolutely not. . . . He would help anyone—black, white, yellow, brown, green—it didn't matter. What mattered was the person.

He also took a tremendous amount of flak in little Cody, Wyoming, in the late sixties for his support of black students, the black college players at Northwest [College, in Powell], and for his support of the Hispanic community. That was something he believed in and he lived by, and he'll have it with him until he dies. That's who he is.

DEAR MR. PRESIDENT

On July 28, 1992, Al Simpson arrived at the White House to talk privately with President Bush about the rising prominence of Democratic presidential candidate Bill Clinton. An extraordinary scene unfolded.

Al began by saying there were things on his heart, troubling things. He pulled out a dozen note cards, onto which he had scribbled his thoughts over several previous days. Motioning to them, he said, "George, some of these things are going to really piss you off." Sensing from Simpson's demeanor that the conversation about his reelection campaign was about to get serious, Bush said, "I'm sure they will."

Al continued: "George, few people know you as I do. You really are a most civilized and decent man. My Pop had a phrase: 'You are one of nature's noblemen.' That's your training, your heritage. That's where you get your loyalty, and it has served you well. I hope you keep all the things you are, and cherish them." He suggested that Bush keep Vice President Quayle on the ticket, then and launched into the heart of his message.

George, I know you are getting tons of advice—and tons of shit. Some of it is stupid, some of it is panicky. Some is banal. But every once in a while you'll find a ruby in the dung.

Some of it makes you defensive—and yet I remember what you told me during the Clarence Thomas hearings. You said, "You can still defend him without being defensive."

"They," whoever "they" are, will be watching you for signs of wear. That concerns all who love you. "They" are saying you are out of touch. That should piss you off—and does. "They" say you don't stand for anything. That too should piss you off. It sure does me.

But don't be defensive. It is unbecoming. It is not really you. You never get ensnarled in self-pity. I was never able to function when I thought I was the human toilet bowl. No one can.

George, stay off that damn boat and off the golf course for just ninety-four more days. That sounds petty, doesn't it? But it's not. It's a "killer" issue out there among the "theys." If you feel you have to do that now, then you'll be doing a lot of it come January, when "Slick Willie" will be running the show.

So what is your old friend saying? I am saying this: Forget this job. It's not about the job. It's not about another term. It is about *you*—what people will think of *you*, win or lose.

It all came to me in the anguish of Clarence Thomas. I suddenly said, "What am I doing to myself? I'm not myself." And Clarence said it too. He said, "I don't care about this job anymore. I just want them to know who I am, how I feel."

This is on my heart: when you go out of here onto the campaign trail, how will you feel? Will you look back and be comfortable with the campaign, the way you did it?

What is it you feel most strongly about? What is in your gut? What would you never compromise on? Share it. Come forward. Say, "This is who I am. This is what I truly believe in. I am going to stop strategizing, because I already know damn well what is right. I don't think about *losing* the job—I think about *doing* the job."

Slip into the old campaign mode, George. You know how to do that so well, with that easy grace and grin. Do it your way, just be sure it's "you." The American people will know the real you—and they'll hire you on one more time, because they will know and trust you—Barbara too.

You are a special man and America needs the real you— desperately. And one more thing: read Kipling's "If"—one more time.

Bush was listening intently and swinging the temples of his glasses in his teeth. When Simpson concluded, he said, "Well, you certainly met your goal!"

A week later, on August 4, 1992, President Bush met with House and Senate Republicans. It was not a confrontational session, although the president did say he found it "disheartening" to have Republicans criticizing him as vigorously as the Democrats were. He emphasized that if he won, it would be good for the Senate Republicans. If he lost, it would be bad for them. "It's simple as that." Al reflected following the session: "He gave me a glance, a look of friendship and mellowness. He is going to do the best he can, and that is all that will be required. Whether that is good enough, who knows?"

At a mid-September White House meeting between the president and Senate Republican leaders, Simpson suggested that Bush should focus on Clinton's inconsistencies over the years. Later that day, in front of the White House, a reporter asked the Wyoming senator what would happen if Bush refused to debate, and Clinton showed up anyway. "I think that would be wonderful," Simpson declared. "It could really be a fine debate, because then Clinton could compare what he said twenty years ago with what he says now—on almost every issue. Clinton has had so many inconsistencies over the years that it would be fascinating for the American people to finally hear him resolve them. Then we'll know which position he is going to take."

Al's concerns over George Bush's sagging campaign were in mind on October 7, 1992, when he participated in a forum discussion at the National Press Club. "Does the media hate George Bush?" asked a panelist. "No, I don't think they hate George Bush, they just don't like him," Al said. "They would like to see somebody new, someone fresh to write about." Columnist Michael Barone countered, "I think the media *does* hate George Bush." Commentator Michael Kinsley added, "I can assure you they do—and list me right there among them."

"So much for media objectivity," Simpson growled into his diary that night.

Regardless of whether the press hated the president, Simpson hit the campaign trail, attending rallies and events in numerous states. Working eighteen-hour days, he served as the president's surrogate, speaking before every organization, meeting, or club that would have him. It was all for naught. In November Bill Clinton scored 43 percent of the vote, 6 percent more than George Bush. Ross Perot proved the spoiler, amassing nearly 20 percent of the total and likely pulling the winning margin away from President Bush.

Al was deflated. His friend's loss of the presidency was bad enough, but it also meant that he would face innumerable new obstacles in his own job. Even if his Republican colleagues reelected him as whip, he would be working with an opposition White House.

Throughout this period there was a matter of even greater personal concern. Al's father was steadily slipping away. "I went to see Pop. He was just lying there, terrible cancers all over his face. His eye was sealed shut and he was just wheezing and gasping. It was ghastly." On November 12, 1992, Milward's ninety-fifth birthday, Al dialed his number and listened hopefully. There was no answer. "It is so sad. It tears me up, to think of the terrible rending of his life. To think of it is to grieve. His life is ending in such apparent and total vagueness—as if in a great colorless void." He knew his father had slipped into the mist and darkness of his final few months.

Chapter Fifteen

WINDS OF CHANGE

~

FOR NINETY MINUTES on November 22, 1992, President-elect Bill Clinton spoke with congressional leaders. He revealed how he intended to run the country and said he would take their calls at any time. That night Simpson summarized the session. "He is very interesting and bright. He had a lot of facts at his fingertips and I think he is ready to go. He may be a unique president. He has all the intelligence—native intelligence, probing intelligence—and the charisma and ability to schmooze like Ronald Reagan—or AKS [Alan K. Simpson]."

In his office, Al was told by staff that the current president's mother, Dorothy Bush, had died. Al phoned George, who said, "You are very dear to call. Barbara and I appreciate it." Simpson referred to Bush's election loss and his impending departure from the White House. "We appreciate you; we know this has been a tough time for you," Al told him. "Enough," came the gentle reply. It was a reminder that Bush was not comfortable with expressions of sympathy and did not want anyone feeling sorry for him.

George and Barbara Bush attended the annual Kennedy Center Honors program in early December. At the end of the program, emcee Walter Cronkite looked up at the president's box and said, "We thank a special man, a man who served us magnanimously well through peace and war. You brought great credit to our country. We wish you well, Mr. Bush." Al described his friend's reaction: "George was taken aback, as he looked out at the very genuine standing ovation. A great paean of praise went up to him. He shuffled and put his hands in his pockets, and then waved. You could see that if they had continued to applaud much longer, he

and Barbara would both have cried. It must truly have been a terribly bittersweet moment for them."

ONE LAST TIME

Before leaving office, President Bush flew to Europe. While returning, he phoned from *Air Force One* to invite the Simpsons to one
last dinner together at the White House. "It was a good conversation, very pleasing. I was just sitting in the living room at 1201
Sunshine Avenue in Cody, no one else home, looking out into the
winter sun in the late afternoon and having a special conversation
with a special friend."

Some of the most detailed pages of Al's diary were devoted to
their final evening together in the presidential mansion. "Ann and I
headed right to the White House and into the southwest gate. More
security than usual. Less knowledge of who is coming and who
is going. It took a few minutes, and then we drove that old gray
Chevrolet straight in and along that road between the White House
and the fountain, in the long curve up to the White House." It was
a beautiful night—cool, invigorating, and clear. They stopped the
car next to the south portico. No other cars were there. They did
not see Martha and Fred Zeder's car and assumed it was parked on
the other side of the White House. Another scheduled guest was
Democrat Lud Ashley, the president's old friend from Yale.

Ann took a picture of me standing by the car at the South
portico. We gulped a big view of it all, and went on in. A
gentleman was there to take our coats. I handed him the
handwritten letter I had penned to George and Barbara,
and asked him to make a photocopy and deliver that to me
upstairs. I planned to give the original to George, keeping a
copy for myself to put into my scrapbook.

We went up the private elevator to the family quarters and
out to the left and across the hall. Barbara and George, and
Lud, and Martha and Fred, were sitting in that marvelous little

room off their bedroom, where we have sat so many times. They were having cocktails and George was watching television—TV news, always watching the evening news. I told him many years ago he ought to get off that diet. But he insisted.

Levity and Sorrow

Not included in Al's dictation was the gift he gave the president that night to lighten the mood. Fifteen years later his daughter Sue, who was regaled about the event the following day, spoke about the uniqueness of her father's presentation to the outgoing leader of the free world. "It was such a sad night that dad brought the remote control fart machine to the White House. It just killed everyone. They are small and you put them under someone's seat, and you've got the remote." She simulated the variety of embarrassing sounds it made and laughed heartily. It was clear that she was her father's daughter when she said, "You just know how *glorious* they are!"

Al remembered that Ann had brought some gifts from Wyoming, little sacks of pinto beans with a drawing of a cowboy in the tub. The caption said, "Take one portion of these to enjoy 'cowboy bubble bath.' Double the portion for Jacuzzi."

> Well, you can imagine that everyone got a hell of a bang out of it, no pun intended. The picture of George opening his surprise package will be a jewel, if Ann has it.
>
> I presented the book of the history of the Buffalo Bill Historical Center in Cody, leather bound. Originally, that was to go to the White House library. Instead, I gave it to George and Barbara. I will get another one for the White House library. They seemed appreciative.
>
> The steward came up with the photocopy of my letter to George. I [gave George the original and] said, "Here, put that in your pocket." Ann had also written a letter to the Bushes. He put that in his pocket too. I said that he should read them later. He said he would.

Ann got a lot of great pictures during the cocktail time, about thirty minutes, and we told some good stories. Then we asked, "How are you doing?" They said they were glad to wind down and had been doing pretty well—until they left Camp David.

Bush said the staff had come forward, at the chapel. They thanked the Bushes for constructing the chapel, with private funds, and presented some small gifts.

As George described it, you could see that it had been totally traumatic for him. I have seen him glisten up and tears come from his eyes, but never really cry. He said, "I cried. It just came right down my cheeks. I was embarrassed." I talked about that.

"Never be embarrassed by that, George. Remember, Dad had that old phrase about never apologizing for his tears. He shed them a lot in his political life. That is the healthiest thing I've heard yet, it is good mental health. It is called healing."

He said, "Yeah, but it was really surprising." His eyes glistened up again as he described it. He said, "I really just couldn't go on. I just had to stop, but everyone seemed understanding."

At Dinner

The cozy atmosphere continued to prevail at the dinner table. For once, current affairs took a back seat and reminiscing was in order.

I said, "Wait a minute. Many times I have sat at this table, or at Kennebunkport, and you have asked me to say grace. You didn't this time, but I am going to give it anyway. Let's hold hands."

Barbara's hands shot out swiftly and I just said, "God bless this house, and God bless the special people who have given us such a total redefinition of the words loyalty and friendship. God bless them as they go on their way." That was it. I don't believe I've ever been that brief, but it seemed appropriate.

We all talked about loyalty and friendship. Those two words are the essence of George and Barbara Bush. We talked about times in the White House, especially the one before the Gulf War, when Ann sat at the other end of the table with George and knew that he was going to end Hussein's reign.

Most fascinating in the course of the evening was that sometimes Barbara and George would say, "I don't remember that." Or, "I hardly remember it."

We said, how *could* you remember? You were doing eighty dramatic things a day, and each time we were in your presence it was one of those unforgettable experiences for us, because we were with our president and first lady. It was an interesting analogy and we all reflected on it.

We talked about all the fun we had had. I reminded them about when I was getting my old ass hammered off because of my comments about Peter Arnett, and George called me that morning at my house and invited us to Camp David. He said, "Read the *Washington Post* this morning?"

I said, "Nope."

"Well," he said, "There is an article on you. It could have been worse—but I don't know how." He said, "How about joining us at Camp David this weekend?"

I recalled exactly how that had taken place, and how we went to the White House in George Bush's greatest hour, with 93 percent popularity. When it came time to depart for Camp David, I said, "We'll board now, so you two can come out by yourselves. The media will want pictures of you departing."

George said to Barbara, "You and Ann go on ahead. Al and I will come behind." As we walked to the helicopter, he said, "There they are, over there. Wave to the press." I did, with a lump in my throat. He put his arm around me as they were taking pictures. He said, "Hop in there, pal."

In the sauna the next day, with just the two of us, I said, "I'm not unmindful of what you are doing here. You are buoying up your old friend who has had his butt torn off. You picked up your wounded comrade and brought him up here, while you are at peak of your game."

He said, "That is what I wanted to do."

When we woke up in our beautiful cabin with the living room and the sitting room and the beautiful fireplace in the bedroom, all of it in beautiful Camp David, the first thing that happened, when we joined the Bushes for breakfast, was that he said, "Look—that's just the picture I had hoped they would have."

It was a picture in the *New York Times* of the four of us walking to the helicopter, and George waving, with his arm around me. Loyalty and friendship. He is a deep believer in the holistic and healing powers of those two attributes.

Then [in the White House] we talked about tears and about politics. We talked about Dad losing in 1940, winning in 1954, losing in 1958, winning in 1962, and just going right on. We talked about how hard it was to deal with the civility of losing, and then the graciousness of losing, and finally getting to the irritation of losing.

We sat there in the dining room, enjoying the last of the wine and dessert. Barbara reflected on Hillary Clinton. She said, "I like her very much. She is a fine person. We had a wonderful visit together."

More talk, more laughs, more fun—no tears, no jerks in the throat. We just stayed right there in that dining room.

Over—and Out

Lingering was appropriate, but only up to a point. The president had a good sense of when that point had come.

Finally, George, in his restive spirit, said the ancient call, which is, "Grab your coats and let's go walk the dogs." This is also easily interpreted by those of us who know him as "after we finish walking the dogs, since you've got your coats on anyway, you've gotta go home."

I said to Ann, "Bring a camera. I've got to go down and see my Lincoln Bedroom." I spent two nights in there on separate occasions in December 1991, when I went bird hunting with George. They were two very special nights.

I showed Fred and Martha and Ann the fifth copy of the Gettysburg address and the copy of the Emancipation Proclamation, and the school books that Lincoln had as a boy, or at least those that were used in his time—and that brooding picture behind a door. When I was there, I left the bedroom door open so that I wouldn't see it. I didn't remember a ghost, but there was a "presence" in that room. Staying there interrupted the time between Christmas and New Year's for me, but it was an interruption I shall remember all my life.

We came back down the hall and there were George and Barbara, sitting on the couch right off their bedroom, in the long hallway just across from the elevator. They were waiting for us and watching our childlike enthusiasm. The dogs were barking and whining, wanting to get out, but George said to take our time. I said, "Boy, we've had some great times in this place."

"So have we," they said together.

We went down the private elevator and outside and started a leisurely walk along the driveway to the west. George and Ann walked arm-in-arm and I was walking with Fred. Martha and Barbara led up front, with the dogs.

Right at the intersection of the fountain and the White House, we looked out toward the Washington Monument and the Jefferson Memorial. The fountain was bubbly with beautiful lights and it was a beautiful dark and clear night. We looked back at the White House and said, "What a place. What a view."

The dogs were kind of hopping around and brushing between our legs as George looked back at the White House and said slowly, "Yes, it is a beautiful place." He wouldn't allow himself to go much further. It was a magic moment. It is frozen in time, in the back of my eye.

We walked on back around the loop to the south portico and around the eastern portion of the driveway. Suddenly we were talking animatedly, because we knew "this was it."

We stopped by our car, the only one sitting there in that huge driveway, Wyoming license plate number 11-1201. The seven of us just stood there, a little overwhelmed and yet feeling almost childlike in our love and affection. The White House and the view awed us. We were excited, sad, nostalgic, proud—damn proud, proud to be friends, proud of what they did. Just proud.

I gave Barbara a big hug and said, "Thanks for everything. It was marvelous."

She said, "We loved it too."

I gave George a big hug and said, "We'll see you at the Bobcat in Cody. You will love it."

He said, "We will—and we will see you in Kennebunkport."

George, Barbara, and the dogs walked over to the south portico as we stood there by the car and said, "See you again soon."

George's last words to us were, "Great evening. Over—and out."

A WINDY KISS

January 20, 1993: William Jefferson Clinton's inaugural. As the incoming president stood at the west front of the Capitol building, ready to take the oath of office as president of the United States, nearby was the outgoing president. Not far from him was Al Simpson, who was visiting good-naturedly with Al Gore Senior, father of the incoming vice president. The elder Gore had served in the Senate with Al's father.

The ceremony began in a stiff, cold wind as hundreds of thousands of people lined the National Mall and Pennsylvania Avenue, all the way to the White House. Al trained his eyes on George and Barbara Bush: "George was really keeping a stiff upper lip. You could see in his eyes that it was tough, tough, tough—especially when he gulped in the scenery and looked out over that huge crowd and thought, 'I could have been doing it one more time.'"

As Al Gore and Bill Clinton were being sworn in as vice president and president, Al Simpson was lost in thought. "It was just a very memorable time. We thought we would all pin our hopes on the man from Hope for a while and see how it goes. I'm willing to help."

When the ceremony concluded, a Secret Service agent asked the Simpsons to line up behind Senator Dole. The procession snaked from the platform through the Rotunda, and when they reached the east front of the Capitol, they saw that perched outside in the parking lot was the presidential helicopter, ready to return the Bushes to private life. "As we stood at the bottom of the steps, Dan and Marilyn Quayle approached first. Dan and I exchanged a big hug. He seemed relaxed, loose, and ready to go on to something else in life."

The Doles and the Simpsons walked to the top of the stairs and through the doorway, where they found George and Barbara Bush standing with Bill and Hillary Clinton. Al turned to Hillary, whom he had not met. "How are you, Mrs. Clinton? Nice to meet you." She responded in kind. President Clinton turned to Al and said, "Dale Bumpers and Dave Pryor [Arkansas senators] told me about you. They said that if you were going to stick it to me, you ought to tell me a couple of stories first—they said you were very good at that."

"I'll give you a better deal than that," Al chuckled. "I'll *not* stick it to you, and I'll *still* tell you a couple of stories."

Clinton said, "Your friend Mike Sullivan [Wyoming's governor] told me you were one hell of a guy—and I take his judgment seriously. Mike is probably one of my finest friends among the governors. Hillary and I are very fond of Mike and Jane."

It was time for George and Barbara, now private citizens, to depart. Al walked sedately over to his friend. There were no emotional hugs, just a handshake. George said, "Well, how about this? We are ready. We'll see you on down the road. See you in Houston or Kennebunkport."

"You've gotta come to the Bobcat Ranch," Al reminded.

Barbara hugged and kissed both Simpsons, then joined her husband for the walk down the stairs. After twelve years as vice president and president, George Bush escorted his wife into the big, dark-green and white helicopter for the final time. They took seats where they could look back on the Capitol as they lifted off.

> Ann and I were holding onto each other's arms. The door
> closed on the helicopter and the steps went up and the engine
> on that big old stallion cranked up. We could see them
> through the window and we threw kisses and waved. Sud-
> denly the craft lifted from the parking lot. The dust came up
> and the wind blew our hair askew. It felt like a glistening,
> windy kiss between four people.

The helicopter roared past the Senate wing of the Capitol and over the vast crowd before turning south, toward Andrews Air Force Base. "It took our breath away. Whether it was the wind of the helicopter or the wind of twelve years that was blowing—or just the winds of change—it sucked the air out of us."

MILWARD LEE SIMPSON

Just before midnight on June 9, 1993, the Simpsons' telephone rang in McLean, Virginia. The call was from Cody. Al's mother had just been taken to the hospital with a racing pulse and loss of blood pressure. An hour later a second call assured that she was resting more comfortably. Al stirred restlessly through the night. He arose early, but because it was two time zones earlier in Wyoming, he did not call immediately for an update. He was watching the clock when the phone rang. A Cody doctor reported that Lorna seemed to be out of danger. But, he said cautiously, there was something else.

"About your father, Al. I don't quite know how to tell you this—but he died."

Al remembers a "warm, hollow rush" flooding his mind as he absorbed the reality of the doctor's words. He dropped the phone, reached out for Ann, and held her tightly. The man so loved and cherished, the Simpson family patriarch, was suddenly gone. Milward's life of ninety-five years and seven months was over.

When they were able, they phoned their children and Al's brother Pete. It was decided that Lorna would not be told until both sons could be by her side. At 10:30 that night Al and Ann joined other members of the grieving family in Cody.

Telling Lorna

In her hospital room Lorna had been isolated from radio and television all day. Outside her room Al, Ann, Pete, and Lynne huddled, planning how to give her the news. Al scribbled a note on his daily schedule card. It was found thirteen years later, tucked into his most personal archive. In black felt-tip pen, he had written these words: "Our Dad Died This Day. So Powerfully Final." The four entered Lorna's room.

"Mom was just sitting in a chair. Pete and I visited with her a short while and gave her big hugs. She seemed to love seeing us, but was teary, even though she didn't know about Pop." Al thought a long moment about the chemistry between his parents, two people who had lived side by side for more than six decades. He and Pete found it significant that their mother had been taken to the hospital just as their father was in his final hours. Later Al said, "It was almost as if they had a spiritual and very real physical bond, as to their extremity."

The family bundled Lorna warmly and drove her home. Once inside, they removed her coat and helped her into her chair. Then, when the time seemed right, Al, Ann, Pete, and Lynne sat beside her. After taking a deep breath and calming himself as best he could, Al looked lovingly at his mother, then turned to his brother. "Pete, if you, as the eldest son, could do this, I would appreciate it."

Pete took one of his mother's hands, Al the other. After speaking a few moments about Christianity and eternity—and death—Pete looked into Lorna's eyes: "Mom, dear Dad has passed into the ages. He is gone. The promise of Christianity is life everlasting. He has gone on to another stage of eternity." Lorna's face wreathed in anguish. "No! No, it cannot be," she cried. After a few minutes, she strengthened. Al recorded the moment in his diary. "You could almost feel it coming through her arms and her body. She asked brief questions about what had happened, and then began to speak of what an inspiration her husband was, that he was 'a man of such courage.'"

That morning the *Casper Star Tribune* ran an extensive article about Milward. It included numerous photos of the former governor and senator. Ann placed the newspaper in front of Lorna and pointed to a 1969 picture of the two. They were both laughing.

"Oh, I love that," Lorna said.

Pete read one of the articles, Al another. Later, in private, Al recorded, "And so it came to pass that the message was conveyed. It was tough. There were hot tears—all around." The family took scores of condolence calls and accepted delivery after delivery of bouquets and cards. The atmosphere remained somber—until Lorna suddenly began taking charge. "Now wait a minute, please," she said. "You are not all listening to me. When you bring those plants and flowers in, be sure you do not remove the cards, so we can tell whom to thank. Do you understand?"

Al was thrilled. "What a woman. What a powerhouse."

In Commemoration

One of many phone calls received at the house that evening was from former president George Bush, who expressed his sympathy. Mrs. Simpson told him, "Thank you so much for calling. I deeply appreciate it. I remember your dear mother and father."

Al and Ann reminded Lorna that it had been Milward's wish to be cremated. Al was not eager for a trip to the funeral home the next day. "None of us really wanted to go. I knew it would be hard to see that beautifully handsome man just returned to clay, with those terrible knots and those skin cancers and one eye covered with matter and with one leg and great rashes on his face."

The next afternoon members of the immediate family stood before Milward's body, each deep in thought. Al said afterward that it was the first time in many years he had seen his father's face becalmed. On the former governor's white shirt was a pin bearing the symbol of the state of Wyoming. They stood silently for many minutes, then said a prayer together. Choking back sobs, they broke into the song heard at every family gathering.

> Oh, the more we are together, together, together,
> the more we are together, the happier we'll be.
> For your friends are my friends, and my friends are your friends.
> The more we are together, the happier we'll be.

Later that afternoon they drove Lorna to the funeral home. Pete, Lynne, Ann, and Al positioned her wheelchair in front of her husband.

> Her little frail hands reached out, but she did not touch him. She kept talking about their heritage, and then she said, "Let's pray." We said the Lord's Prayer together. Her voice was strong, stronger than I had heard it for a long time. She stared intently at the clay before her. Then she said, "I pray, God, for his integrity and his character, and I ask that those traits and attributes be passed down through the generations."

It was one of the most powerful things I have been involved with in my life.

Lorna attempted to stand but was unable. When she felt she had been there long enough, she asked the others to wheel her away. In the car she said, "Oh that was wonderful. It was wonderful. I'm so pleased I did that."

Al, Ann, and their son Bill made one final trip to the funeral home. Later, Al spoke somberly to his diary.

I put my hand on that brow for the last time. I had stroked that head so many times. I knew that one day I would stroke it and it would be icy cold. I held my hand on it until it warmed. It warmed me. I kissed his head—for the last time.

He left us a magnificent heritage, a proud, sturdy and honest heritage. He was all the man there was. I had heard that phrase used about Vince Lombardi. It fit so beautifully. My father was all the man there was.

That evening someone brought dinner to the house. At 10:45 the phone rang. It was President Clinton, calling after midnight, Washington time. "Al, I just wanted to tell you I was thinking of you. I am so sad to learn of the death of your father." The president mentioned that Hillary had "gone through this" several weeks earlier and that he understood some of the pain. Referring to Milward, Clinton said, "He must have been a fine person."

"He was," Al said softly. "You are good to call me. Don't let those bastards in the press grind you down."

Clinton said, "I just wish I had a friend like you were to George Bush in this job."

Sanctuary

Al could not sleep that night. Still awake at 4:45, he got up and walked into his yard. Dawn was just beginning to stir. He listened to the birds and spotted Charlie, Colin's cat.

As protection against the forty-five-degree temperature, he pulled on his Wyoming sweatshirt and a coat over that. He donned his Bobcat Ranch cap, grabbed his camera, and wandered around the yard, taking pictures. Standing there by himself in the predawn glow, he found himself savoring more than the physical scene, recording more than the physical moment. One after another, he revived events in his mind's eye that can only be seen, can only be understood, can only truly be felt by those whose compass star has slipped mercifully from the night sky.

He was back inside at 7:15 when the phone rang. It was George Bush, a second time. "Al, I just wanted to tell you again how I feel about your dad. I'm so sorry." The former president also wanted Al to know something. "The media has been goading me to punch out President Clinton. A guy who cut me to ribbons, Tim Russert of NBC, keeps calling and saying, 'Please come on my show and tell me how you are doing,' and on and on. I told him there would be no postmortems from me. I am through with it. I'm just going to hold my tongue." Al spoke of President Clinton's call the previous evening, including the part about his wishing for a friend like Al had been to Bush.

"Did he really say that?" George asked.

"He sure did," Al told him.

"Well isn't that something? A whole new view of him. Yeah, you went through the fires for me, and I suppose there aren't many who would do that for him."

On Friday, June 18, after breakfast, Simpson family members gathered at the Cody airport and boarded the two airplanes Governor Mike Sullivan had dispatched to fly them to Cheyenne for state funeral services. Family members carried the vessel containing the former governor's cremated remains.

At the crowded service in the rotunda of the State Capitol building, Pete spoke first, then Al. On the last page of the remarks he had carefully prepared, he had written himself a note in felt-tip pen commanding, "Dammit, Al—cry later." He concluded his somber remarks that day with this: "God rest his soaring soul."

The Wyoming flag was lowered, folded in military style, and presented to Lorna by Governor Sullivan and Wyoming National Guard adjutant general Charles Wing. The governor knelt down and spoke to her. The general, standing straight and tall, saluted. Al stood and whispered, "Get down here, Charlie! Mom has known you since you and I were playing ball at U.W." The general dropped to one knee to present the flag. When Lorna reached out and accepted it, he hugged her.

The next day a second service was conducted in Cody's Christ Episcopal Church, where Pete and Al delivered remarks similar to those given in Cheyenne. That evening at home, those closest to Lorna offered tributes to Milward. Finally, Lorna spoke. Her voice was clear and solid as she shared her feelings and thanked her family and friends. They hung on her every word, every expression. No one kept track of how long the evening lasted. They knew only that the moment would never be replicated or forgotten.

Two years later Milward L. Simpson was elected posthumously into the University of Wyoming Athletics Hall of Fame. At the ceremony, Al spoke expansively of his father's talents on the field and in life. "Somewhere out there in the great cosmos, Pop knows of this night. Brother Pete and I hear him cheer his battle cry, 'Hustle, hustle, hustle! Do that all your lives!'"

D-DAY

The Allied invasion of German-occupied France in World War II, known as D-Day, occurred June 6, 1944. Fifty years later, Al Simpson was among the world leaders gathered in somber commemoration. He carried a portable recorder as he boarded an army helicopter along with ten other senators.

> We left Deauville at 5:30 this morning and flew along the coast of France. We are just now crossing the coastline at Omaha Beach. . . .
>
> We can only imagine how those young men felt fifty years ago at this moment. . . . We're just about ready to land on the

deck of the *George Washington*, in the midst of fighter aircraft.
. . .

Certainly, this is one of the most stunning days of my life.
It is cold and gray, a misty, raw and windy day, just as it must
have been on D-Day. . . .

They took us into the ship where we had a reception and
breakfast and awaited the president. He was a half hour late.
Neither he nor Hillary has a topcoat.

President Clinton gave a short speech and placed a wreath upon
the sea. Afterward, knowing that the president would be acutely
aware that the military people present would be focused on his lack
of military service, Simpson said to Clinton, "I know this is a tough
situation for you."

"Thanks," he responded. "This is a most impressive experience for
me, learning more about the military." A few minutes later, Clinton
departed the carrier. The senators followed in a second helicopter,
joining their spouses on Utah Beach as Clinton and the prime minister of France were presiding over the ceremonial firing of cannons
toward the English Channel. Speaking slowly into his recorder, he
described what he saw, and added, "Tears clog our eyes." He recorded
a long while, detailing historical events, many of which hinged on
the beginnings of victory that day on the beaches of France.

It never would have happened without the courage of the men
sitting in this audience. Most are not here to seek any personal
glory. When I said, "Thank you for what you have done," several responded that they didn't do anything as great as "they"
did. Then they would point toward the many graves.

These men are here to find the burial sites of their buddies and to pay thanks to those who had been right alongside
them that day—and were never again seen by their families.

The clouds began to break and shafts of sunlight pierced the gray
scene. A tall senator and his wife walked slowly through the military cemetery.

You look down and see the name, rank, serial number, date of birth, and the state of the young man. Suddenly your heart is torn. You think of your own sons, your father, your brother, your sisters and daughters. These men—their average age was twenty-two—never had the wonder of a home and work, or the peace and joy of sons or daughters and grandparents and family and friends. Their lives were taken from them in a hail of lead and flame.

We asked many veterans at the ceremony, "What were you doing that day, right at this moment?" One guy looked at his watch and said that he was loading his landing craft with wounded soldiers, getting ready to take them back to England, the first of many trips. He said he was later wounded, twice, and he described a sea filled with blood and gore and bits of bodies and wreckage.

Another man said, "I had taken my second wound by now and was hiding under the cliffs. I went to the field hospitals four times, and each time went back into combat."

At an appointed time everyone gathered at a place where Allied paratroopers had dropped into battle. Strom Thurmond had been among them that day, landing in a glider. Some of those who leaped into raging hell fifty years before were preparing to parachute again. Officials warned them against it. "There were about thirty-eight of them. They ranged in age from seventy-one to eighty-three. Somebody said the only noise we would hear would be their teeth falling out when they hit the end of the jerk line. They laughed and said, "What the hell—we're *ready*."

As the plane bearing the aging veterans passed overhead, each jumped out, just as they had a half century before. Some drifted far off course, landing beyond the railroad tracks or beyond a tree line. One drifted especially far, worrying observers. When he finally emerged from the trees on foot, someone shouted, "We're glad to see you."

"So am I!" he exclaimed with a wide grin.

One jumper got his foot caught in his parachute lines. After landing safely, he said, "Oh yes, I was a little worried for a while." The eldest of the group landed in front of the observers, provoking robust cheers of adulation and admiration. Al got the paratroopers' autographs on a special commemorative postal cachet displaying a new United States postage stamp. It bore the image of a glider and paratrooper.

The next day a modern U.S. Air Force jet crossed the Atlantic. Aboard were Al and Ann Simpson, returning to Washington with a profound understanding of the gravity of sending young men to war.

A NEW CHALLENGE

In the weeks leading up to the late 1994 Senate Republican leadership elections, Al Simpson had been lobbying his colleagues, urging their support in his quest to be elected assistant Republican leader a sixth time. Senator Trent Lott of Mississippi had said repeatedly that he would not run for any Republican leadership position currently held by an incumbent seeking reelection, but Al soon realized that Lott had in fact been campaigning for his job: "The curious part of his pitch is that I am not conservative enough, which ought to make some people cringe. The point there is that I've flunked the purity test, since I am pro-choice on abortion. It indicates a division of ideology—like who is the most conservative. I don't think it does us a bit of good, if we are going to lead." He noted that the National Taxpayers' Union had him ranked the seventh most fiscally conservative member of the Senate. Lott was thirty-fifth.

Simpson's diary entry for December 2, 1994, detailed what happened as the Republicans met in secret to pick their leaders for the next two years. A revealing note about politicians: in total, Lott and Simpson received more commitments of support from Republican senators than there were Republican senators—meaning that rather than saying "no" to either of them, some senators promised to support each.

D-Day it was—except that I was on the opposite side of the channel from England. After Bob Dole was reelected GOP leader by acclamation, the vote for assistant leader took place and they gathered the ballots. I felt I had thirty votes going in. Trent told me later that he thought he had thirty-two. Twenty-seven was the magic number.

After the count, Thad Cochran called the meeting to order and said, "Now the results of the race for assistant majority leader. By a vote of twenty-seven for Trent Lott and twenty-six for Al Simpson, we have a new assistant leader."

I stood up immediately—didn't wait a moment. Trent went to shake Bob Dole's hand and those of his supporters. I said, "Trent, come on over here, young man." I put my arm around him and said to everyone, "I pledge every bit of my support and all of my energies, all my interests. He is going to do a good job."

I also said, "I thank you for all the support you have given me over the years. We have to be unified. Let's move forward and stick together. I am very proud to have held this job for ten years. I wish you well, Trent. God bless you all—and thanks."

As you might imagine, there was quite a response to that, an ovation of some note. Of course, I had a lump in my throat but I knew I needed to do that—and at that moment.

At Al's suggestion, the two went together immediately to face the media. A small army of reporters had gathered in a Capitol hallway, behind a bank of microphones. Simpson spoke first: "We just had a very close election, and Trent Lott is the new assistant majority leader. I am pledging him my full support and assistance. He is going to do a great job, and I am going to be at his side for anything he might request of me. I want him to know that, and I want you to know that."

The first question was directed at Simpson: How did he feel about Lott's saying weeks earlier that he would not run against an incumbent? "Well, things changed," Simpson replied. "New members came in, and it energized him." A reporter found Ann and asked how she thought her husband would handle the defeat—the first and last of his life, other than his sixth grade impeachment. "Just like he has handled everything in his life," she responded, "very well." The two found each other at a luncheon. Ann came up, gave him a kiss, and said, "Oh, it's too bad."

"Yep, but that's the way it works in this game," he told her. Probed further by a reporter, he paraphrased a comment by author Kurt Vonnegut. "This loss was no more than a 'sparrow fart' compared with the cataclysmic events of our times." He told his diary: "People don't give a damn how you look when you win around this place. They want to know how you handle things when you lose. You had better just step up there with all the grace, style and magnanimity you have. I didn't have to act. It came naturally."

Years later, Ann looked back on her husband's loss: "I think Al learned from Pete's loss just how deeply you can get into regrets and the rehashing of things. In this case, he just disciplined himself and didn't get into that. We really didn't discuss it much. His disappointment with the people who didn't vote for him was the heaviest part. He had mixed feelings about the pressures of the job, especially under a White House controlled by the Democrats."

That afternoon President Clinton phoned. "I just called to tell you I'm thinking of you," he said. Al thought it odd that if either of them seemed "down" emotionally, it was the president. "This was the flattest I have heard his voice. He was very preoccupied. Perhaps he was reading something while he was talking to me, but it was a weird conversation. He just had no life in his voice at all. None."

Al put down the telephone, but not for long. His several office lines were ringing off the hook, people calling from throughout America, almost exclusively to express regret. "My God! You would think I had *died*! Calls were streaming into my office. I finally told the staff, 'I am alive. Tell them that I am alive—Ann is alive, our children are living, my mother is alive, and we are all well. I *promise*.'"

At home that night Al and Ann looked at the vote list, the note card he had carried in his pocket for weeks as he wrote down commitments of support by his colleagues. He was able to identify the four senators who had promised to support him but had voted for Lott.

Ann said, "Four people *lied* to you."

Al had a ready answer. "Yes, but twenty-six told the truth. That's pretty good odds in any society."

In 2007 Colin described this father's loss of the leadership post differently. "Pop may regret that last whip election. I think that was really painful for him. I think he may regret that he relied on [other senators' support] and didn't lock those up, if he could have."

A few days after Simpson's one-vote defeat, he received a note from former president George Bush.

Dear Alan:

The best man doesn't always win. The guy who served with honor and good grace is not always rewarded—credit is a vapor.

Damn it all. You deserved better. As a President who profited by your advice and loyal support all I can again say is you deserved better but you've got friends—lots & lots—and that *really* counts.

I'm proud to be one of your friends,

GB

Now without the Senate car and driver provided to top leaders, Simpson found himself approaching the Capitol packed tightly into the front-right seat of a staffer's aging Ford Bronco. A Capitol security guard, not recognizing the vehicle, approached and peered through the driver's window. In order to be seen, Al leaned toward him. As the two made eye contact, Simpson faked a grimace. "They took my fucking *car*," he agonized in mock pain. Everyone broke into laughter, Al included.

If Simpson was bitter, he did not show it. Nor did the slightest

hint of bitterness appear in the private diary he faithfully maintained for a decade. He resumed chairmanship of the Veterans'
Affairs Committee, which he had forgone when first elected to the
leadership, and moved forward.

His final diary note on losing his leadership post said this: "Here
we go into a new chapter in the life of Alan K. Simpson—racon-
teur, Cody High School graduate, Cranbrook graduate, University
of Wyoming jock, law student, lawyer, husband of Ann, brother
of Pete, father of Bill, Colin and Susan—a guy who is very, very
blessed in life. Absolutely and totally so."

LORNA HELEN KOOI SIMPSON

In late 1994 Al's ninety-four-year-old mother, Lorna, was failing.
That Christmas, he buoyed her spirits.

> She was a little dotty in the last year of her life. She thought I
> was vice president of the United States. I came home and she
> said, "Alan, dear, how are you?"
>
> I said, "I'm great," and gave her a big hug.
>
> She asked, "How is Mr. Bush?"
>
> I told her, "He's fine."
>
> Then she asked, "Are you enjoying your role as vice presi-
> dent?"
>
> I answered, "Mom, it's amazing. I am enjoying it thor-
> oughly. It is one of the most captivating jobs. I didn't think
> I'd like it, but I do."
>
> It was the damnedest conversation. She had seen much
> of politics, and for her it was political burnout at the age of
> ninety-four.

As he began to decorate his mother's Christmas tree, he realized
that she thought her other son, Pete, was also in the room. Since
Pete had been delayed, Al improvised.

> Pete couldn't get home for a while, so I went ahead and deco-
> rated the Christmas tree. She couldn't see very much, but she

said, "It is wonderful to see you two boys here decorating the tree like you did when you were little."

Hearing that, I darted from one side of the room to the other. Imitating Pete's voice, I said, "Mom, I just heard Handel's *Messiah*. You'll want a copy of it, won't you?"

She responded, "Oh, I will, Peter, dear."

Then I would run to the other side of the room and speak in my own voice. . . . I left her happy.

Sitting on his patio in Cody years later, he reviewed how his relationship with his mother evolved. He always knew her as a deep and multifaceted woman.

I was vicious as a child, but she said that when I was eleven, I turned to her and said I was going to turn my "won't power" into "will power."

Still, it was only when I got to be about thirty-five that I could really tell her that I loved her—without having a drink first. Before, I would have a few beers, hug her, and tell her I loved her. I was about thirty-five years old and sober as a judge when I said, "You are an amazing woman. I love you." That kind of unnerved her.

It was because I was dealing with power—the cell of a tornado, a hurricane, the person who put me together, put the plasma, put the backbone in me. You don't want to give away too much credit, you know. You want to say, "I have cred-ibility of my own." But she was the one who forged me. The old man gave the flavor. She was the forge.

In 2007 Pete agreed. "When you are talking about influences in our lives, those two parents—they were the 'founders of the feast.' They were the ones for whom we still reach for a telephone on occasion."

The Call

Just before 10:00 on Tuesday morning, January 24, 1995, I walked into my boss's office to find him standing at his desk. He was looking into the distance, through the window toward the Capitol dome. Without inflection, he spoke. "Don, I just had a call. They have taken my mother to the hospital. She was not breathing. The reality of that is hard to grasp." I slipped out of the office, locked the door, and instructed the staff to prepare for Al and Ann to depart immediately for Cody.

Later that morning Majority Leader Bob Dole, Al's friend of many years, prepared a statement and took to the Senate floor.

Married to Milward Simpson in Sheridan, Wyoming in 1929, Mrs. Simpson devoted the next 65 years of her life to her family, her community, and to the entire State of Wyoming. Even before her husband's election as governor of Wyoming in 1954, Lorna Simpson was always reaching out to help others. . . .

She was a very special woman who did not seek the limelight and did not wish to boast of her activities. On once being nominated for "Wyoming Woman of the Year" she said, "When I received notification they had nominated me for Woman of the Year, I felt so completely inadequate and unworthy of ever being mentioned as a possibility for the award that I did not reply. But I must say when I saw the rather sparse account of my accomplishments in a booklet sent to me explaining the qualifications of candidates, I felt I owed it to those who organized the entire project to detail some of the activities, that they might have it for their records. I was always taught one should never 'boast' of any charitable activities, but on the other hand, the Bible does say, 'Let your light so shine before men that they may see your good works, and glorify your Father which is in Heaven.' So, as a small justification for the honor bestowed upon me, I shall then 'boast' a bit about some of the fine things that have touched my life."

That life ended peacefully at 7:45 A.M. [MST] January 24, 1995.

Lorna's funeral was conducted at Christ Episcopal Church in Cody, with hundreds of people present, including many of her "other" sons—Al and Pete's friends, whose lives she had influenced. During the service Al spoke powerfully and emotionally about his mother.

> She had seen destruction in other close families caused by a failure of discipline and searing surges of temper and intemperance. She was not going to allow that to happen to me— and yet I assure you I was not always a willing recipient of her ministrations. . . .
>
> We were raised on a rich potion of love and discipline, and the learning of self-esteem. . . .
>
> The thing I remember is her home—a home of such love and joy, one where if you cut your knee playing "mumbley peg" with a rusty, open pocketknife, she was there to hug and kiss you. If you were frightened by lightning and thunder and you were very young—oh, what indescribable joy and comfort, what warmth and safety to scrunch into their bed and snuggle between those two magic people, Mom and Pop. . . .
>
> She missed him so. The great oak was suddenly no longer silhouetted as a part of her horizon. When he was gone, part of Mom's fire was banked and the light of her own life began to dim. On the morning of January 24, her soaring soul fluttered in upward flight toward the heavens, so like the little birds she loved to see playing by her windows. A beautiful little bird she was.

On his copy of the program, he wrote in black felt pen: "Our dear and graceful woman of powerful faith joins our father in Heaven . . . Mom and Pop, eternally one. Love, Al."

Back in Washington not long afterward, Al said, "It is so strange, so very odd after all these years of life with parents, to suddenly feel orphaned." Years later Pete said this about their parents; "The degree to which Al and I have become men, we owe that to our father. The degree to which we have been brothers, we owe that to our mother." Lorna's grandson Colin spoke in 2007 about his grandparents.

My grandfather Milward didn't like to deal with emotional issues in the family. My grandmother was the real force. I never heard her raise her voice, but she was good at cutting to the quick of an issue. Her faith in God was amazing. Her extra-sensory powers that I know she had sustained them for thirty years in their later life, especially in Milward's last five years. They were amazing together, how they kept each other going—how she kept *everybody* going.

She was always presentable, always made up, her hair done, well dressed. She was a modest lady who lived that modesty in her life through her thoughts and her actions. She would tell you, "Be careful what you look at, at the things you put in your head, because they are there forever."

She could tell good from bad, and bad from evil. She dealt with evil and evil people in a more religious way, in terms of ignoring them, sometimes, and believing that they could be overcome by prayer. She didn't hate, or carry around that kind of anger.

I used to love to watch those old home movies with Nana, the very early movies that she took of Rio. She was up in a bi-plane with one of the Brazilian Air Force guys. She had movies of the town. There is a movie of Rudyard Kipling coming out of the hotel . . . there are movies from Egypt and other places, phenomenal stuff.

The Tribute

Three days after Lorna's passing, Al and Ted Kennedy held the weekly recording session for their daily national radio program *Face Off*. It was unlike any other.

This is Al Simpson. Ted, two wonderfully strong, independent, loving, caring women have left this earth in these last days—our beautiful mothers. In a moment, Ted Kennedy and I will face off. [*break for commercial*]

For nearly eight years now, Ted, we've been doing this spirited program—and have often talked of our mothers. Blessed we were to have them in our lives so many years.

Swiftly, in the course of a two-day span, both are now gone from us—part of the fabric of our lives is torn away. Both died in their own homes surrounded by those who love them. What powerful impact these strong women had on our lives. They loved us. Read to us when we were children. Guided us. Instructed us. Buoyed us up when we faltered or failed. They did not judge us—just gave us the grace of unconditional love.

Deepest sympathies to you, old friend—I appreciated your calling to share your condolences. Would that every kid in this old world could have a mother like Rose Kennedy or Lorna Simpson—'twould be a better place. [*in brogue*] God rest their souls.

Kennedy gave this response.

Al, thank you for those thoughts, and my heart goes out to you and your family too.

It's an unusual coincidence that our two mothers, who lived such long and extraordinary lives, passed away within a couple of days of one another—yours at 94, mine at 104. They're probably facing off in Heaven right now—and doing a better job than we are.

Mother liked you, Al, although she thought you were occasionally too rough on me on these broadcasts.

Mother was the best campaigner any Kennedy ever had. We joked about who was the best politician in the family—*after* Mother.

President Kennedy called her the glue that held our family together. Certainly, she was the finest teacher we ever had. Her strength and love, and above all her abiding religious faith, sustained her all her life, and inspired all the members of our family, too.

May both our mothers rest in peace, Al.

Pete Simpson remembers the telephone call from Senator Kennedy in the wake of Lorna's death: "We were in Al's dining room in Cody with a speakerphone on the table while calling relatives and friends, when Ted himself called. He offered his condolences. When he paused, Al said of Rose and Lorna, 'Maybe they're up there clearing the way for you and me.' Ted replied, 'They'll need a bulldozer!'"

Chapter Sixteen

ROUNDING A CORNER

~

AL SIMPSON WAS reflective the day he presented his sons Bill and Colin for admission to practice law before the U.S. Supreme Court, the fourth generation of Simpsons to do so. Seven Supreme Court justices had been installed during Al's years on the Judiciary Committee: "I had a hand in each of them. Some were easy, and some were like sweating blood." The Simpsons dropped by the office of Justice Clarence Thomas, who impressed Bill in particular: "He gave Dad a hug and said, 'You're the reason I'm here, Big Al.' They had a wonderful talk."

A day later the family arrived at the White House. On their way to the Oval Office Al had flashes of nostalgia.

> We went into the Cabinet Room, where I spent many a moon over my ten years as assistant leader. It gave me a very strange feeling. I thought to myself how fortunate I was. When I was elected to the leadership, I had been here just one term. I was in that room an average of once every two weeks and some-times once every two days—sometimes, when things were popping, every day. I realized how privileged I was.

President Clinton greeted Al, Ann, Colin, Bill, Bill's wife Debbie, and their daughter Beth and son Eric. He escorted them into the Oval Office, where Al noted how fresh everything looked; the Remington and Russell bronzes made him feel at home. Again Bill was especially impressed: "Oh my gosh, Clinton was electric. Electric." Bill asked for an autograph and Clinton happily complied, prompting a second request: "Would you also autograph a card for the folks at the Proud Cut Saloon in Cody, Wyoming?"

"Sure will," Clinton replied, adding, "but it might drive out the patrons."

ONE MORE TIME?

In 1995 Simpson gave every appearance of running for a fourth term. To build his war chest for the November 1996 election, he scheduled a second major fundraising gala in New York City. On the weekend of March 25, nearly two hundred supporters gathered for a Broadway performance of *Phantom of the Opera*. Dinner afterward at Sardi's restaurant was attended by Mayor Rudy Giuliani, long a Simpson friend.

But six months later when it was time for the final decision about running again, Al told Ann, "I just don't want to do it anymore." Her first thought was, "I'll have a little more of him soon." Al called me into his office. His introspective mood made it obvious that something important was about to be disclosed. Rather than revealing his decision, he asked, "Do you think I should run again?"

I had been his employee seventeen years, his friend for many more. Memories raced as I said, "Al, I think it is time to move on." He smiled and said he had come to that conclusion. It was time to do something else. His decision was kept under wraps until December 2, 1995, when he and his family appeared before friends and staff members in a large room at Cody's Holiday Inn. Al stepped up to the podium.

> Biblically, there is a wondrously inspirational passage that sets things out so well in life, as the Good Book so often does. We laymen know it as "There is a time."
>
> Tonight I share with my fellow Cody folk . . . that I intend to retire from the United States Senate at the end of my term in January 1997. . . .
>
> On September 2, I turned sixty-four years old. For the past seventeen years, I have spent an average of every other weekend somewhere in, or over, the State of Wyoming. . . . I am usually headed out of Washington on a Friday, and back to Washington on a Sunday afternoon. When other folks might

be with their families or watching a football, basketball, or baseball game or having a cookout, I was usually at 37,000 feet, headed east. I have done that. Don't feel sorry—the pay is good. It was all indoor work and no heavy lifting.

I thought, if I do this again, it is for six full years. One part of me said, "I'd like to go for another two or three years of this, but not six." The old fire in the belly is not there. The edge is off. . . .

I promised you only two things in 1978 when I entered upon these adventures. I said I would work very, very hard and that I would hope to make you proud. I trust that I have done exactly that. I feel honestly that I have.

Helen Dewar observed the next day in the *Washington Post* that "Sen. Alan K. Simpson . . . can be among the most engaging raconteurs in the Senate. Although he is a skilled, serious and persevering lawmaker, he is probably best known for his sharp tongue and earthy humor, which made him one of the most colorful figures in Congress but also frequently got him in trouble."

Al's final opportunity to speak at a Senate Prayer Breakfast in Washington came on January 1, 1996. He gave thanks for the opportunity to serve the public and for the many close relationships he had forged along the way. Simpson remained active for the entirety of his final year in the Senate. In May he brought yet another immigration bill to final passage. At the conclusion of fifty-five hours of Senate debate, during which he "warded off the snakes and the shoats and the toads and the weasels," his legislation passed, 97–3.

Washington Says Goodbye

The May 21 banquet at Washington's Hyatt Regency Capitol Hill Hotel was billed as "A Salute to Al Simpson." Seven hundred people gathered in formal wear to thank, roast, toast, and praise the man who had come to Washington eighteen years before as a "fresh western breeze." Hundreds of Washington officials and corporate representatives helped arrange this biggest honor of Simpson's life.

Tickets to the expensive evening sold out quickly, the proceeds benefiting the University of Wyoming Foundation and the Milward L. Simpson Chair in Political Science. Al's senior staff had selected Dick Cheney to serve as master of ceremonies and former president George Bush to deliver the keynote address.

At a front row table sat Ted Kennedy and former Democratic National Committee chair Robert Strauss. Becky and I shared the table. Not the slightest hint of partisan politics was heard that evening, as Republicans and Democrats reviewed the highs and lows of a career unlikely to be duplicated. The *Washington Post*'s Joel Achenbach summarized the evening in the next day's paper.

> The journey of this unusual man was celebrated last night on Capitol Hill at a black-tie dinner that featured most of the U.S. Senate and former president George Bush, who choked up so badly while toasting his friend that he could barely continue. . . .
>
> Turning to Simpson and his wife, Ann, Bush said with voice cracking, "We love you." He had to stop. The crowd applauded, and then Bush managed to pull himself together and continue. "Things got tough down there at 1600 Pennsylvania Avenue, and this giant would come down, dust us off and put us back in the game."

Mutual Admiration

Work continued in Al's office right to the end of 1996, with a shrinking staff to prepare eighteen years' worth of paperwork and photos for transport to the University of Wyoming, where they would be archived at the American Heritage Center. Meanwhile, he continued to receive a flood of letters from people he had never met and from those he knew well.

> Dear Al:
>
> What is there to say about the most popular guy in the United States Senate who has served his State and Country

with such honor and in the process coined a new word, *gazoo*, which baffled the beltway media—confounded them, irritated them, while his many friends from the White House to Capitol Hill cheered lustily.

Oh my, but the Senate is going to miss you, Al.

George Bush

Ten years later, I asked Al which U.S. president he most admired: "There is no question. George Bush is the most decent man I ever met in life, other than my own dad. George is a man of moral character and loyalty, and love of family and friends. He was amazing. He is amazing."

HARVARD CALLING

The Simpsons moved home to Cody in December 1996, but only briefly. Soon they were off to Boston, where Al had been selected as the visiting lecturer in the Laurence M. Lombard Chair at Harvard. His popular course was titled "The Creating of Legislation: Congress and the Press." It focused on his political experiences, his work as a lawyer in Cody, and especially his lively encounters with the media over the years. Al and Ann lived in a campus dorm two-bedroom suite with a common room but no kitchen: "It was like being on the G.I. Bill again," he said. They were the highest profile occupants of room L-22 at Eliot House since conductor Leonard Bernstein in the late 1970s.

On January 16, 1998, as he continued his lecture series, the university newspaper reported that Simpson had been named director of Harvard's Institute of Politics at the Kennedy School of Government. The article quoted Senator Ted Kennedy: "I'm delighted that Al's agreed to become director. He is an outstanding choice. He served the people of Wyoming and the nation well for 18 brilliant years in the Senate, and he'll do an excellent job at the Institute of Politics. I just hope he remembers it's Harvard Yard, not Harvard Prairie." Al responded: "It is a tremendous honor and privilege to accept this position. It is a critical time to emphasize that you can seriously disagree with a person on a political or partisan basis, but the debate must take place in a civilized manner. In legislating, the word 'compromise' does not mean 'wimp.'"

While at Harvard, Simpson co-hosted the locally produced WGBH public television series *The Long and the Short of It*. His partner was former U.S. labor secretary Robert Reich. The thirty-minute nationally televised program paired the six foot, seven inch Simpson and the less-than-five-foot Reich with a prominent guest to discuss and analyze major political events of the week.

On May 22, 2000, with Simpson's contract completed, Harvard said a formal goodbye. At one point in the banquet, the lights dimmed and former president George H. W. Bush appeared on video: "Al Simpson is one of my closest friends in life. He is one of the people whose opinions I respect the most. He really is the very best. I loved working with him." Senator Ted Kennedy too offered praise, and he recalled the time Al invited him to meet a group of Wyoming constituents.

> I remember when Al asked me to speak. He was introducing me when somebody got up and shouted, "Kennedy is a horse's tail," or words to that effect.
> Al grabbed the guy and threw him out of the room.
> I said, "Al, I didn't know that this was Kennedy country."
> He said, "It isn't. It's *horse* country."

To close the evening a group of students walked across the front of the room. Each one paused at the microphone to recite a single line from Al's favorite poem, "If," by Rudyard Kipling. He was deeply moved.

Not long after Al and Ann returned to Cody and settled in, a few of his old buddies conducted a skeet-shooting contest designed especially for him. He had no idea what they were up to but was intrigued by their having constructed what appeared to be a large catapult. His curiosity deepened when they handed him a shotgun and asked him to shoot whatever object was next launched. With a twang, something familiar bolted skyward. As it reached the zenith of its arc, he aimed and fired. Buckshot met metal, and the crowd roared in approval. Al Simpson had just bagged his last mailbox.

THE FOURTH QUARTER

Predictably, Al scarcely slowed down during his first decade back home in Wyoming. He remained involved in issues of the day, continued to travel the nation on speaking engagements, and stayed in frequent touch with scores of friends, none more often than former president George H. W. Bush.

I asked him in 2008 to compare the two presidents named George Bush—one former, one present.

> Well, when you talk about a sensitivity level, an awareness level, a compassion level, a compromise level, and a diplomacy level—those are all different in those two men.
>
> You don't make any mistakes by engaging in diplomacy with people you hate. For forty years, we had the Soviet Union wanting to tear our ass to shreds, but we had an embassy in each country and a hotline in each president's hands. Can't people remember?
>
> So why the hell won't [the current Bush Administration] get into discussions with our enemies? They say, "We don't negotiate with people that distrust us." [With that approach], soon we wouldn't be talking with anybody in the world. George Bush "the first" would never have allowed diplomacy to go to the back burner, because he was, and is, a diplomat.

Was he speaking specifically about America's relationship with Iran? "Yes! And North Korea. You talk to these people. You talk to Syria, you talk to Iran, and you talk to North Korea. You don't just say, 'We don't like them, and they're ugly and they do nasty things, so we don't talk to them.' I can't imagine anything more unproductive."

Golden Bulldog Summoned

In February 2010 his old friend Vice President Joe Biden phoned Al Simpson with news and a question. President Obama was about to issue an executive order creating the National Commission on Fiscal Responsibility and Reform. Soon to be dubbed the Deficit Commission or Debt Panel, it would be charged with crafting a bipartisan economic blueprint that, if adopted, would lead the nation to a balanced federal budget and long-term national economic security. Would Simpson co-chair the Debt Panel?

The nation's debt had increased $1.6 trillion in the past year to $13 trillion, and it was forecast to deepen another $10 trillion in the coming decade. Al considered it a "practical impossibility" that Congress and the American public would accept the sacrifices necessary to reverse the alarming trend. Yet the appointment was a golden opportunity to make Americans more aware of the nation's disastrous economic path. How many more opportunities would he have to affect national policy on matters that had been close to his heart for nearly forty years? He spoke with the president before making his decision.

On February 18, 2010, he stood at the White House with Vice President Biden and co-chair Erskine Bowles, who had been chief of staff under President Clinton, as President Obama signed the executive order creating the commission. When someone asked Simpson what should be borne in mind about the commission's assignment, he was ready.

> We must all remember we are Americans first. We are not members of political parties first, or lobbying groups first, or unions or corporations or clubs or associations or anything else first. We are Americans first, and for the good of our cherished nation and future generations of Americans, we must come to disregard the next election cycle and think only of the next generational cycle.
>
> The candy store is closed. The facts regarding this huge unconscionable mess will be set before our fellow citizens by

December 1, 2010. We shall then see how much of the strong medicine, if any, they are ready to swallow.

Almost immediately he came under attack from individuals and groups charging that his appointment was an effort to lend a sense of bipartisanship to what would surely be a recommendation to raise taxes. That spiked his ire.

> Most say correctly that these programs of Social Security, Medicare and Medicaid are "unsustainable." I say that they are also unconscionable! This just cannot go on. I decided to take on the cause after being contacted by the vice president and president, as long as I could join with Erskine Bowles of North Carolina, for whom I have such deep respect and admiration. We are both linked at the hip and ready to jump over the cliff. Somebody said, "You'd better pack your own parachutes," and we said, "Hell, we don't even have parachutes!"

Simpson had no idea whether the commission could come to agreement on a package of recommendations to put the nation on a more sustainable financial footing, but even if the effort ended in chaos, he felt it important to educate the populace.

> The people of this country will have a hell of a lot better idea of where our nation is headed. They might not like anything we're doing, but at least the debate will no longer be stuffed with those old five-second sound bites: "just get rid of waste, fraud and abuse, earmarks and foreign aid." Guess what? Foreign aid is 0.07 percent of the national deficit. Lump all of those great and glorious things together and it's about 4 to 5 percent of the entire deficit. Let's all give up on that one. Much more heavy lifting is needed than that!
>   Whenever the emotion, fear, guilt, and hysterical babble begins to take place, we will try to remind Americans that during the recent discussions of Social Security reform over these past years, not one proposal affected anyone over

fifty-five years of age. Does anyone know that? Of course not. The airwaves and the mail are filled with missives from the AARP, the Committee for Preservation of Medicare and Medicaid, the Silver Haired Legislators, the Grey Panthers, the Pink Panthers and all the rest of those similar senior groups who have distorted the issue magnificently.

Before the commission held its first meeting, some conservative groups increased the volume of their charges that he was being used by the president as a political pawn who would endorse higher taxes. In one of his last interviews with me before publication of this book, Al defended his record:

> This "Mr. Tax Hike" business is garbage. It is intended to terrify people and at the same time make money for the groups who babble it. Unlike some folks doing their best to skew the public's perception of my conservatism, I actually have a public record—which, for those inclined to be anchored in reality, could easily be checked.
>
> The nonpartisan *Congressional Quarterly* did a rating in 1993 based on support for the conservative agenda in Congress. My rating was 88 percent. For the previous years, my support for this "conservative coalition" was 87 percent in 1989, 97 percent in 1990, 88 percent in 1993, and 92 percent in 1992. In the 103rd Congress, the National Taxpayers Union Foundation rated me the seventh most conservative Senator based on key votes. Before calling me "Mr. Tax Hike," check the National Taxpayers Union records. From 1992 to 1996, I had one of the very best scores in the Senate for resisting higher taxes. Check with the preeminent small business association, NFIB, who will verify that during my career I was awarded the Friend of Small Business Award eight times. Check the American Conservative Union, where my lifetime rating is 91 percent—or my 100 percent rating from the Chamber of Commerce in 1993—or my Golden Bulldog award from the

Watchdogs of the Treasury. Everyone is entitled to their own opinion. They aren't entitled to concoct their own facts.

Facts, however, were no match for partisanship and self-interest. Coming out one month after a sweep of Republican victories in a general election, the Debt Panel's final report in December 2010 drew too few votes from the panel's members to trigger congressional consideration. No House Republican on the commission would endorse the report.

As Simpson had known from the outset, only elder statesmen with little to lose could take on the rugged partisan and interest group challenges that this commission faced. The political climate had shifted over the decades, but Simpson's convictions had not. Brother Pete predicts that Al will not slow down until his final day: "It's like Joe DiMaggio would say, 'There might be somebody in the stands who has never watched me play.'" Ann agrees, though she notes that Al does enjoy having more time to sit out on the patio late in the evening and listen to music. He is surprised by the very idea of slowing down. "Why even reflect on that? . . . My head is filled with things I want to do."

Asked whether he would choose a different career if starting life anew, he thought for a long moment. "Well, I practiced law. I wouldn't want to do that anymore, although I loved it. The Senate, eighteen years, I didn't want to do any more of that, although I loved it too. The thing about the Senate is, the giants are gone. Whether they were Republicans or Democrats, they were giants in days long past." Prodded to describe the qualities of those who gravitate to public service, he laughed and repeated a line he had last used in the Senate: "We're all here because we're not all there."

As a boy, Al Simpson defied federal laws. As a senator, he defined them. He prevailed in political firefights by valuing correctness over quickness, by accepting a slice when the whole loaf was out of reach, by using truth and humor as his sword and shield, and by listening to others—but never to the exclusion of the man in the

mirror. He learned to forgive himself, to take his work more seriously than himself, and to laugh with others—but not at them.

The former senator remains a very human being—bright, funny,
sometimes controversial, often inspirational—a man who still
expresses complex concepts simply and simple thoughts lyrically.

As he neared his eightieth birthday in 2011, I asked how he hopes
to be remembered. "Just write this on my stone," he said with a
wry smile: "You would have wanted him on your side."

NOTES

PREFACE

1. Weston Kosova, "No One Forgives Anyone," *Newsweek*, April 2, 2010.

CHAPTER 1. PIONEER SPIRITS

1. The idea for this book was spawned during a phone conversation I had with Simpson in early 2005. Work began in earnest that fall. As I started the research, I asked to join a gathering of Simpson's Cody High School friends from the class of 1949. Almost half of the class of forty-nine people attended, as did several spouses and Simpson's wife and brother. While recording equipment was being set up, Al explained that I would be writing the story of his life. He asked everyone to be completely open about events in their early days, and they were eager to oblige. During the ninety-minute session many laughed at length over the youthful adventures of "Alibi Al," stories they had told and retold for more than fifty years.

2. Simpson has shown a lifelong penchant for maintaining detailed records, and it went into overdrive at the end of 1984 when he was elected the Senate's Republican whip, the number two leadership position. Since he would soon have greatly increased access to the White House and other circles of power, he decided to log significant things he did, said, heard, and saw on a daily basis. Today these logs are accompanied by his much larger collection of letters, notes, photographs, newspaper and magazine clippings, drawings and doodles, and awards and certificates that span his entire life.

   When adding to his diary, he dictated events of the day into a Dictaphone. While doing so, he referred to his schedule cards, monthly planner, staff memos, and notes he wrote during meetings. While traveling, he carried the smallest available handheld tape recorder. Although his original intent was to add to his diary every day, in especially busy times this was limited to every week or two. His diary dictation was extensive during his ten years in the leadership, occasional after that. The dictation tapes were transcribed in his office only by his loyal assistant Evora Williams, who placed the sole copies into binders that, when full, were stored in Simpson's home. After the tapes were transcribed, they were erased and used again. Stapled or paper-clipped to many diary pages are schedule cards, invitations, staff memos, and handwritten notes. Simpson's diary entries are so voluminous that only a fraction of them appear in this book.

To ensure accuracy, Al and Ann Simpson were asked to fact check a draft of my manuscript, although I maintained absolute editorial control. Afterward, for use in the book's promotion, Al wrote: "This is no 'puff piece'—indeed not! Don pulls no punches, as you will see. The first chapter almost painfully (for me) details the 'excesses' of my juvenile years. The only other person to have read any selected chapters is my old friend author/historian David McCullough. Because the core of this book is drawn from my private diaries, wherein I recorded details of significant events and exchanges with nationally known individuals shortly after they occurred, David feels this manuscript is of historical value. I agree. The thousands of accounts and quotes that I recorded through the years, and that Don has now lifted from my nineteen-volume diary, should be of keen interest to political aficionados and historians alike. I initially recorded these diaries for personal reflection later, when I have time." To date he has not read them and has made no plans to make them publicly available, now or after his passing.

3. Beyond the material drawn from Simpson's voluminous diary are entries from my own records and recollections of our early encounters a half century ago in Cody and our eighteen years together in Washington. I conducted five formal interview sessions with Simpson and questioned him repeatedly during numerous other in-person and phone conversations between 2006 and 2011. I recorded separate interviews with each of his immediate family members and questioned many people who know or knew him on a personal or professional level. Information was also drawn from the American Heritage Center and the Alan K. Simpson Institute for Western Politics and Leadership in Laramie, and from Simpson's expansive Senate office archives. I examined court records, historical society and museum documents, newspaper archives, *Congressional Record* entries, and Simpson's vast and varied personal collections.

4. This account is from a detailed letter written by Billy Simpson's mother. It was found among numerous other personal Simpson family documents

provided by Al Simpson's second cousin Jon Sneddon. Some details in the letter differ from those in other accounts, such as newspaper articles. Maggie and John subsequently laid out two separate town additions. A 1972 *Jackson Hole Guide* article includes this note about their son Billy: "The first building constructed upon the Jackson town site, after the old clubhouse, was that constructed by William L. [Billy] Simpson for the purpose of establishing the first store in Jackson Hole [in partnership with Charles Deloney]. This building is situated upon lots in the original Simpson Townsite, dedicated in 1897." Oral histories of family members reveal that Mrs. Simpson sold a number of lots for twenty-five dollars and gave away others. Today, building sites in Jackson are among the nation's most expensive.

5. Descriptions and dialogue are taken verbatim from the trial transcript.

6. As this book went to press, the grand opening of the Interpretive Learning Center was scheduled for August 20, 2011. The Heart Mountain Wyoming Foundation planned to dedicate a section as the Friendship Center, to honor Norman Mineta and Alan Simpson.

CHAPTER 3. BIG STEPS

1. See note 3 to chapter 1 for more about how Simpson maintained the diary.

CHAPTER 4. MILESTONES

1. This summary of the Iran-Contra affair is derived from Wikipedia and verified by numerous other historical accounts. The voluminous literature covering the affair includes Ronald Reagan's *An American Life* (New York: Simon and Schuster, 1990); *Report of the Congressional Committees Investigating the Iran-Contra Affair, S. Rep. No. 216, H.R. Rep. No. 433, 100th Cong., 1st Sess.* (Washington, D.C.: U.S. Government Printing Office, 1987); and Howard Zinn, *A People's History of the United States* (New York: Perennial, 2003).

CHAPTER 5. HEADLINERS AND HEADACHES

1. See http://deregulator.blogspot.com/2003_11_30_deregulator_archive.html for a choice example. In response to an attack by Pastor Fred W. Phelps of the Westboro Baptist Church in Topeka, Kansas, over Simpson's support of gay rights, Simpson wrote this classic: "I just wanted to alert you to the fact that some dizzy son of a bitch is sending out mailings and e-mails

from the Westboro Baptist Church—and using your name! I'm certain that you would not want this to continue or some less-alert citizen might think that you, yourself had done it. We know that is surely not the case, because you are a God-fearing Christian person filled to the brim with forbearance, tolerance and love—and this other goofy homophobe nut must be someone totally opposite."

2. See http://johnrlott.tripod.com/op-eds/NRORehnquistMemory0905.html for both Simpson's and Kennedy's remarks.

CHAPTER 6. CAMPAIGNS, COLUMNISTS, AND GAZOOS

1. The individual referenced here was contacted in 2008 and declined to comment on his relationship with Senator Simpson.

2. Burke is similarly quoted at http://www.essex.ac.uk/honorary_graduates/or/1998/colin-wilson-response.aspx.

CHAPTER 10. THE VP THING

1. "Notch babies" refers to people born between 1917 and 1922, for whom Social Security benefits proved disproportionally high and were later adjusted.

CHAPTER 14. HAND-TO-HAND COMBAT

1. For the full text of Simpson's letter as published in the *New York Times,* see http://www.nytimes.com/1991/03/20/opinion/l-the-word-sympathizer-was-not-a-good-one-817991.html?pagewanted=1.

2. See *Congressional Record*, October 15, 1991, pp. S14675–76. Simpson's submission consisted of eight letters from individuals of significant academic, legal, or government standing who felt sufficiently familiar with Thomas or Hill, or both, to offer their observations and opinions. Some letters were critical of Hill's professionalism, ability, or demeanor. Others said little about her but praised Thomas's ability and decorum. One, from a psychiatrist, expressed the view that Hill "could be saying what she believes is true and at the same time be presenting a situation which in fact did not occur." Simpson did not say whether these were all the letters he received "over the transom." Seven years after the hearings, Al Simpson invited Anita Hill to speak at Harvard. In a July 1, 2005, article in *O: The Oprah Magazine*, Hill told author Brigitte Lacombe, "I thought it was

good for me to talk to him. . . . Hearing how he handles conflict, how he expresses himself generally, has allowed me to really understand that his behavior during the hearing was not personal—this was just who he was." During research for this book Anita Hill was contacted about her views of Senator Simpson. She declined to comment.

INDEX

~

Illustrations are indicated by an italicized page number.